SLEEP AND DREAMS

GARLAND REFERENCE LIBRARY
OF SOCIAL SCIENCE
(VOL. 296)

SLEEP AND DREAMS
A Sourcebook

Jayne Gackenbach

GARLAND PUBLISHING, INC. • NEW YORK & LONDON
1986

Library of Congress Cataloging-in-Publication Data

Sleep and dreams.

 (Garland reference library of social science ;
vol. 296)
 1. Sleep. 2. Dreams. I. Gackenbach, Jayne,
1946– . II. Series: Garland reference library of
social science ; v. 296. [DNLM: 1. Dreams. 2. Sleep.
WL 108 S615]
BF 1071.S585 1987 154.6 84-48759
ISBN 0-8240-8764-X (alk. paper)

Fig. 8 reprinted with permission of M. Jouvet and *Science*
163 (3 January 1969): 38 (copyright 1969 by the AAAS);
Fig. 9 reprinted with permission of Springer-Verlag; Fig. 10
reprinted with permission of J. Allan Hobson and *Science* 189
(4 July 1975): 59 (copyright 1975 by the AAAS); Fig. 11
reprinted with permission of Peter Hauri and the Upjohn
Company (Kalamazoo, Mich., 1982) from *The Sleep Disorders*
(Current Concepts series); Table 2 reprinted with permission
of Yale University Press (1973) from *The Functions of Sleep* by
Ernest L. Hartmann.

Printed on acid-free, 250-year-life paper
Manufactured in the United States of America

CONTENTS

v

INTRODUCTION

Unlike many books on sleep and dreams, the emphasis in this volume is on dreaming rather than on sleeping. This reflects the recent emergence of interest in dreaming among professionals, in the general public, and across disciplines. As this introduction is being written the third annual International Conference of the Association for the Study of Dreams is taking form. Under this umbrella organization professionals and lay public alike gather to share their work on dreaming. Also reflective of this new growth in interest in dreams is the emergence of several dream periodicals.

In this book each chapter offers a review of its area with pertinent references. Selected references are annotated. The annotated references represent the cutting edge of the area under review or are classical, historically important pieces or studies that represent a key turning point. Therefore, the number of annotations varies from chapter to chapter.

This book gives the reader a basic grounding in what we know about the sleep state and then details sleep mentation or dreaming. In Part I William Moorcroft introduces the book with two chapters, "An Overview of Sleep" and, with Jennifer Clothier, "An Overview of the Body and the Brain in Sleep," which offer the reader who is completely uninformed about sleep processes a broad overview of this fascinating area of inquiry. For the more sophisticated reader, or the reader who wants more detail, John Zimmerman's chapter, "Neuroanatomical, Neurophysiological, and Biochemical Aspects of Sleep: An Historical Perspective," is recommended. This part on sleep ends with a chapter on the most common form of sleep pathology, "Insomnia." Amy Bertelson and James Walsh offer an engrossing review of this often reported affliction.

The remainder of the book deals with the mentation that goes on during sleep. Part II on dreaming is divided into three sections, "Basic Dream Processes," "Cognitively Based Theoretical Considerations of Dreaming," and "Interdisciplinary Approaches to the Study of Dreaming." Alan Moffitt and Robert Hoffman begin the section by addressing current concerns about dream psychophysiology in "On the Single-Mindedness and Isolation of Dream Psychophysiology." Kathryne Belicki follows with a thorough review of the research on dream recall in her chapter, "Recalling Dreams: An Examination of Daily Variation and Individual Differences." The Dream Processes section closes with David Koulack's chapter, "Effects of Presleep and During Sleep Stimuli on the Content of Dreams." Although this section does not cover all aspects of the dream process, it does examine three key concerns: psychophysiology, recall, and environmental effects.

In the next section under dreams three cognitively based theoretical perspectives are presented. It starts with Donald Kuiken's "Dreams and Self-Knowledge," which takes a purely cognitively based perspective on these nighttime experiences. Harry Hunt goes beyond the boundaries of traditional cognitive psychology in his chapter, "Toward a Cognitive Psychology of Dreams," by arguing that cognitive psychology needs dreams in order to overcome the narrowness which has come to characterize contemporary cognitive perspectives. The third chapter follows along these lines as Charles Alexander and his colleagues at the Maharishi International University offer "Transcendental Consciousness: A Fourth State of Consciousness Beyond Sleep, Dreaming, and Waking." They present a brief but excellent review of the physiological and psychological differences between sleep and dreams, and expand their analysis to include waking and a fourth state of consciousness which they call "transcendental."

The last section on dreams is an interdisicplinary perspective on sleep mentation from anthropological and literary perspectives. With more than 200 references Robert Dentan offers a comprehensive review of "Ethnographic Considerations of the Cross Cultural Study of Dreams." Carol Rupprecht closes the book with a view of the use of dreams in historical literature.

Although this book is not totally comprehensive, it will give the reader a good look at the basic sleep phenomena and a more detailed look at contemporary work on dreaming.

Jayne Gackenbach
University of Northern Iowa
February 25, 1986

Part I
Sleep

Chapter 1

AN OVERVIEW OF SLEEP

William H. Moorcroft

How do you know if someone is asleep? Every child has at one
time or another fooled his parents by lying still with eyes
closed and breathing slowly. At that time the child pretends
to be asleep although is very much awake. At the other extreme, a person in a coma may also be showing outward signs
which cause her or him to appear to be asleep. Obviously,
then, you cannot easily tell if a person is asleep just by
observation. (An alternative is to wake the person up and ask
if she or he was asleep but this requires depending upon that
person's subjective experience, which is not ideal for scientific accuracy.) Furthermore, when the person is awakened, the
very thing being studied has been obtrusively interfered with.

The inability to be absolutely sure another person is
asleep is important for two reasons. (First, sleep has actually
not been studied very much because it was difficult to objectively and unobtrusively measure it until about 35 years ago.)
Thus, much of what is known about sleep is relatively new
knowledge (1). (Second, it is necessary to study sleep in a
sleep laboratory, where the sleeper can be attached to sensitive instruments,* in order to obtain good objective data without disturbing the person's sleep)(2). Since 1953, when
Aserinsky and Kleitman first reported that sleeping people
have two different kinds of sleep (3), many sleep laboratories
all over the world have been engaged in exploring the mysteries
of sleep every night.

Three modes of measurement are used to determine both when
a person is sleeping and what kind of sleep is occurring: EEG,
to measure the pattern of the electrical activity of the center
of the surface of the brain; EOG, to measure eye movements; and
EMG, to measure muscle tone (4). Some laboratories regularly
use another set of EEG leads from the back of the head (over

_____

*Within the last few years portable sleep measuring equipment
has been developed which allows sleep to be accurately assessed
in non-laboratory settings.

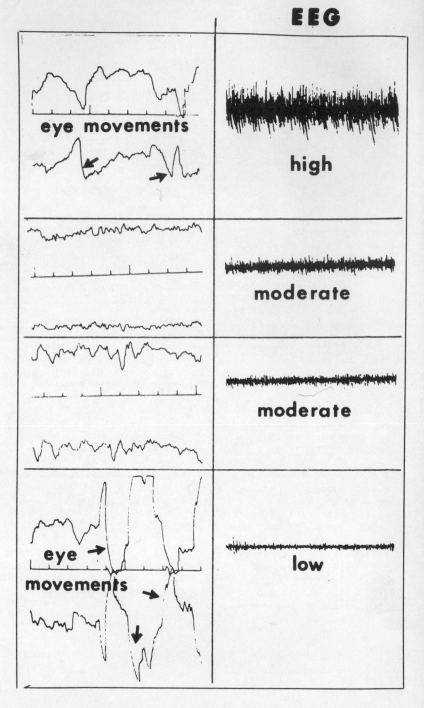

Fig. 1. Criteria for determining the stages of sleep.

EOG	EMG
WAKE	beta waves / alpha waves
NREM — STAGE 2	spindle ^{k} / theta waves
DELTA	delta waves
REM	sawtooth waves

50uv
1sec

the occipital region of the brain) and others eliminate the EMG
(5). Additional measurements such as heart beat and breathing
movements are often also employed (6). Figure 1 summarizes how
the stages of sleep are determined from these measurements.

The waking state (also often called stage 0) is characterized by high EMG, eye movements that are rather constant
but not as abrupt as those occuring in stage REM (rapid eye
movement), and either low voltage (low amplitude on the recording chart), fast irregular waves called beta (over 13 Hz)
or moderate voltage, rather regular somewhat slower waves
called alpha (8-12 Hz) (4).

Sleep onset is characterized by slow rolling eye movements
(see Figure 2) of several seconds' or more duration and a mixture of frequencies of relatively low voltage but typically
dominated by theta waves (4-7 Hz), usually accompanied by or
preceded by a moderation of EMG activity (4).

In stage 2 the EEG shows theta and perhaps a few delta
waves accompanied by K-complexes (a high amplitude negative
wave followed by a positive wave lasting more than 1/2 second)
and sleep spindles (rhythmic 12-14 Hz waves lasting at least
1/2 second). Eye movements are absent and EMG is moderate
during this stage (4).

Delta or slow wave sleep is characterized by high voltage
(more than 75 MV), slow (1/4-3 Hz) waves (7). At least 20%
of the record must show delta waves to be considered this type
of sleep. Eye movements are absent and muscle activity is
moderate. This stage can be further broken down into stages 3
(20 to 50% delta waves) and 4 (greater than 50% delta waves) (4)
Stages 1 through 4 are collectively known as NREM (pronounced
non-REM) sleep (8). Older reports may use terms such as quiet,
slow wave, or S in place of NREM (9;10).

REM sleep is easily distinguished from the other stages.
The EEG is low voltage, random, and fast ("saw tooth" in shape)
waves, the EOG shows bursts of usually sharp waves (reflecting
rapid eye movements), and the EMG is small or absent (4).
This stage of sleep is also known as paradoxical (since the
EEG resembles the waking EEG yet the person is, paradoxically,
asleep), activated, deep, low voltage fast, emergent or ascending stage 1 (because the EEG sometimes resembles stage 1 and
the sleeper is emerging or ascending from deeper sleep), or
D-sleep (9;10).

The physiology of the body during REM is quite different
from that during NREM. NREM is a sleep of tranquility, REM of
physiological storms. During NREM the body processes are very
regular and at a low level, but otherwise similar to the
physiology of wakefulness. During REM some functions like
heart rate and breathing rate can vary wildly and others such
as body temperature regulation operate quite differently from

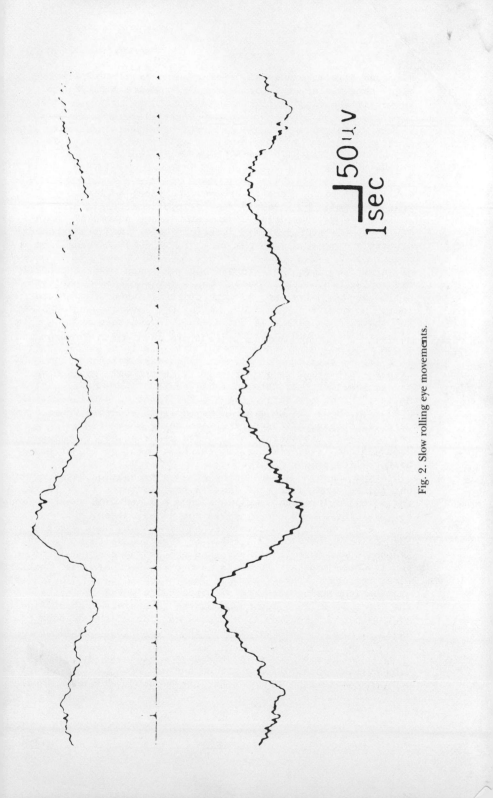

Fig. 2. Slow rolling eye movements.

NREM and even wakefulness. Finally, and importantly, at this
stage the muscles used for body movements are paralyzed so
that they are flaccid (11).

Sleep in the Average Young Adult

The stages of sleep in the average young adult (20 to 30
years of age) show a fairly regular cyclic alteration.
While there is considerable variation from individual to individual, the average times described below indicate a general
pattern and are based on the work of Williams, Karacan, and
Hursch (5).

After the lights are turned out, the beta waves eventually
are replaced by alpha. (Some people may not show alpha, yet
still have normal sleep and wakefulness.) About ten minutes
later the occurrence of slow rolling eye movements accompanies
the onset of stage 1. If the sleeper is awakened at this time,
s/he probably would report feelings of floating. At other
times s/he may experience a myoclonic jerk (a sudden kicking
of a leg or thrusting of an arm) which may awaken her/him
with a start (2). In either case, s/he probably would have
stated that s/he was not really asleep but instead "almost
asleep." However, during stage 1 reactions to outside stimuli
are diminished. In an experiment, college students whose eyes
were taped open no longer reported seeing when stage 1
started (2). The sleeper might have reported experiencing a
"short dream" (12) and her/his thinking might no longer have
been reality oriented.

Stage 1 can best be thought of as a transition between
wakefulness and sleep that lasts 3 to 12 minutes (5). If it
lasts longer it probably will be interspersed with short periods
of wakefulness. It certainly is not a deep sleep.

The emergence of K-complexes and sleep spindles signals
the beginning of stage 2 sleep. If awakened at this time, a
sleeper would most likely say that she/he was truly asleep
yet it would not have been too hard to awaken her/him. This
first period of stage 2 usually lasts from 10 to 20 minutes (5).

The increasing presence of large delta waves indicates
the onset of delta sleep. Waking the sleeper is most difficult
at this time; hence, delta sleep is considered the deepest
stage of sleep. The average length of the first period of
delta sleep ranges from 40 to 90 minutes (5).

Following a brief period of stage 2 sleep again (4 to 10
minutes), which is often preceded and/or ended by a series of
body movements, the signs of REM sleep occur. The neck muscle

tension reduces to its lowest level, the waves become faster and of lower voltage, somewhat resembling those of wakefulness, and bursts of quick eye movement can be noted. Its onset is 80 to 120 minutes after the beginning of stage 1. This period of REM is typically short (7 to 10 minutes) but may be longer (up to 20 minutes) (5). Intense dreaming typically occurs in this stage.

And so the cycle continues throughout the night as shown in Figure 3. About every 90 to 105 minutes another REM period begins (8). But with each succeeding cycle, the duration of REM tends to increase, eventually lasting 1/2 hour or more, while that of delta sleep decreases. In fact, delta sleep rarely occurs during the second half of the night. Most of the rest of sleep is stage 2 with very little stage 1 occurring. This entire pattern is punctuated with an average of 55 movements per night, typically occurring at the point of a stage change and one or two brief arousals to wakefulness (5).

The typical young adult spends about 7 1/2 hours in bed per night. A little over 7 hours of this is spent in sleep (although average total sleep in 24 hours approaches 8 hours if naps are taken into account). Total wakefulness occupies about 1 1/2% of the time between falling asleep and getting up in the morning. REM accounts for about another 25% of this time (or a little less than 2 hours), stage 2 for about 50% (close to 3 1/4 hours), and delta about 20% (about 1 1/4 hours) (1).

Sleep during Other Ages

Not everyone's sleep is like that of the typical young adult. Some normal young adults differ greatly in length and percentage (but not sequence of stages) from these norms. And even casual experience with babies indicates a pattern greatly different from this. The elderly may show dramatic differences, too (1).

Table 1 summarizes the patterns of sleep typical for various ages (5). The lack of information on the newborn does not reflect a lack of study of the sleep at this age. Quite the contrary, this age has been much studied (13). Sleep patterns at this age are so different that direct comparison with older humans is not possible.

When the sleep of newborns is measured, the same basic EEG, EOG, and EMG measurements are taken, plus measurements for respiration via additional sensors applied to the chest. In addition, every 30 seconds an observer must mark on the

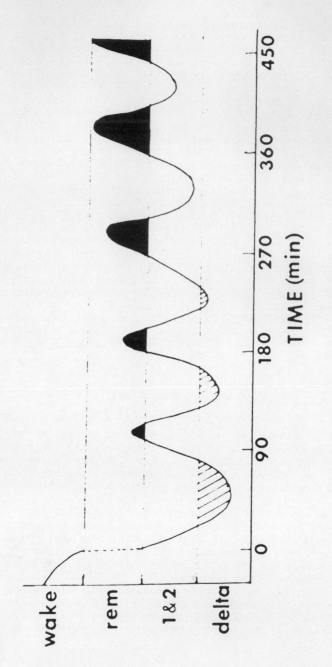

Fig. 3. Idealized night of sleep for a young adult.

Table 1

Average Patterns of Sleep for Various Ages

Variable	Age					
	Newborn	Pre-school	Grade School	High School	Young Adult	Retired
Time in Bed (hrs., mins.)		10h 18m	9h 54m	8h 12m	7h 21m	7h 38m
Total Time Asleep (hrs., mins.)	(17)	9h 53m	9h 30m	7h 48m	7h 4m	6h 46m
Time to Get to Sleep (mins.)		14	15	16.5	9	13
Number of Awakenings (30s or more)		1.5	1.1	2.3	2	5 (♀ less)
Percent of Time Awake		1.3	1.0	1.3	1.2	8.5
Percent REM	(50)	31	28	24	26	22.5
Percent Stage 2		45 (♀ less)	48	48	51	56
Percent Delta		20.5	21	23	16	5
REM Cycle (mins.)	(60)	90 (♀ less)	111	112	105	100
Sleep Efficiency		.96	.96	.95	.96	.88
Number of Stages		34	33	39	36	41

sleep record the condition of the baby--whether eyes are open
or closed and whether she or he is quiet or active and whether
she or he is crying, making body movements, yawning, making
facial expressions, etc. (14).

The characteristics used to categorize newborns are quite
different from those seen in adults. These categories are low
voltage irregular, high voltage slow, mixed (a random mixture
of high and low voltages), and Tracé alternant (several seconds
of high voltage slow waves followed by several seconds of low
voltage fast waves). Additional characteristics necessary to
assess infants' sleep include eye movements and muscle tone
(as in adults), and, as mentioned above, respiration (regular
or irregular), body movements (present or absent), and whether
the eyes are open or shut.

Combinations of these characteristics are used as criteria for various stages of sleep. The names of the stages
as well as their characteristics differ from those used for
adults. They include awake, drowsy, active sleep, quiet sleep,
and indeterminate state (14). Quiet sleep transforms into
NREM as the infant matures. Likewise, active sleep gradually
becomes REM sleep. Indeterminate sleep diminishes with age.

The figures for the newborns that are presented in Table 1
are in parentheses because they are gross approximations.
The rest are absent simply because nothing in newborn sleep
clearly resembles the categories of adult sleep or are otherwise unavailable (6;9;15;16).

By three years of age, a child's sleep has stabilized
enough to clearly compare it with that of adult sleep. As
can be seen in Table 1, the time in bed declines with advancing
age as does total time asleep. In the first five or so years
of life, the number and timing of sleep periods change, as can
be seen in Figure 4. Every 24 hours the newborn has multiple
periods of sleep separated by short (at first) periods of
wakefulness. By one year of age much sleep has "consolidated"
into the evening and night but a daily nap period or two remains. By four years of age, the waking time is longer, partially because the nap is later and shorter. Usually by age
six the regular nap disappears and all sleep occurs at night (1).

In Table 1 we can see that the time it takes to fall
asleep remains relatively stable until young adulthood, as does
percent of time awake after going to bed. The number of
awakenings during sleep dips from 1 1/2 in the preschooler to
about 1 in grade school and rises to 2 by high school. The
percent of REM starts high, going from 75% in premature infants
to 50% in term infants, settling down to around 25% by high
school age. Percentage of stage 2 stays steady at about 50%
throughout maturation to adulthood. The percentage of delta
is also stable but does drop between high school age and

continue

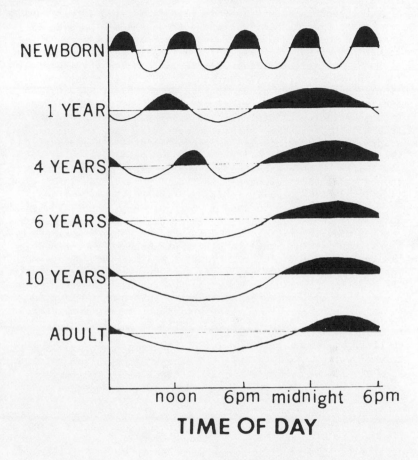

Fig. 4. The number and timing of sleep periods in 24 hours at different ages.

adulthood. Finally, the REM cycle (time from the start of one
REM cycle to the next) increases from 60 minutes to over 100
minutes by grade school age (5).

A somewhat different pattern emerges if the actual amount
of time spent in each stage of sleep is considered rather than
percent of time in bed. This difference occurs because the
change in total sleep time is often different from the change
occurring in the stages at different ages. For example, REM,
stage 2, and delta all show decline in the early years of life
in absolute amounts. The decline in REM is greatest and continues until about the end of high school age. The stage 2
decline occurs almost entirely during pre-adolescence but
gradually increases beginning in mid-young adulthood. The
decline of actual time spent in delta sleep begins during
grade school and continues slowly but steadily throughout the
rest of life (5).

So far we have examined changes in sleep from infancy
through adulthood but have said little about sleep during retirement age. Generally we can say that sleep "frays" in
the retirement years because it is noticeably lighter, with
more awakenings (1). However, individuals differ from one
another more in this age group than in any other; some people
experience little change in sleep while others notice considerable changes in sleep. Time in bed increases progressively
with age in the retirement years, yet total sleep time declines.
The reasons for this can be accounted for by a progressive increase in the amount of time taken to fall asleep and time
awake. A measure called sleep efficiency (derived by dividing
total sleep time by time in bed) dramatically illustrates these
changes. A general decline in this index begins at about 30
years of age when it is .96 with the decline accelerating after
50 years of age to less than .80 in the eighth decade of life.
Finally, the number of awakenings during sleep progresses
steadily from an average of 2 during the fourth decade to 8
during the eighth decade (5).

Other indicators of sleep becoming lighter during the retirement years include the changes in the total duration of
the various stages of sleep. REM shows a decline both in percent of total sleep time and absolute amount. Delta sleep declines also, with few retired males showing any stage 4 sleep
at all. Stage 2 percent increases but its absolute amount remains steady. Stage 1, the lightest sleep, shows a dramatic
increase during the retirement years (5).

Finally, the re-emergence of the nap occurs in the elderly (1)
The significance of this is debatable, however. Later in this
chapter, we will explore napping in general, but suffice it to
say that napping may be more common at all ages than is generally
believed. The relative absence of naps in adulthood in our

culture may be due more to social and work schedules than
anything else. Their re-emergence in retirees may be a result of the absence of the rigid schedule demands of the
workplace which prevent the possibility of napping. On the
other hand, napping, especially excessive napping, may be
both the cause as well as the result of the "fraying" of sleep
in the elderly (17). At any age, daytime sleep tends to reduce
the efficiency of nighttime sleep unless substantial wake time
intervenes (1). However, the issue is not resolved and there
appear to be wide differences among individuals that make a
definitive analysis of the function, cause, and consequences of
napping difficult.

Looking back over all of these data on changes in sleep
that occur with age, what can we say? First there are great
changes in the young in kinds of sleep, their amounts, and in
patterns of sleep followed by relatively stable or gradual
changes in adulthood. The later years again show many changes,
with sleep beginning to fragment, but also greater individual
differences in the amounts and patterns of sleep.

Differences between males and females have not been mentioned because there are very few until late adulthood. As
retirement age approaches, sleep begins to fragment earlier
in males than in females. By postretirement age, changes
in the sleep of females may occur as much as 10 years later
than similar changes in the sleep of males (5).

Sleep Is an Active Process

Not only has the sleep laboratory enabled us to tell when
a person is asleep and in what type of sleep, but also some
things about what sleep is and how it varies among people.
First, it should be obvious that sleep is more than a passive
reduction of bodily processes (2). This is contrary to popular
opinion since it seems that people do everything possible to
reduce body and mental activity and activation when attempting
to go to sleep. Failure to do so usually renders sleep elusive
and difficult.

But laboratory studies show that sleep is anything but
passive. The most compelling evidence is the recurrent REM
episodes with active mind content and aroused internal body
functions at the same time the muscles that produce body movement are actively inhibited (that is, paralyzed) (2). While
it is true that the physiology of the body that accompanies
NREM appears to more closely conform to the notions of passive
sleep, the study of brain functions (see the next chapter)

suggests that this is not entirely true. During any stage of
sleep, some parts of the brain are more, not less, active
than during wakefulness--more active because they are actively
producing sleep. Thus, during sleep the entire brain does not
reduce its activity to a low level, instead some areas become
more activated. And, the relative balance of activity shifts
as sleep progresses through its cycle of stages (15).

Read → Depth of Sleep

Which sleep stage is the deepest? When awakened from
sleep, sometimes it is very easy for a person to regain full
consciousness. But at other times waking up is slow and difficult. In the latter case a person might say that s/he was
very soundly asleep or in a deep sleep. It seems as if it
should be easy to determine which stage of sleep is the
deepest, but actually it is not.

In the laboratory, depth of sleep is determined by the
degree of loudness of a noise necessary to awaken the sleeper.
But it also depends on just what noise is being made. A person awakens, for instance, much more easily and faster to
someone saying her/his name than to someone shouting other
names. There is also the example of the mother sleeping
through the roar of city noises but awakening at the first cry
of her baby. Generally, however, as sleep progresses through
the stages from 1 to 4, it is harder to cause awakening in the
sense that it takes louder and louder noise. REM is somewhere
between stage 2 and delta sleep on this scale (except in the
cat which requires more noise in REM than even in stage 4 to
awaken it) (9). If muscle relaxation is used as the indicator
of depth of sleep, then REM with its muscle paralysis, is
the deepest stage of sleep.

Perhaps, then, the question is too simple. It assumes a
continuum in which various degrees of wakefulness (hyperactive
through alert through drowsy) continue into various degrees of
sleep (light through moderate through heavy) in a straight
line. Instead, it appears that there are perhaps three different states--wakefulness, REM, and NREM--each with its own
characteristics. Rather than being like a continuous hallway
that is very bright at one end and very dark at the other,
the states of sleep and wakefulness are more like separate
rooms in a house--each room with its own furnishings and
function. Just as these rooms may be interconnected and contain some common elements (such as carpeting) so too the
stages of sleep are connected and contain common elements (18).

In fact, there are enough differences to make it more realistic to think of them as separate states.

Sleep Deprivation

(What are the consequences of going without sleep? Although the need for sleep seems to be very compelling, it can be postponed by will power or circumstances. Yet, lack of sleep in and of itself does not result in long-term consequences (19). Furthermore, this sleep loss is permanently and easily reversed by a little extra sleep during the next night or two. And this catch-up sleep is typically considerably less than the amount missed (20). Thus it has been said that the major effect of lack of sleep is simply sleepiness (1;21). For most people, the occasional sleepiness resulting from a lack of sleep is a minor annoyance, but for others it can be a continual devastating factor in their lives (see chapter on sleep disorders). (The sleepiness caused by lack of sleep may, however, result in severe consequences such as a car accident or falling asleep on the job, and thus it is not always totally benign.)

There are some measurable physiological and psychological changes resulting from sleep deprivation (1;19;21). Physiologically, there may be some slowing of the reflexes, heart palpitations, a slight loss of strength, and some difficulty focusing the eyes. Psychologically, a person may experience "illusionations" (something is present but is seen incorrectly), have a lack of "energy," feel depressed, and/or experience a loss of control. In addition, there may be a decrease in ego functioning characterized by a reduction in social adaptation, less tolerance, more immaturity, more irritability, and an increase in basic demands. Also, following a lack of sufficient sleep, a person may have difficulty with concentration and immediate memory.

None of these problems is overwhelming or permanent. With a little effort most people can rally and do many things normally even after several days of sleep loss (1). (A person will become more and more sleepy up to about 60 hours without sleep but become no sleepier after that even with continued sleep loss; other effects may continue to get worse with subsequent sleeplessness (19). Quiet tasks requiring concentration and repetition present the most problems following sleep loss. In fact, most people will experience "micro sleeps" at such times (20). These are quick snatches of sleep lasting only a few seconds (19;22).

Recovery from sleep loss does seem to be necessary (20).
If allowed to sleep undisturbed, a person's total sleep time
will typically be greater than normal for a couple of nights (19)
Most people report that 3 to 4 "good nights of sleep" are sufficient. Interestingly, people make up the lost delta sleep
before the lost REM (9;19)

Most people do not experience successive sleepless nights
as often as they experience successive nights of shortened
sleep. In this situation, the sleep loss seems to accumulate
so that eventually the person begins to show the effects of
the loss. However, it is the end of the sleep cycle of each
night that is lost and since this portion of the sleep period
has a high proportion of REM and no delta, the effects of successive nights of partial sleep loss result in deprivation of
REM sleep only (1).

In the laboratory it is possible to prevent the occurrence of specific stages of sleep in order to assess the
effects of their absence. REM sleep is prevented by awakening
the sleeper every time the chart shows that the person is
entering REM. In this situation the sleeper is allowed to
obtain all the NREM sleep that is desired—only REM is prevented. The original laboratory studies suggested that the
effect was severe mental disorder if the deprivation lasted
several days (20). Without REM, a person could become a
paranoid schizophrenic. Less severe deprivation results in
irritability, poor social interactions, agitation, and increased impulsivity. The results were interpreted at that
time as showing that one needs to dream to maintain mental
stability, since it was believed that dreams occurred only in
REM (1;8;18;23).

Both the results and their interpretation have been subsequently modified (20). First, mental disorder is not the
inevitable outcome of even severe REM deprivation. A number
of normal volunteers have been deprived of REM for several
days with no lasting effects. The procedure is stressful,
however, and like any other stress may cause an unstable
person to manifest a sometimes severe behavioral disorder.
Apparently, that is what happened with the early subjects (9).
Second, it is now known that dreaming is not always confined
to REM but may also occur in NREM (18). Thus, any negative
behavior following REM deprivation cannot unequivocally be
attributed to the loss of dreaming.

REM deprivation does have its effects, but they are subtle.
There is an increase in the number of attempts to start REM
during the sleep period and the length of time between these
attempts decreases. These effects have been given the name
"REM pressure." REM pressure builds with the duration of the
deprivation procedure until a person may make a dozen attempts
per hour to initiate REM (2).

Subsequent uninterrupted sleep also shows REM pressure effects in that the percent of REM is increased, the REM cycle is decreased, and the "density" of eye movements is greater (that is, there are more eye movements per minute than occur normally). These changes have been termed "REM rebound" (8).

The effects of REM deprivation can also be seen during a person's subsequent waking hours. The person is more animated and activated than usual. Memory problems have also been reported. Both humans and animals experience some reduction in their ability to memorize new things as a result of REM deprivation. Even when REM deprivation occurs following learning attempts, a reduction of retention may occur. These effects appear to be more apparent when the material to be learned has an emotional importance for the subject (8).

Delta sleep can also be selectively blocked in the laboratory, but the procedure is different from REM deprivation (10;20;22). Whenever the chart indicates that delta is about to begin, a tone is sounded that is not loud enough to awaken the person but is loud enough to drive sleep back to stage 2 or 1. REM sleep is not affected by this procedure. Delta sleep deprived individuals do not consistently report any behavioral problems but state that they feel lethargic and depressed. They also complain of muscle aches. As a result, they tend to act more subdued and withdrawn.

It is not yet possible to deprive people of only stage 2 or 1 sleep since they normally precede other stages of sleep. Depriving a person of these stages would necessarily deprive them of both delta and REM. Thus, little is known about the importance of these stages of sleep.

Length of Sleep

The effects of variations in the length of prior wakefulness on subsequent sleep are simple. Generally, the longer the period of wakefulness, the more quickly we fall asleep. People who decide to "sleep in" one morning often report difficulty getting to sleep the following night. A similar thing can happen with a long nap during the afternoon or evening (1).

The effects of duration of prior wakefulness on subsequent sleep length are less well known due to a lack of research and more complicated interaction of other factors. Sleep appears to be self-terminating. The body also has rhythms (to be discussed in the next chapter) which make it easier and more efficient to sleep during a certain part of every 24 hours.

When the attempt is made to sleep too long, this sleep starts
to encroach upon the natural awake time and tends to make
subsequent sleep more difficult. Finally, environmental influences such as daylight, traffic noises, and the activity
of other people tend to make prolonged sleep more difficult.
Nevertheless, it is probably safe to say that prolonged wakefulness does tend to lengthen subsequent sleep, and, conversely, shortened wakefulness tends to shorten sleep that
follows. It is difficult to be more specific (1).

The length of prior wakefulness does affect sleep architecture, that is, the amount and distribution of the stages.
The relationship between length of prior wakefulness and the
amount of delta that follows is direct. The longer the period
of wakefulness, the more delta sleep that follows. The effect
on stages 1 and 2 is inverse, with less of these stages following longer periods of wakefulness. There seems to be little
direct effect on REM. REM is indirectly affected because the
need for delta sleep takes precedence and REM sleep appears to
be reduced following a lengthy period of wakefulness, but it
is really just deferred (1).

These effects can be best illustrated by examining the
characteristics of a nap at different times during the day
following a normal night of sleep. A morning nap tends to be
shorter, more difficult to start, and contains more of stages
1 and 2 and perhaps REM. An evening nap tends to be easier to
achieve, lasts longer, and consists of more delta and less
stages 1, 2, and REM (1). Naps in the afternoon appear to be
a special case. People, generally, are sleepier in mid-afternoon than any other time during the waking hours and thus are
able to go to sleep faster (24).

What are the effects of changing the length of the sleep
period? Since delta sleep is present only in the first few
hours of sleep, the sleep period must be drastically shortened
before it can be affected. On the other hand, the amounts of
stages 1, 2, and REM vary directly with sleep length (1).
Think of an old fashioned clock with several springs. One
spring is for delta and another for REM. When you sleep, the
delta spring is wound first. Only when it is tight can the
REM spring be completely wound. But the winding of these
springs takes time and thus shortened sleep may not allow the
REM spring to be fully wound. Stages 1 and 2 are fillers
between the winding periods. During wakefulness the springs
slowly unwind. If they have not been wound enough the night
before, a person may feel the effects. However, a little extra
rewinding the next night or two seems to correct any previous
insufficient winding, but this extra rewinding takes longer.

Timing of Sleep

Changing the sleep schedule is not uncommon in the modern world with changing shift work and jet travel. It has been estimated that 20% of U.S. workers are on shift schedules. Sleep attempted during usual waking hours results in more arousals and more stage 1 and often shorter time asleep. Performance during normal sleep time is greatly reduced especially for long, repetitive, and uninteresting tasks (1). More industrial accidents occur during such times. The body can adapt but it takes several weeks switching from nighttime sleeping to daytime sleeping. (Interestingly, when shifting back to nighttime sleeping, the switch takes place in a much shorter period of time--several days.)

Most people maintain a relatively regular, fixed time of arising (1). Again, society appears to demand regular arousal times due to regular schedules of the job, marketplace, school, and family life. Also the availability of cheap alarm clocks has long made a regular time of arousal possible.

Some people can awaken at a predetermined time without an alarm clock (19). They simply decide what time they would like to awaken before retiring. This is a lot easier if the arousal time is the same every morning but for some people it works even for unusual times. (Besides being a more pleasant way to wake up than being startled by an alarm--usually during the best part of a dream--this phenomenon provides interesting implications about the functioning of the mind during sleep. Just what is the unconscious process of the mind that occurs to allow it to keep time accurately--often with an error of less than 5 minutes--and then be able to interrupt sleep and initiate wakefulness? We need to know more about this often unrecognized yet powerful potential of the mind.)

Most people are less regular about their times of initiating sleep (1). All the indications are that this irregularity is not particularly harmful as long as a person does not con- tinually push back the time of retiring and thus accumulate sleep deprivation.

Napping

Napping has been called any rest period up to 20 minutes long, involving unconsciousness but no pajamas (25). What is known about napping? Is it just for young children? Is it a problem in adults or is it beneficial for them, too?

In our culture the accepted pattern of sleep is one long
period every 24 hours. This is felt to be normal, natural,
and beneficial. Yet non-napping might be the exception rather
than the rule in both humans and animals. In other cultures,
a daily nap, such as the Mexican siesta, is considered appropriate and necessary. In the United States, 50-85% of college
students take several naps per week. (Most of the rest wish
they could but report not having enough time!) In fact, most
non-napping is due to demands of schedules of work or society (1).

Need for naps and effectiveness of naps are most easily
studied using the Multiple Sleep Latency Test (MSLT) (24).
In this test a person is given a 20-minute opportunity to
sleep every 2 hours throughout the day. Using this test,
several things about naps have been discovered. First, almost
everybody is sleepiest in the middle of the afternoon and can
most easily nap then. This is relatively close to being opposite the middle of the night sleep period (i.e., 180 degrees
out of phase with night sleep). Put another way, this is about
the mid-period between successive nights of sleep. During this
time, people feel sleepiest and performance on many tasks
tends to be at its worst. A nap serves to reverse both of
these; subsequent naps take longer to achieve.

Figure 5 compares napping in young adults to that of older
and younger people. As can be seen, pre- and early pubescent
children show little tendency to nap at any time during the
day. In contrast, mid-afternoon sleepiness becomes stronger
in mature adults and the elderly. (It should be noted that
the overall curve does tend to move down following insufficient
sleep on the previous night [24].)

Why do people nap? There appear to be four contributing
factors: compensatory--to "catch up" on lost sleep; environ-
mental--caused by events from outside a person's body; biological rhythm--another example of the influence of internal
rhythms of the body; and recreation--napping for the pure
pleasure of it (25). Compensatory napping is most frequent
following a night of shortened sleep and in night shift or
rotating shift workers. Environmentally caused napping occurs
more in people who live in a hostile environment, especially
one where the afternoons are very hot. Also a part of this
factor are societal/social demands. These account for weekend
napping in the U.S. and other industrialized countries.
People who nap for recreation report they can sleep "anytime,
anywhere." Undoubtedly, all naps are influenced by all four
factors to some degree. Consider classroom napping of college
students; it is frequently compensatory, certainly environmental, influenced by biological rhythms, and mainly recrea-
tional.

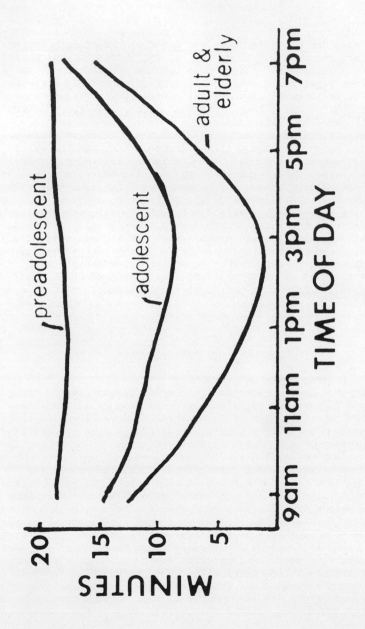

Fig. 5. The average amount of time taken to get to sleep at various times during the day at selected ages.

Sleep Need

Seven and one-half hours per night is the average amount
of sleep required for young adults, but there are wide individual differences (5). Some people do well with 6 hours or
less per night while others cannot live comfortably with less
than 10 or 11 hours of sleep (1). Only the individual can
determine how much sleep is required since only the individual
knows when s/he feels good the next day. The differences
among people in amount of sleep need are not due to differences
in will power, latitude, climate, time of day chosen for sleeping, or demands of society but are rather individual biological
differences. Some people are tall, others short; some people
need more sleep, others less. Not every one needs 8 hours of
sleep a night to be healthy (1).

Very few people sleep too much. Sleep tends to be self-
regulating: when you have had enough you wake up. Too much
sleep, for those few who do manage to get it, has been said
to be as bad as too little (19). Following over-sleeping,
people report feeling lethargic and are slow moving, with
their heads in a fog. These unpleasant sensations may last
the rest of the waking period or slowly diminish with time and
exercise.

Long Versus Short Sleepers

Most of us are close to the average for our age in the
amount of sleep needed per night. The rest fall into three
groups: short sleepers, long sleepers, and variable length
sleepers. People from each of these groups have been studied
in an attempt to find out if they differ in any other way besides sleep needs (8;20). They do.

Short sleepers, for research purposes, are people who
average less than 5 1/2 hours of sleep per night. Insomniacs
and voluntary self-deprivers were excluded from study. Only
those people who felt good and performed well with that amount
of sleep were studied. Likewise, long sleepers are those who
must have more than 8 hours sleep (with 9 hours spent in bed)
each night to feel and function at their best. Variable length
sleepers were people who required short nights of sleep for
long periods of time (months) but long nights of sleep during
other long periods. The results described below are averages
from each group. No one individual showed the entire pattern
nor can you expect to find all or even many of the characteris-

tics to be described in an individual short, long, or variable
length sleeper. Furthermore, the subjects were post-college
age at the time when they were studied. Other research, done
on college students, did not produce the same results. However, these latter subjects probably, like most college students, had not stabilized their sleep patterns and thus observations on them cannot be as readily generalized.

When the sleep of the short and long sleepers was analyzed
in a sleep laboratory, subjects in both groups got about the
same amount of delta sleep and in about the same distribution
throughout the night. In these respects both groups resembled
each other as well as normal length sleepers. However, the
amount of REM sleep they each obtained was different. Short
sleepers accumulated less than average amounts of REM sleep
while long sleepers obtained twice as much REM as short
sleepers, which was above average. Furthermore, long sleepers
showed more rapid eye movements per minute (REM density),
more time awake in bed, took a longer time to get to sleep,
and did not feel as refreshed in the morning.

Short sleepers report themselves to be efficient and
energetic, to be satisfied with themselves and their lives,
and to like to keep busy and work hard. They viewed sleep as
a chore. Long sleepers were less easy to categorize as a
group except that they viewed sleep as a luxury and that it
is very desirable and necessary to get the "right amount."

On psychological tests, short sleepers revealed themselves
to be ambitious, decisive, and extroverted. Furthermore, they
were somewhat conformist and tended to deny rather than worry
about problems. Other than denying problems, they showed
little psychological pathology.

Test results showed long sleepers to be mildly to moderately
neurotic. Some were anxious, inhibited, and depressed. Others
were not very self-assured. They tended to be worriers. There
were some suggestions of high creativity among members of this
group.

Short sleepers were socially adept persons. Long sleepers
were non-conformists, social critics, and politically active.
They also complained about aches and pains. When awakened
during their dreams, long sleepers felt quiet and passive
early in the night but more active and energetic during later
wake-ups. Short sleepers were the same throughout the night
during dream wake-ups. Thus it appears that the long sleepers
experienced psychological change within sleep which the short
sleepers did not experience. Long sleepers also showed more
negative effects when deprived of REM and more REM pressure.

It is not possible to tell from these findings if the
sleep pattern causes the other patterns or vice versa or if
both are caused by something else or, however unlikely, are

totally unrelated. Study of the variable length sleepers, however, does tend to show some cause and effect (20).

Variable length sleepers, when requiring short nights of sleep, showed the characteristics of short sleepers. When they required long nights of sleep they more closely resembled long sleepers. Furthermore, their sleep need increased during times of stress, depression, change in job, increased mental work, increased physical work, increased emotions, and an inward focusing. Their sleep need decreased if all was going well, their work was stable and pleasant, etc. In other words, except for a few individuals who "kept busy" (that is, denied reality), sleep need increased when variable length sleepers were stressed, worried, or changed their lifestyle. The events of waking life, whether physical or emotional, seemed to cause a change in their sleep needs. Thus it appears that sleep length (and thus sleep need) is probably a function of a person's life events.

Similar kinds of changes can be seen in the sleep of average length sleepers although to a much lesser degree. For example, in physically fit individuals either a big increase or big decrease in physical activity increases sleep length a bit. A sudden change in weight will have a similar effect. Another example is the modest but real increase in REM during times of emotional turmoil.

Good Sleep

What then constitutes good sleep? First and foremost, good sleep is very subjective. In the laboratory, when subjects report having had a good night of sleep compared to reports of a poor night, the recording shows more total sleep and, sometimes, fewer awakenings. Interestingly, greater amounts of time in REM have no effect on the degree of feeling sleepy the next day but do tend to improve mood. People who evaluate themselves as consistently good sleepers average more sleep time, less time awake in bed, more REM, but no difference in the amount of delta. Poor nights of sleep may be caused by almost any disturbing environmental conditions and result in a decrease of REM and often less total sleep time and delta as well. Overall, it appears that the amount of delta sleep is relatively unchanged from night to night in most people and probably has little to do with perceived differences in quality of sleep (an exception to this is the rare disorder of alpha-delta sleep). Total sleep time, number of awakenings, and amount of REM do seem to be important in the perceived

quality of sleep but in different ways. Sleepiness and not
feeling refreshed seem to vary inversely with the first two
factors while mood seems to vary directly with the third factor (8).

References

1. Webb, W.B. (1975). *Sleep the Gentle Tyrant*. Englewood
    Cliffs, N.J.: Prentice-Hall, Inc.

    A wonderfully written, thoughtful introduction to the
    world of the scientific study of sleep and dreams. It is
    sometimes somewhat biased toward the conclusions of the author
    and is beginning to be a bit out of date.

2. Dement, W.C. (1976). *Some Must Watch While Some Must Sleep*.
    New York: Norton.

    Although lacking more recent inclusions to the knowledge
    about sleep and dreams, this book is a wonderfully readable
    introduction to the scientific study by an important and
    devoted researcher.

3. Aserinsky, B., and Kleitman, N. (1953). "Regularly Occur-
    ring Periods of Eye Motility and Concommitant Phenomena
    during Sleep." *Science*, *118*, 273-274.

    The classic paper that first reported REM sleep.

4. Rechtschaffen, S., and Kales, S. (1978). *A Manual of
    Standardized Terminology, Techniques and Scoring System
    for Sleep Stages of Human Subjects*. Los Angeles: UCLA
    Brain Information Service/Brain Research Institute.

    The worldwide accepted standards and criteria for "scoring"
    deep laboratory sleep records into stages.

5. Williams, R.L.; Karacan, I.; and Hursch, C.J. (1974).
    Electroencephalography (EEG) of Human Sleep. New York:
    Wiley.

    Presents the characteristics of sleep found in individuals
    from newborns to those well into retirement age in statis-
    tical detail with appropriate verbal interpretations. Ex-
    tremely useful for understanding the characteristics of
    sleep that occur at various ages and the changes that nor-
    mally occur in sleep with aging.

6. Williams, R.L., and Karacan, I. (Eds.) (1978). *Sleep Disorders: Diagnosis and Treatment*. New York: Wiley.

7. Cartwright, R.D. (1977). *Night Life: Explorations in Dreaming*. Englewood Cliffs, N.J.: Prentice-Hall, Inc.

8. Cartwright, R.D. (1978). *A Primer on Sleep and Dreaming*. Reading, Mass.: Addison-Wesley.

    Excellent reviews of the studies of dreaming done in the sleep laboratory with special emphasis on the author's insightful work.

9. Freemon, F.R. (1972). *Sleep Research: A Critical Review*. Springfield, Ill.: Charles C. Thomas.

10. Webb, W.B. (1973). "Sleep Research Past and Present." In W.B. Webb (Ed.), *Sleep: An Active Process* (pp. 1-10). Glenview, Ill.: Scott, Foresman.

11. Orem, J., and Barnes, C.D. (Eds.) (1980). *Physiology in Sleep*. New York: Academic Press.

    Excellent review of the bodily processes in sleep emphasizing those that are different from waking.

12. Faraday, A. (1972). *Dream Power*. New York: Berkley.

13. Hoppenbrouwers, T. (1982). "Electronic Monitoring in the Newborn and Young Infant: Theoretical Considerations." In C. Guilleminault (Ed.), *Sleeping and Waking Disorders: Indications and Techniques* (pp. 239-252). Menlo Park, Calif.: Addison-Wesley.

14. Anders, T.; Emde, R.; and Parmelee, A. (Eds.) (1971). *A Manual of Standardized Terminology, Techniques and Criteria for Scoring of States of Sleep and Wakefulness in Newborn Infants*. Los Angeles: UCLA Brain Information Service/BRI Publications Office.

15. Cohen, David B. (1979). *Sleep and Dreaming: Origins, Nature, and Functions*. New York: Pergamon Press.

    An overview of sleep followed by a review of results of experiments on dreams and dreaming. The writing is rather dry and the organization is a bit awkward.

16. Petre-Quadens, O. (1974). "Sleep in the Human Newborn." In O. Petre-Quadens and J.D. Schlag, *Basic Sleep Mechanisms* (pp. 355-380). New York: Academic Press.

17. Prinz, P.N., and Raskin, M. (1978). "Aging and Sleep Disorders." In R.L. Williams and L. Karacan (Eds.), *Sleep Disorders: Diagnosis and Treatment* (pp. 303-321). New York: Wiley.

18. Dement, W.C., and Mitler, M.M. (1974). "An Introduction to Sleep." In O. Petre-Quadens and J.D. Schlag (Eds.), *Basic Sleep Mechanisms* (pp. 271-296). New York: Academic Press.

19. Kleitman, N. (1963). *Sleep and Wakefulness*. Chicago: University of Chicago Press.

    A masterpiece for its thoroughness. Although of mainly historical importance, it still contains some good basic information in an encyclopedia-like format.

20. Hartmann, E.L. (1973). *The Functions of Sleep*. New Haven: Yale University Press.

21. Webb, W.B., and Cartwright, R.D. (1978). "Sleep and Dreams." *Annual Review of Psychology*, *29*, 223-252.

22. Webb, W.B. (1968). *Sleep: An Experiment Approach*. New York: Macmillan.

23. Van de Castle, R. (1971). *The Psychology of Dreaming*. Morristown, N.J.: General Learning Press.

24. Carskadon, M.A. (1981). "Daytime Sleep Tendency: Implications for Napping." Annual Meeting of Association for the Psychophysiological Study of Sleep. Hyannis, Mass.

25. Webb, W.B. (1981). "The Nature of Naps: A Discussion." Annual Meeting of Association for the Psychophysiological Study of Sleep. Hyannis, Mass.

Chapter 2

AN OVERVIEW OF THE BODY AND THE BRAIN IN SLEEP

William H. Moorcroft and Jennifer Clothier

The Body in Sleep

In recent years it has become apparent that sleep is a
different state not only mentally but physiologically. Quantitative and sometimes qualitative differences have been noted
in many body systems during sleep than those present during
wakefulness. Changes in the cardiovascular system, metabolic
processes, the endocrine system, renal functioning, the ali-
mentary system, the motor system, and, most notably, respiration have been documented in recent years.

Breathing

Of all the physiological differences in sleep versus wakefulness discovered in the last decade, the changes in respiratory control are the most dramatic. The complex and overlapping
neural and biochemical mechanisms that regulate respiration in
awake humans and other mammals (see Guyton [1], for example)
were assumed to function equivalently during sleep. Recent
evidence refutes this.

At sleep onset there is a decrease in breathing rate (2),
mostly because more time is spent breathing in (3). Concurrent-
ly there is an overall decrease in response to carbon dioxide
(more pronounced in males) to about 1/2 of that of waking
values (4;5;6), but of greater importance is the response to
levels of oxygen in the blood (7;8). There is a simultaneous
decrease in the sensitivity to oxygen levels (9). These
changes result in an elevation in the carbon dioxide in the
blood (8). Yet at the same time respiration becomes much more
dependent on levels of carbon dioxide in the blood during sleep
than during wakefulness (7). For example, the immediate,
automatic, adaptive increase in breathing effort that typically
occurs in wakefulness when breathing in is made more difficult

(such as breathing through a restrictive face mask) is totally
absent during NREM sleep (10;11). Only after several inadequate breaths resulting in the elevation of carbon dioxide and
reduction of oxygen in the blood is breathing effort ad-
justed (7).

These changes in respiratory control mechanisms may result
in pauses in breathing when falling asleep, as the sleeper
fluctuates between sleep and wakefulness (5;6). Once sleep
is fully obtained, the increase of carbon dioxide in the blood
persists in NREM due to continued reduced breathing rate.
Breathing during NREM tends to be regular and deeper but of
a reduced (from waking) rate, resulting in overall less air
being exchanged per minute (4;6;12). Most adults do not
awaken due to lower oxygen levels in the blood (13).

Changes in the respiratory mechanisms can be noted during
all phases of sleep (6). It takes more effort to breathe
during sleep because there is more resistance to air flow in
the airways and changes in the efficiency of the muscles used
for breathing. Some of the muscles that help keep the upper
airway open when a person breathes tend to become more relaxed during sleep, especially during REM (8;14). The resistance to the flow of air doubles during sleep because of the
resulting smaller passageway in the throat (15). This appears
to contribute to, or perhaps be the cause of, snoring and other
sleep related breathing disorders. These changes are even
greater in REM than NREM (16). Furthermore, the reflexes of
these same passages are changed during sleep (especially REM)
and the tone of the smooth muscles changes.

The changes that occur during REM sleep are even more
dramatic. Respiratory volume is even lower in REM than NREM
and breathing is more rapid in REM (17) but also more irregular (6), with brief episodes of shallow breathing or absence
of breathing (5). Yet, overall, the level of carbon dioxide
and oxygen in the blood is about what it is during waking (12).

The following have also been noted:

First, the sensitivity to carbon dioxide in the blood
drops to one-third of what it is during wakefulness (4) and
may be even completely absent during the phasic portions of
REM (8;9).

Second, some breathing reflexes are different during REM
sleep. During wakefulness and NREM there are reflex changes
in the larynx when blood oxygen falls or carbon dioxide increases that serve to keep air in the lungs longer; these
reflexes are absent during REM (18). The stretch receptors
of the lungs, which are another important aspect in waking
respiratory regulation, function differently in REM sleep (6).
The threshold for responding to irritants in the airway is
elevated during REM compared to that in NREM. Such irritants

may reflexively cause the cessation of breathing and, if strong
enough, arousal from sleep. This arousal response, which is
slower during REM sleep (6) may be attenuated if the sleeper
is sedated or sleep deprived (19).

Third, it appears that a different mechanism controls
breathing during REM. Instead of the automatic nervous system
plus metabolic receptors it is entirely controlled by the
brain (12). This in many ways resembles the "behavioral"
control of breathing that occurs during wakefulness when talking, swallowing, etc. (20). It has been suggested that a
direct link from the reticular formation to the respiratory
centers of the brainstem function during REM (5). Also important are the brain mechanisms that produce phasic muscle
twitches and eye movements during REM since changes have been
noted to occur in the respiratory neurons of the medulla and
correspond to changes in the nerves that control the diaphragm
(6;19). These neural mechanisms may compete with respiratory
responses to changes in the levels of oxygen and carbon
dioxide in the blood (6). Such changes in breathing and the
controls for breathing during REM are even more dramatic in
the infant (14).

Fourth, while the diaphragm functions no differently in
REM it has to do more of the work of breathing (8), because
the muscles of the rib cage show the same kind of inhibition as
the muscles of body movement (5).

Body Temperature

Temperature regulation also shows some dramatic changes
during sleep. Body temperature tends to decline gradually
during sleep, but may vary a bit with the REM-NREM cycle.
During NREM, and especially during the delta portion (19),
the body still regulates its temperature but apparently at a
lower level (5). Heat production is 9% lower during all of
NREM sleep when compared to resting wakefulness; it is 14%
lower during the delta portion and less variable (21). Just
prior to sleep onset in the presence of cool or neutral ambient
temperatures, a drop in rectal temperature accompanied by
dilation of the blood vessels can be observed (5;22). This
drop is greater if the ambient temperature is cold because the
blood vessels of the skin still dilate rather than constrict
as would be expected during wakefulness and the shivering
response is lessened (22). If the ambient temperature is warm,
exaggerated and persistent sweating and blood vessel dilation
may accompany the onset of sleep (5;22). It is as if the
thermostat regulating body temperature is turned to a lower
setting during NREM sleep.

During REM the situation is dramatically different. In
this stage of sleep there appears to be a total loss of thermoregulation in animals (22). There is no shivering, no sweating,
no vasodilation, no panting in response to dramatic changes
in ambient temperature (5). Such responses are, of course,
present in waking animals and during NREM when the temperature
changes. Although overall heat production during REM is similar to that seen during stage 2 (21), changes in metabolic
heat production for the purpose of regulating body temperature
are unknown (5). It is as if the thermostat was disconnected
during REM.

In humans the change in temperature regulation during REM
does not appear to be as great. Libert, Candas, Muzet, and
Ehrhart (23) have shown that thermoregulatory sweating does
occur in humans during REM but at a greatly depressed level that
allows body temperature to change more drastically before thermoregulatory responses occur. The decrease in sweating begins a
few minutes before the onset of each REM period and lasts
throughout it (6). Even regulatory changes in metabolic heat
production for the purpose of maintaining body temperature are
unknown (5). These changes occur not because the organs themselves are unable to respond (6) but because the brain's temperature regulation mechanisms are not functioning during REM (19).

Candas, Libert, and Muzet (24) found that humans retain
sensitivity to changes in ambient air temperature in all
stages of sleep. Decreases more than increases in air temperature resulted in changes in sleep stage, including awakening,
and such stage changes occurred more often in REM.

The net result of these body temperature regulation changes
is a steady regulated decline in body temperature during NREM.
In REM there is accelerated nonregulated decline in cold environments but unregulated increases during REM in neutral or
warm environments (6). If the ambient temperature is low
enough, the body temperature may drop too much during REM,
resulting in warming during the subsequent NREM. These changes
in temperature regulation do not entirely account for the
rhythmic, 24-hour fluctuation in body temperatures, for such
changes still occur under conditions of continuous bedrest or
sleep deprivation (see 25). However, the difference between
daily high to low was attenuated by such conditions, 25% for
continuous bedrest and 45% for sleep deprivation.

Overall brain temperature decreases during NREM (6;22)
but increases during REM (22;26). These temperature changes
are probably related both to changes in blood flow from the
body to the brain and to the metabolic rate in the brain during
sleep (6;22).

Heart Rate and Blood Pressure

There are also changes that occur in the cardiovascular
system during sleep. Blood pressure, heart rate, and output
from the heart are at their daily lows during sleep (12;19),
especially during delta sleep (6). During delta sleep there
is also less variability in both heart rate and blood pressure
(6;27), but considerable variation typically occurs during
REM (19;27). Blood pressure may show as much as a 40 mm Hg
increase during REM (19), occuring when other phasic REM
events are observed (6). A somewhat similar phenomenon has
been observed in NREM: heart rate increases and constriction
of the blood vessels of the fingers accompany K-complexes (26).
Other differences occur in the internal rhythms of the heart
during sleep as measured by the ECG (28).

There is some evidence that the homeostatic reflexes of
the body that help control blood pressure may function quite
differently during REM than in NREM or when awake (6). Overall
the amount of blood that the heart pumps may decline during
sleep, which partially accounts for the decreased blood
pressure. However, dilation of the body's blood vessels is
also a contributing factor. This vasodilation varies, however, in different parts of the body; some parts may even show
vasoconstriction as a result of local reflexes (6). For example, during REM there is a fall in blood pressure in the
vessels of the heart, kidney, and pelvic region but a corresponding increase in the muscles of movement and brain (12).
Overall there is a net enlargement of the blood vessels of the
body. During REM, brief; generalized vasoconstriction has
been observed which may cause the brief increase of blood
pressure recorded during this stage (6).

The changes in blood flow in the brain during sleep are
especially noteworthy (6;29). During NREM 1/10 to 1/4 of
areas of the brain show increased blood flow of 1/4 to 1/2 or
even more. Many other areas may show simultaneous reductions
of between 1/5 to 1/4 (especially in the brainstem). Blood
flow to the cortex decreases 10-15% in stages 1 and 2, dropping
30% in delta sleep (30). During REM the overall flow of blood
to the brain increases by 1/2 to 1 3/4 and further brief increases may additionally occur during phasic events that take
place during this stage of sleep. Many of these changes in
blood flow to the brain were thought to be in response to increases in metabolism and brain cell activity during sleep
but recent research has failed to show any such increases in
metabolic rate (2;31;32). Many of the changes in body and
brain blood flow are thought to occur to maintain adequate
oxygen to the brain during sleep while simultaneously reducing
energy use (12). During NREM the blood flow to the brain

increases in proportion to the amount of carbon dioxide in the
blood, as during wakefulness. Such a relationship does not
occur during REM, however, since the blood flow is much greater
than changes in carbon dioxide levels in the blood (2).

Hormones

Many diverse changes in the hormones of the body have been
noted during sleep. One of the more interesting changes is
the relationship between sleep and release of the growth hormone (5;33). The onset of sleep is the time during the 24-
hour day associated with the major release of the growth hormone, but other bursts of this hormone occur when sleep re-
sumes after brief awakenings, multiple periods of sleeping
and waking, or significant shifts in the time of sleep (34).
Growth hormone output is significantly reduced by sleep deprivation (29) and sleep following sleep deprivation contains
extra secretion of the growth hormone (34). But this relationship shows developmental variations (19). After three months
of age, almost all of the release of the growth hormone by the
pituitary gland occurs during sleep. In contrast, during
puberty, some is also secreted when the person is awake. In
adulthood, most is secreted during early sleep (probably the
first delta period). With progressive aging, less and then
none are secreted during sleep (5;35). Levels of growth hormone secreted during sleep are also affected by variations in
body metabolism (29). It is interesting to note that administration of the growth hormone prior to sleep inhibits delta
sleep (34).
The sex hormones are also somewhat related to sleep.
Prolactin secretion increases during the sleep period (5) 1/2
to 1 1/2 hours after sleep onset and reaches a peak a few hours
later (6), returning to low levels after sleep ceases (34).
Release of the hormone appears to be directly tied to sleep
since this pattern follows changes in sleep onset to different
times of the day (6) and shows a compensatory increase during
sleep following sleep deprivation (34). Levels of prolactin
production have been reported to fall during REM but increase
during delta sleep (29). Suckling induced release of prolactin is not related to NREM sleep but the release of oxytocin
is, at least in the rat (36). Since the latter hormone is
necessary for milk ejection, sleep deprivation in lactating
rats blocks lactation.
Luteinizing hormone, testosterone (5), and follicle-
stimulating hormone (6) show a slight increase during sleep.
Again, there are differences in this pattern at different
stages of development (6). Children approaching puberty and

during puberty have high luteinizing hormone at sleep onset
but output of this hormone appears to be inhibited by wakefulness. The increase in luteinizing hormone is soon followed
by increases in testosterone in the blood. These changes
occur during sleep no matter when sleep occurs. In pubertal
girls estrogen levels do not increase until about 12 hours
after the increase in luteinizing hormone and follicle-stimu-
lating hormone. In cycling women, there is no increase in
luteinizing hormone that occurs during sleep and, in fact,
there may be an inhibition of its secretion 2-3 hours after
sleep onset (6). In contrast, testosterone levels continue
to peak in the sleep of adults, especially near the end of the
sleep period (34).

Changes in the levels of other hormones typically vary
whether one is asleep or awake but do not readily follow
changes in the sleep period to other times of the day. Thyroid
stimulating hormone decreases at sleep onset (5) from a peak
that just precedes sleep onset (6). While sleep at any time
of the day reduces the output of this hormone, the 24-hour
peak tends to occur during the evening hours. The amount of
delta sleep a person gets correlates somewhat with levels of
thyroid hormones (34). Cortisol output has its daily low
during the first four hours of sleep (37) but peaks at the
end of sleep or soon thereafter. The amount of NREM sleep
between the first and second REM periods of the night is related to both the amount of cortisol secreted during sleep and
the time when this increase in secretion begins (38). This
relationship does not readily follow a shift of sleep to a
different time period of the day (6;38), requiring several
days for complete shift (39).

Melatonin from the pineal gland shows a circadian rhythm
with high levels at night. This rhythm only reluctantly follows changes in sleep time and may never completely shift away
from a nighttime propensity (34). Melatonin is higher in
children than adults. Melatonin has been shown to cause
sleepiness in humans. Thus the higher levels of sleep in
children may be due in part to their higher levels of melatonin.

To a greater or lesser extent then, several hormones show
concentration peaks tied to sleep onset or offset and a regular sleep-wake cycle seems to be important in maintaining
normal hormone cycles (5). On the whole it appears that the
anabolic hormones are more likely to be secreted during sleep
but not the catabolic variety (34) and the levels of the hormones of the anterior portion of the pituitary are mostly
related to sleep (29).

Urine Excretion

The physiology of other organ systems has also been found
to be different in sleep. One example is the excretory system (6). During sleep less urine is produced than during
wakefulness which may be due to the reduced blood flow through
this organ during sleep. Overall the average amount of anti-
diuretic hormone (which reduces the amount of water in the
urine) is the same during sleep as it is when awake but there
are from two to four waves of increased release of it during
sleep. These periodic waves of anti-diuretic hormone release
are not related to the REM/NREM cycle. At the same time there
is less excretion of sodium, potassium, and calcium. Aldosterone (the principal electrolyte-regulating hormone) does increase during sleep with peak levels about every 90 minutes.
Furthermore, the overall level of aldosterone is greater near
the end of sleep. There is no correlation between REM and the
bursts of increase in aldosterone. It has recently been shown
that, paradoxically, renin production (which influences the
level of aldosterone release) is inhibited by REM sleep (39).
The increased levels of aldosterone may account for the reduction of sodium excretion during sleep. The reduced calcium
excretion during sleep may be due to changes in parathyroid
hormone which increases during sleep with peaks during delta
sleep (6). In sum the amount of urine production is lowest
during REM but its concentration is greatest.

Other Effects

Sleep has other miscellaneous effects on the body. Both
the rate of flow of fluid through the eye and the pressure
decrease during sleep but the reduction in flow is much greater
(by 50% of waking values) than the reduction in pressure (41).
One of the more curious physiological differences that occurs
in most people during sleep is a reduction in digestive acid
secretion (19) in contrast to an increase of 20 to 30 times
normal levels in suffering duodenal ulcer patients (6). Both
swallowing and esophageal motility decrease during sleep, resulting in less effective clearance of fluids from the throat
region (19).

One obvious aspect of going to sleep is a reduction of
bodily movement. Yet muscle tone and simple reflexes are at
about the same level in NREM as in wakefulness. In REM many
reflexes and general muscle tone are reduced and there is
almost total absence of bodily movement. All of this is due
to the inhibition (hypolarization) by the brain of the alpha

motor neurons (the cells of the nervous system that stimulate
muscles to contract) (5;42) and motor neurons of the brainstem (3). In spite of this inhibition, muscle twitches and
jerks occur due to a variety of spontaneous action potentials
and other excitations of the alpha motor neurons (42).

Parts of the genital regions are also affected by sleep (6)
During REM there is an erection of the penis in males, and an
enlargement of the clitorus in females. In adolescents, these
same events may also occur during NREM. As a person ages beyond adolescence there is increasingly less erection or enlargement time during sleep.

Overall it appears that during REM sleep the sympathetic
nervous system is aroused (26). This accounts for the great
changes in heart rate, breathing, blood pressure, and so on
that occur during REM. Typically, the sudden changes in these
sympathetically controlled responses occur at the same time as
bursts of rapid eye movements that characterize the REM stage.
One exception to this is the erections of the penis in males
and clitoris in females during REM. Both are primarily the
result of activity of the parasympathetic nervous system (1).

In NREM the overall low, steady levels of physiological
activity appear to be the result of an active parasympathetic
nervous system (26). But, just as in REM, there are exceptions. First, the galvanic skin response (GSR) begins to rise
in stage 2 and peaks in delta but is remarkably low and steady
in REM. At the same time, the GSR is highly bilaterally
asymmetrical during sleep (43). Second, in some sleepers,
K-complexes of stage 2 are accompanied by brief increases in
heart rate, constriction of the blood vessels in the fingers,
and sudden changes in the GSR. Third, the sympathetic system
comes into play if and when it is necessary for homeostatic
regulation (44).

Bodily Effects on Sleep

It is also becoming apparent that certain physiological
processes may affect sleep. For example, people who sleep
longer than the average have higher daytime body temperatures
(5) and increases in body temperature from activities like
exercise or submerging in hot water will greatly increase the
amount of subsequent delta sleep (26). Warm ambient temperatures tend to induce sleep probably because the body loses
more heat during sleep (22). People with hypothyroidism show
a decrease in delta and stage 2 sleep (5). Sensations from
the internal body cavity have been shown to induce sleep (45).

People who are undergoing dramatic gains of weight have
long and generally uninterrupted sleep while those dramatically

losing weight experience shortened and fragmented sleep (19).
Even dietary changes have been reported to change sleep, with
a diet of high carbohydrates and low fat causing a decrease
in delta sleep but low carbohydrates and high fat intake producing an increase in REM (19). Nicolaidis and Danguir (46)
have recently hypothesized that sleep varies with the body's
overall metabolic rate. Many other medical conditions as well
as physiologically toxic substances too numerous to detail
here are also known to affect sleep--usually detrimentally (47).

Brain Structures Involved in Sleep

To the observer, sleep appears to be a passive state--an
absence of activity and reactivity during which an organism
all but "turns off." Although much of the nature and function
of sleep remains unknown, our ability to record the electrical
changes within the brain during sleep shows that there is in
fact much activity taking place. The initiation and maintenance
of sleep requires the coordinated activity of brain structures
other than those responsible for wakefulness. While no single
physiological or chemical model can as yet totally illustrate
the mechanisms controlling sleep, research has provided much
knowledge of the role of brain structures in the sleep-wake
cycle.
     The brainstem is the most primitive part of the brain.
(See Figure 6 for anatomical locations of these brain areas.)
It provides for communication between the brain and body and
is responsible for basic bodily functions. It also appears
to be critical for sleep, as Michael Jouvet, a major contributor
to the current accumulated knowledge of the role of the brain
in sleep, has emphasized. His research has shown that the
cerebellum and spinal cord are not necessary for the occurrence
of sleep and that an animal with only the pons and lower brain
structures intact can still exhibit sleep patterns, including
rhythmic episodes of REM and NREM sleep (see McCarley [48]
for review). But various parts of the brainstem play different
roles in the production of sleep.

REM Sleep

Located upward from the medulla oblongata in the brainstem
is the pons. Areas in the pons, particularly the locus
coeruleus, and the gigantocellular tegmental field (FTG) in
the medial pontine reticular formation, have a function in

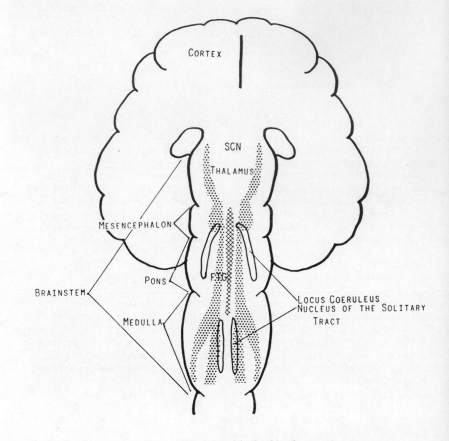

Fig. 6. Parts of the brain involved in sleep and waking.

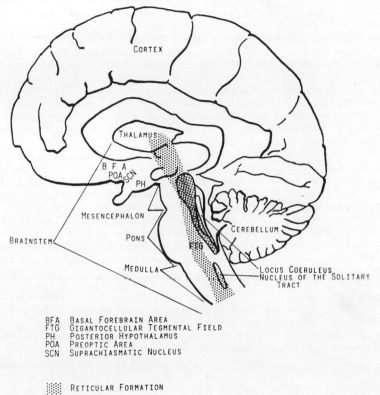

CORTEX

THALAMUS

B F A
POA SCN
PH

MESENCEPHALON

PONS

MEDULLA

FTG

CEREBELLUM

Locus Coeruleus
Nucleus of the Solitary
Tract

BRAINSTEM

BFA Basal Forebrain Area
FTG Gigantocellular Tegmental Field
PH   Posterior Hypothalamus
POA Preoptic Area
SCN Suprachiasmatic Nucleus

Reticular Formation

Raphé

sleep. The neurons of the medial pontine reticular formation
seem to be important for the maintenance of REM (49). Intra-
cellular recordings show that excitability in this area is
greater in REM than in wakefulness or NREM. Tonic depolarization, superimposed with phasic periods of greater depolarization, is also recorded during REM. During NREM, the polariza-
tion of these neurons is increased. That these findings are
related to the occurrence of REM is also demonstrated by extracellular recordings of neuronal activity. Neurons of the
pontine reticular formation are almost silent at the beginning
of NREM and increase firing prior to and during REM.

The nucleus of the gigantocellular tegmental field is so
named because of the presence of giant cells, actually among
the largest in the brain (50). Its axons extend into the
telecephalon, diencephalon, midbrain, and hindbrain. These
neurons show an increase in activity several minutes prior to
the initiation of REM sleep and reach a peak of activity
during this period (51). The giant cells are thought to trigger
some of the events of REM sleep (48).

There are two populations of neurons in the gigantocellular
tegmental field, one that fires phasically during REM and
another that is tonic and fires throughout REM (50). Phasic
firing of giant cells is correlated with PGO spikes (brief,
intense electrical activity in the Pons, lateral Geniculate
nucleus, and Occipital cortex of the brain), rapid eye movements, and muscular twitches, all events characteristic of
REM sleep. Tonic firing could be related to cortical desynchrony
and muscular paralysis. As some giant cells extend into the
reticular formation, they may have a role in the production of
the characteristic wave patterns of REM that are generated in
this area (48).

Pharmacological manipulations of this area provide evidence
of these relationships (50). The giant cells are cholingeric,
utilizing acetylcholine as a neurotransmitter. Pontine injections of substances that either facilitate acteylcholine or
mimic it have been shown to cause cortical desychrony, rapid
eye movements, and paralysis in cats. Cholinesterase inhibition increases cholingeric postsynaptic activity and induces
REM sleep in humans during NREM sleep. This suggests a possible role for the gigantocellular tegmental field as a pacemaker for REM.

While control of REM may be a function of the FTG it is
not specific for this purpose. Large lesions in this area
depress REM sleep, but cell-selective lesions do not exhibit
this effect, and many other metabolic and behavioral functions
are disrupted by large pontine lesions which indirectly may
interfere with sleep. The giant cells are also active in relation to motor activity and are frequently related to head
and neck movements (see 52).

Jouvet suggested in the 1960s that the locus coeruleus was responsible for REM sleep and that lesions of the area would abolish all of its physical and electrical indications (52). Pharmacological manipulations that suppress the synthesis of norepinephrine and the activity of the locus coeruleus do not prevent REM sleep in cats or rats, however. In fact, many manipulations of norepinephrine have shown little or no significant effect on the occurrence of REM (52). Further research has shown that the activity of the locus coeruleus decreases naturally during REM and increases after the REM period is over (51).

Experiments with cats show that small lesions in the pons result in the brain activity of REM sleep without the motor inhibition associated with it (53). The position and size of such lesions determine which muscles become inactive. These results suggest that the lack of muscle tone that normally accompanies REM sleep may be due to activity in the pons. Lesions at the border of the locus coeruleus (dorsal pons) caused REM without atonia (5). While exhibiting an increase in motor activity, cats with locus coeruleus lesions show the same EEG, theta rhythm, and brain temperature as in normal REM (54). It is thought that the noradrenergic nuclei of the locus coeruleus have an inhibitory effect on motor activity, but are not essential to the occurrence of REM sleep as first suggested by Jouvet in 1969 (55).

It is interesting to note that cats with lesions of the locus coeruleus show no abnormal increase of muscle tone when they are awake or during NREM sleep, showing the area's role in control of atonia specifically during REM sleep. Cats are observed to be more active in general after such lesions have been made. Thus there also seems to be a generalized effect of such lesions on motor drive (54).

An interaction of the FTG and the locus coeruleus is suggested by the Hobson-McCarley model of sleep. As we have already noted, the activity of the FTG increases during REM, while the activity of the locus coeruleus quiets during REM and increases again after the REM period is over. The Hobson-McCarley model suggests that the firing of the cholingeric neurons of the FTG activates the locus coeruleus. The activity of the locus coeruleus acts to shut off REM production by way of inhibitory efferents to the FTG. Extended activity in the locus coeruleus tends to inhibit itself, which in turn releases the FTG from inhibition. This reciprocal relationship of cellular activity in these two pontine areas may play a major role in the regulation of the sleep cycle (51).

This relationship is illustrated by experiments involving the neurotransmitter acetylcholine. Perfusion of the locus coeruleus with ACh results in the inhibition of REM in freely

moving cats. This manipulation also prolongs the sleep cycle,
particularly REM sleep, and decreases the number of REM
periods. This is probably similar to the situation that occurs
during the sleep cycle (51).

Wakefulness

The search for a specific center for the control of wakefulness has been a focus for researchers hoping to find a
single neurological system responsible for sleep, attention,
and consciousness. Although this has not been achieved, evidence has accumulated for the involvement of certain brain areas
in wakefulness. The ascending reticular activating system
(ARAS) is such an area. The ARAS is located in the core of
the brainstem and extends upward into the hypothalamus, subthalamus, and thalamus (56). It appears to have an arousal
function and be partially responsible for wakefulness. Stimulation of this area caused EEG desynchronization and behavioral
arousal (53), while its destruction resulted in a slow synchronous EEG and a coma state (54).
The posterior hypothalamus is another brain structure
involved in wakefulness. Research on laboratory animals
shows that stimulation of this area causes a sleeping animal
to awaken. Damage to the posterior hypothalamus results in
pathological sleep (57). The exact mechanisms by which the
posterior hypothalamus is involved in wakefulness is not known,
however.

Sleep

Other brain areas have been found to be important for the
initiation and maintenance of sleep. The basal forebrain area,
including neurons of the anterior hypothalamus and nearby portions of the cortex, seems to have just such a function, as
damage to it reduces the occurrence of sleep in laboratory
animals (19;58;59) and stimulation to this area by electrical
(60;61) and chemical (62) means increases sleep. The raphé
or dorsal raphé nucleus is likewise involved with the initiation
and maintenance of sleep. Neurons in this area show a unique
pattern of firing only at the time of sleep onset (3).
Destruction of raphé nuclei produces a reduction of sleep
proportional to the extent of the lesion. Damage to different
areas of the raphé have different effects. Destruction of the
anterior raphé produces a state of permanent wakefulness interrupted by periods of REM, while lesions in the posterior

raphé cause a proportional reduction of NREM in the absence of REM. An additional function of the raphé may be to prevent the intrusion of characteristic REM events into NREM and waking states (63;64).

Another medullary system, the nucleus of the solitary tract, may also have a role in the initiation of sleep (50). Stimulation of this area induces sleep, but damage to the area does not prevent sleep. Electrical stimulation of the nucleus of the solitary tract has a synchronizing effect on forebrain EEG. Its role may be in inhibiting the arousal effect of the ascending reticular activating system. This area also receives input from the vagus nerve, whose stimulation also produces a synchronized EEG. Dell and Padel (65) have shown that electrical stimulation of this area induces sleep.

The neurons of the preoptic area (POA) have been shown to induce sleep in cats. The majority of the POA neurons discharge rapidly in NREM and REM and show reduced rates of firing in wakefulness. Stimulation of POA neurons in unanesthetized, immobilized cats results in EEG synchronization. Similar EEG synchronization as well as behavioral sleep is observed in unrestrained animals (66). During stimulation of POA neurons the cortical activity induced by stimulation of the reticular system is also abolished. Lesions in this area result in sleeplessness in proportion to the extent of damage.

The thalamus, which acts in regulation and communication between the cortex and lower brain structures, also appears to have a function in the sleep/wake cycle. Dempsey and Morison (67) first provided evidence of this relationship in the 1940s. They found that electrical stimulation of the thalamus of cats resulted in a synchronization of the EEG and spontaneous spindle activity, much like that which normally occurs in sleep. A criticism of this study is that most laboratory cats typically sleep about 60-70% of the time, and it is possible that the testing occurred during this time. Sleep has also been reported as a result of thalamus injury, but the exact role of the thalamus in sleep is as yet unclear (57;68).

Recently, a group of researchers at the National Institute of Mental Health in Washington, D.C., failed to show any increase in metabolic activity in many of these suspected sleep onset, sleep maintenance areas of the brain (31;32). They especially focused attention on the basal forebrain area and the nucleus of the solitary tract (NST) but also observed over 70 other brain areas that have been suggested as playing a role in sleep onset or sleep maintenance. While it would be expected that an area important for sleep would increase its overall metabolic activity during that state, it is possible that it might not. Thus, these results do not com-

pletely rule out these areas but do call their function into
question.
    [A discussion of the role of neurotransmitters and sleep
and sleep inducing substances can be found in the next chapter.]

The Rhythms of Sleep

    Many aspects of sleep show cyclical rhythms. Most obvious
is the one major sleep period alternating with one major wake
period every 24 hours in adult humans. Even animals such as
dogs, cats, and rats that divide their sleep into many smaller
units every 24 hours show a propensity to have more of it
during the same portion of every 24 hours. Such a rhythm is
called a circadian (circa = about; dian = a day) rhythm. But
this is not the only rhythm of sleep; the fairly regular alternation of NREM and REM about every 100 minutes is another
rhythm of sleep. This is called an ultradian (ultra = beyond;
dian = day; thus a frequency higher than once a day).
    As discussed above, there are other circadian rhythms
besides sleep. Many hormone secretions show 24-hour cycles
as do body temperature and metabolism. Likewise, there are
other ultradian rhythms present in the body, such as levels of
certain hormones, activity, and alertness. This ultradian
rhythm has been termed BRAC for Basic Rest Activity Cycle (69).
Other ultradian rhythms include variations in EEG frequencies,
eye movements, the spiral aftereffect, oral food intake, and
waking fantasy reports (5).
    It has been shown that the circadian rhythm of sleeping-
waking is generated by some pacemaker within the body (5)
since it persists even in environments like a deep cave or a
special laboratory that are devoid of clues about time of day
such as changes of light, temperature, noise, clocks, radios,
mealtimes, etc. Under these constant conditions, the rhythms
of the body tend to drift away from being exactly 24 hours
(hence the term "circadian" instead of "dian") and tend to get
out of synchrony (or out of phase) with one another (19;70).
Sleeping-waking rhythms in these constant conditions (also
called free-running conditions) are longer than 24 hours,
averaging 25 hours (70), and are usually between 24 and 28
hours but have gone to 50 hours for one complete cycle (19).
    The length of the sleep-wake cycle appears to diminish
with age (71). Whatever the cycle, the ratio of sleep to wake
time stays relatively constant at 30% while in older people
the time between sleep onset and REM decreases greatly and the

proportion of REM in early sleep increases (72). The free-
running sleep-wake cycle in females averages about 1/2 hour
less than in males, yet 18% more of the cycle is taken up by
sleep (73;74). In some cases, when sleep continued for 14 to
16 hours, delta sleep began to occur again (72). Under free-
running conditions humans are capable of maintaining an endogenous rhythm for a long time; that is, any deviation from
the individual's pattern is compensated for in the next few
cycles. Furthermore, the length of wakefulness influences the
length of the subsequent sleep and, to a lesser degree, vice
versa (74).

The conditions of a more normal environment that involve
clocks, mealtimes, positions of the sun, heat-cold alterna-
tions, etc., act as zeitgebers ("time givers") for the various
circadian rhythms to "entrain" them to 24 hours and to keep
the various rhythms in synchrony with one another. One of the
more important zeitgebers for humans appears to be a fairly
regular time of arousal (19) but "social contacts" are also
very important (73). Without adequate zeitgebers the various
rhythms of the body may "uncouple" (drift out of synchrony with
one another), resulting in, among other things, troublesome
sleep (19).

Circadian rhythms may determine if a person is a night owl
or a day lark. Night owls have been shown to have metabolic
and performance peaks later in the day than day larks (19).
In fact, night owls may not show any increase in these factors
for many hours after awakening. As people get older, they tend
to become "day larks" (72).

There have been several models proposed to explain the
circadian rhythms of sleep and related phenomena. All of them
suggest one or more internal oscillators or timers that run
continuously inside the body. These oscillators are strong
enough to provide the mean 24-hour intervals necessary for
circadian rhythms yet are not so strong that their phases
cannot be reset daily by zeitgebers. The differences among
the theories are in the number of the oscillators, their na-
tures, and their interactions with other factors.

Borbély (75;76) theorizes that two processes regulate
sleep. One is a circadian oscillator that is unaffected by
sleep; he calls this process "C." The other is a process very
much dependent on sleep since its strength declines during
sleep and increases during wakefulness; he calls this process
"S." The processes combine to produce both the likelihood of
sleep onset (or sleepiness) and the subsequent duration of
sleep. Further, process S determines the amount of delta
sleep contained within the sleep period, since it has been
shown that the amount of delta sleep is proportional to the
amount of prior wakefulness. REM, in contrast, is relatively

unaffected by prior sleep or wakefulness but shows a circadian
rhythmicity. Thus REM is controlled by process C. The NREM/
REM cycle is produced by the reciprocal interaction between
these two processes and is not related to any ultradian BRAC
cycle. Body temperature is involved with process C and sleep
since there is an inverse relationship between body temperature
and the likelihood of REM sleep and its subsequent length.

Borbély has recently collaborated with others to modify
his theory (77). First they speculate that process S may be
DSIP (delta sleep inducing peptide) or some similar substance.
Second, they add the notion of dual thresholds--one for sleep
onset and one for waking from sleep--which they speculate are
brain sensitivities to levels of S. When process S rises
above the sleep onset threshold the individual goes to sleep.
When S falls below the waking threshold the individual awakens.
The levels of these thresholds vary regularly and parallelly,
with each showing one peak and one low point at the same time
as the other every 24 hours. The circadian variations in
these dual thresholds are controlled by process C. The sleep
onset threshold is higher than the waking threshold. This
model is analagous to a thermostat that turns off at a higher
threshold than it turns on. Further, like many modern heating
systems, there is a day and a night "cycle," with the night
portion having both thresholds substantially lower than the
day portion. Either threshold can be affected by external
conditions in addition to process C. For example, bedroom
conditions conducive to sleep can lower the sleep onset
threshold. Further, the sleep onset threshold can be will-
fully suspended for a while, allowing S to increase well beyond its threshold limits.

Weitzman (70) proposes two oscillators that intersect with
one another. (Minors and Waterhouse [78] have a very similar
theory.) One of these oscillators is intimately involved with
core body temperature (CBT oscillator). The other more directly affects sleep-wake functions (SWF oscillator). The CBT
oscillator is about four times as effective as the SWF oscillator and entrainment affects only the SWF oscillator. The
CBT oscillator is relatively stable and is located in the brain.
It also controls REM and cortisol rhythms. The SWF oscillator
is much more labile and controls the growth hormone. Social
cues involving culture and interaction with other people are
important aspects of the zeitgeber for this oscillator.

Weitzman (70) also recognizes other factors that influence
sleep. One he calls the "cumulative sleepiness factor" (p. 182)
that affects the amount and timing of delta sleep. It is some
kind of elapsed-timekeeper that biases the effects of the
endogenous circadian oscillators. Another factor is an 80- to
100-minute ultradian oscillator which controls the timing of

the onset of REM. This oscillator is, however, influenced by
the CBT oscillator (79) so that REM is more likely to occur
and be of longer duration when body temperature is rising.

Åkerstedt alone and together with Gillberg (80;81) proposes
that arousal level is governed by two sources. One source
varies directly with amount of prior wakefulness (which makes
it stronger in opposing arousal) and prior sleep (which weakens
its effectiveness in opposing arousal). The other source is
a circadian oscillator that produces an optimal time to be
awake and an optimal time to be asleep every 24 hours. The
effects of both sources are superimposed on one another to
produce both sleep latency and sleep duration. However, delta
sleep is affected more by prior wakefulness but REM and stage
2 more by the circadian oscillator.

Åkerstedt came to these conclusions by studying the effect
of shift work on sleep. Many anecdotal and laboratory reports
agree that working at night and sleeping during the day result
in both poorer sleep and less efficient work. In one experiment, Åkerstedt and associates measured the sleep of six subjects in an isolated laboratory. The bedtime of these subjects
was varied for one night every week. At the conclusion of the
experiment each subject had gone to sleep at 2300, 300, 700,
1100, 1500, 1900, and subsequent 2300 hours after arising at
700 hours the previous day. Thus, both time of day and amount
of wakefulness (from 16 to 40 hours) were simultaneously
varied. (Other experiments by this group using different
sleep deprivation lengths but the same bedtime produced essentially the same conclusions.) The subjects were allowed to
sleep as long as they desired. As the bedtimes went from
2300 to 1100 hours the length of sleep decreased from about
500 minutes to about 250 minutes even though prior wakefulness
in these subjects had increased from 16 to 28 hours. The
bedtimes after noon showed a reverse relationship--increasing
sleep lengths as bedtimes got later. The maximum sleep length
was almost 700 minutes after sleep onset at 1900 hours (which
was also after 36 hours of continuous wakefulness). Time
taken to get to sleep was shortest for the night bedtimes.
Furthermore, the researchers found that the amount of delta
within the sleep period, whenever it occurred, started high but
fell sharply as sleep progressed and the amount of delta sleep
obtained did not vary with sleep onset time. In contrast, REM
amount varied greatly with time of day; it rose as sleep progressed following afternoon bedtimes but fell as sleep progressed after morning bedtimes, resulting in less total REM
during the shorter daytime sleep.

Another interesting finding of this research resulted
from subjective ratings of sleepiness taken just prior to
bedtime and just after arousal. As expected, sleep lowered

these ratings but, surprisingly, ratings at both times were
higher during the day than at night in spite of the fact that
the daytime measurements were done following both longer sleep
deprivation and shorter sleep time.

Although circadian effects on sleep are powerful, behavioral controls can be even stronger (82). Occupational and
social pressures can influence when a person is asleep and
awake as well as how many sleep onsets there are every 24
hours. Within wide limits, people are free to choose when
they sleep and for how long. It has been suggested that body
temperature circadian rhythm influences sleep onset, awakening,
sleep duration, REM latency, and REM duration (83; see also 84).
Indeed, the circadian rhythm of body temperature has an influence on the likelihood to fall asleep and the length of the
subsequent sleep; however, the relationship may be indirect (25).

But the circadian rhythm of sleep also has an effect on
other rhythms of the body. This was partially noted earlier
when discussing the relationship of levels of hormones to
sleep. Three basic patterns have been noted when normal sleep-
wake patterns have been altered (39). First, changes in hormone level immediately and completely follow the sleep period.
Second, the hormone level gradually shifts to the new sleep
period--generally in 5 to 10 days. Third, the hormone level
is related to a particular sleep stage and will immediately
and completely follow its displacement.

A number of experimenters have looked for the brain area
or areas that are a part of the circadian rhythm system controlling sleep and wakefulness (85). A number of studies
have shown the suprachiasmatic nucleus (SCN) of the hypothalamus to have circadian rhythms in its metabolic activity,
firing rate of isolated groups of its cells, and even firing
rate of isolated single cells. Lesions of the SCN abolish the
circadian rhythm of sleep without changing the proportions
of NREM and REM (5). The animals in these studies also show
typical rebound of delta and REM following sleep deprivation (75). The SCN appears to be an important link for en-
training the circadian cycle of wake-sleep to the external
environment light-dark cycles because it receives direct connections from the retina to the SCN or indirectly via the
lateral geniculate nucleus (86). The SCN has input to many
of the brainstem areas that affect the timing of sleep (87).
Most of the results point to the SCN as being either a single
oscillator, a complex of oscillators, or a portion of a
hierarchy of oscillators (see Pickard and Turek [86] for a
review). A recent study by Eastman, Mistlberger, and Rechtschaffen (88) supports the theory that the circadian control
of the SCN is due to many of the brain's oscillators being in
the SCN rather than the entire SCN being a single oscillator

or the SCN acting as a coupler that synchronizes oscillators
of other brain areas.

Ultradian rhythms also affect sleep. Kleitman (69)
originally proposed a basic rest-activity cycle (BRAC) of
about 90 minutes. This BRAC manifested itself in sleep as
the REM-NREM cycle and in wakefulness as subtle but measurable
changes in alertness. Lavie and Zomer (89) have recently
shown a continuation of the 90-minute REM-NREM cycle to waking
hours (especially immediately following sleep) as "sleepability." They found an additional cycle of 3 1/2 to 4 hours
superposed on the 90-minute BRAC and 24-hour circadian rhythms.

Other rhythmic effects on sleep have been noted (90).
Since REM sleep likelihood and durations are phase delayed
from sleep onset and since awakening after sleep of at least
several minutes delays the subsequent REM period, the REM
cycle is either a dependent or renewal process (5). Or, perhaps, REM is the result of an easily reset oscillating ultradian timekeeper that is independent from an ongoing BRAC
but is influenced by the body temperature circadian rhythm (84).

Neural Mechanisms of Sleep: A Model

As yet there is no adequate comprehensive model for the
involvement of the brain in sleep. There are simply too many
unknowns. Yet, it may be helpful to try to fit together what
is known, if only to aid in remembering these facts. Such
model building is only possible by omitting some evidence
that does not fit well with other knowns and, at the same
time, stretching some other facts more than should be toler-
ated. With these things in mind, we offer the following
model (see Figure 7).

Wakefulness is produced and maintained by the action of
the ARAS via the thalamus using acetylcholine (pathway 1 in
Figure 7). At the same time the posterior hypothalamus also
plays a role in wakefulness (pathway 2). But as nighttime
comes, the basal forebrain area begins to exert its influence
causing synchronization of the EEG (pathway 3) while the
raphé inhibits the ARAS using serotonin (pathway 4). The
nucleus of the solitary tract may also play a role in facili-
tating sleep by inhibiting the ARAS (pathway 5). This last
path appears to be triggered by the presence of food in the
digestive tract causing stimulatory activity via the vagus
nerve.

The first stages of sleep are of the NREM variety because
the raphé (using serotonin) and the locus coerulus inhibit the

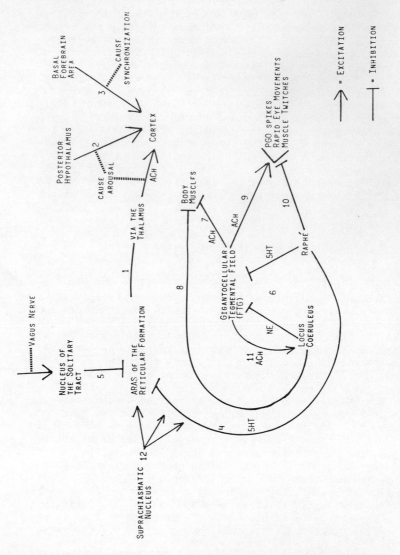

Fig. 7. A model of how the brain produces sleep.

FTG (pathway 6). However, with time the influence of these two areas becomes weaker and weaker due to self-inhibition, thus allowing the FTG to become active. The FTG then produces REM when some of its cells block bodily movements using acetylcholine (pathway 7) with the help of the posterior locus coerulus (pathway 8). Meanwhile, other cells of the FTG activate other brain areas, again with acetylcholine. These areas in turn produce the phasic events (bursts of eye movements, PGO spikes, muscle twitches, etc.) so characteristic of REM (pathway 9). These same phasic events are prevented from occurring in wakefulness and NREM by the inhibitory effects of parts of the raphé (pathway 10). Among the areas activated by the FTG is the locus coeruleus (pathway 11). When activation of this area gains enough strength, it inhibits the FTG, resulting in the end of the REM period and the return to NREM.

The entire sleep system seems to be facilitated on a daily basis by the suprachiasmatic nucleus (pathway 12), resulting in the circadian rhythmicity of sleep and wakefulness.

References

1. Guyton, A.C. (1976). *Textbook of Medical Physiology.* 5th ed. Philadelphia: Saunders.

2. Santiago, T.V.; Guerra, E.; Neubauer, J.A.; and Edelman, N.H. (1984). *Journal of Clinical Investigation, 73,* 497-506.

3. Harper, R.M. (1983). "Neurophysiology of Sleep." *Progress in Clinical Biological Research, 136,* 65-73.

4. Douglas, N.J.; White, D.P.; Weil, J.V.; Pickett, C.K.; and Zwillich, C.W. (1982). "Hypercapnic Ventilatory Response in Sleeping Adults." *American Review of Respiratory Diseases, 126,* 758-772.

5. McGinty, D.J., and Drucker-Colin, R.R. (1982). "Sleep Mechanisms: Biology and Control of REM Sleep." *International Review of Neurobiology, 23,* 391-436.

6. Orem, J., and Keeling, J. (1980). "Appendix A: A Compendium of Physiology in Sleep." In J. Orem and C.D. Barnes (Eds.), *Physiology in Sleep* (pp. 315-335). New York: Academic Press.

   Excellent and up-to-date review of the functioning of

various physiological systems during sleep. Especially noteworthy is the appendix that beautifully summarizes the material from the individual chapters.

7. Skatrud, J.B., and Berssenbrugge, A.D. (1983). "Effect of Sleep State and Chemical Stimuli on Breathing." *Progress in Clinical and Biological Research, 136,* 87-95.

8. Orr, W.C. (1984). "Sleep and Breathing: An Overview." *Ear, Nose, and Throat Journal, 63,* 191-198.

9. Rigatto, H. (1984). "Control of Ventilation in the Newborn." *Annual Review of Physiology, 46,* 661-674.

10. Iber, C.; Berssenbrugge, A.; Skatrud, J.B.; and Dempsey, J.A. (1982). "Ventilatory Adaptations to Resistive Loading during Wakefulness and Non-REM Sleep." *Journal of Applied Physiology, 52,* 607-614.

11. Wilson, P.A.; Skatrud, J.B.; and Dempsey, J.A. (1984). "Effects of Slow Wave Sleep on Ventilatory Compensation to Inspiratory Elastic Loading." *Respiration Physiology, 55,* 103-120.

12. Coote, J.H. (1982). "Respiratory and Circulatory Control during Sleep." *Journal of Experimental Biology, 100,* 223-244.

13. Haddad, G.G., and Mellins, R.B. (1984). "Hypoxia and Respiratory Control in Early Life." *Annual Review of Physiology, 46,* 629-643.

14. Read, D.J.C., and Henderson-Smart, D.J. (1984). "Regulation and Breathing in the Newborn during Different Behavioral States." *Annual Review of Physiology, 46,* 679-685.

15. Hudgel, D.W.; Martin, R.J.; Johnson, B.; and Hill, P. (1984). "Mechanics of the Respiratory System and Breathing Pattern during Sleep in Normal Humans." *Journal of Applied Physiology, 56,* 133-137.

16. Lopes, J.M.; Tabachnik, E.; Muller, N.L.: Levison, H.; and Bryan, A.C. (1983). "Total Airway Resistance and Respiratory Muscle Activity during Sleep." *Journal of Applied Physiology, 54,* 773-777.

17. Douglas, N.J.; White, D.P.; Pickett, C.K.; Weil, J.V.; and Zwillich, J. (1982). "Respiration during Sleep in Normal Man." *Thorax, 37*, 840-844.

18. Walker, D.W. (1984). "Peripheral and Central Chemoreceptors in the Fetus and Newborn." *Annual Review of Physiology, 46*, 687-703.

19. Hauri, P. (1982). *The Sleep Disorders.* Kalamazoo: Upjohn.

20. Badia, P.; Harsh, J.; Balkin, T.; Contrell, P.; Klempert, G.; O'Rourke, D.; and Schoen, L. (1984). "Behavioral Control of Respiration in Sleep." *Psychophysiology, 21*, 494-500.

21. Shapiro, C.M.; Goll, C.C.; Cohen, G.R.; and Oswald, I. (1984). "Heat Production during Sleep." *Journal of Applied Psychology, 56*, 671-677.

22. Obal, F., Jr. (1984). "Thermoregulation and Sleep." In A. Borbély and J.L. Valatx (Eds.), *Sleep Mechanisms* (pp. 157-172). New York: Springer-Verlag.

23. Libert, J.; Candas, V.; Muzet, A.; and Ehrhart, J. (1982). "Thermoregulatory Adjustments to Thermal Transients during Slow Wave Sleep and REM Sleep in Man." *Journal of Physiology (Paris), 78*, 251-257.

24. Candas, V.; Libert, J.P.; and Muzet, A. (1982). "Heating and Cooling Stimulations during SWS and REM Sleep in Man." *Journal of Thermal Biology, 7*, 155-158.

25. Zulley, J.; Wever, R.; and Aschoff, J. (1981). "The Dependence of Onset and Duration of Sleep on the Circadian Rhythm of Rectal Temperature." *Pflugers Archives, 391*, 314-318.

26. Sewitch, L.E. (1984). "Basic Psychophysiology of Sleep." *Sleep Watchers, 2*, 93-100.

27. Zemaityte, D.; Varonekas, G.; and Sobolov, E. (1984). "Heart Rhythm Control during Sleep." *Psychophysiology, 21*, 279-289.

28. Browne, K.F.; Prystrowsky, E.; Heger, J.J.; Chilson, P.S.; and Zipes, D.P. (1983). "Prolongation of the Q-T Interval in Man during Sleep." *American Journal of Cardiology, 52*, 55-59.

29. Passouant, P. (1983). "Pituitary Secretions and Wake-
     Sleep Cycle." *Cephalagia*, *3*, 42-53.

     Condensed but complete review of hormones and sleep.

30. Elmquist, D. (1984). "Cerebral Circulation and Metabol-
     ism in Sleep." In A. Borbély and J.L. Valatx (Eds.),
     Sleep Mechanisms (pp. 188-192). New York: Springer-
     Verlag.

31. Kennedy, C.; Gillin, J.C.; Mendelson, W.; Suda, S.;
     Miyaoka, M.; Ito, M.; Nakamura, R.K.; Storch, F.I.;
     Pettigrew, K.; Mishkin, M.; and Sokoloff, L. (1981).
     "Local Cerebral Glucose Utilization in Slow-Wave Sleep."
     American Neurological Association, *106*, 25-28.

32. Nakamura, R.K.; Kennedy, C.; Gillin, J.C.; Suda, S.;
     Ito, M.; Storch, F.I.; Mendelson, W.; Sokoloff, L.;
     and Mishkin, M. (1983). "Hypnogenic Center Theory of
     Sleep: No Support from Metabolic Mapping in Monkeys."
     Brain Research, *268*, 372-376.

33. Saito, H.; Saito, S.; Kawano, N.; and Tomita, S. (1983).
     "Plasma Somatostatin Level during Natural and Interrup-
     ted Sleep in Man." *Acta Endocrinologica*, *104*, 129-133.

34. Åkerstedt, T. (1984). "Hormones and Sleep." In A. Bor-
     bély and J.L. Valatx (Eds.), *Sleep Mechanisms* (pp. 193-
     203). New York: Springer-Verlag.

35. Prinz, P.N.; Weitzman, E.D.; Cunningham, G.R.; and
     Karacan, I. (1983). "Plasma Growth Hormone during
     Sleep in Young and Aged Men." *Journal of Gerontology*,
     38, 519-524.

36. Voloschin, L.M., and Tramezzani, J.H. (1982). "Reflex
     Arc of Milk Ejection and Prolactin, Their Different
     Dependence on Sleep." *Progress in Clinical and Bio-
     logical Research*, *112*, 31-53.

37. Weitzman, E.D.; Zimmerman, J.C.; Czeisler, C.A.; and
     Ronda, J. (1983). "Cortisol Secretion Is Inhibited
     during Sleep in Normal Man." *Journal of Clinical Endo-
     crinology and Metabolism*, *56*, 352-358.

38. Kupfer, D.J.; Bulik, C.M.; and Jarrett, D.B. (1983).
     "Nighttime Plasma Cortisol Secretion and EEG Sleep--
     Are They Associated?" *Psychiatry Research*, *10*, 191-
     199.

39. Mullen, P.E. (1983). "Sleep and Its Interaction with Endocrine Rhythms." *British Journal of Psychiatry*, *142*, 215-220.

Presents a model of how sleep can interact with other circadian rhythms, then illustrates it nicely with examples of endocrine rhythms.

40. Kolata, G. (1984). "Puberty Mystery Solved." *Science*, *223*, 272.

41. Reiss, G.R.; Lee, D.A.; Topper, J.E.; and Brubaker, R.F. (1984). "Aqueous Humor Flow during Sleep." *Investigative Ophthalmology and Visual Science*, *25*, 776-778.

42. Chase, M.H., and Morales, F.R. (1983). "Subthreshold Excitatory Activity and Inotoneuron Discharge during REM Periods of Active Sleep." *Science*, *221*, 1195-1198.

43. Freixa i Baque, E. (1983). "Electrodermal Asymmetry during Human Sleep." *Biological Psychiatry*, *17*, 145-151.

44. Parmeggiani, P.L. (1984). "Automatic Nervous System in Sleep." In A. Borbély and J.L. Valatx (Eds.), *Sleep Mechanisms* (pp. 39-49). New York: Springer-Verlag.

45. Puizillout, J.J.; Gaudin-Chazal, G.; and Bras, H. (1984). "Vagal Mechanisms in Sleep Regulation." In A. Borbély and J.L. Valatx (Eds.), *Sleep Mechanisms* (pp. 19-38). New York: Springer-Verlag.

46. Nicolaidis, S., and Danguir, J. (1984). "Metabolic Determinants of Feeding and Sleep. The Ischymetric Hypothesis." In A. Borbély and J.L. Valatx (Eds.), *Sleep Mechanisms* (pp. 173-187). New York: Springer-Verlag.

47. Association of Sleep Disorders Centers (1979). *Diagnostic Classification of Sleep and Arousal Disorders*. First Edition, Prepared by the Sleep Disorders Classification Committee, H.P. Roffwarg, Chairman, *Sleep*, *2*, 1-137.

48. McCarley, R.W. (1978). "Where Dreams Come From: A New Theory." *Psychology Today*, *141*, 56-65.

An easily understandable introduction to the activation-synthesis theory of dreaming. Also covers some basic sleep physiology as it relates to this model.

49. Ito, K., and McCarley, W. (1984). "Alterations in Membrane Potential and Excitability of Cat Medial Pontine Reticular Formation Neurons during Changes in Naturally Occurring Sleep-Wake States." *Brain Research, 292,* 169–175.

50. Kelly, P.D. (1981). "Physiology of Sleep and Dreaming." In E.R. Kandel and J.H. Schwartz (Eds.), *Principles of Neural Science* (pp. 472–485). New York: Elsevier.

   A nice, short overview of the brain mechanisms involved in the production of sleep and dreaming.

51. Masserano, J.M., and King, C. (1982). "Effects on Sleep of Acetylcholine Perfusion of the Locus Coeruleus of Cats." *Neuropharmacology, 21,* 1163–1167.

52. McGinty, D.J. (1982). "Sleep Mechanisms: Biology and Control of REM Sleep." *International Review of Neurobiology, 23,* 391–437.

   Thorough review of the interaction of the body and the brain with sleep.

53. Sakai, K. (1984). "Central Mechanisms of Paradoxical Sleep." In A. Borbély and J.L. Valatx (Eds.), *Sleep Mechanisms* (pp. 3–18). Berlin: Springer-Verlag.

54. Morrison, A.R. (1983). "A Window on the Sleeping Brain." *Scientific American, 248,* 94–101.

   An introduction to the neurophysiological processes of the sleep/wake cycle, this article supports its claims with specific research examples.

55. Koella, W.P. (1981). "Neurotransmitters and Sleep." In D. Wheatley (Ed.), *Psychopharmacology of Sleep* (pp. 19–48). New York: Raven Press.

   Although difficult to understand at times, this article provides a detailed look at the role of neurotransmitters in sleep.

56. Dimond, S.J. (1980). *Neuropsychology: A Textbook of System and Psychological Functions of the Human Brain.* London: Butterworths.

57. Schwartz, M. (1978). *Physiological Psychology.* Englewood Cliffs, N.J.: Prentice-Hall.

58. Levinthal, C.F. (1983). *Introduction to Physiological Psychology*. Englewood Cliffs, N.J.: Prentice-Hall.

59. McGinty, D.J., and Sterman, M.B. (1968). "Sleep Suppression after Basal Forebrain Lesions in the Cat." *Science, 169*, 1253-1255.

60. Sterman, M.B., and Clemente, C.D. (1962). "Forebrain Inhibitory Mechanisms: Cortical Synchronization Induced by Basal Forebrain Stimulation." *Experimental Neurology, 6*, 91-102.

61. Sterman, M.B., and Clemente, C.D. (1962). "Forebrain Inhibitory Mechanisms: Sleep Patterns Induced by Basal Forebrain Stimulation in the Behaving Cat." *Experimental Neurology, 6*, 103-117.

62. Hernández-Peón, R., and Chávez-Ibarra, G. (1963). "Sleep Induced by Electrical or Chemical Stimulation of the Forebrain." In R. Hernández-Peón (Ed.), *The Psychological Basis of Mental Activity* (pp. 188-198). New York: Elsevier.

63. Hobson, J.A. (1983). "Sleep: Order and Disorder." *Behavioral Biological Medicine, 1*, 1-36.

64. Monnier, M., and Gaillard, J.M. (1980). "Biochemical Regulation of Sleep." *Experimentia, 36*, 21-24.

    The chemicals in the brain—both neurotransmitters and peptides—that have been implicated in the production of sleep are briefly reviewed.

65. Dell, P., and Padel, Y. (1965). "Rapid Falling Asleep Provoked by Selective Stimulation of Vagal Afferents in the Cat." *Electroencephalography and Clinical Neurophysiology, 18*, 725.

66. Kaitin, K.I. (1984). "Peoptic Area Unit Activity during Sleep and Wakefulness in the Cat." *Experimental Neurology, 83*, 347-357.

67. Dempsey, E.W., and Morison, R.S. (1942). "The Production of Rhythmically Recurrent Cortical Potentials after Localized Thalamic Stimulation." *American Journal of Physiology, 135*, 293-300.

68. Levitt, R.A. (1981). *Physiological Psychology*. New York: Holt, Rinehart and Winston.

69. Kleitman, N. (1963). *Sleep and Wakefulness*. Chicago,
     Ill.: Chicago University Press.

70. Weitzman, E.D. (1982). "Chronobiology of Man: Sleep,
     Temperature, and Neuroendocrine Rhythms." *Human Neuro-
     biology*, *1*, 173-183.

71. Weitzman, E.D.; Moline, M.L.; Czeisler, C.A.; and Zimmer-
     man, J.C. (1982). "Chronobiology of Aging: Temperature,
     Sleep-Wake Rhythms and Entrainment." *Neurobiology of
     Aging*, *3*, 299-309.

72. Weitzman, E.D.; Czeisler, C.A.; Zimmerman, J.C.; Moore-
     Ede, M.C.; and Tonda, J.M. (1980). "Sleep Duration,
     Sleep Stages and Waking Time Are Related to Circadian
     Phase in Young and Older Men during Nonentrained Condi-
     tions." *American Neurological Association Transactions*,
     105, 371-374.

73. Wever, R.A. (1984). "Circadian Aspects of Human Sleep."
     In A. Borbély and J.L. Valatx (Eds.), *Sleep Mechanisms*
     (pp. 258-271). New York: Springer-Verlag.

74. Wever, R.A. (1984). "Properties of Human Sleep-Wake
     Cycles: Parameters of Internally Synchronized Free-
     running Rhythms." *Sleep*, *7*, 27-51.

75. Borbély, A.A. (1982). "A Two Process Model of Sleep
     Regulation." *Human Neurobiology*, *1*, 195-204.

76. Borbély, A.A. (1984). "Sleep Regulation: Outline of a
     Model and Its Implications for Depression." In A.
     Borbély and J.L. Valatx (Eds.), *Sleep Mechanisms* (pp.
     272-284). New York: Springer-Verlag.

77. Daan, S.; Beersma, D.G.M.; and Borbély, A.A. (1984).
     "Timing of Human Sleep: Recovery Process Gated by a
     Circadian Pacemaker." *American Journal of Physiology*,
     246, R161-R178.

78. Minors, D.S., and Waterhouse, J.M. (1984). "The Sleep-
     Wakefulness Rhythm, Exogenous and Endogenous Factors
     (in Man)." *Experientia*, *40*, 410-416.

     A good, readable introduction to and review of cir-
     cadian rhythms.

79. Czeisler, C.A.; Zimmerman, J.C.; Ronda, J.M.; Moore-Ede,
     M.C.; and Weitzman, E.D. (1980). "Timing of REM Sleep

Is Coupled to the Circadian Rhythm of Body Temperature in Man." *Sleep, 2,* 329-346.

80. Åkerstedt, T. (1984). "Work Schedules and Sleep." *Experientia, 40,* 417-422.

81. Åkerstedt, T., and Gillberg, M. (1982). "Displacement of the Sleep Period and Sleep Deprivation." *Human Neurobiology, 1,* 163-171.

82. Campbell, S.S. (1984). "Duration and Placement of Sleep in a 'Disentrained' Environment." *Psychophysiology, 21,* 106-113.

83. Czeisler, C.A.; Weitzman, E.D.; Moore-Ede, M.C.; Zimmerman, J.C.; and Knauer, R.S. (1980). "Human Sleep: Its Duration and Organization Depend on Its Circadian Phase." *Science, 210,* 1264-1267.

84. Carman, G.J.; Mealey, L.; Thompson, S.T.; and Thompson, M.A. (1984). "Patterns in the Distribution of REM Sleep in Normal Human Sleep." *Sleep, 7,* 347-355.

85. Groos, G. (1984). "The Physiological Organization of the Circadian Sleep-Wake Cycle." In A. Borbély and J.L. Valatx (Eds.), *Sleep Mechanisms* (pp. 241-257). New York: Springer-Verlag.

86. Pickard, G.E., and Turek, F.W. (1983). "The Suprachiasmatic Nuclei: Two Circadian Clocks?" *Brain Research, 268,* 201-210.

87. Bloom, F.E.; Lagerson, A.; and Hofstadter, L. (1985). *Brain, Mind, and Behavior.* New York: W.H. Freeman and Co.

88. Eastman, C.I.; Mistlberger, R.E.; and Rechtschaffen, A. (1984). "Suprachiasmatic Nuclei Lesions Eliminate Circadian Temperature and Sleep Rhythms in the Rat." *Physiology and Behaviors, 32,* 357-368.

89. Lavie, P., and Zomer, J. (1984). "Ultrashort Sleep-Waking Schedule. II. Relationship between Ultradian Rhythms in Sleepability and REM-Non-REM Cycles and Effects of the Circadian Phase." *Electroencephalography and Clinical Neurophysiology, 57,* 35-42.

90. Carskadon, M.A., and Dement, W.C. (1980). "Distribution of REM Sleep on a 90-Minute Sleep-Wake Schedule." *Sleep, 2,* 309-317.

Chapter 3
NEUROANATOMICAL, NEUROPHYSIOLOGICAL, AND BIOCHEMICAL ASPECTS OF SLEEP: AN HISTORICAL PERSPECTIVE

John Zimmerman

In order to allow the reader to understand some of the terminology presented in this chapter, the following list of definitions has been prepared.

> Acetylcholine (ACh): an excitatory neurotransmitter
> Acetylcholinesterase (AChE): an enzyme which breaks down acetylcholine
> Agonist: a chemical which mimics the effect of a natural neurotransmitter
> Antagonist: a chemical which blocks the effect of a neurotransmitter
> -ceptive: cells receiving and being influenced by a particular neurotransmitter
> Gamma-aminobutyric acid (GABA): an inhibitory neurotransmitter
> -nergic: a chemical which increases or mimics the action of a neurotransmitter, e.g., GABAnergic
> Norepinephrine (NE): an excitatory neurotransmitter related to adrenalin (epinephrine)

Historical Perspectives

Since ancient times the human race has speculated on the nature of sleep and dreams. Dr. Michael Jouvet illustrated this by recounting an ancient Hindu tale which describes the three states of mind in man:

a) Wakefulness (vaiswanara), in which a person "is conscious only of external objects [and] is the enjoyer of the pleasures of the sense";

b) dreaming sleep (taijasa), in which one "is conscious only of his dreams [and] is the enjoyer of the subtle impressions in the mind of the deeds he has done in the past"; and

c) dreamless sleep (prajna), a "blissful state in
which the veil of unconsciousness envelopes his
thoughts and knowledge, and the subtle impressions
on his mind apparently vanish." (1, p. 62)

Despite the fact that human beings spend fully one-third
of their lives in the second and third states, it has been only
comparatively recently that advances in science and technology
have allowed scientists to investigate and study these states
of consciousness objectively. A number of major scientific
advances have been instrumental in fostering the current
understanding of sleep and the neuroanatomical, physiological,
and biochemical mechanisms that underlie it.

Brain electrical activity was first recorded in rabbits
in the late 1800s by Caton (2) and reported in humans first
by Berger (3). REM sleep was first recognized by the association of regularly occurring periods of ocular motility and
other sleep variables by Aserinski and Kleitman (4). Histochemical fluorescent techniques for visualizing the presence
of specific types of neurotransmitters was pioneered by Bertler,
Carlsson, and Rosengren (5). The distinction between long-
lasting tonic phenomena of REM sleep (such as the EEG desynchronization) and brief bursts of phasic events during REM
sleep was conceptualized by Moruzzi (6). Pontine-Geniculo-
Occipital (PGO) spikes were associated with REM sleep by
Jeannerod, Mouret, and Jouvet (7). A standardized manual and
techniques for scoring sleep stages in human subjects was
produced in the late 1960s (8).

Passive Theories of Sleep

For years, sleep was explained as a passive phenomenon:
the gradual running down of the wakefulness-maintaining system
until it reached a state of inactivity, i.e., sleep. The
process might be likened to a car running out of gas and
gradually coasting to a stop.

When the ascending reticular activating system (ARAS) is
surgically disconnected from the telencephalon, as in the now
classical "cerveau isole" preparations of Bremer (9), the
animal enters a prolonged (but not permanent) state resembling
NREM sleep. Bremer made the transection at the level of the
midbrain and in so doing surgically disconnected the ARAS
from the higher brain centers. This had the same effect as
removing the power source of a car. In this case, the midbrain
transection removed the ascending activating signals which
keep the forebrain awake.

Conversely, Moruzzi and Magoun (10) demonstrated that electrical stimulation of the structures surrounding the ARAS immediately caused an EEG arousal from sleep. This would be comparable to stepping on the gas pedal of a car and making the engine run faster.

The early ideas resulting from these experiments led to the view that normal sleep was the end result of a deactivation "en avalanche" of the neural mechanisms responsible for arousal. It was presumed that the wakefulness-maintaining system was located in the ascending reticular activating system. The neurophysiological mechanisms responsible for normal drowsiness and sleep were originally thought to be caused by synaptic fatigue (11;12).

Active Theories of Sleep

As attractively simple as this idea was, however, it was not reconcilable with some undisputed evidence from a classical experiment of many years prior. First of all, there was the observation that electrical stimulation of certain brain centers *actively produced sleep* in a waking animal much the same way that stepping on the brake pedal of a car actively brings it to a stop. The work of the Swiss neurophysiologist H.R. Hess resulted in the first report that low frequency electrical stimulation of median thalamic nuclei was capable of actively producing a state of sleep in the waking cat (13).

Upon eight cycle per second stimulation of certain brain areas, the waking animal exhibits a progressive decrease in activity, eventually sits down, curls up in its natural sleeping position, closes its eyes and nictating membranes, and goes to sleep. Polygraphic recordings of the animal following electrical brain stimulation revealed a sleep pattern composed of spindles and slow waves, i.e., signs of NREM sleep (14;15).

More recent neurophysiological studies of the sleep inducing effects of electrical brain stimulation have shown that this elicits a volley of thalamocortical inhibitory postsynaptic potentials (IPSPs). The inhibitory brain chemical involved appears to be the neurotransmitter gamma-aminobutyric acid (GABA). Further studies have shown that the commonly used hypnotic class of benzodiazepines act as GABA agonists and increase the IPSP activity of the diffuse thalamic projection system (16).

Other investigators soon repeated Hess's work and found sleep inducing centers in many other parts of the brain as well (17). While these findings supplied evidence that sleep

could be an active process, further proof was needed to counter the arguments of the passive theorists. They pointed out
that most of the sleep-biochemical work was done on cats.
They argued that since cats normally sleep some 60-65% of the
time anyway, showing that electrically stimulating a certain
brain structure could produce sleep does not have a great deal
of statistical significance. Furthermore, the proponents of
the passive theory found it hard to believe that any active
sleep producing system could be so diffuse as to extend from
the spinal cord all the way up to the telencephalon and include structures in the medulla, cerebellum, pons, mesencephalon, hypothalamus, subthalamus, thalamus, and cortex.

Fortunately, further proof was forthcoming in the experiments of Batini and her group. They showed that completely
transecting the brain immediately rostral to the origin of
the trigeminal nerve produced a state of partial insomnia.
Specifically, following a midpontine, pretrigeminal section,
cats were awake more and slept only 20% of the time, instead
of their usual 65% (18). The interpretation of the results
of this and other experiments was that severing the brain at
the pretrigeminal, midpontine level had removed a powerful
sleep inducing mechanism that normally functioned to inhibit
the activity of the reticular activating system (1). Removal
of this active sleep promoting portion of the brain resulted
in prolonged wakefulness, perhaps analogous to disabling the
active braking mechanism of a car. The brain transection experiments forever put to rest the theory that sleep was the
result of *only* a passive decline in the activity of the reticular activating system. The neural regulation of sleep is a
complex topic which is summarized in a short paper by Rossi (19).

Serotonin and NREM Sleep

A serum vasoconstrictor compound, which was called serotonin, was first isolated and characterized by Rapport, Green,
and Page (20). It was later found in the brain (21) and has
subsequently been the focus of much research associating it
as a neurotransmitter of vital importance for sleep.

Beginning in the 1950s, other investigators examined differences in brain biochemistry between the waking and sleeping
states. An important observation for the biochemical study
of sleep was the discovery that the concentration of serotonin
in the rat's brain was higher when the rat is usually asleep
(during the late morning and afternoon hours) and lower when
the animal is usually awake (during the evening and early

morning hours) (22). Furthermore, a decrease in whole brain
serotonin concentration preceded the onset of behavioral activity, indicating that high serotonin concentrations are incompatible with wakefulness.

This discovery, coupled with the gradual acceptance of
the active theory of sleep, prompted neuroscientists to study
the sleep inducing effects of serotonin. Serotonin is ana-
bolized from ordinary L-tryptophan, a common amino acid found
in dairy products, meats, and beans. L-tryptophan is hydroxylated at the number 5 position to form the serotonin precursor,
5-hydroxytryptophan or 5-HTP. The enzyme tryptophane-5-
hydroxylase is necessary for the conversion of L-tryptophan
to 5-HTP. This is the rate limiting reaction in the biosynthesis of serotonin. Once this has occurred, another enzyme,
called aromatic L-amino acid decarboxylase, catalyzes the
removal of the carboxyl group to form serotonin, commonly
called 5-hydroxytryptoamine or 5-HT (23;24). Tryptophan is
the only amino acid precursor of serotonin in the brain (25).

Early experiments had used the immediate serotonin precursor, 5-hydroxytryptophan (5-HTP), which readily crosses the
blood-brain barrier and is converted into serotonin. In these
experiments (26), it was found that intracarotid injections of
22 mg of 5-HTP increased the concentration of brain serotonin
and accentuated EEG synchronization in each of four rabbits.
Higher doses (44 mg) of 5-HTP produced a transient synchronization followed by a persistent desynchronization. Following
the outcome of these serotonin experiments, theorists quickly
began to postulate the existence of a serotonergic mechanism
that was somehow involved in the sleep induction process (27).

Since serotonin does not cross the blood-brain barrier,
the first experiments designed to test the effects of 5-HT on
sleep used chicks since the avarian blood-brain barrier is
poorly developed. This allowed substances like serotonin to
enter the brain through systematic administration. Spooner
and Winters (28) found that subcutaneous injection of serotonin into a chick caused the bird to sleep more. This was
first noted by behavioral observations and verified by electrophysiological recordings. Other experimenters attempted to by-
pass the blood-brain barrier in mammals by injecting serotonin
directly into the brain. Thus, Koella, Trunca, and Czicman (29)
were able to demonstrate a marked increase in cortical recruit-
ing responses following local application of 5-HT to the area
in the postrema.

By combining the results of the histofluorescent tracing
studies of Falck (30) with the detailed neuroanatomical studies
of the efferent pathways of the raphé system (31), it was de-
duced that the perikaryal (cell body) origins of most of the
serotonin containing neurons were in the area of the brainstem
known as the nuclei of raphé (from the Greek word meaning "seam")

Direct proof of serotonin containing cell bodies located in
the raphé nuclei came from the work of Dahlstrom and Fuxe (32)
who used histofluorescent techniques to identify serotonin
containing nerve cell bodies in several raphé nuclei (raphé
centralis, raphé dorsalis, raphé pontis, and nucleus magnus).
   The next step was to demonstrate that sleep was dependent
upon the functional integrity of the serotonergic cells of
the nuclei of raphé. This could only be done by somehow de-
creasing the concentrations of serotonin in the axonal termina-
tions of these cells and observing a decrease in total sleep
time. Three methods of altering brain serotonin were available: a) neuropharmacological alteration of serotonin by inhibiting its biosynthesis; b) neuroanatomical alteration by
surgically destroying the serotonin producing cells of the
raphé nuclei; and c) dietary restrictions of L-tryptophan,
which is the amino acid precursor of serotonin.

Depletion of Serotonin by Means of
Pharmacological Inhibition of Synthesis

   Although it had been known for a long time that many
drugs were capable of reducing sleep time, it was only in
the mid-1960s that new drugs became available that reduced
sleep time by inhibiting the synthesis of serotonin. The
drug para-chlorophenylalanine (PCPA) is such an inhibitor of
serotonin synthesis. It acts by blocking the transformation
of tryptophan into 5-HTP. Serotonin synthesis is also
blocked by (+)-6-fluorortryptophan which also inhibits the
enzyme tryptophan hydroxylase (33).
   When PCPA is given to a cat at the rate of 400 mg/kg, the
following effects are observed: during the first 24 hours there
is no effect on sleep parameters as stored serotonin is available until it is depleted. Afterward, there is a precipitous
decrease in total sleep time as the supply of serotonin runs
out so that by 30 hours, there is near total insomnia. When
the effects of PCPA wear out, sleep reappears after 60 hours
but is accompanied by continuous PGO waves during the NREM
sleep state and "narcoleptic-like" transitions from wakefulness
directly into the REM sleep. Normal sleep patterns are re-
established only after 200 hours following a single 400 mg/kg
injection of PCPA (34).
   Other in vitro and in vivo studies suggest that PCPA acts
to inhibit the synthesis of serotonin by selectively blocking
the enzyme tryptophan hydroxylase (35) and so it should be
possible to reverse the insomnia producing effects of PCPA by

bypassing that enzyme. This was found to be the case since administration of very *small* amounts (2-5 mg/kg) of the serotonin precursor 5-HTP, immediately after administration of PCPA, was able to effectively circumvent the insomnia-causing effect of PCPA, returning both sleep states to normal. One cat in Jouvet's laboratory that was maintained on single daily injections of PCPA had severe and long-lasting insomnia and behavioral disturbances such as anorexia and an inability to walk. Another cat, also getting daily injections of PCPA, was additionally given daily injections of 5-HTP. This cat had normal amounts of sleep time and experienced no behavioral disturbances for several days of continuous observation (36).

Acute administration of PCPA has been shown to produce nearl complete insomnia in rats (34). PCPA also causes insomnia in cats although here it was also suggested that the effects may be due not only to the inhibition of serotonin synthesis but because of the inhibition of catecholamine synthesis by blocking the enzyme phenylalanine hydroxylase which converts phenylalanine to tyrosine (37). The insomnia effect of PCPA, however, is not present in humans (38).

Depletion of Serotonin with
Surgical and Drug Lesioning Techniques

In order to rule out the possibility of any peripheral effects of PCPA and to prove the existence of a serotonergic sleep regulatory mechanism, lesions of the raphé system were performed on cats. Destruction of 80-90% of the raphé system leads to insomnia both behaviorally and electrophysiologically (39). The insomnia persists the first 3-4 days following the lesion, but from days 5-13, the daily percent of the NREM sleep gradually increases up to 10%, but never beyond that (36). Furthermore, partial lesions of the raphé produced data that indicated a significant correlation between the volume of the raphé system destroyed, the degree of resulting insomnia, and measured concentrations of serotonin (36; and see Table 2).

Temporary chemical lesions of the serotonergic nerve terminals are also possible using 5,6-dihydroxytryptamine (5,6-DHT). According to experiments of Baumgarten et al. (40), injection of 5,6-DHT into the lateral ventricle of the rat brain caused a substantial loss of indoleamines (presumably 5-HT) from the brain and caused behavioral hyperexcitability. The effect of such chemical lesions is evident when 5,6-DHT is injected into certain serotoniceptive sites.

Injection of 5,6-DHT into the preoptic area of the hypothalmus suppresses only the cortical synchronization of the slow wave sleep state but does not alter behavioral sleep. Jouvet and Pujol (41) report a 60% decrease in cortical slow waves, lasting at least two weeks, following an intracerebral injection of the compound into the preoptic area.

More recently, Pujol et al. (42) have shown that the method of injection influences the results. Direct injection into the rostral raphé only reduced serotonin and its metabolite 5-hydroxyindoleacetic acid in the cerebellum by 47%. This also led to a transitory increase in REM sleep lasting only 24 hours. In contrast, injections of 5,6-DHT into the brain ventricles produced significant decreases in 5-HT and 5-HIAA in all brain structures and more complex alterations of sleep patterns. Intraventricular 5,6-DHT decreased total sleep time and increased total wake time by 80%, i.e., a chemical insomnia caused by destruction of serotonin terminals. REM sleep was initially greatly suppressed, then first returned to near normal amounts after 4-5 days, then decreased again to 50% of normal for up to 15 days. A significant relationship (r = 0.77) was observed between declines in stage 2 sleep and decreases in cortical 5-HT. This indicates that the rostral projections of the raphé system (raphé dorsalis and centralis) might be important in the expression of stage 2 sleep (42).

One important difference between the insomnia induced by PCPA and by raphé lesions is that subsequent administration of 5-HTP does not reverse the insomnia following destruction of the serotonergic cells of the raphé system; whereas 5-HTP can counteract the effects of PCPA. Ten days after raphé lesions, there is a decrease in endogenous levels of serotonin at the axon terminals and a decrease in the synthesis of labeled serotonin from labeled tryptophan. However, there is no decrease in serotonin synthesis from labeled 5-HTP. The same effects are observed following treatment with PCPA, which blocks the action of tryptophan hydroxylase. This indicates that there must be some other place in the brain where 5-HTP could be converted to serotonin. Perhaps this could occur at the axonal terminals of the destroyed serotonergic cells. One possibility is that 5-HTP may be converted into serotonin via a non-specific 5-HTP-DOPA decarboxylase enzyme, presumably located in brain capillaries or in catecholaminergic neurons. The fact that sleep is not restored by injecting 5-HTP after raphé lesions, even though serotonin is still being synthesized via this alternate pathway, indicates that serotonin must be released from the axonal terminals of the serotonergic neurons onto their target cells in order to induce sleep (43). However, the observation that very low doses (2-4 mg/kg) of 5-HTP can restore sleep in PCPA treated cats can be taken to mean that

exogenous 5-HTP can be preferentially decarboxylated into
serotonin inside serotonergic neurons. Apparently this is true
only if endogenous serotonin is absent, as is the case following PCPA (43).

Depletion of Serotonin by
Dietary Absence of L-Tryptophan

The evidence so far points to the simple conclusion that
serotonin causes slow wave sleep. However, more recent
studies clarify the details of the mechanism and suggest that
serotonin is primarily responsible for the circadian rhythmicity of sleep, not sleep itself. Lanoir, Ternaux, Pons, and
Lagarde (44) studied the effects of a tryptophan free diet
for 16 weeks. They documented 50% reductions in brain serotonin. The only effect on the EEG sleep patterns was the
gradual disappearance of sleep spindles by week 14. However,
there were long-term changes in the 24-hour percentages of
wakefulness and slow wave sleep (7% increase in wakefulness,
6% decrease in slow wave sleep the first month only, then
return to control levels). There was only a slight 5-9% reduction in REM sleep over the 24-hour period. What changed
with dietary reduction of L-tryptophan was the circadian distribution of sleep and wakefulness.

Under control conditions *wakefulness* was twice as great
during the dark period (since cats are nocturnal) than during
the light period and *sleep* was twice as great during the dark
period than the light. Following two months of reductions
in brain serotonin, these normal proportions disappeared and
were replaced with equal amounts of wakefulness and slow wave
sleep occurring during both the dark and the light periods.
Thus, the effect of serotonin on sleep is believed by some to
regulate circadian periodicity, consolidating sleep into the
light (or dark period for humans) portion of the 24-hour day
(44). This conclusion is confirmed by noting an increased
number of nocturnal awakenings in man following a five-day
reduction in dietary tryptophan (45).

The Case for Serotonin's
Causative Influence on Sleep

The results from all of the studies that have been examined so far indicate that the presence of serotonin (5-HTP
at the axonal terminals of serotonergic neurons, originating

in the nuclei of the raphé) is necessary for the production of some sleep inducing factor. In interpreting the sleep inducing effects of serotonin, care must be taken to make a clear distinction between behavioral sleep and EEG synchronization.

Recall that Jouvet and Pujol (41) observed only a decrease in EEG slow waves but not a corresponding decrease in behavioral sleep when 5,6-DHT was injected into the preoptic area of the hypothalamus. The behavioral sleep effect of serotonin is probably brought about by the inhibition of the activity of catecholaminergic neurons of the mesencephalic reticular formation that are responsible for maintaining wakefulness. The later phenomenon (EEG synchronization) is dependent upon the existence and integrity of the telediencephalon (46). There is some experimental evidence (47) that the EEG slow waves characteristic of NREM sleep are the direct result of increased activity of the neurons of the preoptic area of the hypothalamus which may be stimulated by serotonergic neurons whose axonal terminals synapse upon cells of the preoptic area. Bilateral electrical stimulation of this area in behaviorally active and awake cats resulted in the virtually immediate onset (less than one minute) of behavioral and electroencephalographic manifestations of sleep (47).

Evidence that these preoptic neurons are innervated by serotonergic input from the raphé system comes from two types of studies. First are the neuroanatomical studies which demonstrate the existence of serotonin pathways from the raphé system terminating in the preoptic nucleus of the hypothalamus. The second line of evidence supporting this conceptualization comes from the results of injecting serotonin directly into the preoptic area. Yamaguchi et al. (48) have been able to trigger the slow waves of NREM sleep with this procedure. The possibility that seroniceptive cells of the preoptic area are also responsible for the synthesis and/or release of the somatotrophic hormone releasing factor that triggers the adenohypophysis to release growth hormone is most exciting and should be explored in the near future.

The Case Against Serotonin's
Direct Control of Sleep

Until recently researchers have been relatively content with the above explanations of the initiation and maintenance of NREM sleep. It seemed clear that serotonin was necessary for the sleep consolidation process and that either surgical

or biochemical blockage of serotonin resulted in the absence
of sleep, i.e., insomnia. A different interpretation, however,
is also possible. Perhaps the absence of serotonin *increases
wakefulness rather than decreases sleep.* A review of serotonin and sleep is presented by Morgane (49).

For instance, several recent reports have confirmed the
observation that activity of 5-HT neurons is actually higher
during waking than during sleep (50-52). Furthermore, increased firing activity of the serotonergic neurons was accompanied by greater levels of serotonin and its metabolic
byproduct, 5-hydroxyindoleacetic acid (5-HIAA) during
waking (53). This report contrasts with the earlier reported
results in which brain serotonin levels were reported higher
during sleep than waking (22).

Other recent evidence also presents a challenge for the
simplistic serotonin-causes-sleep hypothesis. Administration
of a proposed serotonin agonist (a serotonin receptor stimulant
called quipazine maleate) reduces both NREM and REM sleep in a
dose related fashion. This effect was blocked when the serotonin receptor stimulant was prevented from interacting with
the serotonin receptors by pretreatment with the serotonin
antagonist metergoline which prevents 5-HT receptors from
being activated by either serotonin or quipazine maleate (54).
As wakefulness persists, the synthesis and release of 5-HT
in the dorsal raphé and thalamus increases with increases in
sleep pressure. Transport of 5-HT into the brain may be
necessary for some other sleep inducing mechanisms, but the
sleep inducing chemical is probably not serotonin itself (55).

More recent experiments suggest that serotonin does not
directly cause slow wave sleep itself but regulates the
accumulation of some other sleep factor. When PCPA is given
at the end of a period of sleep deprivation (just before recovery sleep is allowed to begin), the normal amount of NREM
sleep rebound occurs because previously synthesized serotonin
is still available. However, if PCPA is given *during* sleep
deprivation, the resulting inhibition of synthesis of serotonin
may not allow the production of this other sleep factor and
there is little or no rebound of slow wave sleep during the
recovery period (56).

Other researchers observed opposite effects of PCPA with
sleep deprivation, the deprivation starting two hours after
beginning treatment with PCPA. When combined with sleep deprivation, PCPA still effectively reduced total sleep time during
the recovery period but slow wave sleep (SWS) stages 3 and 4
were increased during recovery sleep. Since SWS usually increases following sleep deprivation and PCPA did not interfere
with this increase, it was concluded that the "essential
aspects of sleep regulation are still functioning during PCPA-
induced insomnia" (57).

Not only is serotonin synthesis and release increased during prolonged wakefulness but serotonin metabolism is also increased. In support of this hypothesis is the observation of Toru et al. (55) who noted that 5-HIAA concentrations in the dorsal raphé nuclei increased significantly (140-180%) immediately after sleep deprivation. This suggests that the wakefulness associated with the sleep deprivation increases serotonin metabolism.

It has been suggested that serotonergic neurons are active during waking and are responsible for the biosynthesis for some as yet unidentified sleep factors which accumulate until they initiate sleep. This explains the common observation that the amount of prior wakefulness at least partly determines the amount of subsequent sleep.

Sleep Factors

Much controversy has developed over the possibility of the existence of sleep factors or substances which will produce sleep when injected into an animal and will cause a maintenance of wakefulness when deprived or blocked at certain active brain sites. Pieron (58) was the first to suggest the possibility of a sleep inducing factor in 1913. Since then numerous attempts have been made to identify the compound which produces sleep. Of particular interest is one called delta sleep inducing peptide, or DSIP, reported by Monnier and Hosli (59). This compound has recently been purified and isolated. It is a nanopeptide (9 peptides) of molecular weight 849. This substance has been shown to induce mainly delta sleep (NREM sleep), hence the name DSIP. This action has been demonstrated in rabbits, rats, mice, and humans (see Graf and Kastin, 60, for a review article on sleep peptides). A re-examination of serotonergic sleep mechanisms which discusses both the old supporting evidence and the newer conflicting evidence is presented in a review article (61).

Something called sleep factor-S which accumulates during wakefulness and even during PCPA caused wakefulness, can be transferred from one animal's cerebral spinal fluid (CSF) to another and cause sleep in the recipient (62-65). An effect similar to factor-S has been observed using material extracted from the brains of sleep deprived rats (66). Sleep factor-S has been purified and shown to be different from DSIP (67).

Jouvet has recently accepted this new notion, that the sleep regulating system is still operative even when serotonin synthesis is blocked by PCPA. He has rejected his earlier hypothesis that serotonin itself causes sleep and reformulated

a new one. In his new theory, Jouvet and his group accept the
fact that some sleep triggering factor may still accumulate
in the brain even when serotonin synthesis is blocked by PCPA
and when 5-HT is depleted. Jouvet now suggests that vaso-
intestinal peptide has true hypnogenic effect since it can
overcome the insomnia in PCPA treated rats (46).

The Role of the Raphé System
in Triggering REM Sleep

In the earlier studies in which 80-90% of the raphé system was destroyed and a near total reduction in NREM sleep
was noted, there was also a complete absence of REM sleep,
even after NREM sleep had partially returned. Jouvet (36)
had further observed, from partial lesion studies, that REM
sleep did not appear at all unless the daily proportion of
NREM sleep was greater than 15%. Other studies by Mouret,
Bobillier, and Jouvet (68) have demonstrated that the amount
of REM sleep that remains following various doses of PCPA
treatment was directly related to the brain concentrations of
serotonin. Such experimentation in which cerebral serotonin
is reduced, either by PCPA administration or by raphé lesions,
has shown that a certain critical amount of NREM sleep equal
to at least 16% of the day must be present in order for any
REM sleep to occur at all. From a minimum of 16% and upwards
of daily NREM sleep, the amount of REM sleep increases as a
function of increasing NREM sleep (43).

Other experiments using monamine oxidase (MAO) inhibitors
helped to clarify the purported relationship between serotonin
and REM sleep. It is known that MAO inhibitors such as
nialamide, iproniazid, or phenylisopropryl hydrozide inhibit
the hydrolysis of brain monoamines and thereafter prevent the
formation of deaminated serotonin metabolites, such as 5-
hydroxyindoleacetic acid (5-HIAA). It is also known that one
of the effects of MAO inhibitors is to powerfully suppress both
the tonic and phasic signs of REM sleep (69). This evidence,
together with the fact that a minimum amount of NREM sleep
must precede the appearance of any REM sleep, led to the
hypothesis that a serotonin metabolite (perhaps 5-HIAA) might
be involved in the "priming" mechanism for the "triggering"
of the REM state (39).

Closer analysis of the raphé system lesion data revealed
that it was only the smaller, *caudal* portion of the raphé
nuclei that was involved in the "priming" mechanism that
"triggered" REM sleep. Lesions of only the caudal raphé

nuclei suppressed REM sleep relatively much more than NREM
sleep. On the other hand, lesions of the much larger group
of *rostral* raphé nuclei selectively abolished only NREM sleep,
thus leading to a "narcoleptic-like" condition wherein the
cat would proceed directly from wakefulness into REM sleep (36).
Such sleep onset REM periods and increased REM sleep follow
the administration of the pineal nanopeptide argine vasotocin
in prepubertal boys. The effect is thought to be due to an
interference with serotonin neurotransmission (70).

                 The Role of the Locus Coeruleus and
                 Noradrenalin in the REM State

     In several of his papers, Jouvet (1;27;43) makes the dis-
tinction between those serotonergic structures that are responsible for "priming" or "triggering" REM sleep and other
structures, noradrenergic in nature, that are responsible for
the "executive" mechanisms of REM sleep. The neural structures that are directly responsible for REM sleep are located
in the dorsolateral pontine tegmentum and include a bilateral
structure originating in the locus coeruleus complex and
passing ventrally through the nucleus reticularis pontis
caudalis (71;72). The importance of this relatively small
group of locus coeruleus nuclei is highlighted by surgically
destroying them. Following bilateral, total surgical coagula-
tion of the locus coeruleus complex, REM sleep and all aspects
of it, including PGO spiking, completely disappear (72;73).
Control lesions placed rostrally, caudally, medially, or
laterally do not affect REM sleep (36). The only other
structure in the dorsolateral pontine tegmentum whose destruction was capable of abolishing REM sleep was at the level of
the nucleus reticularis pontis caudalis and nucleus reticularis pontis oralis. Both of these structures probably contain
efferent pathways from the locus coeruleus (71;72;74).
     Less than total destruction of the locus coeruleus re-
vealed that there was a regional specificity in the groups
of locus coeruleus nuclei. When the caudal third of the locus
coeruleus was lesioned, the muscle atonia of the antigravity
muscles, which is characteristic of REM sleep, no longer was
present during REM sleep periods. During REM sleep, cats
with such lesions would suddenly stand up and show behavioral
signs of fear or rage as if acting out an hallucinated
dream (27;75). Thus, it seemed that the caudal portion of
the coeruleus complex was responsible for inhibiting the behavioral expression of ongoing dreams.

In contrast to the caudal third, the medial third of the coeruleus complex is responsible for the ascending phenomena of REM sleep. These include such phasic events as the PGO spikes and rapid eye movements, both of which seem to be triggered by noradrenergic impulses to the vestibular nuclei (76). The tonic EEG desynchronization observed during REM sleep is also under control of the medial third of the coeruleus complex (43;77). By means of these lesion studies involving this nuclear complex in the dorsolateral pontine tegmentum, Jouvet thought he had discovered the center of the REM sleep system, or as he called it, the REM sleep "executive mechanism."

Furthermore, histochemical and histofluorescent mapping techniques (see below) have identified two different noradrenergic pathways originating from the locus coeruleus. The first pathway is the descending system originating in the caudal third of the locus coeruleus and is responsible for the tonic inhibition of muscle tone. It has been suggested that this tonically active inhibitory influence on muscle tone may be due to the noradrenergic inhibition of either the accessory nerve (which innervates the neck muscles) or to an inhibitory influence upon the origins of the reticulospinal tract. In support of this hypothesis is the observation that there is a decrease in the norepinephrine content of the pons and cervical spinal cord following lesions of the caudal third of the locus coeruleus (77). The second system follows the ascending noradrenergic pathway originating in the medial group of locus coeruleus neurons and causes the tonic EEG desynchronization and the phasic PGO spikes and rapid eye movements of REM sleep (77).

The Controversy over Catecholamines
and REM Sleep

After Jouvet's initial lesion studies involving the locus coeruleus (72), Dahlstrom and Fuxe (32;78) discovered that the cells of the locus coeruleus complex contained high concentrations of norepinephrine as indicated by their intense green fluorescence under untraviolet light following exposure to formaldehyde gas. This important histochemical discovery helped pave the way for the development of the biogenic amine theories of sleep. However, this same discovery also marked the beginning of a debate over the relationship between catecholamines and REM sleep.

In one camp, the group headed by Jouvet, are supporters who maintain that REM sleep is *dependent* upon brain concentra-

tions of norepinephrine. In support of this theory, these
investigators have marshalled a great deal of evidence that
seems to indicate that the relationship between norepinephrine
and REM sleep is a *direct* one, by calling upon data that show
a decrease in REM sleep when norepinephrine levels are reduced.

In the other camp, whose main spokesman is Hartmann, a
different theory is adhered to which states that REM sleep
maintains the concentrations of the catecholamines in a homeostatic balance. In support of this maintenance theory is a
wealth of experimental evidence indicating that the amount of
REM sleep is *inversely* related to the concentrations of brain
norepinephrine so that any manipulation which increases the
levels of brain norepinephrine is associated with decreases in
REM sleep and vice versa. The observation that narcoleptics
and hypersomniacs have significantly lower levels of dopamine
in their cerebral spinal fluid is pertinent to this argument
(79).

Evidence for REM Sleep Dependence
upon Catecholamines

The effects of surgically destroying the locus coeruleus
have already been discussed (43;71;72;77). The locus coeruleus
may contain dopamine; therefore, the disappearance of REM
sleep following locus coeruleus destruction suggests that
dopamine is necessary for the executive mechanism of REM
sleep (80). Another way to decrease brain catecholamines is
by chemically inhibiting their synthesis. Reserpine inhibits
serotonin synthesis and depletes monamine storage pools.
When the reserve storage pools of monoamines are depleted by
injecting reserpine, the short-term effect is a reduction in
both states of sleep (81). After a single 0.5 mg/kg dose of
reserpine, NREM sleep is suppressed for 12-14 hours and REM
sleep even longer, for 22-24 hours. Furthermore, PGO spiking
activity becomes dissociated from REM sleep for 50-60 hours
by appearing during wakefulness and NREM sleep. What links
REM sleep with the catecholamines is the fact that REM sleep
is restored in the reserpinized animal following an injection
of the catecholamine precursor, dihydroxyphenylalanine (DOPA)
(75;81).

Since DOPA is converted into both dopamine and norepinephrine, it was not possible to determine which catecholamine
was responsible for restoring REM sleep following reserpine
and DOPA injections. One way to distinguish the effects of

dopamine from norepinephrine would be to administer an alternate norepinephrine precursor, other than dopamine. One such compound is 3,4-dihydroxyphenylserine (DOPS), the carboxylic acid derivative of noradrenalin, which has been shown to be converted into norepinephrine by guinea pig liver and kidney extracts in vitro (82). Evidence suggesting a REM sleep dependence upon norepinephrine comes from experiments in which a single 500 mg/kg, i.v. injection of DOPS was observed to increase the proportion of both states of sleep during subsequent recording periods (83).

Some of the strongest evidence supporting the REM sleep dependence upon catecholamines comes from pharmacological studies in which the synthesis of catecholamines have been inhibited and the effects on REM sleep recorded. While reports differ (see 77), there is some evidence that the drug alpha-methyl-para-tyrosine (AMPT) selectively suppresses REM sleep (84) by interfering with the biochemical synthesis of catecholamines. Since AMPT inhibits the reaction at the level of tyrosine hydroxylase (85) additional studies were needed to determine whether REM sleep was suppressed because of a lack of dopamine or norepinephrine. Use of the dopamine-beta-hydroxylase inhibitor, diethyldithiocarbamate (disulfiram) allows normal dopamine synthesis but blocks the formation of norepinephrine (86). Polygraphic recording experiments have shown that disulfiram significantly reduces REM sleep and behavioral waking (87), suggesting that both waking and REM sleep may be controlled by the similar catecholaminergic mechanisms.

Biochemical changes accompanying varying degrees of locus coeruleus lesions also suggest a REM sleep dependence upon catecholamines. Jouvet (36) has shown that the amount of cerebral norepinephrine is significantly and selectively decreased following bilateral surgical destruction of the locus coeruleus. Since such lesions also selectively suppressed the appearance of REM sleep, Jouvet suggested that noradrenergic mechanisms may also play a role in REM sleep.

Other evidence for REM sleep dependence upon norepinephrine is provided by administering the compound alpha-methyl-DOPA. This compound is readily absorbed by the active uptake mechanisms of catecholaminergic neurons and is rapidly converted into alpha-methyl-dopamine which, in turn, is hydroxylated into the false transmitter alpha-methyl-norepinephrine. The false transmitter thus formed is then stored in the amine-storing granules (88). When it is released by nervous activity, the alpha-methyl-norepinephrine has very little physiological effect on the postsynaptic receptor sites, i.e., it is a norepinephrine competitive antagonist. Of interest here is the fact that when alpha-methyl-DOPA is given to cats at a dose of 100 mg/kg, it causes a marked decrease in REM sleep and behavioral waking (89).

A couple of years after the Dusan-Peyrethon et al. study, a drug was developed which is selectively absorbed by catecholaminergic neurons and results in the pharmacological destruction of catecholamine nerve cells and a concomitant decrease in catecholamines from neuronal perikarya (nerve cell bodies) and axonal terminals (90). When this drug, called 6-hydroxydopamine (6-OHDA), was microinjected into the vicinity of the norepinephrine containing cells of the locus coeruleus, it resulted in the gradual reduction of REM sleep. By the eighth day, there was a total disappearance of REM sleep and PGO spiking activity in animals given 6-OHDA (91).

Jouvet's Biogenic Amine Theory of the Sleep-Wakefulness Cycle

The biochemical and neuropharmacological aspects of the waking state and the two sleep states are summarized in Figure 8 (from Jouvet [36]). In this schematic representation of his monoaminergic theory of sleep, serotonergic cells originating in the raphé system are responsible for NREM sleep (slow wave sleep or SWS), and noradrenergic cells located in the locus coeruleus activate the effector mechanisms responsible for REM sleep phenomena. The drugs that selectively interfere with various aspects of this monoaminergic regulation of the sleep-wakefulness cycle are also shown in Figure 8.

The aspect of Figure 8 not previously discussed is the role of acetylcholine in the sleep-wakefulness cycle, particularly as it relates to the serotonergic "priming" mechanisms of REM sleep. Cholinergic mechanisms first became suspect in the control of REM sleep when it was observed that the muscarinic antagonist, atropine, selectively suppressed REM sleep (72;92). Thus, cholinergic transmission was shown to be necessary for the appearance of REM sleep.

It was later demonstrated that cholinergic mechanisms were capable of increasing REM sleep by direct, microinjections of the acetylcholine agonist carbachol into the mesencephalic reticular formation. When carbachol is thus applied to this area of the reticular formation, there is a considerable enhancement (up to one hour) in the duration of REM sleep (93). Jouvet (36) interpreted the results as evidence that the carbachol stimulated the activity of the locus coeruleus neurons. Other theorists interpreted the results very differently. See section on Hobson and McCarley (below).

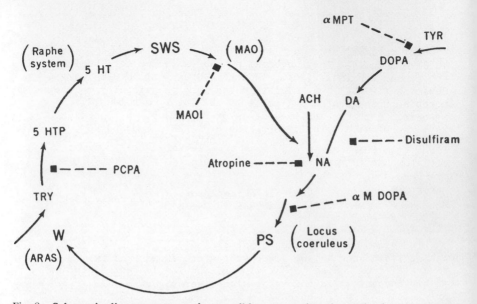

Fig. 8. Schematic diagram representing possible monoaminergic mechanisms involved in the two states of sleep (in the cat). It is postulated that the mammalian brain undergoes cyclical biochemical changes from waking (W), which depends upon the ascending reticular activating system (ARAS), of which the neuromodulator is still unknown, to slow-wave sleep (SWS), which depends upon serotonin (5 HT)-containing neurons of the raphe system, and finally to paradoxical sleep (PS), which depends upon noradrenalin(NA)-containing neurons located in the nucleus locus coeruleus. In the normal adult cat the first two steps of this cycle are reversible (W ⇌ SW ⇌ PS), whereas the final step from PS to W is never reversed. The actions of several drugs which may block certain steps of this cycle are represented. p-Chlorophenylalanine (PCPA), which inhibits the enzyme tryptophan hydroxylase (TRY), decreases cerebral 5 HT by impairing its synthesis, and thereby leads to total insomnia, which is reversed by a secondary injection of 5 HTP, the immediate precursor of 5 HT. Monoamine oxidase inhibitors (MAOI) which prevent the catabolism of serotonin lead to an increase in slow-wave sleep and to total suppression of paradoxical sleep. Thus the action of a deaminated metabolite of 5 HT may possibly be involved in the triggering of paradoxical-sleep mechanisms. Atropine, which suppresses the final steps of paradoxical sleep, inhibition of muscle tonus, may act upon a cholinergic mechanism that may be responsible for the triggering of noradrenergic mechanisms of paradoxical sleep. The latter mechanisms may be altered by numerous drugs, all of which may selectively suppress paradoxical sleep in the cat: α-methyl-p-tyrosine (α MPT), which impairs the synthesis of DOPA and NA at the level of tyrosine hydroxylase (TYR); disulfiram, which inhibits the action of the enzyme dopamine β-hydroxylase and thus prevents the synthesis of NA from DOPA; and, finally, α-methyldihydroxylalanine (α M DOPA), which may act as a false transmitter when it is converted to α-methylnoradrenalin.

The results from the cholinergic drug experiments led
Jouvet to speculate that the serotonergic priming mechanisms
of REM sleep (located in the caudal raphé) "would trigger a
cholinergic link which in turn would activate the executive
noradrenalin neurons (of the locus coeruleus) impinging upon
the effector neurons" of REM sleep along the descending and
ascending noradrenergic fiber tracts emanating from the dorsolateral pontine tegmentum (77,p. 240).

The cytoarchitectonic (cell structure) organization and
neuropharmacological pathways of the monoamine system responsible for the sleep-waking cycle is summarized in Figure 8 (from
Jouvet [77]). In this schematic diagram, serotonergic connections from the rostral raphé are seen to terminate in the
striatum and in the cerebral cortex. In the substantia nigra,
the 5-HT neurons are thought to inhibit the dopaminergic neurons that normally are responsible for behavioral waking, thus
causing behavioral sleep. The cortical hypersynchronization of
NREM sleep is probably controlled by synchronizing impulses
from the preoptic area, which in turn, is activated by the
serotonergic neurons of the anterior raphé. The perikarya of
the caudal raphé sends projections to terminate on the cells of
the locus coeruleus (31). In Jouvet's conceptualization the
serotonergic system is thought to act upon intermediate cholinergic mechanisms to induce REM sleep. As seen in the figure,
this executive mechanism is noradrenergic in nature and is
divided into two oppositely directed pathways. The descending
system is responsible for the tonic inhibition of the antigravity muscles, whereas the ascending noradrenergic system, which
passes through the medial forebrain bundle, is the source of
the tonic EEG desynchronization and the phasic PGO spikes and
rapid eye movements characteristic of REM sleep.

Evidence for the Catecholamine
Maintenance Theory of REM Sleep

As eloquent as Jouvet's theory sounds, it is unable to
explain an increasingly large body of experimental evidence
which runs counter to the predictions of the REM sleep
dependence-upon-catecholamines theory. To explain these disparate findings, Hartmann (94) has proposed an alternate REM
sleep theory. In Hartmann's theory, REM sleep (or, as he calls
it, D-sleep) functions to *maintain* the brain catecholamine
system at a certain homeostatic, optimum level of performance.
The relationship, then, between REM sleep and catecholamines
is an *inverse* one: when catecholamine levels are reduced, REM

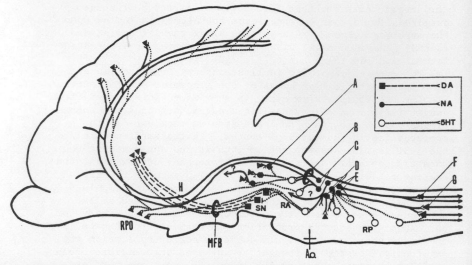

Fig. 9. *Organization of the MA systems responsible for the sleep-waking cycle.* On a sagittal map of the brain of the cat (Ao is the reference Horsley Clark zero) are highly schematized some possible organization of the MA systems. The posterior or caudal raphé system (*RP*) is responsible for the priming of PS and sends terminals to the locus coeruleus complex (*CDE*). The caudal part of the locus coeruleus (*E*) is responsible for the CA mechanisms which are responsible for the total inhibition of muscle tone, either by acting upon n. nervi accessorii (*F*) which innervates the neck muscle, or by acting upon the origin of the reticulo-spinal tract (*G*). The medial part of the locus coeruleus and subcoeruleus (*D*) is responsible for the innervation of the reticular formation of the pons and for the triggering of PGO activity and rapid eye movements during PS.   From the anterior part of the locus coeruleus (*C*) starts the ascending NA bundle (*B*). This bundle is responsible for an important NA innervation of the tele-diencephalon since its destruction is followed by a 50 % decrease of NA. It is also possible that collaterals from this bundle may act upon the anterior raphé system (*RA*) since there is an increase of tryptophan and 5-HIAA after lesion in B.   Thus the anterior part of the locus coeruleus is concerned with the control of waking (and not with PS). The anterior or rostral raphé (*RA*) is responsible for the maintenance of slow-wave sleep, either by acting upon the waking system [substantia nigra (*SN*) or group A 6 and A 8 of the Ponto-mesencephalic tegmentum (*A*) (*C*)], or by acting upon effector mechanisms located in the preoptic area (*RPO*). Some 5-HT neurons ascend through the medial forebrain bundle (*MFB*) but others certainly ascend more dorsally in the cat. EEG arousal is tonically prolonged by the CA mechanism located in group A 6 and A 8 (*A*). (*C*). These groups contribute to the CA innervation of the adjacent mesencephalic reticular formation. (Note that a lesion destroying group A 8 may also destroy the dorsal NA bundle in the mesencephalic tegmentum.) Behavioral waking is under the influence of the dopaminergic nigro-striatal system which ascends from the substantia nigra (*SN*) to the striatum (*S*) through the medial forebrain bundle. The lesion of this system decreases DA in the striatum and strongly impairs behavioral alertness, whereas it does not interfere with the cortical activity. Lesions of the lateral and medial hypothalamus (*H*) may interfere with both ascending NA and DA systems and thus alter EEG and behavioral waking but this does not imply that the hypothalamus is a waking center. The ventral NA pathway originating from the medulla is not represented in this schema.

sleep time is increased but when catecholamine levels are increased, there is a reduced need or "pressure" for REM sleep.

Some of the evidence in support of the REM sleep catecholamine maintenance theory is clearly at variance with earlier
reports. For instance, there have been several studies which
have reported that REM sleep *increases* following administration
of the tyrosine hydroxylase inhibitor, alpha-methyl-para-
tyrosine (AMPT) (95-98). Most recently, even Jouvet's group
has conceded that AMPT can increase REM sleep (as well as
NREM sleep) (99). Also at odds with earlier reports is evidence that 5-hydroxydopamine (the drug that destroys catecholamine nerve endings) significantly decreases brain norepinephrine levels and *increases* REM sleep for as long as four
months following drug adminsitration (100). Finally, two recent publications have provided evidence that alpha-adrenergic
blockers (such as phenoxybenzamine) are capable of increasing
REM sleep (101;102). These reports would seem to be in dis-
agreement with an earlier study in which the false transmitter
alpha-methyl-norepinephrine was found to result in a reduction
in noradrenergic stimulation of postsynaptic receptors and a
corresponding direct reduction in REM sleep (81;89).

While not in direct conflict with earlier reports, there
is other evidence that cannot be explained by Jouvet's theory
but that bolsters the framework of Hartmann's theory. This
other evidence demonstrates that when more catecholamines are
made available at brain synapses, therefore reducing the need
for REM sleep to restore them, the biological response is a
drastic reduction in REM sleep. This inverse relationship
between brain catecholamine levels and REM sleep is presented
in Table 2, adapted from Hartmann (92). A critical review and
consolidation of the REM sleep dependence versus REM sleep
maintenance theories are presented by Ramm (103).

Catecholamines and the Maintenance
of Wakefulness

In spite of the fact that there is so much conflicting
evidence over the effects of diminished catecholamine levels
on REM sleep, one thing is clear: the catecholamines do play
a role in the maintenance of wakefulness since wake time
during periods of reduced catecholamine levels is always decreased. A division in the function of the two catecholamines
is apparent when one considers the fact that dopamine seems
to be responsible for the behavioral aspects of wakefulness,
alertness, and responsiveness, whereas norepinephrine functions
to maintain a desynchronized EEG (43;94;104).

Table 2

Relationship between REM Sleep and
Functionally Available Catecholamines

Condition	Catecholamines Available at Brain Synapses	REM Sleep Time (or REM Pressure)*
Imipramine	+	−
Amitriptyline	+	−
Monoamine oxidase inhibitors	+	−
Dextroamphetamine	+	−
Intrathecal injection of norepinephrine	+	−
Electroconvulsive shock	+	−
Clinical mania	+	−
Reserpine	−	+
Methyldopa	−	+
Alpha-methylparatyrosine (AMPT)	−	+
6-hydroxydopamine	−	+
Clinical endogenous depression	−	+
Withdrawal from amphetamines	−	+

Note: See text for details of some of these studies and for references.

*REM time changes in the direction indicated in all situations with the exception of some depressions. Here the situation is more complex (see text). Some depressed patients show increased (+) REM time, while others show decreased (−) REM time, but with short REM latencies, long first REM periods, and high REM density in REM periods, all usually interpreted to indicate increased "REM pressure" or "tendency toward REM." Table and caption adapted from Hartmann (94).

Higher levels of norepinephrine in aged (as compared to younger) subjects may explain the greater amount of wakefulness and sleep fragmentation in the elderly (105).

Studies of the circadian variation of norepinephrine (NE) support the concept that NE is necessary for the maintenance of wakefulness. Both NE and epinephrine levels were shown to peak during late morning hours and exhibited lowest values at night during sleep (106).

The Hobson-McCarley Theory of the
REM-NREM Sleep Cycle

The importance for electrophysiological recordings in developing new theoretical models has been exemplified by the report by Hobson, McCarley, and Wyzinski (107) of reciprocal discharge rates of two different brainstem neuronal groups during the two states of sleep. In this article, they provide evidence that the cells of the giganto-cellular tegmental field (FTG) fire at a high rate during REM or D-sleep but are actively inhibited by the cells of and near the locus coeruleus during NREM or S-sleep.

In contrast, the cells of the locus coeruleus (LC) have a moderate discharge rate during NREM sleep (just the opposite of Jouvet's view) and have the lowest firing rate during REM sleep. During wakefulness locus coeruleus cells fire over 30 times more frequently than during REM sleep and even higher than during NREM sleep (10 times higher [108]). The same is true for the firing rate of serotonin-containing raphé cells. The cell discharge rate of the LC is inhibited by the FTG cells prior to REM sleep and is maintained at a low level during REM sleep by recurrent collateral inhibition. That is, LC cells actively inhibit their own firing rate during REM sleep (108). A proposed schematic diagram of the relation between the FTG cells and the LC group of neurons is given in Figure 10, adapted from McCarley and Hobson (109).

In their model, the activity of the noradrenergic cells of the locus coeruleus gradually declines during NREM or S-sleep and reaches a minimum at a couple of minutes prior to the onset of REM or D-sleep. This produces a disinhibition of the cells of the FTG and their discharge rates correspondingly begin to increase just prior to D-sleep onset. At the actual onset of REM sleep, the FTG firing rate suddenly begins to increase even more, accelerating rapidly under the influence of the positive feedback collaterals of the FTG cells back onto themselves, as shown in Figure 11 from Hobson,

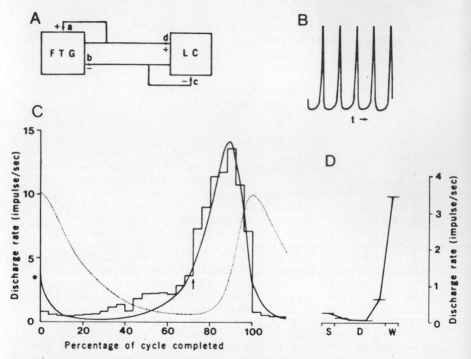

Fig. 10. Structural model of interaction between FTG and LC cell populations. The plus sign implies excitatory and the minus sign inhibitory influences. The letters *a*, *b*, *c*, and *d* correspond to the constants associated with the strength of the connections and included in the text equations. (B) Theoretical curve derived from the model that best fits the FTG unit in Fig. 1. In this fit, $a = 0.3029$, $c = 0.1514$, and the initial conditions (amplitude unscaled) were $x(0) = 1$ and $y(0) = 4.5$. (C) The solid line histogram is the average discharge level of FTG unit 568 over 12 sleep-waking cycles, each normalized to constant duration. The cycle begins with the end of desynchronized sleep, and the arrow indicates the bin with the most probable time of desynchronized sleep onset. The solid curve describes the FTG fit and the dotted line the LC fit derived from the model with the values $a = 0.5490$, $c = 0.2745$, $x(0) = 1$, and $y(0) = 3.0$ (amplitude unscaled). The dot in the ordinate scale indicates the equilibrium values for the two populations. (D) Geometric mean values of the discharge activity of ten LC cells before (synchronized sleep, *S*), during (desynchronized sleep, *D*), and after (waking, *W*) a desynchronized sleep episode. Each time epoch is equal to one-quarter of a desynchronized sleep period. Note that the discharge rate increase begins in the last quarter of *D*.

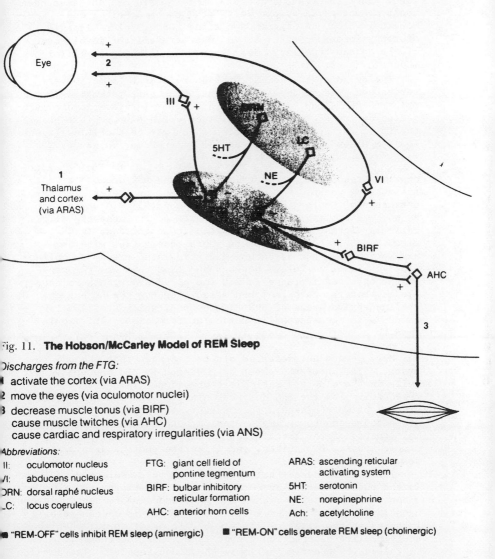

Eye

+
2
+

III

5HT

LC

NE

VI

1
Thalamus
and cortex
(via ARAS)

+

+

BIRF

+

AHC

−

+

3

Fig. 11. **The Hobson/McCarley Model of REM Sleep**

Discharges from the FTG:

1 activate the cortex (via ARAS)

2 move the eyes (via oculomotor nuclei)

3 decrease muscle tonus (via BIRF)
  cause muscle twitches (via AHC)
  cause cardiac and respiratory irregularities (via ANS)

Abbreviations:

III:	oculomotor nucleus	FTG:	giant cell field of pontine tegmentum	ARAS:	ascending reticular activating system
VI:	abducens nucleus	BIRF:	bulbar inhibitory reticular formation	5HT:	serotonin
DRN:	dorsal raphé nucleus			NE:	norepinephrine
LC:	locus coeruleus	AHC:	anterior horn cells	Ach:	acetylcholine

■ "REM-OFF" cells inhibit REM sleep (aminergic)   ■ "REM-ON" cells generate REM sleep (cholinergic)

McCarley, and Wyzinski (107). This excitatory input to the LC cells and the positive feedback stimulation of the FTG cells onto themselves is mediated by the neurotransmitter acetylcholine. Such recurrent collaterals of the FTG neurons have been amply demonstrated by the Golgi studies of Scheibel and Scheibel (110). A diagram depicting the cellular elements, neurophysiological effects, and neurotransmitter involvement of the Hobson-McCarley model is presented in Figure 11 (also shown in Hauri, 111).

The cells of the medial pontine reticular formation experience a gradual depolarization in membrane potential just prior to REM sleep. On top of this tonic increase in depolarization during REM sleep proper, such cells also exhibit phasic bursts of further depolarization which may be a critical event for REM sleep phasic phenomena (112), such as PGO waves, rapid eye movements, and muscle twitches.

Since the cells of the FTG are assumed to be both cholinoceptive (responsive to acetylcholine) and noradrenoceptive (responsive to NE), this puts a new light on the earlier experiments of George, Haslett, and Henden (93), in which carbachol was applied to the general area of the mesencephalic reticular formation, which resulted in an increase in REM sleep. Jouvet (36) interpreted this observation with the assumption that the carbachol had stimulated presumed cholinoceptive, locus coeruleus neurons and that this was the cause of the observed increase in REM sleep. However, others concluded that the carbachol had stimulated not the LC but the cholinoceptive areas of the FTG neurons, which are also located in the mesencephalic reticular formation. This would lead to a further increase in FTG firing and the onset of REM sleep.

More recent and detailed studies suggest that the EEG desynchronization of REM sleep is mediated by cholinoceptive cells in the midbrain reticular formation. This site also is responsible for the EEG desynchronization and the behavioral arousal of wakefulness. In contrast, the pontine reticular formation seems to be implicated in both the initiation and maintenance of the electrographic signs of REM sleep such as muscle atonia, PGO spikes, and (like the pontine area) EEG desynchronization (113).

There is evidence that endogenously released acetylcholine in the pontine reticular formation (PRF) initiates the REM sleep state naturally. When the acteylcholinesterase inhibitor, neostigmine, is injected into the PRF there is a dose related increase in the signs of REM sleep. In other words, when the acetylcholine destruction enzyme (acetylcholinesterase) is inhibited (by neostigmine) more REM sleep results. The percentage, frequency, and duration of REM periods increase and REM latency decreases following neostigmine administration (114).

Other evidence supportive of the Hobson-McCarley model comes from the results of experiments stimulating the locus coeruleus (LC) with acetylcholine (ACh). Since the LC is assumed to be cholinoceptive, application of ACh would increase the firing rate of LC cells, which would inhibit the firing of FTG cells. This would shift the state from REM to NREM (115). See Figure 10.

Conclusions

As should be obvious by now, the neuropharmacological mechanisms underlying the sleep-wakefulness cycles are extraordinarily complex and cannot be fully explained by such simplistic theories as have been presented here. The complex situation and the relationship between mutually interactive biochemical causes of sleep and resultant biochemical changes have prompted one author to state:

> The problem of defining sleep in biochemical terms is extremely difficult, yet studies in this area are numerous and go back to the early part of this century. Many of these provide observations that are peripheral to the central question as to what biochemical manifestations are causative of, or directly the result of, sleep. (Morgane, 49, p. 13)

Based upon our current knowledge, it would be safe to surmise that the catecholamines are responsible for the behavioral and EEG aspects of wakefulness. Behavioral alertness and subjective wakefulness are mediated by dopamine and the desynchronization of the EEG is controlled by norepinephrine. All available evidence seems to support the notion that NREM sleep, at least, is initiated and maintained by the activity of the serotonergic cells of the raphé system. Serotonin, however, is not directly responsible for the induction of sleep. Since the activity of serotonergic cells is higher during wakefulness but the levels of serotonin in the brain are higher during sleep, this presents us with somewhat of a paradox. Perhaps circadian alterations in brain neurotransmitter receptor sensitivity may explain why serotonin nerve cell activity is higher during wakefulness in spite of the previously established fact that serotonin concentration levels are higher during sleep (116). It is possible that the higher activity of serotonergic cells during daytime wakefulness leads to an accumulation of the synaptic storage of serotonin in presynaptic vessicles. When this reaches a critical level, sero-

tonin is released into the synaptic clefts, diffuses across
postsynaptic membranes, binds to postsynaptic receptor sites,
and is then metabolized into 5-hydroxyindoleacetic acid. This
may trigger brain sensitivity to a circulating humoral factor
such as deep sleep inducing peptide, or some sleep factors
(such as factor-S) or other neurohumoral agent which directly
causes both behavioral sleep and the EEG slow waves characteristic of NREM sleep.

Once a certain amount of NREM sleep has occurred, the
metabolism of serotonin into 5-HIAA may trigger cholinergic
neurons to begin to fire. The activity of these cholinergic
neurons may affect the cholinoceptive cells of the gigantocellular tegmental field in an excitatory fashion causing them
also to fire. This would further increase the firing rate of
the FTG cells because of collateral positive feedback upon
themselves and lead to REM sleep. Prior to REM sleep the
cells of the locus coeruleus and of the raphé nuclei would
gradually decrease their firing rate and reach a minimum.
This would produce a disinhibition of the cells of the FTG and
their discharge rates would accelerate and fire even faster
than before, as shown in Figures 10 and 11.

The cortical hypersynchronization so characteristic of
NREM sleep is controlled by the preoptic area of the hypothalamus. The behavioral quiescence of NREM sleep is probably
effected by the serotonergic inhibition of the substantia
nigra, striatum, and neocortex which in turn is influenced by
the activity of the cells of the anterior raphé system.

It also seems clear that a certain amount of NREM sleep
must be necessary to build up an adequate amount of some metabolic byproduct (perhaps a deaminated serotonin metabolite)
in order to "trigger" the onset of REM sleep. Unfortunately,
the executive mechanisms of REM sleep remain somewhat ambiguous
Jouvet's evidence, especially from his studies involving
lesions of the locus coeruleus, seem to provide clear evidence
that the locus coeruleus is the center of the REM sleep executive mechanism and that REM sleep depends upon the level of
brain catecholamines.

On the other hand, Hartmann has marshalled considerably
more evidence that leads to the conclusion that REM sleep
functions to maintain the catecholamine system. Furthermore,
the recent electrophysiological evidence of Hobson (108) and
Hobson, McCarley, and Wyzinski (107) has allowed them to
develop a neuroanatomical model that is consistent with Hartmann's theory. It is also possible that both the locus
coeruleus and the cells of the giganto-cellular tegmental field
function in different ways in the service of REM sleep. It
must be admitted, though, that the current weight of evidence
tips the theoretical scales in favor of Hartmann's maintenance

theory, especially when one considers the tremendous number of drugs that decrease REM sleep and the one thing that many of these drugs have in common is that they increase the amount of catecholamines available in the synaptic clefts of brain synapses.

The dynamic balance between the concentration of various neurochemicals may be more important in regulating the sleep-wake cycle rather than absolute levels (117). The ultimate integration of these facts with the obvious dependence of REM sleep on the noradrenergic cells of the locus coeruleus must await the results of future research. Several recent review articles have attempted to integrate these disparate findings into a cohesive theory of the biochemical regulation and neurophysiological control mechanisms of sleep (REM and NREM) and wakefulness (118;119). More recently, Koells (120) has developed a novel integrated model of the regulation of sleep and wakefulness. It is hoped that in the near future converging evidence from anatomical, electrophysiological, neuropharmacological, and lesion studies will allow us to forge a comprehensive theory of that circle of events we spend our entire existence in from birth until death--the sleep-wake cycle.

References

1. Jouvet, M. (1967). "The States of Sleep." *Scientific American, 216* (2), 62-72.

2. Caton, R. (1875). "The Electric Currents of the Brain." *British Medical Journal, 2*, 978.

3. Berger, H. (1969). "On the Electroencephalograph in Man." *Archives of Electroencephalography and Chemical Neurophysiology* (Suppl. 290). (Pierre Gloor, Trans. and Ed.) (Originally published in 1929.)

4. Aserinsky, E., and Kleitman, N. (1953). "Regularly Occurring Periods of Eye Motility and Concomitant Phenomena during Sleep." *Science, 118*, 273-274.

    This paper elaborates upon the newly discovered association between rapid eye movements and other physiological variables which later were defined in a consolation of parameters known as REM sleep. Subsequent work showed that this combination of electro-physiological variables was associated with the behavioral state of dreaming.

5. Bertler, A.; Carlsson, A.; and Rosengren, E. (1958). "A Method for the Fluorometric Determination of Adrenalin and Noradrenalin in Tissues." *Acta Physiologica Scandinavica*, *44*, 273-292.

This paper describes the development of the histo-fluorescent technique which has been so helpful in delineating the neuroanatomical pathways of the various neurotransmitter systems.

6. Moruzzi, G. (1963). "Active Processes in the Brain Stem during Sleep." *The Harvey Lectures* (Series 58; pp. 233-297). New York: Academic Press.

This paper describes the two temporal aspects of REM sleep in terms of long-lasting tonic changes and brief phasic events.

7. Jeannerod, M.; Mouret, J.; and Jouvet, M. (1965). "Effets recondaires de la deafférentation visuelle sur l'activité électrique phasique ponto-geniculo-occipitale du sommeil paradoxal." *Journal de Physiologie* (Paris), *57*, 255-256.

8. Rechtschaffen, A., and Kales, A. (Eds.) (1968). *A Manual Standardized Terminology, Techniques and Scoring System for Sleep Stages of Human Subjects*. Washington, D.C.: Public Health Service, U.S. Government Printing Office.

9. Bremer, F. (1935). "Cerbeau 'isole' et physiologie du sommeil." *Comptes Rendues des Séances de la Société de Biologie*, *118*, 1235-1241.

This report was the basis of the passive theories of sleep because it showed that surgical destruction of the wakefulness-maintaining system located in the ascending reticular activating system resulted in an animal preparation incapable of maintaining wakefulness and that would passively sleep as a result.

10. Moruzzi, G., and Magoun, H.W. (1949). "Brain Stem Reticular Formation and Activation of the Electroencephalogram." *Electroencephalography and Clinical Neurophysiology*, *1*, 455-473.

11. Bremer, F. (1954). "The Neurophysiological Problem of Sleep." In E.D. Adrian, F. Bremer, and H.H. Jasper (Eds.), *Brain Mechanisms and Consciousness* (pp. 137-162). Springfield, Ill.: Charles C. Thomas.

12. Kleitman, N. (1939). *Sleep and Wakefulness*. Chicago: University of Chicago Press.

13. Hess, W.R. (1927). "Stammganglien-Reizversuche. 10. Tagung der Peutoschen Physiol. Gesi, Frankfurt A.M." *Berichte des Physiol.*, *42*, 554-555.

14. Hess, W.R. (1954). *Diencephalon-Autonomic and Extrapyramidal Functions* (pp. 1-24). New York: Grune and Stratton.

15. Hess, W.R. (1954). "The Diencephalic Sleep Centre." In J.F. Delafrepnage and C.C. Thomas (Eds.), *Brain Mechanisms and Consciousness* (pp. 117-136). Springfield, Ill.: C. Thomas Pub.

    This paper was the first report that suggested that sleep may be an active mechanism. Low frequency electrical stimulation of the brain resulted in immediate behavioral sleep in an otherwise waking cat.

16. Tissot, R. (1984). "Activation of the Diffuse Thalamic Projection System by GABA-ergic Stimulation." *Encephale.*, *10*(1), 21-24.

17. Parmeggiani, P.L. (1964). "A Study on the Central Representation of Sleep Behavior." In W. Bargmann and J.L. Schade (Eds.), *Progress in Brain Research, Vol. 6. Topics in Basic Neurology* (pp. 180-190). Amsterdam: Elsevier.

18. Batini, C.; Moruzzi, G.; Palestini, M.; Rossi, G.F.; and Zanchetti, A. (1958). "Persistent Patterns of Wakefulness in the Pre-trigeminal Midpontine Preparation." *Science*, *128*, 30-32.

    This report describes the importance of an active sleep promoting mechanism in the brainstem by showing that surgical destruction of this active sleep promoting center resulted in a state of prolonged, although temporary, wakefulness because of the insomnia produced by the removal of the sleep center.

19. Rossi, G.F. (1980). "Neural Regulation of Sleep." *Experientia*, *36*, 19-20.

    This review is a brief overview of the neuroregulation of sleep.

20. Rapport, M.M.; Green, A.A.; and Page, I.H. (1948). "Serum
     Vasoconstrictor (Serotonin). IV. Isolation and Charac-
     terization." *Journal of Biological Chemistry, 176*,
     1243-1251.

21   Twarog, B.M., and Page, I.H. (1953). "Serotonin Content
     of Some Mammalian Tissues and Urine and a Method for
     Its Determination." *American Journal of Physiology,
     175*, 157-161.

22. Albrecht, P.; Vissher, M.B.; Bittner, J.J.; and Halberg,
     F. (1956). "Daily Changes in 5-hydroxytryptamine
     Concentration in Mouse Brain." *Proceedings of the
     Society for Experimental Biology and Medicine, 92*,
     703-706.

     This group reported that there is an association be-
     tween an increase in brain serotonin levels and the time
     of day when sleep usually occurs, suggesting that serotonin
     may play a functional role in the onset and maintenance
     of sleep.

23. Smith, B.H., and Sweet, W.H. (1978). "Monoaminergic
     Regulation of Central Nervous System Function: II.
     Serotonergic Systems." *Neurosurgery, 3*(2), 257-272.

24. Bender, D.A. (1983). "The 5-hydroxyindole Pathway of
     Tryptophan Metabolism: Serotonin and Other Centrally
     Active Tryptophan Metabolites." *Molecular Aspects of
     Medicine, 6*(2), 113-144.

25. Moir, A.T.B., and Eccleston, D. (1968). "The Effects of
     Precursor Loading in the Cerebral Metabolism of 5-hydroxy
     indoles." *Journal of Neurochemistry, 15*, 1093-1108.

26. Costa, E.; Pscheidt, G.R.; van Neter, W.G.; and Himurch,
     H.E. (1960). "Brain Concentrations of Biogenicamines
     and EEG Patterns of Rabbits." *Journal of Pharmacology
     and Experimental Therapeutics, 130*, 81-88.

27. Jouvet, M. (1967). "Neurophysiology of the States of
     Sleep." *Physiological Reviews, 47*(2), 117-177.

     Neurophysiology of the states of sleep. This review
     paper summarizes a major conceptualization regarding the
     neural physiological and biochemical control mechanisms
     of wakefulness, NREM sleep, and REM sleep integrating a
     number of diverse findings into a well-developed logical
     theory.

28. Spooner, C.E., and Winters, W.D. (1965). "Evidence for
     a Direct Action of Monoamines on the Chick Central
     Nervous System." *Experientia, 21*, 256-258.

29. Koella, W.P.; Trunca, C.M.; and Czicman, J.S. (1965).
     "Serotonin: Effects of Recruiting Responses of the Cat."
     Life Sciences, 4(1), 173-181.

30. Falck, B. (1964). "Cellular Localization of Monoamines."
     In H.G. Himwich and W.A. Himwich (Eds.), *Progress in
     Brain Research, Vol. 8, Biogenic Amines* (pp. 28-44).
     Amsterdam: Elsevier.

31. Brodal, A.; Taber, E.; and Walberg, F. (1960). "The Raphé
     Nuclei of the Brain Stem in the Cat. II. Efferent Con-
     nections." *Journal of Comparative Neurology, 114*,
     239-259.

32. Dahlstrom, A., and Fuxe, K. (1964). "Evidence for the
     Existence of Monoamine Containing Neurons in the Cen-
     tral Nervous System. I. Demonstration of Monoamine in
     the Cell Bodies of Brain Stem Neurons." *Acta Physio-
     logica Scandinavica, 62* (Suppl. 232), 1-55.

     This report describes the application of a technique
     tracing the biochemical pathways of monoamine containing
     neurons in the central nervous system from the cell
     bodies along the axon pathways to the axon end terminals.
     These synapse on other areas of the brain which have
     important regulatory mechanisms in their control of the
     sleep-wakefulness states.

33. Nicholson, A.N., and Wright, C.M. (1981). "(+)-6-fluor-
     tryptophan, an Inhibitor of Tryptophan Hydroxylase:
     Sleep and Wakefulness in the Rat." *Neuropharmacology,
     20*(4), 335-339.

34. Delorme, F.; Froment, J.L.; and Jouvet, M. (1966). "Sup-
     pression du sommeil par la p. chlormethamphetamine et
     la p. chlorophenylamine." *Comptes Rendus des Séances
     de la Société de Biologie, 160*(2), 2347-2351.

35. Koe, B.K., and Weissman, A. (1966). "P-chlorophenylala-
     nine: A Specific Depletor of Brain Serotonin." *Journal
     of Pharmacology and Experimental Therapeutics, 154*,
     499-516.

36. Jouvet, M. (1969). "Biogenic Amines and the States of
     Sleep." *Science, 163*, 32-41.

37. Koella, W.P.; Feldstein, A.; and Cziecman, J.S. (1968). "The Effect of Para-chlorophenylalanine on the Sleep of Cats." *Electroencephalography and Clinical Neurophysiology*, *25*, 481-490.

38. Watt, R.J. (1972). "The Serotonin-Catecholamine-Dream Bicycle: A Clinical Study." *Biological Psychiatry*, *5*, 33-64.

39. Jouvet, M., and Renault, J. (1966). "Insomnie persistante après lesions des moyaux du raphé chez le chat." *Comptes Rendus des Séances de la Société de Biologie*, *160*, 1461-1465.

40. Baumgarten, H.G.; Evetts, K.D.; Holman, R.B.; Iverson, L.L.; Vogt, M.; and Wilson, G. (1972). "Effects of 5,6-dihydroxytryptamine on the Monoaminergic Neurons in the Central Nervous System in the Rat." *Journal of Neurochemistry*, *19*(2), 1587-1597.

41. Jouvet, M., and Pujol, J.F. (1974). "Effects of Central Alterations of Serotonergic Neurons upon the Sleep-Waking Cycle." *Advances in Biochemical Psychopharmacology*, *2*, 199-209.

42. Pujol, J.F.; Keane, P.; Bobillier, P.; Renaud, B.; and Jouvet, M. (1972). "5,6-dihydroxytryptamine as a Tool for Studying Sleep Mechanisms and Interactions between Monaminergic Systems." *Annals of the New York Academy of Sciences*, *305*, 576-589.

43. Jouvet, M. (1974). "Monoaminergic Regulation of the Sleep-Waking Cycle in the Cat." In F.O. Schmitt and F.G. Warden (Eds.), *The Neurosciences, Third Study Program* (pp. 499-507). Boston: Massachusetts Institute of Technology.

44. Lanoir, J.; Ternaux, J.P.; Pons, C.; and Lagarde, J.M. (1981). "Long-Term Effects of a Tryptophan-Free Diet on Serotonin Metabolism and Sleep-Waking Balance in Rats." *Experimental Brain Research*, *41*(3-4), 346-357.

45. Al-Marashi, M.S., and Freemon, F.R. (1977). "Dietary Tryptophan Effects on the Sleep of Normal Subjects." *Waking and Sleeping*, *1*, 163-164.

46. Jouvet, M. (1984). "Neuromediators and Hypnogenic Factors." *Revue Neurologique*, *140*(6-7), 389-400.

This paper revises somewhat part of Jouvet's original theories regarding the neurophysiological and biochemical control factors of the sleep-wakefulness cycle and includes a discussion on neuromediators and hypnogenic factors.

47. Sterman, M.B., and Clemente, C.D. (1962). "Forebrain Inhibitory Mechanisms: Sleep Patterns Induced by Basal Forebrain Stimulation in the Behaving Cat." *Experimental Neurology, 6*, 103-117.

48. Yamaguchi, N.; Ling, G.M.; and Marczynski, T.J. (1963). "The Effects of Chemical Stimulation of the Preoptic Region, Nucleus Centralis Medialis, or Brain Stem Reticular Formation with Regard to Sleep and Wakefulness." *Recent Advances in Biology and Psychiatry, 6*, 9-20.

49. Morgane, P.J. (1981). "Monoamine Theories of Sleep: The Role of Serotonin--A Review Proceedings." *Psychopharmacology Bulletin, 17*(1), 13-17.

This paper summarizes the monoamine theory of sleep and emphasizes the role of serotonin in the control of the sleep states.

50. Trulson, M.E., and Jacobs, B.L. (1979). "Raphé Unit Activity in Freely Moving Cats: Correlation with Level of Behavioral Arousal." *Brain Research, 163*(1), 135-150.

51. Jacobs, B.L.; Heym, J.; and Trulson, M.E. (1981). "Behavioral and Physiological Correlates of Brain Serotoninergic Unit Activity." *Journal of Physiology, 77* (2-3), 431-436.

52. Heym, J.; Steinfels, G.F.; and Jacobs, B.L. (1982). "Activity of Serotonin-containing Neurons in the Nucleus Raphé Pallidus of Freely Moving Cats." *Brain Research 251*(2), 259-276.

53. Cespuglio, R.; Faradji, H.; and Jouvet, M. (1983). "Voltammetric Detection of Extracellular 5-hydroxyindole Compounds at the Level of Cell Bodies and the Terminals of the Raphé System: Variations during the Wake-Sleep Cycle in the Rat in Chronic Experiments." *Académie des Sciences, Paris, Comptes Rendus Hebdomadaires des Séances, Série 3: Sciences de la Vie, 296*(13), 611-616.

54. Fornal, C., and Fadulovacki, M. (1981). "Sleep Suppressant Action of Quipazine: Relation to Central Serotonergic Stimulation." *Pharmacology and Biochemistry in Behavior, 15*(6), 937-944.

55. Toru, M.; Mitsushio, H.; Mataga, N.; Takashima, M.; and Arito, H. (1984). "Increased Brain Serotonin Metabolism during Rebound Sleep in Sleep-deprived Rats." *Pharmacology and Biochemistry in Behavior, 20*(5), 757-761.

56. Sallanon, M.; Janin, M.; Buda, C.; and Jouvet, M. (1983). "Serotoninergic Mechanisms and Sleep Rebound." *Brain Research, 268*(1), 95-104.

57. Tobler, I., and Borbély, A.A. (1982). "Sleep Regulation after Reduction of Brain Serotonin: Effect of p-chlorophenylalanine Combined with Sleep Deprivation in the Rat." *Sleep, 5*(2), 145-153.

58. Pieron, H. (1913). "Le problème physiologique du sommeil." Unpublished thesis, Paris. Maisson cie.

     This was the first published paper to suggest the possibility of a circulating sleep inducing factor in either the cerebral spinal fluid or blood.

59. Monnier, M., and Hosli, L. (1965). "Humoral Regulation of Sleep and Wakefulness by Hypnogenic and Activating Dialysable Factors." *Progress in Brain Research, 18*, 118-123.

60. Graf, M.V., and Kastin, A.J. (1984). "Delta-Sleep-inducing Peptide (DSIP): A Review." *Neuroscience and Biobehavior Physiology, 8*(1), 83-93.

     This report describes the possible sleep promoting activity of a compound referred to as delta sleep inducing peptide.

61. Puizillout, J.J.; Gaudin-Chazal, G.; Sayadi, A.; and Vigier, D. (1981). "Serotoninergic Mechanisms and Sleep." *Journal de Physiologie* (Paris), *77*(2-3), 415-424.

62. Pappenheimer, J.R. (1979). "'Nature's Soft Nurse': A Sleep Promoting Factor Isolated from the Brain." *Johns Hopkins Medical Journal, 145*, 49-56.

63. Pappenheimer, J.R.: Miller, T.B.; and Goodrich, C.A.

(1967). "Sleep Promoting Effects of Cerebral Spinal Fluid from Sleep Deprived Goats." *Proceedings of the National Academy of Sciences*, *58*, 513-518.

64. Pappenheimer, J.R.; Koski, G.; Fencl, V.; Karnovsky, M.L.; and Krueger, J. (1975). "Extraction of Sleep Promoting Factor S from Cerebrospinal Fluid and from Brains of Sleep-deprived Animals." *Journal of Neurophysiology*, *38*(6), 1299-1311.

65. Borbély, A.A., and Tobler, I. (1980). "The Search for an Endogenous Sleep Substance." *Trends in Pharmacological Science*, *1*, 356-358.

    This paper discusses the search for endogenous sleep promoting substances in the blood or cerebral spinal fluid.

66. Nagasaki, H.; Iriki, M.; Inoue, S.; and Wchizono, K. (1974). "The Presence of a Sleep-promoting Material in the Brain of Sleep Deprived Rats." *Proceedings of the Japanese Academy*, *50*, 241-246.

    The authors discuss sleep factor S, describe the techniques used to purify this compound, and show how it is different from a similar compound called deep sleep-inducing peptide.

67. Krueger, J.M.; Pappenheimer, J.R.; and Karnovsky, M.L. (1978). "Sleep-promoting Factor S: Purification and Properties." *Proceedings of the National Academy of Sciences*, *75*(10), 5235-5238.

68. Mouret, J.; Bobillier, P.; and Jouvet, M. (1967). "Effets de la parachlorophenylalanine sur le sommeil du rat." *Comptes Rendus des Séances de la Société de Biologie*, *161*(2), 1600-1603.

69. Jouvet, M.; Vimont, P.; and Delorme, F. (1965). "Suppression élective du sommeil paradoxal chez le chat par les inhibiteurs de la monoamineoxidase." *Comptes Rendus des Séances de la Société de Biologie*, *159*(2), 1595-1599.

70. Pavel, S.; Goldstein, R.; Petrescu, M.; and Popa, M. (1981). "REM Sleep Induction in Prepubertal Boys by Vasotocin: Evidence for the Involvement of Serotonin Containing Neurons." *Peptides*, *2*(3), 245-250.

71. Jouvet, M. (1961). "Telencephalic and Rhombencephalic Sleep in the Cat." In G.E.W. Wolstenholine and M. O'Connor (Eds.), *The Nature of Sleep* (pp. 188-206). London: Churchill.

72. Jouvet, M. (1962). "Recherches sur les structures nerveuses et les mécanismes responsable des différentes phases du sommeil physiologique." *Archives Italiennes de Biologie, 100,* 125-206.

73. Pujol, J.F. (1972). "The Role of the Monaminergic Neurons in the Sleep-Waking Cycle." In M.H. Chase (Ed.), *The Sleeping Brain: Vol. 1. Perspectives in the Brain Sciences* (pp. 146-150). Los Angeles: Brain Information Service/Brain Research Institute, UCLA.

74. Roussel, B.; Buguet, A.; Bibillier, P.; and Jouvet, M. (1967). "Locus coeruleus, sommeil paradoxal, et noradrenaline cérébrale." *Comptes Rendus des Séances de la Société de Biologie, 161*(2), 2537-2541.

75. Jouvet, M. (1967). "Mechanisms of the States of Sleep: A Neuropharmacological Approach." *Research Publications of the Association for Research in Nervous and Mental Disease, Vol. 45, Sleep and Altered States of Consciousness* (pp. 86-126). Baltimore: Williams & Wilkins.

76. Morrison, A.R., and Pompeiano, O. (1966). "Vestibular Influence during Sleep. IV. Functional Relations between Vestibular Nuclei and Lateral Geniculate Nucleus during Desynchronized Sleep." *Archives Italiennes de Biologie, 104,* 425-458.

77. Jouvet, M. (1972). "The Role of Monoamines and Acetylcholine Containing Neurons in the Regulation of the Sleep-Waking Cycle." *Ergebnisse der Physiologie, 64,* 166-307.

78. Dahlstrom, A., and Fuxe, K. (1965). "Evidence for the Existence of Monoamine Neurons in the Central Nervous System. II. Experimentally Induced Changes in the Interneuronal Amine Levels of Bulbospinal Neuron Systems." *Acta Physiologica Scandinavica, 64* (Suppl. 247), 1-36.

79. Montplaisir, J.; deChamplain, J.; Young, S.N.; Missala, K.; Sourkes, T.L.; Walsh, J.; and Remillard, G. (1982). "Narcolepsy and Idiopathic Hypersomnia: Biogenic Amines and Related Compounds in CSF." *Neurology, 32*(11), 1299-1302.

80. Gerady, J.; Zuimaux, N.; Maeda, T.; and Dreese, A. (1969).
    "Analysis of Monoamines in the Locus Coeruleus and
    Other Brain Structures by Thin-Layer Chromotography."
    *Archives Internationales de Pharmacodynamic et de
    Thérapie*, *177*, 942-949.

81. Matsumoto, M., and Watanabe, S. (1967). "Paradoxical
    Sleep: Effects of Adrenergic Blocking Agents." *Pro-
    ceedings of the Japanese Academy*, *43*, 680-683.

82. Blaschko, H.; Burns, J.H.; and Langemann, H. (1950).
    "The Formation of Noradrenalin from Dihydroxyphenyl-
    serine." *British Journal of Pharmacology*, *5*, 431-437.

83. Havlicek, V. (1967). "The Effect of dl-3,4-dihydroxy-
    phenylserine (Precursor of Noradrenalin) on the ECOG
    of Unrestrained Rats." *International Journal of Neuro-
    pharmacology*, *6*, 83-89.

84. Weitzman, E.D.; McGregor, P.; Moore, C.; and Jacoby, J.
    (1969). "The Effect of Alpha-methyl-para-tyrosine on
    Sleep Patterns of the Monkey." *Life Sciences*, *8*(2),
    751-757.

85. Spector, S.; Sjoerdsma, A.; and Udenfriend, S. (1965).
    "Blockade of Endogenous Norepinephrine Synthesis by
    Alpha-methyl-tyrosine, an Inhibitor of Tyrosine Hydroxy-
    lase." *Journal of Pharmacology and Experimental Thera-
    peutics*, *147*, 86-95.

86. Goldstein, M., and Nakajima, K. (1967). "The Effect of
    Disulfiram on Catecholamine Levels in the Brain."
    Journal of Pharmacology and Experimental Therapeutics,
    157, 96-103.

87. Dusan-Peyrethon, D., and Froment, J.L. (1968). "Effets
    du disulfiram sur les états de sommeil chez le chat."
    Comptes Rendus des Séances de la Société de Biologie,
    162(2), 2141-2145.

88. Carlsson, A.; Meisch, J.; and Waldeck, B. (1968). "On
    the Beta-hydroxylation of (+-)-alpha-methyldopamine in
    Vivo." *European Journal of Pharmacology*, *5*, 85-92.

89. Dusan-Peyrethon, D.; Peyrethon, J.; and Jouvet, M. (1968).
    "Suppression élective du sommeil paradoxal chez le chat
    par alpha methyl-DOPA." *Comptes Rendus des Séances de
    la Société de Biologie*, *162*(1), 116-118.

90. Ungerstedt, U. (1969). "6-hydroxy-dopamine Induced De-
    generation of Central Monoamine Neurons." *European
    Journal of Pharmacology*, *5*, 107-110.

91. Buguet, A.; Petitjean, F.; and Jouvet, M. (1970). "Sup-
    pression des pointes ponto-geniculo-occipitales du
    sommeil par lesion ou injection in situ de 6-hydroxy-
    dopamine au niveau de tegmentum pontique." *Comptes
    Rendus des Séances de la Société de Biologie*, *164*(3),
    2293-2298.

92. Khazan, N., and Sawyer, C.H. (1964). "Mechanisms of
    Paradoxical Sleep as Revealed by Neurophysiologic and
    Pharmacologic Approaches in the Rabbit." *Psychopharma-
    cologia*, *5*, 457-466.

93. George, R.; Haslett, W.L.; and Jenden, D.J. (1964). "A
    Cholinergic Mechanism in the Brainstem Reticular Forma-
    tion: Induction of Paradoxical Sleep." *International
    Journal of Pharmacology*, *3*, 451-552.

94. Hartmann, E.L. (1973). *The Functions of Sleep*. New
    Haven: Yale University Press.

    This book describes a theory diametrically opposed to
    that promoted by Jouvet with respect to the role of
    catecholamines in the functional control of REM sleep.

95. Hartmann, E.; Bridwell, T.J.; and Schildkraut, J.J.
    (1967). "Alpha-methyl-paratyrosine and Sleep in the
    Rat." *Psychopharmacologia*, *21*, 157-164.

96. King, C.D., and Jewett, R.E. (1971). "The Effects of
    Alpha-methyltyrosine on Sleep and Brain Norepinephrine
    in Cats." *Journal of Pharmacology and Experimental
    Therapeutics*, *177*, 188-194.

97. Henriksen, S.J., and Dement, W.C. (1972). "Effects of
    Chronic Intravenous Administration of 1-alpha-methyl
    Paratyrosine on Sleep in the Cat: A Preliminary Report."
    Sleep Research, *1*, 55.

98. Stern, W.C., and Morgane, P.J. (1973). "Effects of Alpha-
    methyltyrosine on REM Sleep and Brain Amine Levels in
    the Cat." *Biological Psychiatry*, *6*, 301-306.

99. Stein, D.; Jouvet, M.; and Pujol, J. "Effects of Alpha-
    methyl-p-tyrosine upon Cerebral Amine Metabolism and
    Sleep States in the Cat." *Brain Research*, *72*, 360-365.

100. Hartmann, E.; Chung, R.; Draskoczy, P.R.; and Schild-
      kraut, J.J. (1971). "Effects of 6-hydroxydopamine
      on Sleep in the Rat." *Nature, 233,* 425-427.

101. Hartmann, E.; Zwilling, G.; and List, A. (1973). "Ef-
      fects of Alpha-adrenergic Blocker on Sleep in the Rat."
      Sleep Research, 2, 58.

102. Oswald, I.; Thacore, V.R.; Adam, K.; Brezinova, V.; and
      Burack, R. (1975). "Alpha-adrenergic Receptor Blockade
      Increases Human REM Sleep." *British Journal of Clini-
      cal Pharmacology, 2*(2), 107-110.

103. Ramm, P. (1979). "The Locus Coeruleus, Catecholamines,
      and REM Sleep: A Critical Review." *Behavioral and
      Neural Biology, 25*(4), 415-448.

      This paper attempts to integrate the divergent theories
      of Jouvet and Hartmann regarding the role of the locus
      coeruleus, catecholamines, and REM sleep and presents
      the available evidence in the form of a critical review.

104. Jones, B.; Bobillier, P.; and Jouvet, M. (1968). "Effets
      de la destruction des neurons contenant des catecho-
      lamines du mesencephalon sur le cycle veille-sommeil
      du chat." *Comptes Rendus des Séances de la Société de
      Biologie, 163,* 176-180.

105. Prinz, P.N.; Vitiello, M.V.; Smallwood, R.G.; Schoene,
      R.B.; and Halter, J.B. (1984). "Plasma Norepinephrine
      in Normal Young and Aged Men: Relationship with Sleep."
      Journal of Gerontology, 39(5), 561-567.

106. Prinz, P.N.; Halter, J.; Benedetti, C.; and Raskind, M.
      (1979). "Circadian Variation of Plasma Catecholamines
      in Young and Old Men: Relation to Rapid Eye Movement
      and Slow Wave Sleep." *Journal of Clinical Endocrino-
      logical Metabolism, 49*(2), 300-304.

107. Hobson, J.A.; McCarley, R.W.; and Wyzinski, P.W. (1975).
      "Sleep Cycle Oscillation: Reciprocal Discharge by Two
      Brain Stem Neuronal Groups." *Science, 189,* 55-58.

108. Hobson, J.A. (1974). "The Cellular Basis of Sleep Cycle
      Control." *Advances in Sleep Research, 1,* 217-250.

      This review paper summarizes the Hobson and McCarley
      theories of sleep, describing the cellular basis of the
      control of the sleep-wakefulness cycle.

109. McCarley, R.W., and Hobson, J.A. (1975). "Neuronal Ex-
      citability Modulation over the Sleep Cycle: A Struc-
      tural and Mathematical Model." *Science, 189*, 58-60.

      This is another milestone paper integrating a number
      of diverse neurophysiological findings from micro-elec-
      trode studies of various brainstem nuclei. The paper
      describes a reciprocal relationship between cells of the
      giganto-cellular tegmental field and cells of the locus
      coeruleus and the initiation and maintenance of the REM
      and NREM sleep states.

110. Scheibel, M.E., and Scheibel, A.B. (1973). *Brain In-
      formation Service Conference Report* (No. 32, p. 12).
      Los Angeles: Brain Information Service/Brain Research
      Institute.

111. Hauri, P. (1982). *The Sleep Disorders*. Kalamazoo,
      Mich.: Upjohn Publishing.

112. Keihachiro, I., and McCarley, R.W. (1984). "Alterations
      in Membrane Potential and Excitability of Cat Medial
      Pontine Reticular Formation Neurons during Changes
      in Naturally Occurring Sleep-Wake States." *Brain Re-
      search, 292*, 169-175.

113. Baghdoyan, H.A.; Rodrigo-Angulo, M.L.; McCarley, R.W.;
      and Hobson, A. (1984). "Site-specific Enhancement
      and Suppression of Desynchronized Sleep Signs Following
      Cholinergic Stimulation." *Brain Research, 306*, 39-52.

114. Baghdoyan, H.A.; Monaco, A.P.; Rodrigo-Angulo, M.L.;
      Assens, F.; McCarley, R.W.; and Hobson, J.A. (1984).
      "Microinjection of Neostigmine into the Pontine Reticu-
      lar Formation of Cats Enhances Desynchronized Sleep
      Signs." *The Journal of Pharmacology and Experimental
      Therapeutics, 231*(1), 173-180.

115. Masserano, J.M., and King, C. (1982). "Effects on Sleep
      of Acetylcholine Perfusion into the Locus Coeruleus
      of Cats." *Neuropharmacology, 21*(11), 1163-1167.

      The authors describe the effects of acetylcholine per-
      fusion into the locus coeruleus of cats and delineate
      the role of acteylcholine in triggering REM sleep.

116. Kafka, M.S.; Wirz-Justice, T.; Naber, D.; Moore, R.Y.;
      and Benedito, M.A. (1983). "Circadian Rhythms in Rat
      Brain Neurotransmitter Receptors." *Federation Pro-
      ceedings, 42*(11), 2796-2801.

117. Monti, J.M. (1982). "Catecholamines and the Sleep-Wake-
      Cycle. I. EEG and Behavioral Arousal." *Life Sciences*,
      30(14), 1145-1157.

      The paper develops a synthetic approach to understand-
      ing the biochemical regulation of sleep and wakefulness.
      This is based upon the relative concentrations and ratios
      of various neurochemicals rather than their absolute
      levels. It suggests a way of ending the controversy
      over which chemicals are more important for which states.
      Furthermore, it eliminates the possibility that relative
      concentrations of certain chemicals may be more impor-
      tant than their absolute levels.

118. Monnier, M., and Gaillard, J.M. (1980). "Biochemical
      Regulation of Sleep." *Experientia*, *36*(1), 21-24.

      This is a brief overview of the biochemical regulation
      of sleep.

119. McGinty, D.J., and Druker-Colin, R.R. (1982). "Sleep
      Mechanisms: Biology and Control of REM Sleep." *Inter-
      national Review of Neurobiology*, *23*, 391-436.

120. Koella, W.P. (1984). "The Organization and Regulation
      of Sleep. A Review of the Experimental Evidence and
      a Novel Integrated Model of the Organizing and Regu-
      lating Apparatus." *Experientia*, *40*(4), 309-338.

      This relatively recent paper is a review article on
      the organization and regulation of sleep and presents
      an integrated model of neurophysiological and biochemical
      mechanisms regulating the sleep-wakefulness states.

Chapter 4
INSOMNIA

Amy D. Bertelson and James K. Walsh

Sleep appears to have an important bearing on physical and psychological well-being. Yet, after a half-century of sleep research, the relationship between sleep and "well-being" is still unclear. Most of us take for granted the alliance between our sleeping habits and our daily activity, but the relatedness of sleep and daytime functioning is ever present for those suffering from insomnia. The complaint of insomnia may focus upon difficulty falling asleep (onset insomnia), difficulty staying asleep (maintenance insomnia), or both.

Insomnia is one of the most common health-related complaints in our society. Data from surveys estimate that 15% to 30% of adults report occasionally to frequently disturbed sleep. According to the 1973 Gallup Poll, about 50% of all Americans over 15 years of age have had difficulty sleeping at some point in their lives and over 35 million individuals report chronic insomnia (1). The 1979 Institute of Medicine (2) report summarized research on the prevalence of insomnia by stating, "between 29 to 38 percent of individuals over 18 in the United States perceive themselves as having had 'trouble' sleeping within a given year ..." (p. 6). By sheer numbers alone, the complaint of disturbed sleep is a problem of significant magnitude.

In the past few years information has begun to accumulate which suggests that insomnia deserves attention for reasons other than simple prevalence. Indeed, persistent complaints of poor or insufficient sleep have been shown to be related to (although not necessarily a cause of) a number of medical and psychosocial factors. Insomniacs report discomfort and loss of work efficiency, increased prevalence of emotional tension and domestic and vocational adjustment difficulty, and more frequent health problems and hospitalizations. Recent evidence even suggests that habitually short nightly total sleep time (as well as very long nightly sleep time) is associated with an increased mortality risk.

Why is insomnia associated with such a wide range of life
disturbances? This is, of course, a very complex question.
In fact, some of these problems (e.g., depression) may cause
insomnia rather than result from it. However, it is clear
that many individuals feel that their lives are markedly influenced by the lack of satisfactory sleep.

The stereotypical insomniac is a tired-looking, lethargic
individual who sleeps very little, or not at all. However,
the concept that insomnia is a simple unitary disorder is an
inaccurate stereotype. Research of the past twenty years has
led to a more accurate understanding of insomnia which includes the following concepts:

a) Insomnia is actually a complaint, rather than a disorder. It is a complaint of poor, insufficient, or non-
refreshing sleep. For health professionals, insomnia is also
a symptom, a symptom of an underlying problem. Just as ab-
dominal pain can be a symptom of appendicitis, ulcers, food
poisoning, or many other conditions, insomnia can result from
a variety of disorders.

b) Insomnia is a common, significant health problem, not
merely a nuisance for rare individuals.

c) Disturbed sleep has an impact on waking behavior.
Therefore, insomnia is a twenty-four hour problem, not simply
a problem of the night. In fact, virtually all aspects of
our lives can be influenced by poor sleep.

d) Sleeping pills do not cure insomnia; they simply mask the
symptom of a problem. Although quite helpful in specific
situations, there are many conditions for which sleeping pills
are inappropriate.

These concepts of insomnia and others to be discussed are
the result of hundreds of research studies. The methodology
of many early studies limits the generalizability of the data.
Nevertheless, these years of research are of interest for both
historical and scientific reasons. In fact, it was these
early research efforts and the lack of uniformity among insomniacs which broadened our perspective and led to more recent
conceptualizations of insomnia.

Early Descriptive Research

Most research performed before 1980 attempted to describe
some characteristics of insomniacs in general. These studies
almost universally included any individual with the complaint
of insomnia with little regard for subtype or etiological factors. In short, insomnia was typically being investigated as

if it were a single disorder, rather than a symptom. The duration of the complaint was also frequently ignored and we know now that individuals with transient insomnia complaints differ in a number of ways from those with persistent insomnia. Further, the impact or consequence of insomnia was virtually ignored. Keeping these limitations in mind, let us review research describing the polysomnographic and reported measurement of sleep as related to the psychological and physiological characteristics of insomniacs.

Objective and Subjective Characteristics of Sleep

To determine whether the insomniac has differing sleep stage patterns from the non-insomniac, most researchers have compared insomniacs with a sex- and age-matched control group. Subjects are observed for an average of three nights with the first night (for adaptation) exempt from analysis. In most studies, insomniac subjects discontinued their medication from 10 days to four weeks prior to the study, and all subjects were asked to refrain from alcohol, caffeine, and naps while participating in the experiment.

A number of studies have examined the polysomnographic differences between good sleepers and insomniacs. From these studies, the most consistent findings have been a significantly longer sleep onset latency for insomniacs, greater time awake after sleep onset, more frequent awakenings, and consequently a lower sleep efficiency index (ratio of total sleep time to time in bed) when compared to good sleepers. Other sleep architectural changes (e.g., percent REM, delta, etc.) have shown less consistent results. One clear outcome of most studies is the extreme variability in the polysomnographic sleep patterns among a group of insomniacs. While the sleep of non-insomniacs is basically the same every night, the sleep of insomniacs can vary tremendously across nights. On some nights, sleep onset may come easily with only a few short awakenings, while on other nights it may be the total opposite. This variability may be a significant part of the insomniac's difficulty. That is, the insomniac is unable to predict whether or not the night's sleep will be a satisfactory one. Hence, he or she frequently worries about sleep, which only exacerbates the problem.

In addition to the objective parameters of sleep, the insomniac's subjective estimate of sleep is also of interest. Compared to non-insomniacs, the concordance between polysomnographic and subjective estimates of sleep is substantially poorer. On the average, insomniacs overestimate sleep latencies and underestimate total sleep time and sleep efficiency. Yet

Frankel et al. (3) state that "even though insomniacs consistently overestimated their sleeplessness, their polygraph sleep patterns could be predicted from their subjective estimates as accurately as those of the controls" (p. 618). In other words, the predictability of the objective data from the subjective estimates, although low, was still significantly better than chance. These findings are important for two reasons: a) in most (but not all) cases, clinicians can rely on the patient's complaint as being relatively accurate, although perhaps overestimated, and b) insomnia involves both objective and subjective parameters which are not perfectly correlated (i.e., insomniacs frequently report their sleep to be much more disturbed than EEG recordings indicate). Measurement of only objective (i.e., polysomnographic) aspects of sleep is not sufficient to explain all complaints of insomnia nor should it be the only yardstick of therapeutic benefit. Why is there such a discrepancy between polysomnographic and subjective estimates of sleep for many⁻insomniacs? There are several possible explanations although none has been proven to date:

a) Polysomnography may not measure some critical aspects of sleep. That is, physiological activity not reflected in the EEG, EMG, etc., may be important in the perception of sleep.

b) Some individuals may simply sleep in a relatively activated condition. If physiological activation remains high during sleep, it may lead to the experience of being awake despite what the EEG displays.

c) Some individuals may have a very low threshold for reporting disrupted sleep. That is, minimal sleep disturbance may not bother most people, but may disturb insomniacs which leads to the complaint.

d) An individual's sleep need may be involved. If a patient sleeps seven hours a night, but physiologically requires nine hours to maintain optimal daytime function, he or she may complain of disturbed sleep simply because of daytime tiredness.

e) Some individuals may be less capable of tolerating sleep loss. Therefore, small amounts of sleep loss are more significant in terms of daytime functioning.

f) The quality of sleep may depend on the placement of sleep hours within the circadian rhythm of sleepiness/alertness. That is, sleep "at the wrong time" may be perceived as being wakefulness or poor sleep.

g) The complaint of insomnia may simply be an acceptable complaint for individuals experiencing psychological problems.

In future years, it is likely that researchers will determine that more than one of the above explanations are in-

volved in the difference between perceived and polysomnographic
sleep of insomniacs.

Physiological Characteristics

Although surveys revealed poor sleepers to have more
physical symptoms and health problems than good sleepers, few
studies have been designed specifically for examination of
physiological differences between insomniacs and controls.
The first study was by Monroe (4) who took physiological
measures at 5-minute intervals during the presleep period and
at 10-minute intervals through the 7-hour sleep period for
both good and poor sleepers. Poor sleepers had significantly
higher mean rectal temperatures, higher mean number of phasic
vasoconstrictions during both sleep and presleep periods,
higher heart rates during the presleep period, and more body
movement activity and higher basal skin resistance while sleeping than good sleepers. Monroe concluded that "poor sleepers
not only sleep less, but the sleep they obtain is more 'awake-
like' than that of good sleepers" (p. 263). Other researchers
have reported that insomniacs displayed higher physiological
activity than normal sleepers prior to sleep onset, but as
sleep onset was approached, physiological activity diminished
and no differences were noted during sleep (5).
Whether significant physiological differences exist in the
waking state between insomniacs and controls has only been
investigated minimally. Johns et al. (6) had good and poor
sleepers collect their urine three times a day for three days.
Poor sleepers excreted more free 11-OHCS (free cortisol, cor-
ticosterone, and 20 hydroxycortisol) than good sleepers
throughout each day and night. These results (and others) led
to the hyperarousal hypothesis of insomnia. Increased activation of the central nervous system may predispose or underlie
sleep disturbance.
Perhaps insomniacs sleep worse because they are lighter
sleepers and more easily awakened by noise. Such a question
was answered by assessing arousal threshold differences during
sleep by presenting tones to good and poor sleepers during
different stages of sleep. No significant differences in
arousal threshold between the two groups were found regardless
of sleep stage, even though poor sleepers claim they are
easily awakened by noise (7). In another study, various
light and tone intensities were presented to insomniacs and
controls several hours before bedtime and average evoked responses were recorded. Insomniac subjects had less cortical
reactivity to auditory stimuli in comparison with the control

group, which suggests that insomniacs are actually less reactive to external stimulation (8).

Some researchers have suggested that muscle tension (EMG) may play a role in delaying sleep for some insomniacs. Unfortunately, there have been little confirming data. Hauri and Good (9) reported that poor sleepers in general did not show higher waking EMG levels when compared with good sleepers. Nor were significant correlations found between frontalis EMG and sleep latency when EMG was measured five minutes prior to "goodnight" and 30 minutes after sleep onset (10;11).

Hauri and others have speculated that there may be a sleep-specific physiological system that may cause insomnia in some individuals. The sensory motor rhythm (SMR), originating in the sensorimotor cortex, can be operantly conditioned in cats to produce greater sleep length (12). On a human level, Jordan and colleagues (13) found that, while awake, insomniacs produce weaker SMR signals than good sleepers.

Physiological data which distinguish insomniacs from good sleepers are scarce. The few studies that have demonstrated significant findings have not been replicated. Those studies with significant results do indicate that insomniacs are more physiologically aroused than non-insomniacs, but whether or not this arousal has anything to do with sleeping difficulties has yet to be determined.

Psychological Characteristics

Survey information from metropolitan Los Angeles and Houston residents revealed that people with difficulty sleeping were significantly more lonely, tense, depressed, and unhappy than people with no sleep problems (14;15). Other research has shown that insomniacs have had major disappointing incidents, such as marital problems, broken love affairs, and failure in professional life, prior to the onset of insomnia. In an extensive study by Healey et al. (16) chronic insomniacs, compared to good sleepers, were found to experience more stressful life events (e.g., illness or loss) during the year in which their insomnia began than in previous years. Thus, emotionally laden environmental factors, especially crisis events, appear to have a precipitating role in the onset of insomnia for some individuals.

Psychological characteristics of insomniacs are frequently examined with personality measurements. Most studies tested insomniacs who were free from medication and from major medical or psychiatric problems. The most widely used and researched personality measure has been the Minnesota Multiphasic Person-

ality Inventory (MMPI). Results have been fairly consistent
over many studies and across age groups. Insomniacs have a
remarkably high percentage of MMPI elevations. Many MMPI
studies with control groups consistently have shown insomniacs
to be significantly higher than good sleepers on the scales
of Hypochondriasis, Depression, and Hysteria. These three
scales are commonly called the neurotic triad scales, reflecting depression, feelings of inferiority, and hypochondriacal
symptoms. Nearly every MMPI investigation has described
insomniacs as being anxious and excessive worriers, hypochondriacal or concerned with body symptoms, depressed, withdrawn,
obsessed, having feelings of inadequacy, inferiority, and lacking self-confidence.

Insomniacs have also been compared to non-normal control
groups. Studies of the psychological profiles of emotionally
disturbed adolescent poor sleepers indicate that they are
anxious, tense, obsessed, and depressed as compared to emotionally disturbed adolescent good sleepers who were characterized as provocative, resentful, flippant, and denying (17;
18;19). However, in a comparison of adult psychiatric outpatients with and without a complaint of insomnia, only the
Psychasthenia scale differed between groups (20). These
results may suggest that characteristics such as obsessional
worry are related to insomnia, whereas elevations on the
Depression, Hysteria, and Hypochondriasis scales are also
characteristic of emotionally troubled adults without a sleep
complaint.

Other personality measures (e.g., Taylor Manifest Anxiety
Scale) have also demonstrated a relationship between anxiety
and insomnia. In sum, many insomniacs display abnormal personality traits and, for some, these psychological disturbances
are likely to play an integral role in their sleep disturbance.

While most of the studies on psychological variables and
insomnia discussed to this point have attempted to differentiate
good from poor sleepers, or non-insomniacs from insomniacs,
more recent research has focused on differences among subtypes
of insomniacs. The severity of insomnia may be related to
different personality characteristics so that generalizations
over all insomnias may be inappropriate. Two studies (21;22)
investigated sleep-onset insomniacs, separating them according
to severity. Using the MMPI, they found the insomniac sample
to be more neurotic than normals, but there were no differences
among insomniacs with respect to severity. In other words,
people with severe insomnia were not more disturbed than those
with mild insomnia.

Beutler, Karacan, Thornby, and Salis (23) also looked at
MMPI differences for insomniacs with problems of sleep onset
and those with problems of sleep maintenance (difficulty

remaining asleep). The onset group was found to show a "neurotic profile with depressive, hypochondriacal, and hysterical
features," while the maintenance group was described as "somewhat more confused, schizoid, and agitated than normal"
(p. 181). These findings suggest that sleep-onset insomnia
is related to conditions of anxiety and neuroticism, while
sleep maintenance insomnia may be associated with more serious
forms of psychopathology. Thus, it may be that people with
sleep maintenance insomnia are more resistant to treatment.

The only published MMPI data for insomniacs in varying
diagnostic categories (see explanation of categories below)
suggests that the degree of psychopathology is significant in
only three of ten diagnostic groups (24). Patients diagnosed
as having insomnia related to a) psychiatric disorder, b) drug
or alcohol use, and c) atypical polysomnographic features
lack abnormal MMPI scores relative to normal controls. Clearly,
psychopathology is not universal for insomniacs.

In summary, the psychological characteristics which have
been most consistently associated with sleep disturbance are
anxiety, worry, depression, and somatic concerns. Obviously,
psychological variables play a role in some insomnia. The
question is how best to determine which patients' insomnia
has a psychological origin and what is the appropriate treatment.

Treatment Research

Pharmacological Treatment

The treatment of the complaint of insomnia has classically
been pharmacological. That is, "sleeping pills" were prescribed for individuals reporting difficulty with sleep. The
terms "sleeping pills" and "hypnotic medication" include all
substances which are central nervous system depressants and
are taken for the purpose of inducing or improving sleep.
Benzodiazepines are clearly the most widely used and preferred
drug for the induction and maintenance of sleep.

Benzodiazepines. The introduction, in 1970, of the first
benzodiazepine hypnotic, flurazepam (Dalmane) began a marked
decrease in the frequency of barbiturate administration for
sleep disturbance. This change in prescribing habits occurred
because of physicians' recognition of two major advantages of
benzodiazepines over barbiturates and other CNS depressants.
First, benzodiazepines are much less toxic than other available
compounds. The toxicity of a sleeping pill is generally ex-

pressed as the ratio between the lethal dose (LD) and the effective dose (ED). The larger the ratio, the safer the drug.
For barbiturates the ratio is relatively small; that is, the
lethal dose and the effective dose are relatively close. The
benzodiazepines, on the other hand, have very large LD-ED
ratio. In fact, there is virtually no overlap between the
distributions of the effective dose and the lethal dose. When
used in isolation, then, benzodiazepines are very safe compounds. Like all central nervous system depressants, if benzodiazepines are combined with other CNS depressants (including
alcohol), toxicity potential is increased.

The second major reason that benzodiazepines are preferred
to barbiturates relates to drug interactions. Because barbiturates induce the production of hepatic enzymes, which are
active in the metabolism of the barbiturate compounds, the
potential for interaction with other drugs is high. In general, taking barbiturates in conjunction with most other drugs
will reduce the effectiveness of the other drug. Benzodiazepines, on the other hand, interact only with other CNS depressants since they do not induce hepatic enzymes to a clinically
significant degree.

Hypnotic efficacy. All benzodiazepines, as well as other
CNS depressants, are effective in inducing and maintaining
sleep at some dose. The more appropriate issues are the
safety of the medication at that effective dose and the specific type of insomnia for which these compounds should be
utilized. The property of sleep induction is principally related to absorption characteristics of the drug, in addition
to the dosage. If the drug is absorbed rapidly enough into
the blood and the dose is large enough, rapid sleep induction
is likely. Virtually all benzodiazepines are absorbed rapidly
enough to promote sleep onset if taken 20-45 minutes before
bedtime.

Whether or not a drug improves sleep maintenance is primarily related to the dosage and duration of action of the
medication. An individual compound's duration of action is
closely related to a pharmacological characteristic known as
half-life. Half-life refers to the time it takes for the
amount of any given drug in the circulatory system to be reduced to 50% of the initial amount through distribution to
body tissue or elimination. Marketed benzodiazepines have a
wide range of half-lives from about 3 hours to over 80 hours.
It is important not to confuse the term half-life with the
drug's actual duration of action. A drug can remain biologically active for periods much longer than the drug's half-
life, if the dose administered is high enough. In fact, when
administered in appropriate doses, even the shortest acting
benzodiazepines have durations of action that are sufficiently

long to promote sleep in most situations. In general, the
half-life of a drug will be longer in an elderly person than
in a younger individual.

Daytime function. The same two pharmacological properties
of a compound, dosage and half-life, also are the primary
determinants of the drug's impact on daytime function. The
larger the dose and/or the longer the half-life, the more
likely that a hypnotic medication will impair daytime alertness and performance. This effect is commonly termed "hang-
over" or "carryover." Hypnotic medications are a unique type
of drug, in that the same pharmacological effect (i.e., sedation) is the desired therapeutic effect during the sleep period
but becomes the major unwanted side effect at any other time
of the day. (In a minority of cases the prolonged sedation
may be desirable. For example, an extremely anxious individual
may benefit not only from nighttime sedation but daytime sedation as well.)

It is also very important to realize that even if a patient
reports no daytime impairment following administration of a
hypnotic, some impairment may actually exist. This situation
is analogous to those who claim no impairment from alcohol
ingestion, yet are unable to drive a car without swerving from
lane to lane.

Tolerance. Another clinical property of hypnotics is
tolerance. Tolerance refers to the lack of, or reduced effect
of, a compound as the dosage is kept constant. Another way of
saying this is that a larger and larger dose is required to
produce the desired effect. It is now well known that barbiturates and other non-benzodiazepine hypnotics lose their
effectiveness within two weeks of nightly use. This loss
appears to be related to the induction of hepatic enzymes by
these compounds. Benzodiazepines, on the other hand, appear
to be effective for at least 30 days of consecutive use. Very
little is known about the long-term clinical efficacy of benzodiazepines, although clinically some patients report reduced
effectiveness after months of nightly administration. Some
investigators feel that such clinical tolerance may develop
due to changes in benzodiazepine receptor sensitivity in the
central nervous system.

Withdrawal effects. Another area of clinical concern re-
lating to the use of sleeping pills is withdrawal effects.
That is, what happens when nightly hypnotic administration is
terminated. This area is of considerable controversy at the
present time (circa 1984). Some scientists believe that a
patient's sleep disturbance will frequently become much worse
than it was originally following termination of hypnotic medication, particularly with shorter acting benzodiazepines (25).
This phenomenon has been termed "rebound insomnia." Other

investigators feel that rebound insomnia occurs very rarely
or not at all and others suggest that it occurs with longer
acting as well as shorter acting benzodiazepines (26). There
is no doubt that when hypnotic medication is terminated that
recrudescence occurs. That is, the patient's original degree
of insomnia is likely to return. The question is whether the
patient's insomnia becomes significantly worse after drug
withdrawal (and this determines whether rebound insomnia has
occurred) or whether the observed sleep disturbance is simply
recrudescence of the original symptoms. At the present time,
it is probably safe to assume that if rebound insomnia occurs
it is more likely to occur if the nightly dose of the medication is large, if the duration of nightly ingestion is long,
and if the compound has a short duration of action. In any
case, the clinical significance of rebound insomnia is very
questionable. For a patient to actually determine that the
insomnia following drug withdrawal is worse than or equal to
the original problem is very difficult. The clinical significance of the problem comes when the patient decides to resume
the use of medication following withdrawal because insomnia
has returned. The physician prescribing the medication should
warn patients about withdrawal effects (whether they be recrudescence or rebound insomnia) and tell them that their sleep
may worsen after a night or two following withdrawal (in the
case of rebound insomnia). In either case, the patient must
understand that there is a reason for termination of medication
and that the return of the insomnia is not a reason to resume
consumption.

Effects upon sleep physiology. Benzodiazepines do alter
sleep. In particular, they decrease amounts of stage 1, slow
wave sleep, and REM, while increasing the amount of stage 2
and REM latency. Currently, the significance of these changes
in sleep architecture is not understood and does not influence
the selection of hypnotics. However, casual administration
of medication without documentation of significant sleep disturbance is inappropriate.

Hypnotics also have the potential to influence other aspects of physiology during sleep. Since physiological laws
which govern wakefulness may change during sleep, the effect
of benzodiazepines upon various systems may also change. For
example, while benzodiazepines do not alter heart rate during
wakefulness, they appear to increase heart rate slightly during
sleep (27). Although this increase is probably clinically
insignificant, at about five beats per minute, it is an example
of a differential effect of a drug during sleeping and waking.
Much research is necessary to describe the effects of hypnotics
upon all physiological systems during sleep.

Antihistamines. Despite the fact that about 30 million
containers of over-the-counter sleeping aids (e.g., Nytol,
Sleep-Eze) are purchased annually (2), little is known about
their effectiveness and their safety is questionable. Virtually all of these products contain one or more antihistamines
as the sedating agent. Clinical trials have produced little
supportive evidence for hypnotic efficacy as studies have
found no improvement in sleep after ingestion of over-the-
counter sleeping pills.

L-tryptophan. This is an essential amino acid which has
been reported to decrease sleep latency when administered in
doses of 1.0 to 15.0 grams. There seems to be nearly as much
negative data as positive, however. Therefore, no firm conclusions are possible at this time. A recent preliminary report suggests that particular types of insomnia patients may
respond very well, whereas others may respond poorly. Lindsley,
Hartmann, and Mitchell (28) suggest that patients having subjective multiple discrete awakenings as the major characteristic of sleep disturbance were likely to improve significantly
with L-tryptophan. Insomniacs with one discrete awakening or
a sense of having only "light sleep" were unlikely to improve.
Clearly, further investigation is necessary to determine the
characteristics of hypnotic efficacy for L-tryptophan. Similarly, although it has been suggested that L-tryptophan may
promote sleep because of its conversion to the neurotransmitter
serotonin, no convincing evidence has been published.

Endogenous sleep inducing substances. A number of endogenous substances have been examined in relation to sleep and have
been found to promote sleep in some fashion. However, this
field of research is truly in its infancy and much work needs
to be done with such a compound before clinical problems can
be addressed. Nevertheless, the benefits of identifying a
"natural" compound which might be utilized is intriguing.
Early clinical studies with one substance, delta sleep inducing
peptide (DSIP), hold promise for the treatment of insomnia (29;
30).

Behavioral Treatments

As mentioned earlier, one of the most frequently postulated
explanations for insomnia has been hyperarousal. Many researchers have hypothesized that insomniacs are unable to discharge their feelings outwardly and that they cope with stress
by excessive rumination which leads to internalization of
psychological disturbances. This inability to express conflict
may cause physiological activation that makes sleep difficult.

Relaxation therapy. This hypothesis of increased physiological activity quite naturally led to the application of relaxation therapies to treat insomnia. There are various methods of relaxation therapy, such as progressive muscle relaxation, hypnotic relaxation, autogenic training, EMG biofeedback, and meditation, but there is little evidence of differential effectiveness. In fact, in a combined analysis of three well-controlled studies there were no group differences comparing biofeedback, progressive relaxation, or control manipulations (31).

Improvement in latency to sleep onset is usually measured in these studies by self-report on a daily sleep questionnaire. Reductions in subjective sleep latency average 45% from pretherapy reports (32). However, the validity of self-report data is questionable, particularly since such reports may suggest significant treatment effects in studies which demonstrate no change in polysomnographic measures. In addition, they may also indicate improvement in individuals having no objective sleep onset problem prior to treatment.

Only a few sleep laboratory studies have been conducted to determine the effects of relaxation therapies on objective sleep parameters, some showing reductions in sleep latency following training (10;33;34;35), while others (31;36) have found no significant group effect. Therefore, relaxation therapy appears to be an effective treatment for some but not all insomniacs.

Why should relaxation training work? The original hypothesis was that relaxation training works by reducing arousal, thereby helping the insomniac calm down and enabling faster sleep onset. Perhaps relaxation training works not by reducing arousal but by forcing the insomniac's attention on relaxation rather than on cognitive activity incompatible with sleep. Since relaxation training does teach people cognitive control, it is possible that insomniacs improve by gaining control of their cognitive ruminations rather than by reducing arousal levels.

Stimulus control. A second theory for the cause of insomnia is a conditioning hypothesis that suggests the bed and bedroom have become associated with sleep incompatible behaviors such as eating, watching TV, fighting with spouse, worrying, etc. In other words, the bed is no longer a discriminative stimulus for sleep. Treatment, called stimulus control, is aimed at pairing rapid sleep onset with bed cues. Bringing sleeping behaviors under stimulus control may help eliminate cognitive and/or other behaviors associated with elevated arousal. The instructions (37) used include: a) go to bed only when sleepy; b) if you cannot fall asleep within 10 minutes, leave the bedroom and engage in some other activity,

return to bed when drowsy again, and repeat this every time
10 minutes of no sleep has passed; c) awaken at the same time
every morning regardless of how much sleep you got the night
before; d) do not nap during the day.

Although no polysomnographic studies have been completed,
subjective reports of improvement are higher for stimulus control than for any other behavioral technique. Reductions in
reported sleep onset latency frequently average 70% (38;39;
40;41;42).

The fact that stimulus control appears to help some insomniacs does not necessarily demonstrate that the bed and bedroom have been re-aligned as a discriminative stimulus for
sleep. Some researchers have attempted to isolate the active
ingredient(s) causing stimulus control to be effective. Zwart
and Lisman (42) compared stimulus control with a procedure
called countercontrol. In stimulus control, insomniacs must
leave the bedroom and engage in some non-sleep behavior,
whereas in countercontrol, insomniacs were to remain in bed,
sit up, and engage in some activity (e.g., reading) when unable to sleep. Both procedures were effective in reducing
sleep onset latency. Zwart and Lisman argue that stimulus
control works, not by establishing the bed as a cue for sleep,
but rather by disrupting sleep-incompatible activities, especially cognitions, that maintain arousal and occur during
the difficult period prior to sleep onset.

Thus, it is possible that both relaxation and stimulus
control procedures do not necessarily decrease sleep latency
by reducing arousal. Rather, they appear to work by providing
attention-focusing techniques which disrupt cognitions that
inhibit sleep.

Paradoxical intention. Another approach for dealing with
the arousal problems inherent in the insomniac's effort to
fall asleep is the procedure of paradoxical intention. Basically,
this theory assumes that performance anxiety about falling
asleep develops quickly after a few nights of transient insomnia and this may lead to chronic insomnia. Such a treatment
requires subjects "to perform responses that appear to be incompatible with the goal for which they are seeking therapeutic
assistance" (43, p. 547). In the case of sleep-onset insomnia,
that means that the subject is told to try to remain awake as
long as possible. To provide subjects with a rationale for
this seemingly irrational behavior, they are usually told that
the therapeutic sessions that are part of their sleep improvement program can advance more rapidly if the therapist has
additional information. For example, the therapist may say
that he or she needs to know specific details of the thoughts
experienced while trying to go to sleep. The subject is told
that falling asleep too quickly may prevent the necessary

information from being acquired. Thus the subject's new instructions help to relieve the performance anxiety associated
with falling asleep.

There have only been a few investigations of paradoxical
intention as a treatment for insomnia, and none of them has
used a polysomnographic evaluation (39;43;44). Some researchers have used paradoxical intention with severe cases of insomnia when other behavioral treatments (especially relaxation)
have failed to work. The subjects showed an average subjective
improvement in sleep latency of 58% from pre-therapy levels.
However, one study found that only subjects with severe insomnia improved with paradoxical intention, while those with mild
insomnia had a worsening of symptoms (39). Since paradoxical
intention appears to work by removing the client from the
anxious situation, it is possible that only severe insomniacs
who are abnormally high in performance anxiety respond well to
this treatment.

To date, no investigations of behavioral treatment for insomnia have examined effects of treatment upon daytime function. This would seem to be a fruitful area of investigation
in future studies.

Insomnia and the Aging Process

Certainly, the prevalence of the complaint of insomnia
increases with age. Miles and Dement (45) have summarized two
dozen survey studies, nearly all of which provide some evidence of an increase in sleep disturbance in the elderly compared to other adults. However, it is extremely difficult to
estimate the prevalence of insomnia in the elderly because
of the differences in the exact questions asked across
surveys.

Changes in sleep architecture do occur with aging. Briefly, these changes include an increase in a) wake time during
the sleep period, b) number of awakenings, c) nocturnal sleep
latency, and d) percent of stage 1 sleep. Decreases are also
seen in amount of slow wave sleep and sleep efficiency. The
changes in nighttime sleep have led to the commonly held belief that people need less sleep when they get older. However, daytime somnolence and napping behavior also increase
with age. If napping behavior and daytime sleepiness increase
as nocturnal sleep becomes disturbed, how can we conclude that
less sleep is required? Perhaps, the *ability* to maintain continuous sleep is what changes. If sleep need actually decreased

with age, one would logically expect briefer, uninterrupted
sleep to be the hallmark of the aged. In fact, the sleep of
the elderly is markedly fragmented and very inefficient.
Total sleep time remains about the same as it was earlier in
adulthood, but more time is required to accumulate sleep each
night.

Recent research provides some insight into this sleep
fragmentation in the elderly. The incidence of periodic leg
movements during sleep (PMS) and sleep apnea increases with
age. For example, studies of individuals 55 years or older
with and without sleep complaints showed that between 58% and
63% have PMS and/or sleep apnea (46). Both PMS and breathing
disorders during sleep produce sleep fragmentation, the hallmark of sleep of the aged, resulting in increased daytime
sleepiness.

Aging also appears to bring about an alteration in circadian rhythmicity. This finding suggests that aging may
alter the neural control of circadian rhythmicity and,
theoretically, may contribute to the early morning awakenings
and fragmentation of sleep and wakefulness. The reduction in
zeitgeibers (indicators of time) that frequently occurs with
age (e.g., retirement removes the need to arise at the same
time each morning and go to bed at a reasonably regular time)
may also contribute to changes in circadian influences upon
sleep and wakefulness.

It may be useful to conceptualize the sleep disturbance
of aging as including not only fragmentation of sleep but
also fragmentation of wakefulness (i.e., daytime drowsiness
and napping are increased). This concept is particularly
relevant when considering the influence of various medications
upon sleep and wakefulness. Many elderly individuals take
medication related to the increase in medical disorders of
this population, and these compounds have the potential to
increase the instability of sleep and wakefulness. For example, analgesics taken for arthritic pain generally produce
some CNS depression, furthering the likelihood of daytime
sleepiness and naps, which in turn may disturb nocturnal sleep.
Of course, the medical disorders themselves (pain, urinary
frequency, etc.) can also disturb sleep with resultant negative
effects on daytime alertness. One can quickly understand how
sleep and wakefulness coexist and can never be independent of
one another (this, of course, is true for all individuals, not
just the elderly).

Sleeping pills are frequently used by the aged. In fact,
in the U.S. forty percent of all sleeping pills are consumed
by the elderly despite the fact that they comprise only
eleven percent of the population.

Current Diagnoses and Treatment of Insomnia

Like any other symptom, insomnia varies in degree. That
is, the insomnia complaint may be quite severe (e.g., "I have
not slept in six months") or more moderate (e.g., "it takes me
an hour to fall asleep each night"). Another aspect of the
severity of the sleep disturbance is the impact upon daytime
function. Individuals with very similar reports about their
sleep at night may experience widely different daytime impairment. One individual may claim a nearly total inability to
hold a job because of fatigue, whereas a second person may
complain of only mild lethargy.

The duration of the insomnia complaint also varies. Nearly
everyone has experienced an occasional night of poor sleep and
subsequent tiredness, lack of energy, or irritability the following day. It is useful to divide individuals into those
having transient or short-term and those having long-term
insomnia.

Frequently, the type of complaint (sleep onset or sleep
maintenance difficulty) will aid in establishing the likely
course of the sleep disturbance. For example, a sleep onset
complaint is more likely to be voiced if the insomnia is related to psychophysiological factors or long-term use of
hypnotic drugs, whereas a sleep maintenance complaint is common when insomnia is related to depression or periodic leg
movements (see below for descriptions of these subtypes of
insomnia). Caution should be taken in interpreting a patient's
complaint, however. It is not at all unusual for an individual
to complain of sleep onset difficulty and for researchers to
find during polysomnographic recording that sleep latency was
very short. Because people are amnesic for what occurs during
sleep, and because those with disturbed sleep are often very
poor judges of sleep quantity, polysomnographic recording is
currently the only method which leads to a definitive diagnosis
for patients with sleep-wake disorders.

Whenever possible, treatment efforts should be directed
at the specific cause of the insomnia. It is logical that
chronic headaches should not routinely be treated with aspirin
(or another analgesic) until possible organic causes (e.g.,
brain tumor), which should be directly treated, have been
ruled out. Similarly, symptomatic relief for insomnia should
be provided, in most situations, only when the cause of the
insomnia cannot be directly treated or manipulated. In other
words, the key to treatment of an insomnia complaint is accurate diagnosis. Therefore, brief summaries of current treatment for the various insomnia conditions are presented below
by diagnostic category.

Transient Insomnia

Transient insomnia is experienced by many individuals (who generally have normal sleep) in response to a specific acute situation. For example, many students experience disturbed sleep for one night prior to an important examination. Transient insomnia refers to a sleep complaint which lasts only a few nights or less. Typically, transient insomnia is of minimal concern to the affected individual since he or she is aware of the cause of disturbed sleep and knows when the situation will end. An example would be an executive who flies frequently from the West Coast to the East Coast. Because of the time discrepancy between these locations, some disturbance of sleep is likely.

As most of us know from experience, one or two nights of poor sleep associated with acute stress, jet lag, or the like, is generally tolerable. In most cases treatment is unnecessary. If, however, there is a need to be optimally productive the following day, and the sleep disturbing event can be anticipated, the use of a short-acting sleeping pill may, for a night or two, be quite beneficial. Self-relaxation techniques may also be helpful in some situations which produce transient insomnia.

Short-term Insomnia

Short-term insomnia refers to a complaint of poor sleep which lasts from about a week to two or three months. Usually, short-term insomnia is related to continuing stress of one type or another or some other emotional response (e.g., grief following death of a loved one). The stress response to beginning a new job frequently will disturb sleep until the individual feels confident and accepted in the new position. Typically, the person's sleep will return to normal as the stress abates.

Generally the situation or condition leading to short-term insomnia is reasonably unavoidable and may not be as predictable as those resulting in transient insomnia (e.g., death of a loved one). During the period of continuing stress, the practice of good sleep hygiene may minimize sleep difficulty. Ordinarily, sleep will improve as the situation (or reaction to the situation) resolves. Some experts feel that use of sleeping pills for symptomatic relief during periods of short-term insomnia may prevent the development of chronic psychophysiological insomnia by eliminating the worry and concern over sleep as well as avoiding conditioned wakefulness in the sleep setting.

Chronic Disorders of Initiating and Maintaining Sleep (DIMS)

Chronic, or long-term, insomnia refers to disturbed sleep which persists for more than a few months. There are numerous conditions which cause or contribute to a report of chronic insomnia: psychophysiological disorders, psychiatric conditions medical illnesses and their treatments, sleep-specific physiological abnormalities (i.e., central sleep apnea, nocturnal myoclonus), disorders of circadian rhythms, consumption of drugs and alcohol, etc. Not uncommonly, more than one factor is involved in perpetuating an individual's sleep disturbance. Some of the more common diagnostic categories for chronic insomnia are briefly described below. The diagnostic categories discussed are essentially those described in the Diagnostic Classification of Sleep and Arousal Disorders, which was published by the Association of Sleep Disorders Centers (47).

Psychophysiological. Patients classified with this diagnosis are individuals who are overly concerned and worried about their sleep and who as a consequence of such worry have difficulty sleeping. Often, the sleep disturbance begins because of a stressful event or situation. Individuals who respond to short-term insomnia by fretting and worrying about sleep or by "trying" harder and harder to fall asleep are likely to develop persistent psychophysiological insomnia. Frequently, there is a conditioning factor involved. That is, the bedroom, bedtime ritual, or thought of retiring for sleep becomes an unconscious stimulus which regularly produces an "awake" response. Although these individuals can be thought of as having maladaptive behavior regarding sleep, their behavior in other situations is generally quite normal.

Since these individuals display abnormal psychological and/or physiological responses to sleep or the sleep environment, one logical therapeutic approach is behavior therapy aimed at changing the person's response to the "sleep stimuli." For example, if a person finds himself or herself becoming anxious whenever bedtime approaches, practicing progressive relaxation may, over time, establish physical relaxation (rather than anxiety) as the learned response to the stimulus of "bedtime." Similarly, worrying about finances, relationships, etc., may become a learned response to the bedroom environment because there are no distractions to aid in avoiding such thoughts. If this rumination occurs, stimulus control procedures may be helpful. That is, if an individual finds himself or herself awake and worrying after 20 or 30 minutes in bed, he or she should get up, go to a different room, and engage in a calm, but not too interesting, activity. In this way, neither lying awake nor worrying become learned responses to the bedroom environment stimulus.

Some clinicians feel that the judicious administration of hypnotic medication early in a bout of persistent psychophysiological insomnia may prevent the development of a strong, inappropriate stimulus-response relationship. That is, if an occasional good night of sleep is "available" by taking a sleeping pill, the pressure to try to fall asleep quickly may be relieved simply because the patient knows that he or she can obtain a good night's sleep the next night by taking medication. Similarly, intermittent use of hypnotics for psychophysiological insomnia during particularly stressful times may avoid worsening the problem. Rarely, if ever, is the chronic, nightly use of hypnotics beneficial. Additionally, the intermittent use of hypnotics in chronic psychophysiological insomnia should not be the total therapeutic strategy. It is generally useful to also utilize behavioral strategies and/or patient education regarding sleep needs and sleep hygiene.

It is not uncommon for patients in this diagnostic category to have unrealistic expectations about their sleep which lead to concern, which leads to sleep disruption. Occasionally, simply explaining that individual sleep needs vary widely may be sufficient to relieve an individual's concern which, in turn, may lead to improved sleep. Another aspect of patient education which is important to communicate is the remarkable ability of humans to deal with and recover from sleep loss. Some patients feel that they will be completely incapacitated if they do not sleep at least eight hours each night. This worry also makes sleep more elusive.

Psychiatric. The complaint of insomnia is quite frequent for individuals with a number of psychiatric disorders including: depression (both primary and reactive), generalized anxiety, panic, and phobias, hypochondriasis, psychoses, and personality disorders. With psychiatric conditions the severity of the insomnia generally parallels the severity of the patient's psychiatric symptoms (i.e., periods of worst depression are associated with times of most significant sleep disturbance) and with successful treatment of the psychiatric disorders, the patient's sleep usually becomes significantly better. Therefore, treatment should be directed toward amelioration of the psychiatric disorder.

Since many psychiatric patients ingest psychoactive medication for long periods of time, some individuals' sleep disturbance may also be related to chronic drug use and/or tolerance to sedative effects. This may pose a therapeutic dilemma of sorts, since medication may be important for psychiatric symptom control and, at the same time, disturb sleep. Clearly, a decision to terminate medication in the interest of improving sleep must be made cautiously.

Use of drugs or alcohol. Any chemical which is active in
the brain can potentially influence sleep. Sleep disturbance
frequently develops during and after long periods of nightly
ingestion of drugs or alcohol. Obviously, the use of stimulant compounds (e.g., caffeine, amphetamines, etc.) will produce high levels of neural activity which are often incompatibl
with sleep. Acute use of central nervous system depressants
generally will induce sleep; however, chronic use may result
in tolerance to the compound and the sleep disturbance will
return. If drug use is terminated, the insomnia will become
worse for days or weeks (termed "drug withdrawal insomnia").
It is as if the brain "forgets how to sleep on its own" and
must relearn this process.

In many cases, drug use is begun because of insomnia that
is related to chronic or acute anxiety, acute medical illness,
or other conditions. In the case of sleep disruption secondary
to medication prescribed for another medical condition, treatment involves adjustment of dose or a change to another medication.

Insomnia related to chronic use of CNS depressants must
be thoroughly explained to the patient. That is, the reason
sleep is disturbed during drug ingestion is because of toleranc
and the worsening of sleep upon withdrawal is *not* a return of
the original insomnia. Rather, it is a temporary condition
due to long-term drug use. Once the patient understands and
is likely to comply, a gradual withdrawal process can begin.
Frequently, patients with this diagnosis take multiple drugs
in large doses. Therefore, step one is to stabilize the dose
and minimize the number of drugs taken. Then, withdrawal is
conducted at the rate of one therapeutic dose per week. This
slow withdrawal usually prevents abrupt worsening of sleep.
Patients quickly begin to realize that their sleep does not
change much as the dose is reduced, which helps them understand
the lack of benefit the medication provides. Following withdrawal, if the insomnia persists, further evaluation may be
necessary to determine the original cause of the insomnia.

Sleep-related respiratory disorders. Breathing abnormalities during sleep, in individuals who have no (or little)
breathing difficulty while awake, are quite common. Typically,
these patients complain about excessive daytime sleepiness
rather than insomnia; however, a small minority report disturbe
sleep as their principal problem. The majority of insomnia
patients with respiratory abnormalities as the primary cause
of disturbed sleep have central sleep apnea. This is a condition in which, periodically during sleep, there is no effort
to breathe. Central apnea episodes typically last 10 to 45
seconds, but some last as long as two minutes. Individuals
with this condition are almost always unaware of a breathing

problem despite the fact that they wake up after each apnea
episode. It is not unusual for a patient to experience 100
to 200 central apnea episodes each night without realizing the
reason for the awakenings.

The specific cause of central sleep apnea is unknown and
treatments to date are not totally satisfactory. Respiratory
stimulants (medroxyprogesterone, theophyline) may be helpful
for some individuals. Acetazolamide appears to be a promising
pharmacological treatment because it increases baseline CO_2
levels and decreases pH which serve as exitatory stimuli to
respiratory system chemoreceptors. Diaphragmatic pacing via
the phrenic nerve also may be helpful. All treatments for
reducing central apnea, however, appear to have the potential
to increase other types of apnea (e.g., obstructive) and,
therefore, caution is necessary.

Periodic leg movements and restless legs syndrome. Periodic
leg movements during sleep (PMS), also called nocturnal myoclonus, is a condition characterized by repetitive, stereotyped leg movements which result from brief muscle contractions during sleep. Generally, these movements are very
periodic, occurring every 15 to 40 seconds, and are specific
to the sleeping state. They may occur in runs from several
minutes to an hour or more in length throughout the night (in
some patterns 300-1000 leg jerks occur in a single night).
Although PMS frequently produce awakenings and/or prevent
deeper stages of sleep from regular occurrence, they are virtually always imperceptible to the patient. Patients may complain of frequent awakenings or report non-refreshing, light,
and fragmented sleep but are unaware of the cause. Bed part-
ners occasionally will report "kicking" or abnormal motor activity during the night.

Restless legs syndrome (RLS) is a related disorder in that
virtually all patients with RLS also display PMS. The reverse
is not true; only a minority of individuals with PMS experience
RLS. RLS refers to an irritating paresthesia which occurs in
the legs while at rest. Descriptions of the sensations are of
uncomfortable aching, drawing, "nervousness," or creeping
feelings deep within the legs. Many times the sensations require frequent, perhaps vigorous, movement to provide relief.
Some individuals term the paresthesia as unbearable and leg
movement, stretching, or walking, is irresistable. Clearly,
such activity is incompatible with sleep. Amazingly, some
patients fail to recognize the connection between RLS and disturbed sleep. As far as is known RLS never remits.

The causes of PMS and RLS are not known. Chronic uremia
and other metabolic disorders seem to increase the likelihood
of PMS, as does the withdrawal from CNS depressants or the
administration of tricyclic antidepressants, at least for a

few weeks (48). PMS also occurs in patients with other sleep
disorders (e.g., narcolepsy, sleep-wake schedule disturbances)
more frequently than in non-complaining individuals. Both
conditions become more common in older age groups. PMS may
also be associated with a primary complaint of daytime sleepiness and recent evidence suggests that the longer the disorder
persists, the more likely that waking somnolence will be the
complaint as opposed to insomnia.

Because the etiologies of these disorders are not understood, specific treatment is not currently available. The
arousals secondary to PMS are frequently minimized by administration of benzodiazepines and may reduce the number of actual
leg movements. Certainly, the possibility that PMS is secondar
to metabolic disorders, administration of tricyclic antidepressants, or recent discontinuation of CNS depressants
must be taken into account when treatment alternatives are
considered. Treatment of RLS syndrome is also largely symptomatic. Benzodiazepines may be beneficial, but many patients
require oxycodone or carbamazepine if the symptoms are moderate
to severe. Some reports suggest that propranolol or L-dopa
type compounds may also be beneficial.

Medical, toxic, and environmental conditions. A long list
of medical, toxic, and environmental conditions may result in
a persistent complaint of insomnia. Some examples are arthri-
tis and other conditions resulting in chronic pain, disorders
leading to chronic pruritis (itching), hyperthyroidism, dys-
pepsia, chemical toxin reaction (e.g., arsenic, copper, carbon
monoxide), allergies, ulcers, "teething" in infants, and poor
sleeping conditions (excess heat, cold, noise, danger, movement
of bed partner, etc.). When any of these conditions are removed or improved, sleep becomes better. Environmental issues
related to sleep are discussed further under "Sleep Hygiene"
below.

Because of the considerable heterogeneity of conditions
in this category, treatment approaches must be just as variable.
When a medical condition is responsible for disturbed sleep
and appropriate treatment of that condition does not alleviate
the insomnia, intermittent use of hypnotics may be appropriate
and beneficial (some medical conditions, however, could be
exacerbated by hypnotics). If the medical condition remits,
even partially, hypnotic use should be ceased and the sleep
problem reassessed.

In the case of insomnia related to toxic or environmental
conditions, once the suspected condition is identified, the
treatment is to remove or counteract the condition (eyeshades
for light in bedroom, earplugs or masking noise for noisy
sleeping environment, etc.).

Childhood onset insomnia. Rare individuals appear to have "primary" insomnia. That is, the sleep disturbance was recognized early in childhood and has persisted throughout life in the absence of an identifiable cause. These factors suggest a CNS abnormality affecting sleep-wake mechanisms.

Very little is known about the treatment of these patients. If there is a CNS dysfunction of sleep-wake mechanisms, as proposed by some investigators, then behavioral strategies are not likely to help. On the other hand, if this condition develops because of poor learning of sleep-wake behavior early in life, then behavioral treatment may be "just what the doctor ordered." Until research sheds light on the precise etiological progression of this type of insomnia, treatment alternatives are essentially identical to those discussed under psychophysiological DIMS, above. In fact, the determination of which treatment strategy appears most beneficial for these patients may be our best clue to precise etiology.

Alpha-delta sleep. Patients with this condition generally complain of poor, non-restorative sleep and of being unrefreshed and tired during the day. Polysomnography reveals high voltage alpha EEG (a "waking" pattern) activity superimposed upon slow waves during NREM sleep. Numerous brief bursts of alpha may also be noted in the recording. Although individuals with alpha-delta sleep may experience themselves to be asleep for 7 to 8 hours, the restorative nature of sleep is markedly compromised. Other patients report considerable wakefulness during the night.

The speculation that numerous factors may underlie the appearance of alpha-delta sleep has yielded no specific determinant nor inspired any systematic treatment studies. Clinical benefit, at least for a few weeks, has been observed with the administration of amitriptyline. If a disorder of serotonin metabolism is involved, as speculated by Moldofsky and colleagues (49), treatment with agents affecting this system may be beneficial.

Insomnia without objective findings. Some healthy individuals with a convincing complaint of poor sleep are found to have essentially normal sleep, at least as defined polysomnographically. For unknown reasons these individuals consistently overestimate sleep latency and/or underestimate total sleep time. It is important to determine if an individual's complaint is a manifestation of hypochondriasis or contrived with the purpose of obtaining drugs, instead of an honest misappraisal of his or her sleep.

Individuals who express a genuine complaint of poor sleep, despite an absence of polysomnographic abnormality, are a treatment puzzle. Perhaps there is something about their sleep, not reflected in polysomnographic data, which is abnormal

and deserves treatment. Conversely, perhaps their insomnia
is a neurotic complaint. In this case the treatment should be
directed at the neurosis rather than toward sleep per se.
However, recent work by Borkovec and colleagues (33) suggests
that the subjective report of sleep in such patients improves
following behavioral therapy, despite a lack of change in polysomnographic patterns. This suggests, although does not prove,
that a neurotic complaint is not involved and that some sleep
disturbance exists.

A second type of individual in the "insomnia without objective findings" category is one who consistently sleeps a
limited number of hours (perhaps 4 to 6 hours) each night and
reports an insomnia problem because of an expectation that
"anything less than eight hours of sleep per night" is abnormal.
This misconception exists despite an absence of complaint about
sleep quality and daytime function. Polysomnographic recordings reveal normal sleep in terms of continuity and staging,
although the total sleep time per 24 hours is less than con-
ventionally accepted as typical. Such individuals do not
generally have difficulty sleeping unless they attempt to extend sleep, which fails.

For those individuals categorized as "DIMS--without objective findings" because of misperceptions about "normal" sleep,
reassurance and education about the variability in individual
sleep requirements may be sufficient therapy.

Frequency. The relative frequency of each of the above
diagnostic categories among 1,919 chronic insomnia patients
has been reported by Coleman (50). The majority of these insomniacs were referred to a sleep center by their family
physicians so they probably are representative of chronic insomniacs seeking medical assistance. In this study, the most
common diagnosis was DIMS related to psychiatric disorders which
accounted for approximately 35% of insomnia patients. About
15% were classified as psychophysiological insomniacs and about
10-12% were diagnosed as DIMS associated with periodic leg
movements/restless legs syndrome or with chronic drug use.
Clearly, these data indicate that insomnia is associated with
a number of diverse conditions. Follow-up data suggest that
specific insomnia diagnosis leads to beneficial treatment.

Daytime Consequences

No matter which condition underlies insomnia, probably the
most important aspect of disturbed sleep is its impact upon
wakefulness. A small minority of insomniacs may emphasize the

frustration of lying awake at night while "everyone else in
the world is sleeping soundly," but most insomniacs (consciously or unconsciously) measure the severity of insomnia by their
feelings, mood, or ability to perform adequately during waking
hours. They complain of lethargy, lack of energy, tiredness,
irritability, inability to concentrate, nausea, and a myriad
of other symptoms which they directly attribute to poor or insufficient sleep.

Sleep deprivation frequently, although not always, results
in some measurable change in waking function. Should not
chronic insomniacs display such changes since they (at least
many of them) have been deprived of some sleep over a long
period of time? Amazingly, little work has been performed in
this area despite a rather voluminous literature dealing with
sleep deprivation in normal sleepers, most of which was published more than 10 years ago. Recently, the focus of some
research dealing with insomnia has shifted from night to day.

Johnson and Spinweber (51) have compared performance of
almost 3,000 Navy personnel (over a six-year period) who
judged themselves to be "good" sleepers against that of self-
reported "poor" sleepers. Poor sleepers were found to have
fewer promotions, fewer recommendations for re-enlistment, a
higher attrition rate, and more hospitalizations. However,
an examination of the same career data for a smaller sample
of poor sleepers failed to support the notion that the Navy
personnel with objectively defined poor sleep would have the
poorest career records. They compared 30 individuals with the
complaint of poor sleep *and* poor laboratory sleep to an equal
number of self-reported poor sleepers with essentially normal
laboratory sleep and found that the groups were equally poor
with regard to career performance.

Examination of multiple sleep latency test (MSLT) data for
insomniacs provides some insight into the daytime sleep tendency of insomniacs (52). It showed that 29% of the insomniacs
showed no daytime sleepiness, but 11% were as sleepy as narcoleptics. Interestingly, there was no relationship between
sleep tendency during the day and polysomnographic aspects of
nighttime sleep.

Sugerman and colleagues (53) have reported that patients
with the diagnosis of "DIMS--no objective findings" had more
errors of omission on a vigilance task than did either persistent psychophysiological DIMS or normal sleepers. There were
also non-significant trends for "DIMS--no objective findings"
subjects to have increased sleep tendency in the morning on
the MSLT and more total time of eye closure (presumably an
indication of low arousal) during the vigilance task than the
other two groups.

Clearly, little is known about the specific daytime consequences of insomnia. It is likely that future research will
illustrate that there is wide variability in terms of sequelae
of insomnia, since sleep needs and sleep-wake schedule adapti-
bility vary widely among individuals.

Sleep Hygiene

As common sense tells us, poor sleep habits can cause insomnia. Staying up later than usual, the use of alcohol,
coffee, or medication, hunger, and worry (among other things)
affect how we sleep. Certainly the first night in an unfamilia
place will alter how we sleep as do unusual noises and any
source of anxiety.
Noise. The awakening threshold varies greatly among individuals. Some people respond to a whimper, while others
need the radio on full blast in order to awaken. In addition,
sensitivity to noise increases with age, and women are more
sensitive to noise than men (54;55).
Whether or not one awakens from sleep depends on the stage
of sleep one is in. More noise is needed to awaken someone
from delta sleep than from any other stage. In REM sleep,
the noise may be incorporated into the dream content, thereby
allowing the dreamer to sleep through the noise.
Occasional noises are more disruptive than constant noises.
In fact, some people sleep better if there is a white noise
(e.g., air conditioner hum) background to mask outside distractions. LeVere et al. (56) studied the effects of occasional
jet airplane overflights at night and found that sleepers
awoke for 5 minutes during each overflight. Interestingly,
the sleepers had no morning recall of any awakening.
It is possible to adapt to a noisy environment to some
degree, but never completely. Globus et al. (57) studied two
neighborhoods--one adjacent to the Los Angeles airport and one
in a quieter neighborhood. Those people living close to the
airport believed they had adapted to the noise, and yet they
slept 45 minutes less and showed less delta sleep than people
from the quieter neighborhood.
Temperature. According to Phillips (58), ideal room temperature for sleep is between 64° and 66° F. Cool temperatures
will consolidate sleep by causing fewer awakenings while
temperatures above 75° F. disturb sleep by causing more movements and less REM and delta sleep.
Mattresses. Sleep does not seem to be affected by the
kind of mattress one uses with the exception of a hard board

which produces more awakenings, more stage 1 sleep, and more
body movements than do softer surfaces (59). Water beds and
other specialty beds may make people more comfortable but do
not seem to alter sleep (60).

Sleeping with someone may also affect sleep. Monroe (16)
studied the impact of sleeping apart on those who habitually
slept together and found sleeping alone increased delta sleep
and decreased REM.

Food consumption. Weight gain is associated with uninterrupted sleep while weight loss is associated with short
and fragmented sleep. From a survival point of view, "starving
animals ought to be awake and looking for food; satiated animals are safest if they hide and sleep" (62). A light snack
before bed can be helpful, but a heavy meal can impair sleep.
Milk before bed can improve sleep since it contains the amino
acid called tryptophan which is a precursor of serotonin, a
transmitter associated with sleep. Indeed, research has shown
that drinks that contain milk do improve sleep (63). One to
15 grams of tryptophan nightly is probably needed to be effective as a sleeping aid.

Alcohol in moderation does help people fall asleep. Unfortunately, the effects of alcohol wear off causing awakenings
from sleep and poor quality sleep. Thus, alcohol may actually precipitate sleep maintenance insomnia. Likewise,
stimulants disturb sleep. Caffeinated coffee, tea, and soft
drinks should be avoided in the evening. Nicotine is also a
stimulant. Hence, heavy smokers sleep worse than non-smokers;
and sleep improves after one stops smoking (64).

Exercise. The impact of exercise on sleep is still in
debate. A regular exercise program seems to deepen sleep as
athletes have more delta sleep than non-athletes. However,
whether exercise affects sleep seems to depend on the time of
day the exercise is performed. Exercise during the morning or
late evening has less impact than exercise in the afternoon or
early evening (65;66). Excessive exercising (e.g., tennis)
close to bedtime may stimulate the cardiovascular system making
it difficult to relax and fall asleep. The best suggestion
appears to be a regular exercise program in the afternoon or
early evening.

Sleep schedules. The body has a circadian rhythm that can
be desynchronized by something as major as travel through time
zones or by something as seemingly minor as not having a
regular sleep-wake schedule. It is important to go to bed only
when sleepy and not to force sleep. Sleep is one of the few
things that working harder at will not help. Even more important is having a regular awakening time in the morning. Staying in bed longer may help recover sleep, but it also makes it
more difficult to fall asleep that night. Daytime naps also

decrease the quality and quantity of nighttime sleep. In particular, naps in the late afternoon or early evening are very
disruptive to night sleep, making it difficult to fall asleep
and producing lighter and/or fragmented sleep.

Sleeping pills as part of a regular sleep schedule should
be avoided. A pill once or twice a week during periods of
stress may be helpful but regular use leads to restless sleep
with increased awakenings. Sleeping pills also have a carry-
over effect causing dull thinking and impaired performance the
next day. And, of course, sleeping pills in combination with
alcohol can be deadly.

Summary

It is important to recognize that insomnia is a complaint
or symptom, rather than a disorder. Scientific research had
ignored this fact until recent years and, therefore, no clear
description of an insomniac has emerged with regard to physiological, psychological, or polysomnographic characteristics.
Nor has an accepted understanding of etiology or treatment
been advanced.

The severity of an insomnia disorder includes the impact
of disturbed sleep upon the waking function. Further, treatmen
efficacy must be judged not only by the effect upon sleep, but
also the resultant change in daytime performance and feelings.

Sleeping pills should not be viewed as the only available
treatment. In fact, some insomnia conditions may be enhanced
by hypnotic medications. The chronic use of sleeping pills
is virtually never in the best interest of the patient, althoug
short-term or intermittent utilization can provide beneficial
symptomatic relief and may help avoid prolonged sleep disturbance. There is a multitude of conditions and situations which
can lead to an insomnia complaint. These can be temporary or
chronic, situational, psychological, or physical. A more
exact conception of DIMS conditions and rational treatment approaches will be forthcoming as research endeavors to focus
on specific DIMS conditions rather than on insomnia as a unitary disorder.

References

1. Mayer, L. (1975). "That Confounding Enemy of Sleep."
    Fortune, *91*, 158–170.

2. Institute of Medicine (1979). *Sleeping Pills, Insomnia
    and Medical Practice*. Washington, D.C.: National
    Academy of Science.

3. Frankel, B.L.; Coursey, R.D.; Buchbinder, R.; and Snyder,
    F. (1976). "Recorded and Reported Sleep in Chronic
    Primary Insomnia." *Archives of General Psychiatry*, *33*,
    615–623.

4. Monroe, L.J. (1967). "Psychological and Physiological
    Differences between Good and Poor Sleepers." *Journal
    of Abnormal Psychology*, *72*, 255–264.

5. Freedman, R.R., and Sattler, H.L. (1982). "Physiological
    and Psychological Factors in Sleep-onset Insomnia."
    Journal of Abnormal Psychology, *91*, 380–389.

6. Johns, M.W.: Gay, T.J.A.; Masterton, J.P.; and Bruce,
    D.W. (1971). "Relationship between Sleep Habits, Adreno-
    cortical Activity and Personality." *Psychosomatic Medi-
    cine*, *33*, 499–507.

7. Johnson, L.C.; Church, M.W.; Seales, D.M.; and Rossiter,
    V.S. (1979). "Auditory Arousal Thresholds of Good
    Sleepers and Poor Sleepers with and without Flurazepam."
    Sleep, *1*, 259–270.

8. Coursey, R.D.; Buchsbaum, M.; and Frankel, B.L. (1975).
    "Personality Measures and Evoked Responses in Chronic
    Insomniacs." *Journal of Abnormal Psychology*, *84*, 239–
    249.

9. Hauri, P., and Good, R. (1975). "Frontalis Muscle Tension
    and Sleep Onset." *Sleep Research*, *4*, 222.

10. Freedman, R., and Papsdorf, J.D. (1976). "Biofeedback and
    Progressive Relaxation Treatment of Sleep-onset Insomnia:

A Controlled, All-Night Investigation." *Biofeedback and Self-Regulation*, *1*, 253-262.

11.   Good, R. (1975). "Frontalis Muscle Tension and Sleep Latency." *Psychophysiology*, *12*, 465-467.

12.   Sterman, M.B.; Howe, R.C.; and MacDonald, L.R. (1970). "Facilitation of Spindle-burst Sleep by Conditioning of Electroencephalographic Activity while Awake." *Science*, *167*, 1146-1148.

13.   Jordan, J.B.; Hauri, P.; and Phelps, P.J. (1976). "The Sensorimotor Rhythm (SMR) in Insomnia." *Sleep Research*, *5*, 175.

14.   Bixler, E.O.; Kales, A.; Soldatos, C.R.; Kales, J.D.; and Healey, S. (1979). "Prevalence of Sleep Disorders in the Los Angeles Metropolitan Area." *American Journal of Psychiatry*, *136*, 1257-1262.

15.   Karacan, I.; Thornby, J.I.; and Williams, R.L. (1983). "Sleep Disturbance: A Community Survey." In C. Guilleminault and E. Lugaresi (Eds.), *Sleep/Wake Disorders: Natural History, Epidemiology, and Long-Term Evolution* (pp. 37-60). New York: Raven.

16.   Healey, E.S.; Kales, A.; Monroe, L.J.; Bixler, E.O.; Chamberlain, K.; and Soldatos, C.R. (1981). "Onset of Insomnia: Role of Life-Stress Events." *Psychosomatic Medicine*, *43*, 439-451.

17.   Bertelson, A.D., and Monroe, L.J. (1979). "Personality Patterns of Adolescent Poor and Good Sleepers." *Journal of Abnormal Child Psychology*, *7*, 191-197.

18.   Marks, P.A., and Monroe, L.J. (1976). "Correlates of Adolescent Poor Sleepers." *Journal of Abnormal Psychology*, *85*, 243-246.

19.   Monroe, L.J., and Marks, P.A. (1977). "Psychotherapists' Descriptions of Emotionally Disturbed Adolescent Poor and Good Sleepers." *Journal of Clinical Psychology*, *33*, 263-269.

20.   Piccione, P.; Tallarigo, R.; Zorick, F.; Wittig, R.; and Roth, T. (1981). "Personality Differences between Insomniac and Non-insomniac Psychiatry Outpatients." *Journal of Clinical Psychiatry*, *42*, 261-263.

21. Levin, D.; Bertelson, A.D.; and Lacks, P. (1984). "MMPI Differences among Mild and Severe Insomniacs and Good Sleepers." *Journal of Personality Assessment*, *48*, 126-129.

22. Shealy, R.C.; Lowe, J.D.; and Ritzler, B.A. (1980). "Sleep Onset Insomnia: Personality Characteristics and Treatment Outcome." *Journal of Consulting and Clinical Psychology*, *48*, 659-661.

23. Beutler, L.; Karacan, I.; Thornby, J.; and Salis, P. (1978). "Personality Characteristics Associated with Four Subtypes of Primary Insomnia." *Sleep Research*, *7*, 181.

24. Zorick, F.J.; Roth, T.; Hartze, K.M.; Piccione, P.M.; and Stepanski, E.J. (1981). "Evaluation and Diagnosis of Persistent Insomnia." *American Journal of Psychiatry*, *138*, 769-773.

25. Kales, A.; Scharf, M.B.; and Kales, J.D. (1979). "Rebound Insomnia. A Potential Hazard Following Withdrawal of Certain Benzodiazepines." *Journal of the American Medical Association*, *241*, 1692-1695.

26. Mitler, M.M.; Seidel, W.F.; van den Hoed, J.; Greenblatt, D.J.; and Dement, W.C. (1983). "Comparative Hypnotic Effects of Flurazepam, Triazolam and Placebo: A Long-Term Simultaneous Nighttime and Daytime Study." *Sleep Research*, *12*, 113.

27. Muzet, A.; Johnson, L.C.; and Spinweber, C.L. (1982). "Benzodiazepine Hypnotics Increase Heart Rate during Sleep." *Sleep*, *5*, 256-261.

28. Lindsley, J.G.; Hartmann, E.L.; and Mitchell, W. (1983). "Selectivity in Response to L-tryptophan among Insomniac Subjects: A Preliminary Report." *Sleep*, *6*, 247-256.

29. Schneider-Helmert, D., and Schoenenberger, G.A. (1981). "The Influence of Synthetic DSIP (Delta-Sleep-inducing-Peptide) on Disturbed Human Sleep." *Experientia*, *37*, 913-917.

30. Schneider-Helmert, D., and Schoenenberger, G.A. (1983). "Effects of DSIP in Man." *Neuropsychobiology*, *9*, 197-206.

31. Freedman, R.; Hauri, P.; Coursey, R.; and Frankel, B. (1978). "Behavioral Treatment of Insomnia: A Collaborative Study." *Sleep Research*, *7*, 179.

32. Van Oot, P.H.; Lane, T.W.; and Borkovec, T.D. (1984). "Sleep Disturbances." In H.E. Adams and P.B. Sutker (Eds.), *Comprehensive Handbook of Psychopathology*. New York: Plenum Press.

33. Borkovec, T.D.; Grayson, J.B.; O'Brien, G.T.; and Weerts, T.C. (1979). "Relaxation Treatment of Pseudoinsomnia and Idiopathic Insomnia: An Electroencephalographic Evaluation." *Journal of Applied Behavior Analysis, 12,* 37-54.

34. Borkovec, T.D., and Weerts, T.C. (1976). "Effects of Progressive Relaxation on Sleep Disturbance: An Electroencephalographic Evaluation." *Psychosomatic Medicine, 38,* 173-180.

35. Coursey, R.D.; Frankel, B.L.; Gaarder, K.B.; and Mott, D.E. (1980). "A Comparison of Relaxation Techniques with Electrosleep Therapy for Chronic, Sleep-onset Insomnia: A Sleep-EEG Study." *Biofeedback and Self-Regulation, 5,* 57-73.

36. Hauri, P.J.; Percy, L.; Hellekson, C.; Hartmann, E.; and Russ, D. (1982). "The Treatment of Psychophysiologic Insomnia: A Replication Study." *Biofeedback and Self-Regulation, 7,* 223-235.

37. Bootzin, R.R. (1972). "Stimulus Control Treatment for Insomnia." *Proceedings of the 80th Annual Convention of the American Psychological Association, 1,* 395-396.

38. Haynes, S.N.; Price, M.G.; and Simons, J.B. (1975). "Stimulus Control Treatment of Insomnia." *Journal of Behavior Therapy and Experimental Psychiatry, 6,* 279-282.

39. Lacks, P.; Bertelson, A.D.; Gans, L.; and Kunkel, J. (1983). "The Effectiveness of Three Behavioral Treatments for Different Degrees of Sleep-onset Insomnia." *Behavior Therapy, 14,* 593-605.

40. Puder, R.; Lacks, P.; Bertelson, A.D.; and Storandt, M. (1983). "Short-Term Stimulus Control Treatment of Insomnia in Older Adults." *Behavior Therapy, 14,* 424-429.

41. Turner, R.M., and Ascher, L.M. (1979). "A Within Subject Analysis of Stimulus Control Therapy with Severe Sleep-onset Insomnia." *Behaviour Research and Therapy, 17,* 107-112.

42. Zwart, C.A., and Lisman, S.A. (1979). "Analysis of Stimulus Control Treatment of Sleep-onset Insomnia." *Journal of Consulting and Clinical Psychology*, *47*, 113-118.

43. Ascher, L.M., and Efran, J.S. (1978). "Use of Paradoxical Intention in a Behavioral Program for Sleep Onset Insomnia." *Journal of Consulting and Clinical Psychology*, *46*, 547-550.

44. Ascher, L.M., and Turner, R.M. (1979). "Paradoxical Intention and Insomnia: An Experimental Investigation." *Behaviour Research and Therapy*, *17*, 408-411.

45. Miles, L., and Dement, W.C. (1980). "Sleep and Aging." *Sleep*, *3*, 119-220.

46. Ancoli-Israel, S.; Kripke, D.F.; Mason, W.; and Messin, S. (1981). "Sleep Apnea and Nocturnal Myoclonus in a Senior Population." *Sleep*, *4*, 349-358.

47. Association of Sleep Disorders Centers (1979). *Diagnostic Classification of Sleep and Arousal Disorders*, 1st ed., prepared by Sleep Disorders Classification Committee, H.P. Roffwarg, Chairman, *Sleep*, *2*, 1-137.

48. Ware, J.C.; Brown, F.W.; Moorad, P.J.; Pittard, J.T.; Murphy, M.; and Franklin, D. (1984). "Nocturnal Myoclonus and Tricyclic Antidepressants." *Sleep Research*, *13*, 72

49. Moldofsky, H.; Scarisbrick, P.; England, R.; and Smythe, H. (1975). "Musculo-skeletal Symptoms and Non-REM Sleep Disturbance in Patients with 'Fibrositis Syndrome' and Healthy Subjects." *Psychosomatic Medicine*, *37*, 341-351.

50. Coleman, R.M. (1983). "Diagnosis, Treatment, and Follow-up of about 8,000 Sleep/Wake Disorder Patients." In C. Guilleminault and E. Lugaresi (Eds.), *Sleep/Wake Disorders: Natural History, Epidemiology, and Long-Term Evolution* (pp. 87-98). New York: Raven.

51. Johnson, L.C., and Spinweber, C.L. (1983). "Quality of Sleep and Performance in the Navy: A Longitudinal Study of Good and Poor Sleepers." In C. Guilleminault and E. Lugaresi (Eds.), *Sleep/Wake Disorders: Natural History, Epidemiology and Long-Term Evolution* (pp. 13-28). New York: Raven.

52. Seidel, W.F., and Dement, W.C. (1982). "Sleepiness in
     Insomnia: Evaluation and Treatment." *Sleep*, *5*, 180s-
     190s.

53. Sugerman, J.L.; Stern, J.A.; and Walsh, J.K. (1985).
     "Daytime Alertness in Subjective and Objective Insomnia."
     Biological Psychiatry, *20*, 741-750.

54. Rousey, C.L. (1979). "Auditory Acuity during Sleep."
     Psychophysiology, *16*, 363-366.

55. Wilson, W., and Zung, W. (1966). "Attention, Discrimina-
     tion, and Arousal during Sleep." *Archives of General
     Psychiatry*, *15*, 523-528.

56. LaVere, T.E.; Bartus, R.T.; and Hart, F.D. (1972). "Elec-
     troencephalographic and Behavioral Effects of Nocturnal-
     ly Occurring Jet Aircraft Sounds." *Aerospace Medicine*,
     43, 384-389.

57. Globus, G.; Friedmann, J.; and Cohen, H. (1973). "Effects
     of Aircraft Noise on Sleep as Recorded in the Home."
     Sleep Research, *2*, 116.

58. Phillips, E.R. (1983). *Get a Good Night's Sleep*. Engle-
     wood Cliffs, N.J.: Prentice-Hall.

59. Kinkel, H.J., and Maxion, H. (1970). "Schlafphysiolo-
     gische Untersuchungen zur Beurteilung verschinder
     Matratzen." *International Zeitschrift für Angewandte
     Physiologie Einschliesslich Arbeitsphysiologie*, *28*,
     247-262.

60. Anch, A.M.; Shurley, J.T.; Orr, W.C.; and Wooten, G.D.
     (1977). "Effect of the Airfluidized Bed on the Sleep
     of Normal Male Adults." *Waking and Sleeping*, *1*, 195-
     198.

61. Monroe, L.J. (1969), "Transient Changes in EEG Sleep
     Patterns of Married Good Sleepers: The Effects of
     Altering Sleeping Arrangement." *Psychophysiology*, *6*,
     330-337.

62. Hauri, P. (1982). *The Sleep Disorders*. Kalamazoo, Mich.:
     Upjohn.

63. Southwell, P.R.; Evans, C.R.; and Hunt, J.N. (1972). "Ef-
     fect of a Hot Milk Drink on Movements during Sleep."
     British Medical Journal, *2*, 429-431.

64. Soldatos, C.R.; Kales, J.D.; Scharf, M.B.; Bixler, E.; and Kales, A. (1980). "Cigarette Smoking Associated with Sleep Difficulty." *Science*, *207*, 551-553.

65. Hauri, P. (1968). "Effects of Evening Activity on Early Night Sleep." *Psychophysiology*, *4*, 267-277.

66. Horne, J.A., and Porter, J.M. (1976). "Time of Day Effects with Standardized Exercise upon Subsequent Sleep." *Electroencephalography and Clinical Neurophysiology*, *40*, 178-184.

Bibliography

Borkovec, T.D. (1982). "Insomnia." *Journal of Consulting and Clinical Psychology*, *50*, 880-895.

Presents theoretical causes and behavioral treatments for two of the most frequent kinds of insomnia: psychophysiological and insomnia without objective findings. This is a good review article of the psychological literature on insomnia.

Dement, W.D.; Seidel, W.; and Carskadon, M. (1984). "Issues in the Diagnosis and Treatment of Insomnia." In I. Hindmarch, H. Ott, and T. Roth (Eds.), *Sleep, Benzodiazepines and Performance*. Berlin: Springer-Verlag.

Discusses how to diagnose insomnia, the daytime consequences of insomnia, when to prescribe a hypnotic for treatment, and how to tell if the hypnotic has been effective.

Institute of Medicine (1979). *Sleeping Pills, Insomnia and Medical Practice*. Washington, D.C.: National Academy of Science.

Reports prevalence of sleep complaints, common medical treatments, health problems associated with hypnotic drugs, and other treatment options. Includes a section on insomnia in the elderly.

Part II
Dreams

SECTION A
BASIC DREAM PROCESSES

Chapter 5
ON THE SINGLE-MINDEDNESS AND ISOLATION
OF DREAM PSYCHOPHYSIOLOGY*

Alan Moffitt and Robert Hoffmann

The purpose of this chapter is to review the current state of knowledge and opinion concerning the psychophysiological study of dreams, dreaming, and dreamers. This can be done simply and briefly. In the opinion of Foulkes (1;2) the area is nearly bankrupt and his judgment appears to be widely shared (3;4). The result, noted by Koella (5) is that progressively fewer people are doing dream research of any sort, especially dream psychophysiology. Therefore, in addition to reviewing the reasons for the apparent failure of more than 30 years of psychophysiological dream research to contribute to "an explanation or interpretation of dreams" (1, p. 93), we will also examine new directions which suggest the possibility of a renewal of interest in the area. Since these new directions emerge out of the study of the central correlates of dreaming, the focus of the discussion will be on electroencephalography (EEG), electrooculography (EOG), and electromyography (EMG).

Bankruptcy

There is an emerging consensus that the scientific study of dreams has not lived up to the potential that motivated much of the research following the discovery of REM sleep in 1953 (6;7;8). Foulkes has been a leader in this emerging view, arguing that the three foundation disciplines of dream psychology--psychoanalysis, psychophysiology, and evolutionary biology--have contributed very little to a scientific understanding of dreaming. The remedy he proposes is the development of a

---

*Preparation of this paper was supported by operating grant #A7503 from the National Science and Engineering Research Council of Canada.

cognitive theory which views dreaming as a unique form of species-specific higher symbolic activity (1;2;9;10). According to Foulkes (1) psychophysiology, "... however useful it may be as a method of dream collection ... cannot, at present, be expected to make any substantial contributions to the explanation or interpretation of dreams" (p. 93). A surprising conclusion, but one which merits serious consideration if only because Foulkes has used those methods with such skill and fecundity. Moreover, he is not alone in his opinion. Fiss (11), for example, has claimed:

> the fact that sleep researchers have ... emphasized the biological substratum of dreaming and by and large neglected the psychological experience of dreaming has given rise to a curious paradox: despite the monumental achievements in sleep research in recent years, our prevalent notions of dreaming continue to be derived principally from clinical practice and psychoanalysis—as if REMs had never been discovered. In brief, the technological breakthrough of the fifties and sixties has had relatively little impact on our understanding of dreaming. (p. 41)

Are these opinions accurate? Reviews of psychophysiological dream research (12-18) indicate that they are. Rechtschaffen, in an interesting turn of phrase, has noted that we do not know the "intimate" correlates of dreaming (16). Similarly, Pivik (18) states quite unequivocally:

> The efforts to determine physiological correlates of sleep mentation have been largely negative or inconclusive. Although much had been learned about descriptive physiology of sleep, the strongest psychophysiological association remained that between eye-movements and dream content in REM sleep, with only frail hints of possible physiological correlates of NREM mentation. *The situation was not very different from that which existed just after Aserinsky published his initial (1953) report.* (p. 253, italics added)

The problem is compounded by the realization that reports of dreaming can be obtained from awakenings from all stages of sleep (19-23). The early identification of stage REM with dreaming and of the NREM stages with dreamless sleep has proved incorrect (24). Similar dream reports can be obtained upon experimental awakenings from stage REM sleep as well as from stages 1, 2, 3, and 4 of NREM sleep. The probability of obtaining a report varies as a function of the stage of

awakening (REM > 2 > 4; see 25). However, dream psychophysiology has been able to find few reliable within-stage electrophysiological correlates of the qualitative characteristics
of dreaming and dream recall. The best correlates of dreaming
still appear to be the global stages of sleep rather than the
microstructural characteristics of electrophysiological activity within any particular stage of sleep. Such appearances
merit a closer examination. They have the power to determine
the nature and direction of dream research for decades to
come.

Dream Psychophysiology and the
Mind-Body Problem

The search for electrophysiological correlates of dreams
and dreaming has been hampered by commitments to what we have
referred to as "unfortunate habits of mind and practice" (25).
Chief among these was the belief that the delineation of electrophysiological correlates of the qualitative and quantitative characteristics of dreams and dreaming would lead to an
early and expeditious resolution of the mind-body problem.
Most investigators appear to have had prior commitments on
this issue in terms of strongly held beliefs about the nature
of the relation of experience and the brain. Many discussions
of this issue are available (26-30) so our presentation of
the alternatives will be brief.

Mental activity and subjective experience can be regarded
as isomorphic with brain activity, epiphenomenal to brain
activity, or as an independent domain which interacts causally
with brain activity. Most dream psychophysiology seems to
have been done in order to prove that one or the other of
these positions was correct. The most popular scientific
view is that mental experience generally and dreams in particular are epiphenomenal to brain activity. This view is
also reductionist in the sense that it is assumed or asserted
that linguistic terms describing subjective experience can be
translated unambiguously into physical predicates—often,
numerical descriptors of EEG, EOG, and EMG activity—and it
is this latter level of description which has reality status,
at least as far as causality is concerned. Psychophysiological
isomorphism is somewhat more humble in granting probationary
reality status to mental predicates but it asserts that mind
and brain terms can be coordinated in a one-to-one mapping.
Interactionism grants reality status to both domains and permits them to causally interact in a manner entailing mappings

of different sorts between the domains—particularly one-to-
many and many-to-one mappings. A careful reading of the historical and contemporary literature of dream psychophysiology
(31-33) suggests that most researchers have had prior philosophical commitments to epiphenomenal reductionism or isomorphism but have been forced to live with interactionism.
A contemporary example of reductionism is Crick and Mitchison's
(34) theory of dreaming based on neural net theory; a famous
example of isomorphism is the activation-synthesis theory of
Hobson and McCarley (35;36); and an interesting modern version of interactionism is Koukkou and Lehmann's (37-39) functional state shift theory. The problem with the first two
theories is that neither is based on concurrent measurements
of dreams and electrophysiological activity in humans. Moreover, they are probably untestable in that sense, except perhaps in exceptional medical circumstances. The problem with
interactionism is that one-to-many or many-to-one mappings
guarantee a certain level of ignorance. Some input and/or
output terms will not map unambiguously. Nevertheless, it
was the possibility of scientifically specifying reductionist
or isomorphic mind-brain relations which attracted many researchers to the psychophysiological study of dreams. The
results of their efforts have been judged deficient, as we
indicated above. We turn our attention now to how they went
about their business.

Traditional Dream Psychophysiology:
An Evaluation

    Electrophysiological correlates of sleep mentation have
generally fallen into three categories: phasic events, asymmetries of hemispheric activation, and tonic EEG characteristics. Pivik (18) has concluded that "... phasic activity is
not the determinant of sleep mentation *per se*" (p. 268). His
conclusion still stands. Nevertheless, the search for these
correlates persists, largely because phasic events such as
eye movements, pips, memas, K-complexes, spindles, etc., are
relatively easily measured and because it is difficult to
give up the hope that these more or less conspicuous aspects
of electrophysiological activity should be related reliably to
some quantitative or qualitative characteristic of dreams or
dreaming. Nevertheless, phasic events, by themselves, seem
not to be strongly related to dreams or dreaming.
    Another durable myth which persists in spite of inadequate
initial evidence and mounting evidence to the contrary concerns

the relation of asymmetrical hemispheric activation to the
qualitative characteristics of sleep mentation. Dreams are
asserted to have certain characteristics--visuo-spatial,
metaphoric, analogical, syncretic, wholistic, bizarre--because
they are the product of the activation of the right hemisphere
(40-44). McCarley and Hobson (29) have concluded that support for this hypothesis "... is so tenuous and indirect as
to be nonexistent" (p. 110). In fact, Snyder (45) has pointed
out that evidence going back to the turn of the century indicates that the preceding characterization of dreaming is generally incorrect, regardles of the nature of the underlying
brain activity.

Contemporary evidence establishing that the right hemisphere is activated during dreaming or during stage REM sleep
is not strong (46-58). Many of the studies which claim to
find such a relation are inadequate in terms of subject selection, methodology, measurement, and conceptualization. Not
the least of these failures is the continuing misidentifica-
tion of stage REM sleep and dreaming, obviating the investigator from the necessity of collecting both dream reports and
EEG measurements from the same subjects at the same time
(41;59). Another unfortunate habit is the practice of making
inferences concerning activation (power variations in the
higher frequency regions) in one hemisphere based on amplitude
asymmetries between the two hemispheres measured by variations
in total power rather than by asymmetries of power within
specific frequency bands. More recent studies meeting minimal
conditions of adequacy, specifically, simultaneous measurement
of EEG activity at homologous locations using human subjects,
and obtaining dream reports using experimental arousals, have
not supported the claim that dreaming is the result of activation of the right hemisphere. Those differences which do exist
in preawakening EEG activation between the hemispheres are
generally miniscule (53;56), and they are not always related
to dream recall and report characteristics (55). When they
are found, as often as not they favor the left hemisphere
rather than the right, depending on individual differences in
dream recall and the particular dependent variables of the
dream report under consideration (47;53). When found, activation of the right hemisphere prior to awakening is associated
with poorer rather than richer dream phenomenology (53). In
addition, total power variations in one hemisphere do not in
general correlate inversely with power variations in the
higher frequency categories in the opposite hemisphere (53).
Thus, the association of dreaming with activation of the right
hemisphere seems to be incorrect rather than tenuous and indirect. Even this conclusion must be regarded as tentative,
however, since all dream psychophysiology studies to date have

only measured one or a few homologous locations over each
hemisphere of the sleeping human brain. What is needed, of
course, are studies taking concurrent measurements from 16 to
32 electrodes per hemisphere for each subject as well as
dream reports. The technologies for the storage and analysis
of data sets of this size are only now becoming readily available for dream psychophysiologists with limited means, so it
will probably be some years before we see an adequate test of
the relation of dream recall and report characteristics to
hemispheric asymmetries in EEG activity. If such relations
exist, they will likely prove to be very subtle.

What about tonic EEG correlates of dreaming? The answer,
with certain reservations, is the same as for the other classes
of correlates. For example, Pivik (18) has observed that
"... there is much variation in the incidence and quality of
mental activity within a sleep stage where a given EEG pattern
is essentially constantly maintained" (p. 249). In other words,
repeated waking of a person from a particular stage of sleep,
such as tonic stage REM (no rapid eye movements), routinely
produces reports of differing preawakening experience. Dream
reports following awakenings from different stages of sleep
support the same general conclusion. It was thought that one
of the major between-stage differences in dream reports
from stages REM and 2 was that the former were "dream-like,"
meaning visuo-spatial, while the latter were "thought-like"
(see 22). Foulkes (2), however, has emphasized that the
differences between dream reports from these stages are distri-
butional rather than categorical. Many reports from all stages
of sleep are indistinguishable. In summary, there appear to
be few distinguishing tonic EEG correlates of dreaming, as
Pivik claimed. This appears to leave dream psychophysiology
exactly where it was shortly after the discovery of stage REM
sleep.

New Directions

The question now facing dream psychology in general and
dream psychophysiology in particular is where do we go from
here. We can continue what Fodor (4) has called the traditional game of mentalists and physicalists, each accusing the
other of intellectual bankruptcy. We can follow Kuhn's (60)
lead as Foulkes has recommended and eventually abandon the
psychophysiological paradigm. Or we can do what Stewart and
Tall have observed happens in mathematics and presumably other
disciplines as well: "It is a cardinal principal of mathematics

not to throw away a good idea just because it doesn't work"
(61). In our opinion, dream psychophysiology may just be one
of those good ideas which we should not throw away just because it didn't work.

Why didn't dream psychophysiology work? It didn't work
for reasons which are fairly simple, and most of which had
nothing to do with psychophysiology per se. First among these
is a commitment to a rationalistic view of the waking and
sleeping mind which restricts rational consciousness, also
known as normal (in the sense of normative) waking consciousness, to a particular segment of the waking state, defined
electrophysiologically and behaviorally. In addition to
dreams and other mentation during sleep, waking fantasies and
hallucinations are viewed as technically irrational, at least
at the level of surface structure (psychoanalysis) but also
at deeper levels (most of logical positivism, logical empiri-
cism, behaviorism, cognitive psychology--dreams are "notional"
objects for Fodor [4]). The restriction of rational consciousness to the waking state enforces the view of sleep as an expression of the unconscious mind, the irrational mind, or in
Kramer's elegant if inaccurate terms, "the mind in pure culture" (62). Assumptions such as these lead to a truncated
view of dreaming and sleep mentation as derivative in relation
to normal waking consciousness (63-65). Consequently, within
Western epistemology the mind can only know itself correctly
during the waking state, and what it knows correctly is that
it *is* awake. It is not possible on this account for the
sleeping mind to correctly know its own state.

Lucid Dreaming

Phenomenological descriptions of dream experience going
back to the foundations of Western views of the mind have
described a curious experience occurring within some dreams
in which the dreamer becomes aware of dreaming while dreaming,
known now as lucid dreaming. In fact, the experience of lucid
dreaming is central to Descartes' method of doubt and Western
epistemology in general (see 66, Principle IV). Viewed from
normal waking consciousness, the impression that one is awake
while asleep is false, because one is in fact asleep. This
is how cognitive psychology gets to run a univocal interpretation on the meaning of the expression "being awake," producing
among other things Malcom's amusing book on dreaming (67) and
Fodor's (4) cryptic view of dreams as "notional" objects.

Thus, most of the traditions of Western science (excluding
perhaps phenomenology) simply dismissed lucid dreaming as

irrelevant or, worse, denied its existence. There are two
problems with this approach. The first is the claim that it
is possible to correctly tell that we are awake while awake
is undemonstrable, as Descartes (66) and O'Flaherty (68) have
noted. A limitation on this impossibility postulate, however,
comes from the methods of psychophysiology. The postulate is
correct as long as methods other than phenomenological and intellectual are excluded. This is where psychophysiological
methods might become relevant since they give us an additional
perspective concerning the physical organization of states
to which the expression "being awake" may be applied. It is
precisely at this point that evolutionary biology becomes very
important. Foulkes is quite incorrect when he says that evolutionary biology is irrelevant to modern dream psychology.
Both deal with the question of the forms of "being awake."
The available data indicate that there are many different
forms of wakefulness and sleep within the vertebrate line,
including diverse forms of wakefulness during sleep (69).
The second problem is that the intuition is in fact correct
at the time of its occurrence that what one is experiencing
during a lucid dream is a dream. So the assertion that
rational consciousness occurs only during normal waking consciousness would appear to be questionable if not incorrect.
The problematic implication of this fact is that the intuition
that one is awake while recognizing that one is dreaming is
also correct. This entails two apparent contradictions, that
one is both awake and asleep, and that one is also not awake
because one is in fact electrographically asleep, usually in
stage REM of sleep (70;71). Similar apparently paradoxical
conditions have been documented in other areas of sleep psychophysiology (72-75). In any event "being awake" and "being
asleep" are not univocal expressions nor are they mutually
exclusive. One wonders how Hofstadter (76;77) missed this
one.

   Other possibilities exist, however. Maybe one had a
dream, awakened, and then fell back asleep, and upon awakening
again confused the two experiences, attributing the wakefulness incorrectly to sleep but correctly remembering having
dreamed. Not much reason for movement here as far as dreaming
is concerned, especially without good electrophysiological
data.

   As a result of the dispersal of the Tibetan culture in
the early 1950s at about the same time as the discovery of
REM sleep, scholars in the West gradually became aware of the
practices of the unique form of Buddhism developed within the
traditions of that culture (78). Among these was a dream yoga
which cultivated lucid dreaming as an epistemologically desirable state (79). A number of dream researchers inter-

nationally and at about the same time began to take seriously
the possibility suggested by the testimony of the phenomenological record of their own culture and other cultures as well,
and in some cases the testimony of their own experience, that
lucid dreaming might really exist (80-87). But how to *prove*
it?

By now the details of what is being called "LaBerge's proof"
are becoming well known (88-100). The lucid dreamer while
dreaming makes an intentional sequence of eye movements with
his/her dream eyes, the sequence having been determined before-
hand as a code which could be recognized as distinguishably
different from the typical rapid eye movements of stage REM
sleep by someone watching the EOG tracings from the sleeper on
a polygraph. If psychophysiological isomorphism held, or even
a weak form of parallelism or interactionism were true, maybe
the dreamed eye movements would be evident on the EOG tracings
of the polygraph. The dreamer could then be awakened and
queried about his or her preawakening experience, including the
awareness of dreaming while dreaming and the nature of the
dreamed eye movement gestures they executed while asleep and
dreaming. If the latter report matched the sequence of eye
movements recorded on the polygraph during the preawakening
period, it would constitute clear and distinct evidence of the
existence of lucid dreaming.

Surprisingly, it worked. The awakened dreamer reported
both lucidity and having executed the sequence of dreamed
eye movements which were in fact reflected on the EOG tracings
of the polygraph during the preawakening period of sleep,
normally stage REM. Even more surprising, the effect has been
independently replicated a number of times in different sleep
laboratories and generated additional research, the former an
almost vanishingly rare event in dream psychophysiology (101-
108). For our present concerns, what is important about the
psychophysiological proof that lucid dreaming does exist as
an apparently paradoxical state of sleep is that the proof
depended upon the use of *traditional* techniques of dream
psychophysiology, those same methods which had been judged
unproductive. It is perhaps an interesting commentary on the
business of dream research that the judgment and the proof
were both happening at about the same time.

Notice that the proof entails a different interpretation
of the meaning of a phasic electrophysiological event. Patterned EOG activity is not a correlate of lucidity which in
any sense "explains" such dreaming. Rather, it is a sign
of the existence of the experiential state of conscious awareness and intentionality during sleep. It indicates the existence of a particular form of dreaming but it does not explain
such dreaming. Instead of contributing to the explanation or

interpretation of dreaming, with LaBerge's proof traditional
dream psychophysiology has proved useful in demonstrating
that the traditional scientific and psychoanalytic view of
dreams and dreaming were, if not incorrect, then limited in
ways that have fundamental implications for dream psychophysiology (cognitive and neurocognitive), dream psychology,
cognitive psychology, and, finally, cognitive and ecological
epistemology (109-116). That is worth the cost of 30 years
of psychophysiological dream research.

The proof has some significant implications for psychophysiological studies of dreaming. The claims, advanced by
some skeptics, that dreams are confabulations can safely be
dismissed. At least lucid dreams are not, and it probably
would not be worth the time and effort to prove that dreams
or sleep mentation generally are not simply postawakening
confabulations. More importantly, the proof creates an opportunity to explore the relation of quantitative variations of
tonic EEG during stage REM sleep (see below) with the qualitative characteristics of the dream experience during "windows"
of signalled lucidity, as LaBerge has already noted (100), and
with nonlucid dreaming as well. LaBerge has also implied that
the proof indicates that mind-brain relations are isomorphic
in general during dreaming (100). This is incorrect. Neither
eye movements nor other phasic or tonic electrophysiological
parameters are reliably isomorphic with dream experience
during nonlucid dreaming in any stage of sleep, as the preceding reviews have indicated. All one can assert about isomorphism is that under the conditions of lucidity and activated intention, dreamed and physical eye movements are
strongly linked. In nonlucid dreaming they are only weakly
coupled, if at all (117-119). It remains to be determined
whether isomorphism or strong or weak interactions will occur
between variation in other electrophysiological parameters and
the qualitative characteristics of lucid dream experience.
The proof also creates the possibility of a clinically relevant
experimental psychology of dreaming, a hope expressed by
Fiss (3) and shared by LaBerge (100). Lucid dreaming and its
use of traditional psychophysiological methods may be the
means by which dream psychophysiology extends its influence
into the broader domain of clinical psychiatry and psychology.

Dream Psychophysiology: Picture Science or
  Quantitative Science

Some problems, however, remain unresolved. Dream psychophysiology has not been very willing to move beyond what we
call "picture science" in dealing with the problem of the

quantification of tonic EEG activity. By this we mean the
description of tonic EEG activity in any stage of sleep through
the use of a picture of an apparently representative polygraph
tracing of an epoch of the electrohpysiological activity in
that stage along with some form of verbal description of that
activity. The alternative to characterizing tonic EEG during
any stage of sleep by visual inspection of polygraph tracings
has been available at least since 1965 when Digital Equipment
Corporation introduced the PDP/8 series of minicomputers.
This machine became the workhorse of psychophysiological
laboratories because it was equipped with analog to digital
converters and mass storage devices. During the subsequent
20 years the computer industry has undergone developments
which make the routine conversion of analog electrophysiological signals to digital values quite practical for the dream
psychophysiologist. Analog to digital conversion is the only
practical way to quantify tonic EEG activity. It permits the
investigator to sample such activity very rapidly (for example,
at a rate of 1000 samples per second) and produce a number for
each successive sample. The EEG waveform can then be characterized in terms of its quantitative variation through time
rather than through verbal descriptions such as "low amplitude
desynchronized activity" as in stage REM, or "higher amplitude slow wave activity." There is nothing intrinsically ob-
jectionable to such verbal descriptions or "picture science"
if they are adjuncts to quantitative numerical descriptions.
By themselves, however, they represent only a nominal form of
quantification.
     Analog to digital conversion is not, however, a panacea.
It is only a first step in data acquisition. It suffers from
the problem of producing an enormous amount of numbers
describing the characteristics of the EEG, EOG, and EMG signals. Data reduction and analysis must follow, and here the
investigator faces basically two options--to describe the
amplitude and frequency characteristics of the complex EEG
signal by remaining in the time domain or by converting to
the frequency domain. The latter option is the most popular
and can be accomplished through the use of commercially available programs which implement versions of the fast Fourier
transform (FFT). Such analyses produce estimates of the
amplitude and phase or power at any given frequency in the
EEG signals up to the Nyquist frequency (half the sampling
rate). There are numerous time-domain analyses available to
the investigator, such as fast Walsh transforms, various
wave-form stripping algorithms, and relatively simple and efficient versions of half-wave and full-wave period analysis
routines (120-146). In most of these procedures the amplitude
of the signal is integrated during an interval such as suc-

cessive crossings of electrical zero. The period between
such crossings is then classified in the appropriate frequency
category and the amplitude value is stored in that category.
Such analyses produce estimates of the percentage of time in
a given epoch which is occupied by EEG activity in that frequency category, as well as the integrated amplitude of the
waveforms occurring in that frequency category. Analog to
digital conversion and subsequent FFT or period analysis are
inherently more powerful than the techniques of EEG quantification used in traditional dream psychophysiology. These more
traditional techniques usually employ some version of amplitude integration, either of total power or power within a
given frequency band, but seldom both. FFT analyses can produce quantitative descriptions of a given segment of EEG activity in terms of power or amplitude and phase. Period
analyses, depending on the algorithm, can produce many different quantitative estimates of the characteristics of the
EEG waveform. Many good sources are available for these
types of analyses, and the reader is encouraged to pursue
them (147-155). In our opinion, these types of techniques
represent the direction that an evolving dream psychophysiology
will take during the remainder of this century.

Psychophysiological studies of dreaming using these sorts
of techniques have already produced interesting results. The
claim that the right hemisphere is activated during stage REM
sleep has been dispelled. Hemispheric asymmetries in the frequency and amplitude characteristics of EEG activity during
dreaming have been found to be *very* small (53). In fact,
they are so small that one wonders if the myth of dreaming
and dominance of the right hemisphere might not have been advanced had the measurements been available earlier. Dream
recall and report characteristics have been associated with
tonic EEG activity in a number of recent studies using more
adequate quantification procedures, as we noted above. It
seems reasonable to expect that digital quantification procedures will lead to a better characterization of the "intimate
correlates of dreaming and dream recall than we have had so
far. As we have suggested elsewhere, it is no longer reasonable to ignore within-stage variation in tonic EEG activity
as a potential correlate of dreaming and dream recall (128).
Such variation exists; it is measureable; it correlates with
dream recall and report characteristics; and these relations
are different among self-reported high and low frequency
dream recallers (53). The use of digital quantification of
tonic EEG activity during signal-verified lucid dreaming
might move dream psychophysiology beyond the limitations
imposed by earlier unfortunate habits of mind and practice.
It has already been used effectively in the study of the EEG
correlates of nonlucid and prelucid dreaming (156-160).

The importance of this conclusion cannot be overemphasized. On the one hand, the apparent lack of fruitfulness of dream psychophysiology can just as reasonably be viewed as evidence for the inadequacy of the traditional measurement procedures as opposed to being evidence for the bankruptcy *in principle* of the psychophysiological enterprise. Thus, Foulkes' and Fiss' conclusions are more or less correct, contingent on the continued use of traditional measurement procedures. However, *quantitative* studies of tonic, phasic, and hemispheric EEG and autonomic correlates of dreaming using multiple electrode arrays and multivariate statistical analysis strategies may well prove fruitful for dream psychophysiology.

The relation between measurement and theory in any scientific area is fundamentally developmental. Better measurement produces new knowledge, whether by chance or design. The two in combination lead to re-evaluation of older theories, to new questions, new theories, and sometimes to new answers to old questions, some of which were previously thought to be unanswerable. This much is common knowledge. What is less well understood is that the relation of the researcher to his or her measurement techniques is fiduciary (161), i.e., based on an assumption of trust that the measurement procedures are adequate to provide at least a partial answer to the questions being asked. The evidence and opinion surveyed to this point in the chapter indicate paradoxically that the methods of traditional dream psychophysiology were quite adequate to answer a set of questions which were not being asked within traditional dream psychology and psychophysiology, although they have proved to be inadequate to answer those questions which were being asked. As Thomas Pynchon has observed in one of his Proverbs for Paranoids: if they get you asking the wrong questions, they don't have to worry about your answers (162). Good methods will not help to answer bad questions, but more adequate measurement and the theory associated with these methods of measurement, particularly signal processing and biophysiological systems theory (163-166) can lead to better questions. Practically, the advent of cheap, efficient, and reliable analog to digital conversion, good software and operating systems, and cheap, fast, and powerful micro- and minicomputers bodes well for the future fruitfulness of dream psychophysiology. The impact of these machines on the study of mind-brain relations during both sleeping and waking may be as revolutionary as the original discovery of the EEG by Berger, the descriptions of REM sleep by Aserinsky and Kleitman, and the proof of the existence of lucid dreaming by La-Berge and others. However, unlike the former discoveries each of which had an obvious and immediate impact, the practical and theoretical impact of digital technologies will probably

be slower and more subtle. Still, a real possibility does
exist that the use of digital technologies will permanently
change the way contemporary research in dream psychophysiology
is done.

Stage, State, and the Ordinary Language
of Dream Psychophysiology

The concept of stage is the centerpiece of the conceptual
and empirical methods of dream psychophysiology. An early
stage scoring system with considerable popularity was that
of Loomis, Harvey, and Hobart (167)--it worked reasonably
well until Aserinsky and Kleitman reported that the eyes of
sleeping individuals behaved rather oddly. However, it took
until 1968 for a widely used sleep stage scoring system which
included REM to evolve under the editorial guidance of
Rechtschaffen and Kales (168). This scoring system defined
a canonical form of data classification for dream psychophysiology which undoubtedly constitutes another one of
Stewart and Tall's "good ideas," one which dream researchers
will be very slow to give up solely on the grounds that it
doesn't always work.
     An unfortunate habit of mind and practice of both tradi-
tional and contemporary dream psychophysiology is the assumption, often implicit, that the canonical stage labels of
Rechtschaffen and Kales (168) identify states which are functionally equivalent, at least in the sense that within-stage
variations of tonic EEG activity are random and unrelated to
the qualitative characteristics of sleeping and waking conscious experience. For example, different epochs of stage REM
are taken as equivalent instances of the same state because
they meet the electrophysiological conditions for the application of the stage label. However, electrophysiologically
homogeneous states within a given stage of waking and sleeping
sometimes endure for no more than a few seconds (169-171).
Stage labels and "picture science" encourage a static, pictoria
form of thinking about mind-brain relations. This view has
been challenged recently in an interesting psychophysiological
theory of dreaming proposed by Koukkou and Lehmann called the
Functional State Shift Theory (37, pp. 172-175). In this
theory, the canonical sleep stages define functionally different states and electrophysiological variations within any
given instance of a stage can also define further functional
states of the particular stage. On this account two instances
of a stage with the same label, such as stage REM, are not

necessarily functionally equivalent states, even on average.
This claim directly challenges the assumption of traditional
cognitive epistemology that the expressions "being awake" and
"being asleep" can be given a univocal interpretation by means
of electrophysiological procedures.

   We have recently reported data which support Koukkou and
Lehmann's approach. We have used digital period amplitude
analysis to quantify the EEG (C3, C4), EOG, and EMG activity
of eight adult males during sleeping and waking, four of whom
were self-reported high frequency dream recallers ($\geq$ 5 dreams
recalled per week) and four were self-reported low frequency
dream recallers ($\leq$ 1 dream recalled per week). These subjects
participated in a dream psychophysiology study, the methodological details of which have been reported elsewhere (53).
The experimental awakenings from stage REM in this study occurred after 5 minutes in the stage and were followed by a
four-minute postawakening rehearsal interval prior to the
dream report. The quantitative measures gathered during each
30-second epoch of sleeping and waking are presented in
Table 3. For all stage REM awakenings which produced a dream
report we correlated the various EEG, EOG, and EMG measures
with each other, averaged across hemispheres and preawakening
epochs among the four subjects in each group. The results
for the self-reported high frequency recallers are presented
in Table 4 and for the self-reported low frequency recallers
in Table 5. For the sake of simplicity only the correlations
with EEG power measures in the various frequency bands, as
well as EOG and EMG, are presented in these and subsequent
tables. No correlations below +/- .70 are reported. There
are a great many differences which emerge from a comparison
of these tables. The most conspicuous difference is that the
various EEG measures are more strongly intercorrelated for the
high than for the low recall subjects. For the low recallers
variation in tonic EEG power in any given frequency band is
much more independent of variations of EEG frequency and
power in the remaining bands than for the high recallers.
Electrophysiological activity during stage REM sleep is
more organized or structured in the high than in the low recall subjects. For example, total power variation (TOTP) is
inversely related to high frequency activity (beta.zero cross,
beta first derivative, and beta power) in the high recallers
but not in the lows. This contradicts the assumption that
total power variations can be used to index activation. The
assumption is correct for the highs but not for the lows.
In the lows only alpha and theta power variations co-vary
with other variables, most notably EOG and EMG activity.
Delta power variations are independent. In the highs, however, delta power co-varies strongly with other EEG frequency

Table 3

Measures per Epoch

Stage: REM, 2, or 4
Epoch number: 1 to 960 (= 8 hours)

EOG count: number of eye movements
EOG power: integrated amplitude of eye movements

EMG power: integrated amplitude of EMG

EEG Measures (C3, C4)

Hemispheric Averages		Hemispheric Differences
	Zero Cross	
Beta	(>= 16 Hz.)	LR Beta
Sigma	(12 to < 16 Hz.)	LR Alpha
Alpha	(8 to < 12 Hz.)	LR Alpha
Theta	(4 to < 8 Hz.)	LR Theta
Delta	(.5 to < 4 Hz.)	LR Delta
	First Derivative	
Beta		LR Beta
Sigma		LR Sigma
Alpha		LR Alpha
Theta		LR Theta
Delta		LR Delta
	Power	
Beta		LR Beta
Sigma		LR Sigma
Alpha		LR Alpha
Theta		LR Theta
Delta		LR Delta
Total		LR Total

Averages = (Left+Right)/2
LR = (Left-Right/Left+Right) x 100

Table 4

Intercorrelations* of Preawakening Measures
with Preawakening EOG, EMG, and EEG Power Measures
from Stage REM for High Recallers

	EOG	EOGP	EMG	BP	SP	AP	TP	DP	TOTP
Average Measures									
EOG		.90							
EOGP			-.75						
EMG									
BZ				.97				-.85	-.81
SZ					.95	.90	.74	-.85	
AZ				.74	.93	.97		-.91	
TZ					.76	.80	.94	-.70	
DZ				-.74	-.88	-.95	-.71	.96	
BD				.96			.72	-.86	-.85
SD					.94	.81			
AD									
TD				-.84	-.81	-.86		.95	.80
DD					-.78	-.80		.79	
BP								-.78	-.73
SP						.92	.74	-.80	
AP								-.88	
TP									
DP									.80

* $p < .01$, n = 6

Table 5

Intercorrelations* of Preawakening Measures
with Preawakening EOG, EMG, and EEG Power Measures
From Stage REM for Low Recallers

	EOG	EOGP	EMG	BP	SP	AP	TP	DP	TOTP
				Average Measures					
EOG		.91				-.71	-.74		
EOGP						-.75	-.83		
EMG									
BZ									
SZ									
AZ									
TZ							.83		
DZ									
BD						-.83			
SD									
AD									
TD						-.80			
DD					-.80				
BP					.81				
SP					.72				
AP									
TP									
DP									.74

* p < .01, n = 5

and power variations. Notice also that for the highs, EOG
and EMG variations are independent of variations in EEG activity. The conclusion is clear. To talk about "stage REM
sleep" in these different subjects as though one were referring
to the same thing is not correct. The states denoted by the
same stage label are different in these different types of
subjects.

The same conclusion applies to similar correlations com-
puted on the postawakening epochs immediately following the
arousal from stage REM. These data from the awake stage are
presented in Tables 6 and 7 for the high and low recall subjects. Again, the organization of the awake state/stage is
different in these subjects. Among the highs, variations in
theta power and total power are independent of variations in
the other variables. In addition, variations in delta power
are inversely related to frequency and power variations in
the higher frequency categories. In the lows, variations in
delta power during the waking state are positively rather
than negatively correlated with higher frequency and power
variations. Thus, from the point of view of the electrophysiological organization of stage and state, "being awake" does
not mean the same thing in these subjects any more than does
"being asleep" in stage REM.

Finally, we correlated the averaged preawakening EEG,
EOG, and EMG values of the variables in Table 3 with averaged
EEG power, EOG and EMG variations from the immediately following awake stage for these different groups of subjects. The
data are presented in Tables 8 and 9. The differences are
striking. Pre- and postawakening states/stages are largely
independent in the low recallers. For the highs there is a
rich set of intercorrelations between these states. Note
especially that in the self-reported high recall subjects,
preawakening EOG and EMG activity during stage REM are correlated with subsequent postawakening variations in sigma and
alpha power. In effect, the process of "waking up" is different in these two types of subjects. The quantitative
organizational characteristics of the waking state are much
more dependent on the preawakening organization of state in
the self-reported high frequency recallers than in the lows.
It is worth emphasizing that these stage/state differences
occur in the context of successful but qualitatively different
dream recall characteristics in these subjects (see 53). The
data in these tables are consistent with Koukkou and Lehmann's
assertion that the functional organization and interrelation
of states of sleeping and waking can differ in important ways
which are implicated in dreaming and dream recall. Explorations in this area are only beginning. The important point
for our present purposes is that the *quantitative* psycho-

Table 6

Intercorrelations* of Postawakening Measures
with Postawakening EOG, EMG, and EEG Power Measures
Following Stage REM Arousals
for High Recallers

	EOG	EOGP	EMG	BP	SP	AP	TP	DP	TOTP
EOG		.96							
EOGP									
EMG									
BZ				.88					
SZ				.75	.97	.92		-.90	
AZ					.95	.98		-.81	
TZ							.88		
DZ				-.76	-.88	-.85		.99	
BD				.73					
SD									
AD									
TD									
DD				-.86	-.76			.78	
BP					.75			-.73	
SP						.96		-.84	
AP								-.81	
TP									
DP									
TOTP									

* $p < .01$, n = 6

Table 7

Intercorrelations* of Postawakening Measures
with Postawakening EOG, EMG, and EEG Power Measures
Following Stage REM Arousals
for Low Recallers

	EOG	EOGP	EMG	BP	SP	AP	TP	DP	TOTP
				Average Measures					
EOG		.87						.74	
EOGP									
EMG									
BZ			.94	.86				.88	.85
SZ									
AZ					.83	.76			
TZ							-.85		
DZ					-.71	-.85			
BD			.73					.78	
SD					-.94	-.87			
AD					.75				
TD									
DD									
BP					.91			.92	.97
SP								.73	.91
AP						.88			
TP									
DP									.90
TOTP									

* p < .01, n = 5

Table 8

Intercorrelations* of Preawakening Measures
from Stage REM
with Postawakening EOG, EMG, and EEG Power Measures
for High Recallers

Average Measures

	Postawakening								
	EOG	EOGP	EMG	BP	SP	AP	TP	DP	TOTP
STAGE REM									
EOG					.84	.86			
EOGP					.70	.74			
EMG					-.77	-.78			
BZ				.77					
SZ				.70	.82	.81		-.96	
AZ				.84	.74			-.86	
TZ								-.78	
DZ				-.80				.84	
BD				.81					
SD					.72	.73		-.85	
AD									
TD				-.83	-.75	-.70		.78	
DD								.81	
BP				.76					
SP				.71	.81	.80		-.91	
AP				.75				-.85	
TP								-.73	
DP				-.87	-.74			.83	
TOTP				-.78					

* p < .01, n = 6

Table 9

Intercorrelations* of Preawakening Measures
from Stage REM
with Postawakening EOG, EMG, and EEG Power Measures
for Low Recallers

Average Measures

				Postawakening					
	EOG	EOGP	EMG	BP	SP	AP	TP	DP	TOTP
STAGE REM									
EOG						-.71			
EOGP	.70	.75							
EMG									
BZ									
SZ									
AZ									
TZ		-.70							
DZ									
BD									
SD									
AD						-.76	-.85		
TD									
DD									
BP									
SP									
AP									
TP		-.81							
DP									
TOTP									

* p < .01, n = 5

physiological investigation of the functional organization
and interrelation of states within and among the stages of
sleeping and waking depends critically upon the modern data
acquisition and analysis techniques of digital signal processing. Without these techniques it will not be possible
to address fundamental questions of dream psychophysiology,
whether old or new, in a quantitative manner.

Conclusion

    The apparent bankruptcy of dream psychophysiology was due
in large measure to a collection of unfortunate habits of
mind and practice. Chief among these were a single-minded
dependence on a nearly intellectually bankrupt dream psychology
and on a minimally quantitative approach to the measurement
of electrophysiological parameters. Consequently, one should
perhaps take with a certain reservation current suggestions
concerning the development of a strictly cognitive dream
psychology (2). In fact, a little thought will convince one
that psychology as phenomenology always informs psychophysiology
with meaning. It is historically unfortunate that dream
psychology has been forced to operate under the relatively
restrictive regimen of a reductionist interpretation of the
goals of dream psychophysiology. It was, and is, philo-
sophically and methodologically inappropriate. Mind predicates and physical thing predicates are not unambiguously
interchangeable. As Davidson (176) claims "there is no important sense in which psychology can be reduced to the
physical sciences" (p. 354). In other words, Foulkes and
Fiss did not have to *declare* the independence of dream
psychology from dream psychophysiology. It has always been
independent. Consequently, it seems reasonable to suggest
that the proper intellectual home of dream psychophysiology
is as much with the historical and contemporary traditions
of experimental phenomenology (see 45) as with an asemantic,
structural, cognitive, or neurocognitive dream psychology.
    Why then would one want to do dream psychophysiology?
One answer, we think, is that we know a good deal more about
the mind than about the brain. Dream psychophysiology can
help us learn about the brain, maybe. It is clearly useful
to know that the magnitude of the hemispheric asymmetries
occurring during sleeping and waking are not large. Similarly,
it has clearly helped us appreciate the limitations of traditional dream psychology in the case of lucid dreaming. More
importantly, dream psychophysiology can help in arriving at a

better understanding of some absolutely fundamental categories
of the ordinary language of science and of everyday life,
specifically "being awake," "being asleep," "waking up,"
"having a dream," "being conscious and awake," "being unconscious and asleep," "being conscious and asleep," and so
on. Modern dream psychophysiology can help to shed significant new light on our understanding of some of these archaic
categories of experience in the context of the development of
what Humphrey has called a "natural" psychology.

References

1. Foulkes, D. (1976). *A Grammar of Dreams*. New York: Basic
   Books.

   A very important book.

2. Foulkes, D. (1985). *Dreaming: A Cognitive-Psychological
   Analysis*. Hillsdale, N.J.: Lawrence Erlbaum Associates.

   An even more important book.

3. Fiss, H. (1983). "Toward a Clinically Relevant Psychology
   of Dreaming." *Hillside Journal of Clinical Psychiatry*,
   5, 147-159.

   Interesting discussion.

4. Fodor, J. (1981). "Methodological Solipsism Considered
   as a Research Strategy in Cognitive Psychology." In
   J. Haugeland (Ed.), *Mind Design: Philosophy, Psychology,
   Artificial Intelligence* (pp. 307-338). Cambridge,
   Mass.: The MIT Press.

   Difficult and provocative chapter.

5. Koella, W. (Ed.) (1981). *Sleep, 1980*. Basel: S. Karger.

6. Aserinsky, E., and Kleitman, N. (1953). "Regularly Occurring Periods of Eye Motility and Concomitant Phenomena,
   during Sleep." *Science*, *118*, 273-274.

   The early report.

7. Aserinsky, E., and Kleitman, N. (1955). "Two Types of
   Ocular Motility Occurring in Sleep." *Journal of Applied
   Physiology*, *8*, 1-10.

   A continuation of their ideas.

8. Dement, W., and Kleitman, N. (1957). "Cyclic Variations
    in EEG during Sleep and Their Relation to Eye Move-
    ments, Body Motility and Dreaming." *EEG and Clinical
    Neurophysiology, 9,* 673-690.

    Further discussion.

9. Foulkes, D. (1982). "A Cognitive-Psychological Model of
    REM Dream Production." *Sleep, 5,* 169-187.

    A very important article.

10. Foulkes, D. (1983). "Cognitive Processes during Sleep:
    An Evolutionary Perspective." In A. Mayes (Ed.),
    *Sleep Mechanisms and Functions in Humans and Animals:
    An Evolutionary Perspective* (pp. 332-353). London:
    Van Nostrand Reinhold.

    A curious article.

11. Fiss, H. (1979). "Current Dream Research: A Psychobio-
    logical Perspective." In B. Wolman (Ed.), *Handbook
    of Dreams* (pp. 20-75). New York: Van Nostrand Reinhold.

    An insightful review, with a light touch.

12. Dement, W. (1966). "The Psychophysiology of Dreaming."
    In G. Von Grunebaum and R. Callois (Eds.), *The Dream
    in Human Societies* (pp. 77-108). Los Angeles: Univer-
    sity of California Press.

13. Foulkes, D., and Vogel, G. (1974). "The Current Status
    of Laboratory Dream Research." *Psychiatric Annals, 4,*
    7-27.

14. Foulkes, D. (1978). *A Grammar of Dreams.* New York:
    Basic Books.

    See especially Chapter 5, "Psychophysiological Dream
    Research."

15. Foulkes, D. (1983). "Dream Ontogeny and Dream Psycho-
    physiology." In M. Chase and E. Weitzman (Eds.), *Ad-
    vances in Sleep Research, Vol. 8* (pp. 347-362). New
    York: Spectrum Publications.

    Another important article.

16. Rechtschaffen, A. (1973). "The Psychophysiology of Men-
    tal Activity during Sleep." In F. McGuigan and R.
    Schoonover (Eds.), *The Psychophysiology of Thinking*
    (pp. 153-205). New York: Academic Press.

    Good review.

17. Rechtschaffen, A. (1983). "Dream Psychophysiology." In
     M. Chase and E. Weitzman (Eds.), *Advances in Sleep Re-
     search, Vol. 8* (pp. 401-414). New York: Spectrum Pub-
     lications.

18. Pivik, T. (1978). "Tonic States and Phasic Events in
     Relation to Sleep Mentation." In A. Arkin, J. Antrobus,
     and S. Ellman (Eds.), *The Mind in Sleep: Psychology and
     Psychophysiology* (pp. 245-271). Hillsdale, N.J.:
     Lawrence Erlbaum Associates.

     Aptly described by Foulkes as a lucid review.

19. Foulkes, D. (1962). "Dream Reports from Different Stages
     of Sleep." *Journal of Abnormal and Social Psychology*,
     65, 14-25.

20. Foulkes, D., and Vogel, G. (1965). "Mental Activity at
     Sleep Onset." *Journal of Abnormal Psychology, 70*,
     231-243.

21. Goodenough, D. (1978). "Dream Recall: History and Cur-
     rent Status of the Field." In A. Arkin, J. Antrobus,
     and S. Ellman (Eds.), *The Mind in Sleep* (pp. 113-140).
     Hillsdale, N.J.: Lawrence Erlbaum Associates.

     Excellent article.

22. Schwartz, D.; Weinstein, L.; and Arkin, A. (1978). "Qual-
     itative Aspects of Sleep Mentation." In A. Arkin, J.
     Antrobus, and S. Ellman (Eds.), *The Mind in Sleep* (pp.
     143-241). Hillsdale, N.J.: Lawrence Erlbaum Associates.

     A long but important chapter.

23. Snyder, F. (1969). "The Physiology of Dreaming." In
     M. Kramer (Ed.), *Dream Psychology and the New Biology
     of Dreaming* (pp. 7-31). Springfield, Ill.: C.C. Thomas.

24. Dement, W. (1969). "The Biological Role of REM Sleep
     (circa 1968)." In A. Kales (Ed.), *Sleep: Physiology
     and Pathology*. Philadelphia: Lippincott.

25. Moffitt, A.; Hoffmann, R.; Wells, R.; Armitage, R.;
     Pigeau, R.; and Shearer, J. (1982). "Awakening EEG
     Correlates of Dream Reports Following Arousals from
     Different Stages of Sleep." *Psychiatric Journal of
     the University of Ottawa, 7*, 111-125.

26.   Dennett, D. (1981). *Brainstorms*. Cambridge, Mass.: MIT
      Press.

      See especially Chapter 8: "Are Dreams Experiences?"

27.   Feigl, H. (1953). "The Mind-Body Problem in the Develop-
      ment of Logical Empiricism." In H. Feigl and M. Brod-
      beck (Eds.), *Readings in the Philosophy of Science*
      (pp. 612-626). New York: Appleton-Century-Crofts.

      Foundation reading.

28.   McCarley, R. (1981). "Mind-Body Isomorphism and the
      Study of Dreams." In W. Fishbein (Ed.), *Advances in
      Sleep Research, Vol. 4* (pp. 205-238). New York: Spec-
      trum Publications.

29.   McCarley, R., and Hobson, A. (1979). "The Form of Dreams
      and the Biology of Sleep." In B. Wolman (Ed.), *Hand-
      book of Dreams* (pp. 76-130). New York: Van Nostrand
      Reinhold.

30.   Rechtschaffen, A. (1983). "Dream Psychophysiology and
      the Mind-Body Problem." In M. Chase and E. Weitzman
      (Eds.), *Advances in Sleep Research, Vol. 8* (pp. 335-
      346). New York: Spectrum Publications.

31.   Arkin, A.; Antrobus, J.; and Ellman, S. (Eds.) (1978).
      The Mind in Sleep. Hillsdale, N.J.: Lawrence Erlbaum
      Associates.

      A core book.

32.   Diamond, E. (1962). *The Science of Dreams*. Garden City,
      N.Y.: Doubleday.

33.   McCarley, R. (1983). "REM Dreams, REM Sleep, and Their
      Isomorphisms." In M. Chase and E. Weitzman (Eds.),
      Advances in Sleep Research, Vol. 8 (pp. 363-392). New
      York: Spectrum Publications.

34.   Crick, F., and Mitchison, G. (1983). "The Function of
      Dream Sleep." *Nature, 30*, 111-114.

      Devotional literature in the Church of Science.

35.   Hobson, A., and McCarley, R. (1977). "The Brain as a
      Dream State Generator: An Activation-Synthesis Hypothesis
      of the Dream Process." *American Journal of Psychiatry*,

134, 1335-1348.

You will love or hate this article. Ask yourself whether you think the title might work if the order of the major terms were reversed?

36. McCarley, R., and Hoffman, E. (1981). "REM Sleep Dreams and the Activation-Synthesis Hypothesis." *American Journal of Psychiatry*, *138*, 904-912.

37. Koukkou, M., and Lehman, D. (1983). "Dreaming: The Functional State-Shift Hypothesis." *British Journal of Psychology*, *142*, 221-231.

The best psychophysiological theory around.

38. Koukkou, M.; Lehmann, D.; and Angst, J. (Eds.) (1980). *Functional States of the Brain: Their Determinants*. Amsterdam: Elsevier/North Holland Press.

39. Lehmann, D.; Meier, B.; Meier, C.; Mita, T.; and Skrandies, W. (1983). "Sleep Onset Mentation Related to Short Epoch EEG Spectra." *Sleep Research*, *12*, 180.

40. Goldstein, L. (1979). "Some Relationships between Quantified Hemispheric EEG and Behavioral States in Man." In J. Gruzlier and P. Flor-Henry (Eds.), *Hemisphere Asymmetry of Function in Psychology* (pp. 237-254). Amsterdam: Elsevier/North-Holland Biomedical Press.

41. Goldstein, L.; Stolzfus, N.; and Gardocki, J. (1972). "Changes in Interhemispheric Amplitude Relations in EEG during Sleep." *Physiological Behavior*, *8*, 811-815.

42. Allen, M. (1983). "Models of Hemispheric Specialization." *Psychological Bulletin*, *93*, 73-104.

An important article.

43. Broughton, R. (1975). "Biorhythmic Variations in Consciousness and Psychological Function." *Canadian Psychological Review*, *16*, 217-239.

An interesting article. Notice the term "consciousness" in the title. Very rare.

44. Springer, S., and Deutsch, G. (1981). *Right Brain-Left Brain*. San Francisco: Freeman.

45. Snyder, F. (1970). "The Phenomenology of Dreaming." In L. Madow and L. Snow (Eds.), *The Psychodynamic Implica-*

tions of the Psychophysiological Studies on Dreams
(pp. 124-151). New York: C.C. Thomas.

A beautiful article. Timeless.

46. Armitage, R.; Hoffmann, R.; Moffitt, A.; and Shearer,
    J. (1985). "Ultradian Rhythms in Interhemispheric
    EEG during Sleep: A Disconfirmation of the Guild Hy-
    pothesis." *Sleep Research*, *14*, 286.

47. Antrobus, J., and Erlichman, H. (1981). "The 'Dream'
    Report: Attention, Memory, Functional Hemispheric
    Asymmetry, and Memory Organization." In W. Fishbein
    (Ed.), *Sleep, Dreams and Memory* (pp. 135-146). New
    York: Spectrum Publications.

    An important chapter.

48. Antrobus, J.; Erlichman, H.; and Weiner, M. (1978). "EEG
    Asymmetry during REM and NREM: Failure to Replicate."
    Sleep Research, *7*, 24.

49. Bertini, M.; Violani, C.; Zucolotti, P.; Antonelli, A.;
    and DiStephano, L. (1984). "Right Cerebral Activation
    in REM Sleep: Evidence from a Unilateral Tactile Recog-
    nition Test." *Psychophysiology*, *28*, 418-423.

50. Bertini, M.; Violani, C.; Zuccolotti, P.; Altomare, P.;
    Doricchi, R.; and Evangelisti, L. (1985). "Verbal and
    Spatial Tasks during Waking and upon Awakenings from
    REM and NREM." *Sleep Research*, *14*, 88.

51. Hershkowitz, M.; Turner, D.; Ware, J.; and Karacan, I.
    (1979). "Integrated Amplitude Asymmetry during Sleep."
    Sleep Research, *8*, 25.

52. Hershkowitz, M.; Ware, J.; and Karacan, I. (1980). "EEG
    Amplitude Asymmetry during Early and Late REM and NREM
    Periods." *Sleep Research*, *9*, 291.

53. Moffitt, A.; Hoffmann, E.; Wells, R.; Armitage, R.;
    Pigeau, R.; and Shearer, J. (1982). "Individual Dif-
    ferences among Pre- and Post-awakening EEG Correlates
    of Dream Reports Following Arousals from Different
    Stages of Sleep." *Psychiatric Journal of the University
    of Ottawa*, *7*, 111-125.

54. Rosekind, M.; Coates, T.; and Zarcone, V. (1979). "Lateral
    Dominance during Wakefulness, NREM Stage 2 Sleep and REM
    Sleep." *Sleep Research*, *8*, 36.

55. Pivik, R.; Blysma, F.; Busby, K.; and Sawyer, S. (1982).
     "Interhemispheric EEG Changes in Relationship to Sleep
     and Dreams in Gifted Adolescents." *Psychiatric Jour-
     nal of the University of Ottawa*, 7, 56-76.

56. Spire, J.; Jacobson, J.; Chen, C.-T.; and Cooper, M.
     (1975). "Positron Emission Tomography (PETT) in
     Sleeping Normal Humans and Narcoleptics." *Sleep Re-
     search*, 14, 285.

57. Williamson, P.; Galin, H.; and Mamelak, M. (1983). "Spec-
     tral EEG Correlates of Mentation during Sleep." *Sleep
     Research*, 12, 58.

58. Sugerman, A.; Goldstein, L.; Mayerrison, G.; and Stolzfus,
     N. (1973). "Recent Research in EEG Amplitude Analysis."
     Disorders of the Nervous System, 34, 162-166.

59. Cohen, D. (1977). "Changes in REM Dream Content during
     the Night: Implications for an Hypothesis about Changes
     in Cerebral Dominance across REM Periods." *Perceptual
     and Motor Skills*, 44, 1267-1277.

60. Kuhn, T. (1970). *The Structure of Scientific Revolutions*.
     2nd ed. Chicago: The University of Chicago Press.

     Essential for an understanding of an important view of
     the process of change in science.

61. Stewart, I., and Tall, D. (1983). *Complex Analysis: The
     Hitchhiker's Guide to the Plane*. Cambridge: Cambridge
     University Press.

     Essential reading for oneironauts.

62. Kramer, M. (1982). "The Psychology of the Dream: Art or
     Science?" *Psychiatric Journal of the University of
     Ottawa*, 7, 87-100.

     Dream science as an art form.

63. Hartmann, E. (1967). *The Biology of Dreaming*. Spring-
     field, Ill.: C.C. Thomas.

64. Hartmann, E. (1973). *The Functions of Sleep*. New Haven:
     Yale University Press.

65. Rechtschaffen, A. (1978). "The Single-Mindedness and
     Isolation of Dreams." *Sleep*, 1, 97-109.

     How many of us dream much of the time.

66. Descartes, R. (1955). "The Principles of Philosophy."
    In E. Haldane and G. Ross. *The Philosophical Works of*
    Descartes: Vol. 1 (p. 220). Cambridge, England: Dover
    Publications.

    As usual, Descartes gets it backwards: "Sum ergo cogito."

67. Malcom, N. (1959). *Dreaming*. London: Routledge & Kegan
    Paul.

    What "being awake" means to one philosopher.

68. O'Flaherty, W. (1984). *Dreams, Illusions and Other*
    Realities. Chicago: University of Chicago Press.

    Scholarship, insight, and beautiful prose.

69. Karmanova, I. (1982). *Evolution of Sleep: Stages of the*
    Formation of the 'Wakefulness-Sleep' Cycle in Verte-
    brates. Basel: Karger.

    The context for human forms of the wakefulness-sleep
    cycle. Essential reading.

70. LaBerge, S.; Nagel, L.; Dement, W.; and Zarcone, V.
    (1981). "Lucid Dreaming Verified by Volitional Com-
    munication during REM Sleep." *Perceptual and Motor*
    Skills, *52*, 727-732.

71. LaBerge, S. (1985). "The Temporal Distribution of Lucid
    Dreams." *Sleep Research*, *14*, 113.

72. Badin, P.; Harsh, J.; Balkin, T.; and Frost, M. (1985).
    "Consistency of Arousals to Signals across Nights and
    Conditions." *Sleep Research*, *14*, 118.

73. Engle-Friedman, M.; Baker, E.; and Bortzin, R. (1985).
    "Reports of Wakefulness during EEG Identified Stages of
    Sleep." *Sleep Research*, *14*, 152.

74. Kennedy, W.; Czeisler, C.; and Richardson, G. (1985).
    "Electroencephalographic Recordings at the Transition
    from Wakefulness to Sleep." *Sleep Research*, *14*, 119.

75. Ogilvie, R., and Wilkinson, R. (1985). "Behavioral
    versus EEG-based Wakefulness Discrimination of Wakeful-
    ness from Sleep." *Sleep Research*, *14*, 101.

76. Hofstadter, D. (1979). *Godel, Escher, Bach: An Eternal*
    Golden Braid. New York: Basic Books.

77. Hofstadter, D. (1985). *Metamagical Themas: Questions
     for the Essence of Mind and Pattern.* New York: Basic
     Books.

     Notice the "blah blah" theory. It applies to dreams
     as well.

78. Gyatso, T. (1975). *The Buddhism of Tibet and the Key to
     the Middle Way.* London: George Allen & Unwin.

79. Chang, G. (1974). *Teachings of Tibetan Yoga.* Secaucus,
     N.J.: The Citadel Press.

80. Brown, A. (1936). "Dreams in Which the Dreamer Knows He
     Is Asleep." *Journal of Abnormal and Social Psychology,
     31,* 59-66.

81. Evans-Wentz, W. (1958). *Tibetan Yoga and Secret Doc-
     trines.* London: Oxford University Press.

82. Faraday, A. (1972). *Dream Power.* New York: Coward,
     McCamer and Geohagen.

83. Gackenbach, J. (1978). "A Personality and Cognitive
     Style Analysis of Lucid Dreaming." Unpublished doc-
     toral dissertation, Virginia Commonwealth University.

84. Green, C. (1968). *Lucid Dreams.* Oxford: Institute of
     Psychophysical Research.

85. Tart, C. (1979). "From Spontaneous Event to Lucidity."
     In B. Wolman (Ed.), *Handbook of Dreams* (pp. 226-268).
     New York: Van Nostrand Reinhold.

86. Reed, H. (1978). "Meditation and Lucid Dreaming." *Sun-
     dance Community Dream Journal, 2,* 237-238.

87. Van Eden, F. (1972). "A Study of Dreams." In C. Tart
     (Ed.), *Altered States of Consciousness* (pp. 147-160).
     New York: Anchor Books.

88. LaBerge, S. (1979). "Lucid Dreaming: Some Personal Ob-
     servations." *Sleep Research, 8,* 153.

89. LaBerge, S. (1980). "Lucid Dreaming as a Learnable
     Skill: A Case Study." *Perceptual and Motor Skills, 51,*
     1039-1042.

90. LaBerge, S. (1980).   "Induction of Lucid Dreams." *Sleep Research, 9*, 138.

91. LaBerge, S.; Nagel, L.; Taylor, W.; Dement, W.; and Zarcone, V. (1981).   "Evidence for Lucid Dreaming during REM Sleep." *Sleep Research, 10*, 148.

92. LaBerge, S.; Nagel, L.; Taylor, W.; Dement, W.; and Zarcone, V. (1981).   "Psychophysiological Correlates of the Initiation of Lucid Dreaming." *Sleep Research, 10*, 150.

93. LaBerge, S.; Owens, J.; Nagel, L.; and Dement, W. (1981). "'This Is a Dream': Induction of Lucid Dreams by Verbal Suggestion during REM Sleep." *Sleep Research, 10*, 150.

94. LaBerge, S. (1980).   "Induction of Lucid Dreams." *Sleep Research, 9*, 138.

95. LaBerge, S. (1981).   "Lucid Dreaming: Directing the Action as It Happens." *Psychology Today, 15*, 48-57.

96. LaBerge, S.; Nagel, L.; Dement, W.; and Zarcone, V. (1981).   "Lucid Dreaming Verified by Volitional Communication during REM Sleep." *Perceptual and Motor Skills, 52*, 727-732.

97. LaBerge, S. (in press).   "The Paradox of Lucid Dreaming." In A. Alisen, A.T. Dalan, and C.S. Jordan (Eds.), *Handbook of Imagery Research and Practice*. New York: Brandon House.

98. LaBerge, S. (July 1982).   "The Paradox of Lucid Dreaming." Paper presented at the 22nd annual meeting of the Association for the Psychophysiological Study of Sleep, San Antonio, Texas.

99. LaBerge, S., and Dement, W. (July 1982).   "Voluntary Control of Respiration during Lucid REM Dreaming." Paper presented at the 22nd annual meeting of the Association for the Psychophysiological Study of Sleep, San Antonio, Texas.

100. LaBerge, S. (1985).   *Lucid Dreaming*. Los Angeles: J.P. Tarcher, Inc.

      The leading edge of a wave.

101. Covello, E. (1984). "Lucid Dreaming: A Review and Ex-
     perimental Study of Waking Intrusions during Stage
     REM Sleep." *Journal of Mind and Behavior*, 5, 81-98.

102. Dane, J. (1984). "A Comparison of Waking Instructions
     and Post-hypnotic Suggestion for Lucid Dream Induc-
     tion." Unpublished doctoral dissertation, Georgia
     State University.

103. Fenwick, P.; Schatzman, M.; Worsley, A.; and Adams, J.
     (1984). "Lucid Dreaming: Correspondence between
     Dreamed and Actual Events in One Subject during REM
     Sleep." *Biological Psychology*, 18, 243-252.

104. Gillespie, G. (1984). "Problems Related to Experimenta-
     tion while Dreaming Lucidly." *Lucidity Letter*, 3,
     1-3.

105. Hearne, K.A. (1981). "'Light-Switch Phenomenon' in
     Lucid Dreams." *Journal of Mental Imagery*, 5, 97-100.

106. Hearne, K. (1983). "Lucid Dream Induction." *Journal
     of Mental Imagery*, 7, 19-23.

107. Tholey, P. (1983). "Techniques for Inducing and Manipu-
     lating Lucid Dreams." *Perceptual and Motor Skills*,
     57, 79-90.

108. Ogilvie, R.; Hunt, H.; Tyson, P.; Lucescu, M.; and
     Jeakins, D. (1982). "Lucid Dreaming and Alpha Activi-
     ty: A Preliminary Report." *Perceptual and Motor
     Skills*, 55, 795-808.

109. Fodor, J. (1983). *Representations: Philosophical Essays
     on the Foundations of Cognitive Science*. Cambridge,
     Mass.: MIT Press.

110. Gibson, J. (1970). "On the Relation between Hallucina-
     tions and Perception." *Leonardo*, 3, 425-427.

111. Gibson, J. (1977). "The Theory of Affordances." In
     R. Shaw and J. Bransford (Eds.), *Perceiving, Acting
     and Knowing* (pp. 67-82). Hillsdale, N.J.: Lawrence
     Erlbaum Associates.

112. Gibson, J. (1979). *The Ecological Approach to Visual
     Perception*. Boston, Mass.: Houghton Mifflin.

113. Haugeland, J. (1981). *Mind Design*. Cambridge, Mass.: MIT Press.

114. Kitchener, K. (1983). "Cognition, Meta-cognition and Epistemic Cognition." *Human Development, 26*, 222-232.

115. Marcel, A. (1983). "Conscious and Unconscious Perception: An Approach to the Relations between Phenomenal Experience and Perceptual Processes." *Cognitive Psychology, 15*, 238-300.

116. Shepard, R. (1984). "Ecological Constraints on Internal Representation: Resonant Kinematics of Perceiving, Imagining, Thinking and Dreaming." *Psychological Review, 91*, 417-447.

117. Herman, J.; Barker, D.; and Roffwarg, H. (1983). "Similarity of Eye Movement Characteristics in REM Sleep and the Awake State." *Psychophysiology, 20*, 537-543.

118. Herman, J.; Erman, J.; Boys, R.; Peiser, L.; Taylor, M.; and Roffwarg, H. (1984). "Evidence for a Directional Correspondence between Eye Movements and Dream Imagery in REM." *Sleep, 7*, 52-63.

119. Moskowitz, E., and Berger, R. (1969). "Rapid Eye Movements and Dream Imagery: Are They Related?" *Nature, 224*, 613-614.

120. Bremer, G.; Smith, J.; and Karacan, I. (1970). "Automatic Detection of the K-complex in Sleep Electroencephalograms." *IEEE (Institute of Electrical and Electronics Engineers, Inc.) Transactions on Biomedical Engineering, 4*, 314-323.

121. Burser, D. (1980). "Analysis of Electrophysiological Signals: A Comparative Study of Two Algorithms." *Computers and Biomedical Research, 3*, 73-86.

122. Degler, H.; Smith, J.; and Black, F. (1979). "Automatic Detection and Resolution of Synchronous Rapid Eye Movements." *Computers and Biomedical Research, 8*, 393-404.

123. Feinberg, J.; March, G.; Fein, T.; Floyd, J.; Walker, J.; and Price, L. (1978). "Period and Amplitude Analysis of 0.5 - 3 c/sec Activity in NREM Sleep of Young Adults." *Electroencephalography and Clinical Neurophysiology, 44*, 202-213.

124. Feinberg, I.; Fein, G.; and Floyd, T. (1980). "Period
      and Amplitude Analysis of NREM EEG in Sleep: Repeata-
      bility of Results in Young Adults." *Electroencephal-
      ography and Clinical Neurophysiology, 48*, 212-221.

125. Frost, J.; Hillman, C.; and Kellaway, P. (1980). "Auto-
      matic Interpretation of EEG: Analysis of Background
      Activity." *Computers and Biomedical Research, 13*,
      242-257.

126. Larsen, L., and Walter, D. (1970). "On Automatic
      Methods of Sleep Staging by EEG Spectra." *Electro-
      encephalography and Clinical Neurophysiology, 28*,
      459-467.

127. Gaillard, J., and Tissot, R. (1973). "Principles of
      Automatic Analysis of Sleep Records with a Hybrid
      System." *Computers and Biomedical Research, 6*, 1-13.

128. Hoffmann, R.; Moffitt, A.; Shearer, J.; Sussman, P.;
      and Wells, R. (1979). "Conceptual and Methodological
      Considerations towards the Development of Computer-
      controlled Research on the Electrophysiology of Sleep."
      Waking Sleeping, 3, 1-16.

129. Itil, T. (1969). "Digital Computer 'Sleep Prints' and
      Psychopharmacology." *Biological Psychiatry, 1*, 91-95.

130. Itil, T. (1970). "Digital Computer Analysis of the
      Electroencephalogram during Rapid Eye Movement Sleep
      State in Man." *Journal of Nervous and Mental Diseases,
      150*, 201-208.

      Suggests the possibility that dreaming is associated
      with specific quantitative patterns of tonic EEG during
      stage REM.

131. Itil, T. (1977). "Computer Analysis of Sleep EEG in
      Psychiatry." *Waking and Sleeping, 1*, 343-357.

132. Kay, C.; Pickworth, W.; Neidert, G.; Falcone, D.;
      Fishman, P.; and Othmer, E. (1979). "Opioid Effects
      on Computer-derived Sleep and EEG Parameters in Non-
      dependent Human Addicts." *Sleep, 2*, 175-191.

      An interesting example of wave-form stripping.

133. Ktonas, P.; Luoh, W.; Kejariwal, M.; Reilly, E.; and
      Seward, M. (1981). "Computer Aided Quantification

of EEG Spike and Sharp Wave Characteristics." *Electro-encephalography and Clinical Neurophysiology, 51,* 237-243.

134. Ktonas, P., and Gosalia, A. (1981). "Spectral Analysis *vs* Period Analysis of Narrowband EEG Activity: A Comparison Based on the Sleep Delta Frequency Band." *Sleep, 4,* 193-206.

Quantifies some ambiguities inherent in spectral analysis.

135. Ktonas, P., and Smith, J. (1976). "A Software Package." *Computers and Biomedical Research, 9,* 109-124.

136. Laird, C., and Burger, D. (1979). "System for Studying the Delta Rhythm during Sleep and Its Topographical Amplitude Distribution." *Electroencephalography and Clinical Neurophysiology, 47,* 115-118.

137. Martin, W.; Johnson, L.; Viglione, S.; Naitoh, P.; Joseph, R.; and Moses, J. (1972). "Pattern Recognition of EEG-EOG as a Technique for All-Night Sleep Stage Scoring." *Electroencephalography and Clinical Neurophysiology, 32,* 417-427.

138. Pigeau, R.; Hoffmann, R.; and Moffitt, A. (1981). "A Multivariate Comparison between Two EEG Analysis Techniques: Period Analysis and Fast Fourier Transform." *Electroencephalography and Clinical Neurophysiology, 52,* 656-659.

139. Roessler, R.; Collins, F.; and Ostman, R. (1970). "A Period Analysis Classification of Sleep Stages." *Electroencephalography and Clinical Neurophysiology, 29,* 358-362.

140. Saletu, B.; Itil, T.; Saletu, M.; Klingenberg, H.; and Akpinar, S. (1973). "Computer Sleep Stage Classification in Relation to Physiological Measures." In U. Jovanovic (Ed.), *The Nature of Sleep.* Stuttgart: Fischer-Verlag.

142. Smith, J.; Karacan, I.; and Yang, M. (1978). "Automated Analysis of Human Sleep EEG." *Waking and Sleeping, 2,* 75-82.

143. Smith, J.; Karacan, I.; and Yang, M. (1979). "Automated

Measurement of Alpha, Beta, Sigma and Theta Burst Characteristics." *Sleep*, *1*, 435-443.

144. Smith, J.; Karacan, I.; and Yang, M. (1978). "Automated Analysis of Human Sleep EEG." *Waking and Sleeping*, *2*, 75-82.

145. Smith, J.; Funke, W.; Yeo, W.; and Ambuehl, R. (1975). "Detection of Human Sleep EEG Waveforms." *Electroencephalography and Clinical Neurophysiology*, *38*, 435-437.

146. Su, S., and Smith, J. (1974). "Micro and Macro Analysis of Sleep Data Using Hybrid and Digital Computers." *Computers and Biomedical Research*, *7*, 432-448.

147. Basar, E. (1976). *Biophysical and Physiological Systems Analysis*. Reading, Mass.: Addison-Wesley.

     Necessary reading for those interested in brain dynamics, waking, and sleeping.

148. Basar, E. (1980). *EEG-Brain Dynamics*. Amsterdam: Elsevier/North-Holland Biomedical Press.

     Scholarly, technical, and imaginative.

149. Brazier, M. (1961). "Computer Techniques in EEG Analysis." *Electroencephalography and Clinical Neurophysiology*, *13* (Supplement 20).

150. Brigham, O. (1974). *Fast Fourier Transform*. Englewood Cliffs, N.J.: Prentice-Hall.

     A good place to start if you don't understand fast Fourier transforms.

151. Gottman, J. (1981). *Time-Series Analysis*. London: Cambridge University Press.

     Important analytic tools and concepts.

152. Johnson, L. (1972). "Computers in Sleep Research." In M. Chase (Ed.), *The Sleeping Brain*. Los Angeles: Brain Information Services, U.C.L.A.

153. Niedermeyer, E. (1982). "The Normal EEG of the Waking Adult." In E. Niedermeyer and F. Lopes da Silva (Eds.), *Electroencephalography* (pp. 71-92). Munich: Urban & Schwarzenberg.

     Everything you wanted to know about EEG.

154. Oppenheim, A., and Schafer, R. (1975). *Digital Signal Processing*. Englewood Cliffs, N.J.: Prentice-Hall.

155. Hoffmann, R.; Moffitt, A.; Wells, R.; Sussman, P.; Pigeau, R.; and Shearer, J. (1984). "Quantitative Descriptions of Sleep-Stage Electrophysiology Using Digital Period Analytic Techniques." *Sleep*, 7, 356-364.

156. Ogilvie, R.; Hunt, H.; Sawicki, C.; and McGowan, K. (1978). "Searching for Lucid Dreams." *Sleep Research*, 7, 165.

157. Ogilvie, R.; Hunt, H.; Tyson, P.; Lucescu, M.; and Jeakins, D. (July 1982). "Alpha Activity and Lucid Dreams." Paper presented at the 22nd annual meeting of the Association for the Psychophysiological Study of Sleep, San Antonio, Texas.

158. Ogilvie, R.; Hunt, H.; Tyson, P.; Lucescu, M.; and Jeakins, D. (1982). "Lucid Dreaming and Alpha Activity: A Preliminary Report." *Perceptual and Motor Skills*, 55, 795-808.

159. Ogilvie, R.; Hunt, H.; Kushniruk, A.; and Newman, J. (July 1983). "Lucid Dreams and the Arousal Continuum." Paper presented at the 4th International Congress of Sleep Research, Bologna, Italy. (Also in *Lucidity Letter*, 2, 1-2.)

160. Tyson, P.; Ogilvie, R.; and Hunt, H. (1984). "Lucid, Prelucid and Nonlucid Dreams Related to the Amount of EEG Alpha Activity during REM Sleep." *Psychophysiology*, 21, 442-451.

161. Polanyi, M. (1964). *Personal Knowledge: Towards a Post-critical Philosophy*. New York: Harper & Row.

162. Pynchon, T. (1973). *Gravity's Rainbow*. New York: Viking Press.

163. Chen, C. (1982). *Nonlinear Maximum Entropy Spectral Analysis Methods for Signal Recognition*. New York: Research Studies Press.

164. Gardner, F. (1979). *Phaselock Techniques*. New York: John Wiley & Sons.

165. Rabiner, L., and Gold, B. (1975). *Theory and Application of Digital Signal Processing.* Englewood Cliffs, N.J.: Prentice-Hall.

166. Simonsen, E.; Thomas, C.; and Wildschiedtz, G. (1985). "Computerized Classification of EEG Using Power Spectrum Analysis and Unsupervised Learning." *Sleep Research, 14,* 284.

167. Loomis, A.; Harvey, E.; and Hobart, G. (1937). "Cerebral States during Sleep as Studied by Human Brain Potentials." *Journal of Experimental Psychology, 21,* 127-144.

168. Rechtschaffen, A., and Kales, A. (Eds.). (1968). *A Manual of Standardized Terminology. Techniques and Scoring System for Sleep Stages of Human Subjects.* National Institute of Health Publication No. 204. Washington, D.C.: United States Government Printing Office.

      A must for the potential sleep researcher.

169. Lehmann, D., and Koukkou, M. (1980). "Classes of Spontaneous Private Experiences and Ongoing Human EEG Activity." In G. Pfurtscheller, P. Breser, F. Lopez da Dilva, and H. Petsche (Eds.), *Rhythmic EEG Activities and Cortical Functioning* (pp. 289-297). Amsterdam: Elsevier.

170. Lehmann, D., and Koukkou, M. (1974). "Computer Analysis of EEG Wakefulness-Sleep Patterns during Learning of Novel and Familiar Sentences." *Electroencephalography and Clinical Neurophysiology, 37,* 73-84.

171. Lehmann, D.; Koukkou, M.; and Andreae, L. (1981). "Classes of Day Dream Mentation and EEG Power Spectra." *Sleep Research, 10,* 151.

172. Koukkou, M., and Lehmann, D. (1980). "Brain Functional States: Determinants, Constraints and Implications." In M. Koukkou, D. Lehmann, and J. Angst (Eds.), *Functional States of the Brain: Their Determinants* (pp. 13-20). Amsterdam: Elsevier.

      An important article in an important book.

173. Lehmann, D. (1980). "Fluctuations of Functional State: EEG Patterns and Perceptual and Cognitive Strategies."

In M. Koukkou, D. Lehmann, and J. Angst (Eds.), *Functional States of the Brain: Their Determinants* (pp. 189-202). Amsterdam: Elsevier.

174. Lehmann, D.; Dumermuth, G.; Lange, B.; and Meier, C. (1981). "Dream Recall Related to EEG Spectral Power during REM Periods." *Sleep Research, 10,* 151.

175. Lehmann, D., and Koukkou, M. (1981). "Dream Formation in a Psychophysiological Model: A State-change Theory." In W. Koella (Ed.), *Sleep, 1980* (pp. 170-174). Basel: S. Karger.

176. Davidson, D. (1981). "The Material Mind." In J. Haugeland (Ed.), *Mind Design: Philosophy, Psychology, Artificial Intelligence* (pp. 339-354). Cambridge, Mass.: MIT Press.

177. Humphrey, N. (1983). *Consciousness Regained.* Oxford: Oxford University Press.

Worth reading.

Chapter 6

RECALLING DREAMS: AN EXAMINATION OF
DAILY VARIATION AND INDIVIDUAL DIFFERENCES

Kathryn Belicki

With the development of sleep monitoring technology came
several surprises concerning the nature of sleep and dreams.
One of these was the realization that we experience many more
dreams than we typically recall. For example, the average
adult when awakened from rapid eye movement (REM) sleep will
report dreams about 80% of the time (1). In addition, it is
now accepted that dreaming also occurs to some extent during
non-rapid eye movement (NREM) sleep (2). However, despite
the frequent experience of dreaming, surveys conducted by
Belicki (3) and others (4) have found that people at home
only recall, on average, between two and three dreams a week.
The mystery of why we tend to forget dreams has been
studied for several decades. One major issue which has been
addressed is whether our inability to recall dreams is due to
problems in transferring the experience *into* memory (impaired
encoding) or in retrieving it *from* memory. This issue is
based upon a theory of memory which suggests that the act of
remembering involves three phases: encoding (the transfer of
information into memory), storage (the organization of information in memory), and retrieval (successfully recalling information from storage). Cohen (5) and Goodenough (1) have re-
viewed in detail the literature pertaining to this issue of
dream forgetting, and while these two researchers draw slightly
different conclusions, they concur that a probable reason for
dream recall failure is an inability to retrieve dream experiences which have been stored in memory.
Goodenough has further contended that this retrieval problem is not specific merely to dreams but reflects a general
difficulty related to the memory of experiences during sleep.
He noted that studies have shown that we have difficulty recalling other experiences (such as experimental tasks) which
occur either during sleep or in periods of brief wakefulness.
In order for experiences to be stored in a retrievable form,
he hypothesized that active cognitive processing is required--

processing which is impaired by sleep. Given, then, that
forgetting may be a natural consequence of sleep, a question
which becomes of interest is why do we occasionally remember
dreams? It is this question that the remainder of this chapter will address.

When we turn our attention to dream recall, it becomes
apparent there are two somewhat different phenomena which
need to be explained. The first is a question of within subject or *intraindividual* variation in recall. Specifically,
within an individual, why are dreams recalled following some
nights and not others? In addition to this issue there also
exist differences across people in terms of the number of
dreams they typically recall (a question of *interindividual*
variation). While "average" recall, based on a calculated
mean, appears to be two to three dreams a week, some people
never recall dreams, while others fairly consistently remember
several a night. What accounts for such differences?

Unequivocal answers do not exist for either question.
However, there is greater agreement among investigators concerning explanations for within individual fluctuations in
recall than for between individual differences. Therefore,
we will first examine the issue of daily variation in recall
and then consider the more controversial issue concerning
differences across people in quantity of recall.

Intraindividual Differences (Daily Variation) in Recall

Four classes of variables have been identified which may
account for dreams being recalled following one night and not
another: the conditions of awakening, the individual's motivation to recall dreams, the characteristics of the dream experience, and life stress.

Conditions of awakening. Webb and Kersey (4) have argued
that the simplest explanation for variability is the stage of
sleep from which a person awakens. Specifically, they suggest that if individuals awaken from REM sleep they are much
more likely to recall a dream than if they awaken from NREM
sleep. While decades of laboratory experience have confirmed
that dream recall is more frequent following REM than NREM
awakenings, nevertheless, one study (6), which duplicated
home awakening (alarm clock) conditions in a laboratory,
found that even when subjects awoke from NREM sleep they often
were able to report dreams. Therefore, awakening from REM
may facilitate remembering dreams but is not the only factor
accounting for recall.

Another factor is the degree of attention people pay to
their dreams immediately upon awakening. Specifically, if we

are distracted by other concerns, or by events in the environment, we are less likely to recall dreams. The most direct evidence for the deleterious effects of distraction or inattention comes from a study by Cohen and Wolfe (7). These investigators compared the dream recall of subjects who were instructed to immediately telephone the Weather Bureau upon awakening to that of subjects who lay quietly in bed. The simple distraction of calling the Weather Bureau dramatically reduced subjects' abilities to recollect dream content.

Motivation. It has been my experience that when people who only infrequently recall dreams participate in a study of dreaming, they become more interested in the phenomenon of dreaming and subsequently recall more dreams even when increased recall is not the intention of the research. Cartwright (8) reported a similar phenomenon in an investigation of 28 poor recallers whose ability to recall dreams increased as a function of their participation.

A study by Reed (9) suggests that motivation may facilitate recall by increasing attention to dreams postawakening. He described the observations of 17 students who as part of a course attempted to increase their recall. These subjects felt that their recall was best on days when they were motivated to remember and poorest on days when motivation was low due to other preoccupations.

Characteristics of the dream experience. In terms of dream experience two factors have been examined: the time of dream occurrence and the qualities of the experience. Dreams which occur toward the end of the night are more easily recalled than dreams occurring early in the night (10;11;12). An example of a study demonstrating this phenomenon is one conducted by Meier, Rueff, Ziegler, and Hall (11). These investigators studied one man who slept in a laboratory for 50 consecutive nights. He was awakened several times per night in order to obtain dream reports. In addition, each morning he was asked to re-recall the dreams he had reported during the night. One of the factors predicting whether or not he could re-recall a dream was the time of occurrence: dreams occurring later were more likely to be recalled.

A second finding of the Meier et al. study addresses the other relevant factor—the qualities of the dream experience. Specifically, dreams that were longer or of high intensity were better re-recalled than short and/or low intensity dreams. Consistent with the first finding, there is considerable concurrence that longer dreams are more likely to be re-recalled than shorter dreams (11;12). However, the results are mixed concerning the effect of dream salience on re-recall. (The term "dream salience" refers to the vividness and intensity of the experience.) While Trinder and Kramer (12) found that

dramatically intense dreams were better recalled than those
less intense, Baekeland and Lasky (10) did not observe such a
relationship. A further problem in drawing conclusions from
these studies is the limitations of their samples: Meier et
al. studied only one man, Trinder and Kramer 14 male war
veterans (who were emotionally disturbed), and Baekeland and
Lasky 20 males.

   Life stress. There are mixed feelings concerning the impact of stress on dream recall frequency. Naturalistic studies
which have examined naturally occurring stress have found that
dream recall increases in difficult times. For example, Cartwright (13) in a survey of 167 women found that they reported
increased "dreaming" following stressful events. Similarly,
Cohen (14) compared subjects' dream recall following nights
they rated themselves as low in self-confidence rather than
high in self-confidence. Dream recall was greater following
the low self-confidence night (particularly in subjects who
typically recalled dreams infrequently). A major limitation of
both these investigations is that they studied only women;
as gender differences are fairly common in dream research
(e.g., Spanos, Stam, Radtke, and Nightingale [15]), we cannot
assume these findings would hold true of men.

   In contrast to the above results, studies which have
experimentally induced stress by having subjects watch a presleep film (summarized in Goodenough [1]) or participate in
assertiveness training (16) tend to observe either no effect
on recall or a subsequent decrease. Both Segall (16) and
Goodenough (1) interpret a decrease in recall as being caused
by anxiety distracting the individual from thoughts of their
dreams.

   The discrepancy between the findings from naturalistic
versus experimental studies may be due to several factors
(including sampling differences). The most important reason
may be that the stress invoked by the experimental manipulations is likely quite different from the naturalistic stress
studied by Cartwright and Cohen. For example, it was not
clear to what degree Segall's assertiveness training was
stressful; similarly, stressful films may agitate and arouse
subjects (and therefore distract them from their dreams)
but not truly disturb or threaten them.

   Taking all the data together, I think we can tentatively
conclude that at least in women there exists a tendency to
recall more dreams during times of upset. Why this would be
the case is, of course, another question. Perhaps at such
times dreams are more salient (and therefore memorable), or
it could simply be that sleep is more disrupted resulting in
more awakenings (and therefore more opportunities for recall).

Summary. It would seem that awakening from REM sleep increases the likelihood of recalling a dream, as does paying
immediate attention to the dream upon awakening. Being motivated to recall dreams appears to facilitate postsleep attention and therefore improves recall. On the other hand, being
distracted, either externally by environmental events or
internally by competing preoccupations or concerns, decreases
the likelihood of recall. In addition, there is some evidence
(with men) that salient dreams are better recalled, particularly if they occur late in the night. Further, dream recall
may increase, at least in women, during times of upset. However, by now it will probably be clear to the reader that all
of these conclusions must be accepted with some caution due
to the small number of studies addressing each issue and the
methodological limitations of the research. When we turn
our attention to interindividual variation (differences across
people) in typical dream recall, even less can be concluded
with confidence.

Interindividual Differences in Recall

There are great differences across people in the number
of dreams typically recalled. By way of illustration, Table 10
summarizes the survey results from two studies in which I
asked undergraduate university students from a range of academic disciplines to estimate the number of dreams they
typically recalled in the prior year. While most people reported one to three dreams per week, a sizeable number reported
never recalling dreams (15.6% and 16.8% respectively for the
two studies), while a few (3.4% and 5.9% reported remembering
more than one dream a night, ranging up to four dreams a
night).

As a matter of convenience, explanations for such variations in recall can be divided into two groups. The first
group states that a subset of the factors which account for
daily fluctuations in recall are sufficient to account for
differences among people in typical recall. The second group
turns to other factors, specifically personality and ability
variables, to explain recall differences.

Turning to the first group, it has been argued, for example, that frequent recallers awaken more often from REM
sleep (4). While a reasonable hypothesis, it has not been
thoroughly investigated. There is some evidence (summarized
in Goodenough [1]) that frequent recallers spend slightly more
time in REM, although they have the same number of REM periods
as infrequent recallers. However, such small differences in

Table 10

Distribution of Dream Recall Frequency
in Subjects Asked to Estimate the Number of
Dreams They Typically Recalled per Week

Number of Dreams	Study 1 (436 subjects) % of sample	Study 2 (392 subjects) % of sample
0	15.6	16.8
1	26.6	24.2
2	25.2	24.7
3	18.1	13.3
4	3.9	5.4
5	6.2	8.2
6	0.9	1.5
7	0.7	2.8
8-28	2.8	3.1

REM time seem insufficient to account for the rather dramatic differences in dream recall. Further, as already noted, Wiesz and Foulkes (6) demonstrated that dreams can be recalled following alarm clock awakenings from NREM sleep. In addition, Cohen (5) presented tentative data suggesting that frequent (in contrast to infrequent) recallers are particularly adept at recalling dreams from NREM sleep. If replicable, his finding suggests that stage of awakening may not be important to this group as they may be able to recall almost as well from NREM as REM sleep.

Another hypothesis, for which there is stronger support, is that frequent recallers may be more highly motivated to recall their dreams (and therefore pay closer postsleep attention to them). For example, Cernovsky (17) in a recent study found a significant relationship between frequency of dream recall and motivation to recall dreams. Interestingly, however, the author argued that the size of the relationship was small and insufficient to account fully for recall differences. This is consistent with the findings from a study I recently completed which examined the responses of 200 undergraduates to an eight-item questionnaire assessing both attention to dreams upon awakening and, more generally, motivation to recall dreams. Although subjects' estimates of dream recall were correlated significantly with their scores on the motivation scale, the relationship was small ($r = .23$). One must be cautious about drawing conclusions from small relationships as they may reflect unreliable or invalid measures. However, while frequent recallers appear to be more motivated to recall dreams, it has not been established that motivation is sufficient to account for their increased recall.

The previous two hypotheses (concerning motivation and stage of awakening) have received only minimal research attention. In contrast, considerable research has been directed toward examining the hypothesis that frequent recallers have more salient or memorable dreams than infrequent recallers. A major problem in investigating this issue is that it is very difficult to validly assess the salience of dream content. This is a difficult task when comparing one dream to another from the same individual, as described above with the studies comparing dreams collected during the night with dreams re-recalled in the morning. It is even more difficult when we are attempting to compare one person's dreams to another's. In order to make such comparisons the quality of dream reports must be equal so that any differences that exist among dream reports can be attributed to the dreaming experience.

Unfortunately, several factors other than the dream itself may differentially influence measures of dream content. For example, the reporting or narration skills of the dreamer will

affect the quality of dream reports: an individual who is
skilled at describing experiences may inadvertently present
a more salient report than one who has great difficulty
describing events. Second, Goodenough (1) has pointed out
that quality of recall will likely influence the salience of
reports: presumably a dream well recalled will be described
more saliently than a dream only dimly remembered.

Finally, some research I conducted with Patricia Bowers
(18) demonstrated that personality can affect the way people
rate and describe their experiences. Our work followed up an
investigation by Spanos and his colleagues (15) which found
that a personality trait of Absorption (which reflects the
tendency to become very involved and engrossed in fantasy and
aesthetic stimuli, such as movies) was correlated both with
dream recall and the tendency to rate dreams saliently.
Spanos et al. interpreted their findings to indicate that frequent recallers (and Absorbers) had more salient dreams than
infrequent recallers. In our study we explored an alternative
hypothesis: that Absorbers are inclined to exaggerate the
salience of their experiences. We did not think this was
deliberate exaggeration but an inadvertent one caused by de-
voting such intense attention to their experiences.

To test this hypothesis, we conducted two studies, each
with 100 undergraduate students. Each subject completed an
inventory of Absorption, rated the salience of their dreams
on several five-point scales (measuring dream vividness, emo-
tionality, activity, and bizarreness), and then listened to
a tape-recorded story ("The Oval Portrait" by Edgar Allan Poe),
which they subsequently rated on the same scales of salience
on which they scored their dreams. We then compared the
ratings of their dreams with their ratings of the standardized
event (the story). If such ratings vividly tap the qualities
of the event being rated there should be no correlation between these two sets of ratings. If, on the other hand, as
we hypothesized, Absorbers are inclined to exaggerate all
their experiences, ratings of the story and of dreams would
be significantly correlated with each other, and both would
be correlated with Absorption. (For the reader unfamiliar
with statistics, correlation coefficients range in value from
zero to minus or plus one with zero indicating no relationship
between two variables and one indicating a perfect relationship.) As apparent in Table 11 the findings supported our
hypotheses, suggesting that if a high and low Absorber were
to both hypothetically experience the same dream, the high
absorber would likely rate it more saliently.

It is a consistent finding that frequent recallers rate
their dreams more saliently than do infrequent recallers (5;
18;19;20). However, given the preceding concerns, it is not

Table 11

Correlations among Absorption, Ratings of
Dream Salience, and Ratings of
Story Salience in Two Studies

	Absorption	Ratings of Dream Salience	Ratings of Story Salience
Absorption	-	.41**	.33*
Ratings of Dream Salience	.52**	-	.35**
Ratings of Story Salience	.28*	.30*	-

*p < .01   ** p < .001

Note: Findings from the first study are above the diagonal,
      findings from the second are below.

clear what this finding means. It could merely be that frequent recallers have qualitatively better memories of their
dreams (1) or that they pay closer attention and become more
absorbed in the memory of their dreams and in so doing inflate
the salience of their experience. Clearly, frequent recallers
rate (and presumably experience) their dreams saliently: what
remains unanswered is whether this is due to the content of
their dreams or due to their memory and/or subjective perception of that content.

   Personality and ability factors in recall. Several investigators have suggested that to fully account for differences
among people in recall, we need to consider stable personality
or ability characteristics which may increase the likelihood
of remembering (or forgetting) dreams. There have been many
studies addressing a variety of hypotheses. This section will
review only the major issues which have been examined.

   One of the earliest popular hypotheses concerning personality and dream recall derived from Schonbar's study (21) in
1959 which observed strong relationships between dream recall
and defensive style; specifically, on pencil and paper
measures, high recallers tended to be more anxious whereas
low recallers showed greater tendencies toward repression.
This study occurred at a time when investigators were clearly
preoccupied with explaining dream *forgetting*, and led to the
hypothesis that infrequent recallers repressed memories of
their dreams. However, the studies that followed produced
findings which either contradicted or only mildly supported
this hypothesis (7;16;19); Cohen (5;22) offers excellent
critical reviews of this literature. Recently there has been
renewed interest in the possibility that defensive style may
affect dream recall, with proponents arguing that better
measures of defensive style need to be employed (23;24) in
order to observe a relationship with recall.

   Another factor which has been examined is subjects' memory
ability. While tests of general memory do not appear to distinguish frequent from infrequent recallers (summarized in
Cory, Ormiston, Simmel, and Dainoff [19]), it is possible that
specific types of memory are. For example, memory for visual
material has been examined both by Cohen (25) and Cory et
al. (19). Cohen found no relationship between dream recall
and visual memory; however, Cory et al. in a more extensive
study did obtain a significant relationship.

   In a different vein, Sehulster (26), in a factor analytic
study of people's perceptions of their memory, found memory
for dreams to be unrelated to a factor tapping factual memory
(such as the capacity for studying and memorization) but related to a factor assessing memory of feelings, smells, and
personal events from the past. Unfortunately, he did not

include in his survey memory for visual material, so we do
not know to what extent, if any, visual memory might overlap
with his factor of memory for personal and sensory experiences.

Weighing the three studies together, we are able to conclude with reasonable confidence that dream recall is unrelated
to general memory capacity; however, it is possibly related
to specific types of memory such as for images and for personal or sensory experiences.

A third major area which has been examined is subjects'
cognitive style (style of thinking), specifically, the tendency to use imagery and creative processes while awake.
There are at least two reasons why such a cognitive style
might facilitate recall. Creative and imaginative individuals
may be more interested in and therefore motivated to recall
dreams (5). Additionally, it is well established in the memory
literature that we can more easily remember events or material
which are consistent with the way we view and think about the
world. Dreams would presumably be more consistent with the
waking thoughts of individuals who typically make use of
imagery and fantasy, and therefore would be more easily recalled.

The earliest support for this hypothesis was a study by
Schechter, Schmeidler, and Staal (27) which found that arts
majors tended to recall more dreams than science majors, who
in turn recalled more dreams than engineering students. Further, Hiscock and Cohen (28) and Richardson (29) have found
small but significant correlations between dream recall and
subjects' ratings of the vividness of their waking imagery.
In work with P. Bowers (3) I have found correlations between
dream recall and creative interests, the ability to control
dreams, and the ability to fall asleep effortlessly and at
will. Finally, a relationship between dream recall and hypnotic ability has been observed by Spanos et al. (15) and by
Belicki and P. Bowers (3). For the reader unfamiliar with
the concept of hypnotizability, stable differences exist among
people in the ability to be hypnotized. It is not fully
understood what accounts for such differences, but high hyp-
notizables seem to more readily employ fantasy in their
waking lives: specifically, they report more vivid imagery on
tests of imagery ability (30), more readily become absorbed
in fantasy-like experiences (30), and are more creative (31).
Thus, there seems to be considerable evidence that frequent
recallers tend to be more imaginative and creative than infrequent recallers.

We have considered several variables which may facilitate
or impede recalling dreams. However, a major problem that
exists with all the research on personality and ability factors is that the observed relationships tend to be disappoint-

ingly small. One possible reason for this state of affairs
is that it has been widely assumed that differences among
people in dream recall are stable differences, consistent
over time. However, in my early research when I regularly
asked subjects to estimate their typical weekly dream recall,
many individuals would insist they did not have a typical
amount of recall, that their recall fluctuated dramatically
from one time period to the next. Clearly, it would be inappropriate to expect stable factors such as ability and personality to correlate with recall in people whose quantity
of recall varies from one week to the next. Perhaps by excluding such people from analyses, higher correlations could
be obtained between dream recall and personality or ability
variables.

     To examine this possibility, I conducted with P. Bowers
(3) a study of 100 undergraduates (70 men and 30 women) in
which I examined the relationship of several variables known
to correlate with hypnotic ability (listed in Table 12). In
addition to estimating their recall, I had subjects rate the
consistency of their recall over time on a five-point scale
from one "extremely variable" to five "quite stable" with the
midpoint labelled "somewhat variable." Only 46 of the subjects rated their consistency as three or higher, and these
were designated (on the basis of a median split) as having a
consistent style; the remaining 54 were designated as having
an inconsistent style. We predicted that stronger relationships would be obtained between personality and dream recall
within the subsample of consistent subjects than within inconsistent subjects. As evident in Table 12 the findings were
consonant with our hypotheses. To further illustrate this
pattern, stepwise multiple regressions were calculated within
each group. (Multiple regressions estimate the relationship
between a single variable and a group of variables yielding a
value between zero and positive one, which is interpreted in
a similar fashion to correlation coefficients.) Before
dividing the sample, the multiple R was equal to .44, which
while statistically significant, was again quite low. In
contrast, when divided into subgroups, the consistent group
obtained an R of .80, while the inconsistent group yielded a
nonsignificant R of .37, indicating that personality was much
more strongly related to recall within the consistent group.

Summary and Future Directions

     The study above describing consistency of recall would
suggest that we should divide people into at least two groups:
individuals with a consistent style of frequent and infrequent

Table 12

Correlations of Dream Recall
with Personality Measures within Consistent
and Inconsistent Subjects

Name of Measure	Description of Measure	Entire Sample	Subsample of Consistent Subjects	Subsample of Inconsistent Subjects
Tellegen & Atkinson Absorption	Measures the tendency to experience states, without the aid of hypnosis, which are similar to those achieved in hypnosis.	.42**	.54**	.27
Effortless Experiencing	Measures the ability to effortlessly imagine upon request specific images and scenes. This measure correlates reliably with creativity.	.17	.24	.15
Creative Interests	Measures subjects' self-assessment of their creativity and their degree of participation in, and enjoyment of, creative activities.	.29*	.46**	.21
Evans' Control of Sleep	Measures the ability to fall asleep or nap at will in a variety of settings.	.05	.41*	.22
Evans' Control of Dreaming	Measures the ability to volitionally affect dream content by deciding prior to sleep what to dream about or by changing the dream as it occurs.	.23	.56**	.11

*p < .05   **p < .01

recall, and individuals whose recall fluctuates over time.
In this latter group it seems reasonable to hypothesize that
recall would be determined by the processes which may influence daily fluctuations in recall (conditions of awakening,
motivation, dream salience, and life stress). However, this
hypothesis remains to be empirically tested.

Only in individuals with a consistent style is it reasonable to hypothesize that personality or ability factors would
predict recall. Unfortunately, almost all studies have not
differentiated this group from the large group of individuals
who are inconsistent. With consistent people, the literature
points to four possible reasons for differences in recall.
There is fairly strong evidence that frequent recallers tend
to be more creative and imaginative than infrequent recallers.
It is also possible that they are more skilled in recalling
visual stimuli or sensory experiences; however, this possibility clearly requires more investigation. Third, they may
have more salient dreams. Finally, the role of defensive
style remains an intriguing question. While many of the more
productive researchers in this area, such as Cohen (5) and
Goodenough (1), have concluded that defensive style is not an
important factor in recall, some investigators have more recently revived an interest in this dimension, arguing that
prior studies employed inadequate measures. It may be that
defensive style will prove to be particularly relevant in
accounting for people who consistently never recall dreams.

References

1. Goodenough, Donald R. (1978). "Dream Recall: History and
    Status of the Field." In Arthur M. Arkin, John S.
    Antrobus, and Steven J. Ellman (Eds.), *The Mind in
    Sleep: Psychology and Psychophysiology* (pp. 113-140).
    New York: John Wiley & Sons.

    Reviews the literature addressing why dreams (and other
    events during sleep) are harder to recall than waking ex-
    periences. Advances an "arousal-retrieval" model of dream
    recall which argues, first, that failure to recall dreams
    is due to difficulty in retrieving memory of the experience
    and that, second, recall is facilitated both by awakening
    before a dream ends and by paying immediate attention to
    the dream upon awakening.

2. Herman, John H.; Ellman, Steven J.; and Roffwarg, Howard
    P. (1978). "The Problem of NREM Dream Recall Re-

examined." In Arthur M. Arkin, John S. Antrobus, and Steven J. Ellman (Eds.), *The Mind in Sleep: Psychology and Psychophysiology* (pp. 59-92). New York: John Wiley & Sons.

Reviews the literature concerning NREM dream recall and presents data suggesting that rates of NREM recall (in contrast to REM recall) are very sensitive to experimenter bias.

3. Belicki, Kathryn, and Bowers, Patricia (1982). "Consistency in the Ability to Recall Dreams as a Moderator in Predicting Dream Recall." Paper presented to the 22nd Annual meeting of the Association for the Psychophysiological Study of Sleep, San Antonio.

Examines the relationship of several personality variables (related to hypnotic ability) to dream recall within two groups: subjects with a consistent style of dream recall and subjects with an inconsistent style. Personality was significantly related to recall only in consistent subjects.

4. Webb, Wilse B., and Kersey, Joseph (1967). "Recall of Dreams and the Possibility of Stage 1 REM Sleep." *Perceptual and Motor Skills*, *24*, 667-670.

5. Cohen, David B. (1979). *Sleep and Dreaming: Origins, Nature and Functions*. Oxford: Pergamon Press.

Contains a chapter which reviews the literature on dream recall and elaborates his earlier arguments (see item 22) concerning the importance of interference and dream salience.

6. Weisz, Robert, and Foulkes, David (1970). "Home and Laboratory Dreams Collected under Uniform Sampling Conditions." *Psychophysiology*, *6*, 588-596.

Compares dream reports recalled at home with those collected in a laboratory under similar conditions of awakening (alarm clock). Of interest to this chapter, the authors observed that in the laboratory subjects were able to frequently recall dreams even when the alarm aroused them from NREM sleep.

7. Cohen, David B., and Wolfe, Gary (1973). "Dream Recall and Repression: Evidence for an Alternative Hypothesis." *Journal of Consulting and Clinical Psychology*, *47*, 349-358.

Describes five studies, four of which addressed (and failed to find empirical support for) the role of repression (and related constructs) in dream recall. Two of the five studies examined the effects on dream recall of distraction following awakening, and observed that the simple act of calling a weather bureau dramatically reduced subjects' ability to report dream content.

8.   Cartwright, Rosalind D. (1977). *Night Life: Explorations in Dreaming*. Englewood Cliffs, N.J.: Prentice-Hall.

Examines research and theories concerning the nature and function of dreams.

9.   Reed, Henry (1973). "Learning to Remember Dreams." *Journal of Humanistic Psychology*, *63*, 33-48.

Describes the attempts of 17 participant-observer subjects to increase their dream recall over a twelve-week period. Subjects were generally successful but concluded that motivation was an important variable in accounting for fluctuations in recall.

10. Baekland, Frederick, and Lasky, Richard (1968). "The Morning Recall of Rapid Eye Movement Period Reports Given Earlier in the Night." *Journal of Nervous and Mental Disease*, *147*, 570-574.

Compares dream reports obtained in the morning to those collected during the night from REM awakenings; the principal finding was that longer reports (in contrast to shorter) were more likely to be re-recalled in the morning. Differences between frequent and infrequent recallers were examined. Several were noted, including better morning re-recall and greater field independence in frequent recallers.

11. Meier, C.A.; Rueff, H.; Ziegler, A.; and Hall, C.S. (1968). "Forgetting of Dreams in the Laboratory." *Perceptual and Motor Skills*, *26*, 551-557.

Reports the study of a single individual sleeping for 50 nights in a laboratory with multiple nightly awakenings for dream reports. Argues that, compared to a repression theory of dream forgetting, classical memory theory better predicts which dream reports were re-recalled in the morning.

12. Trinder, John, and Kramer, Milton (1971). "Dream Recall." *American Journal of Psychiatry*, *128*, 296-301.

Compares dream reports of 14 subjects collected through the night by laboratory awakenings with dreams re-recalled in the morning. Argues that classical memory theory, particularly the recency effect, best accounts for which dreams are re-recalled in the morning.

13. Cartwright, Rosalind D. (1979). "The Nature and Function of Repetitive Dreams: A Survey and Speculation." *Psychiatry, 42,* 131-137.

Examines the responses of 167 women to a survey concerning repetitive dreams. Of interest to this chapter is the finding that subjects reported increases in dreaming during times of stress and upset.

14. Cohen, David B. (1974). "Effect of Personality and Pre-sleep Mood on Dream Recall." *Journal of Abnormal Psychology, 83,* 151-156.

Compares subjects' recall following evenings in which they were high in self-confidence versus evenings when they were low. In infrequent recallers, dream recall was best after nights of low self-confidence.

15. Spanos, Nicholas P.; Stam, Henderikus J.; Radtke, H. Lorraine; and Nightingale, Mary E. (1980). "Absorption in Imaginings, Sex-Role Orientation, and the Recall of Dreams by Males and Females." *Journal of Personality Assessment, 44,* 277-282.

Documents that Absorption was related to dream salience and dream recall in female (but not male) subjects. Interprets these findings as supportive of a salience theory of dream recall on the assumption that Absorbers are likely to have more salient dreams.

16. Segall, Seth R. (1980). "A Test of Two Theories of Dream Forgetting." *Journal of Clinical Psychology, 36,* 739-742.

Argues that a theory based on "interference" better accounts for dream forgetting than a theory of repression. Bases his argument on his finding that dream recall decreased in subjects undergoing assertiveness training, and that this decrease was not predicted by repression as assessed by the Defense Mechanism Inventory.

17. Cernovsky, Zack A. (1984). "Dream Recall and Attitude toward Dreams." *Perceptual and Motor Skills, 58,* 911-914.

Presents data indicating a significant correlation between dream recall and a positive attitude toward dreams.
However, on the basis of the small size of the observed
relationship, argues that motivation to recall dreams
is insufficient to fully account for differences in dream
recall.

18. Belicki, Kathryn, and Bowers, Patricia (1982). "Ratings
    of Absorption and the Validity of Dream Ratings."
    Paper presented to the 22nd annual meeting of the
    Association for the Psychophysiological Study of Sleep,
    San Antonio.

    Questions the conclusions of Spanos et al. (see item
    15) that Absorbers are more likely to have salient dreams
    by reporting two studies in which Absorption was observed
    to significantly correlate not only with ratings of dreams
    but also with ratings of a standardized event (a tape-
    recorded story). Argues, therefore, that salience ratings
    in part reflect a response style which is affected by the
    degree of attention devoted to an experience.

19. Cory, Thomas L.; Ormiston, Donald W.; Simmel, Edward;
    and Dainoff, Marvin (1975). "Predicting the Frequency
    of Dream Recall." *Journal of Abnormal Psychology*, *84*,
    261-266.

    Presents data in support of the hypothesis that fre-
    quent recallers have better memory of visual stimuli
    than infrequent recallers.

20. Cohen, David B., and MacNeilage, Peter F. (1974). "A
    Test of the Salience Hypothesis of Dream Recall."
    Journal of Consulting and Clinical Psychology, *42*,
    699-703.

    Directly tests the hypothesis that dream salience is
    greater in frequent than infrequent recallers by comparing
    both dream reports and subjects' salience ratings of
    their dreams following laboratory awakenings. Compared
    to infrequent recallers, frequent recallers rated their
    dreams more saliently and reported more salient dream
    accounts (as assessed by judges' ratings).

21. Schonbar, Rosalea A. (1959). "Some Manifest Characteris-
    tics of Recallers and Nonrecallers of Dreams." *Journal
    of Consulting Psychology*, *23*, 414-418.

    Compares frequent and infrequent recallers on several
    characteristics including defensive style. Frequent

recallers were found to be higher on anxiety and lower on ego strength.

22. Cohen, David B. (1974). "Toward a Theory of Dream Recall." *Psychological Bulletin, 81,* 138–154.

    Reviews the literature on dream recall and argues that there is no consistent support for a hypothesis that repression is a significant factor in dream forgetting. Instead, presents a model of dream recall which stresses the importance of two variables: dream salience and "interference" (situational and person factors which interfere with dream recall).

23. Reitav, Jaan (1985). "Psychological Defenses and the Prediction of Dream Recall Failure." *Association for the Study of Dreams Newsletter, 1,* 10–11.

    Argues that defensive style is a relevant predictor of dream recall; however, improved measures are required (over what has been used in the past) as is the consideration of defenses other than repression.

24. Silverman, Edward G. (1980). "Effects of Stress and Repression-Sensitization on Home Dream Reports." *Dissertation Abstracts International, 41-B,* 1931.

    Argues for the relevance of repression in dream forgetting, suggesting that to demonstrate a relationship with recall, more sophisticated measures of repression are required than have been used in past studies.

25. Cohen, David B. (1971). "Dream Recall and Short-term Memory." *Perceptual and Motor Skills, 33,* 867–871.

    Describes two studies employing different strategies for assessing short-term memory, in which no relation was observed between memory ability and frequency of recall.

26. Sehulster, Jerome R. (1981). "Structure and Pragmatics of a Self Theory of Memory." *Memory and Cognition, 9,* 263–276.

    Describes a factor analytic study of the responses of 893 subjects to a 60-item questionnaire concerning memory ability. Memory for dreams loaded on a factor tapping memory of sensory and personal experiences.

27.   Schechter, Naomi; Schmeidler, Gertrude R.; and Staal,
      Murray (1965). "Dream Reports and Creative Tendencies
      in Students of the Arts, Sciences and Engineering."
      Journal of Consulting Psychology, *29*, 415-421.

      Compares fine arts, science, and engineering students'
      responses to a creativity scale and a questionnaire
      concerning their most recent dream. Arts majors were
      most likely to be able to recall (report) a dream, fol-
      lowed by science and then by engineering students.
      Creativity was unrelated to recall but correlated with
      the imaginativeness of dream reports.

28.   Hiscock, Merrill, and Cohen, David B. (1973). "Visual
      Imagery and Dream Recall." *Journal of Research in
      Personality*, *7*, 179-188.

      Presents evidence suggesting frequent recallers have
      more vivid visual imagery than infrequent recallers.

29.   Richardson, Alan (1979). "Dream Recall Frequency and
      Vividness of Visual Imagery." *Journal of Mental
      Imagery*, *3*, 65-73.

      Reports small, but significant, correlations between
      frequency of dream recall and Marks' Vividness of Visual
      Imagery Questionnaire.

30.   Bowers, Kenneth S. (1976). *Hypnosis for the Seriously
      Curious*. Monterey, Calif.: Brooks/Cole Publishing
      Company.

      Reviews the literature on various issues concerning
      hypnosis and hypnotic ability.

31.   Bowers, Patricia (1979). "Hypnosis and Creativity: The
      Search for the Missing Link." *Journal of Abnormal
      Psychology*, *88*, 564-572.

      Describes studies demonstrating a relationship between
      hypnotic ability and creativity.

Chapter 7
EFFECTS OF PRESLEEP AND DURING-SLEEP
STIMULI ON THE CONTENT OF DREAMS

David Koulack

Since we spend approximately one-third of our lives sleeping,
it is no surprise that the essence and function of sleep has
always been a source of interest and concern to mankind.
Perhaps no facet of sleep has attracted more attention or
been the source of more speculation than dreaming.

Why do we dream? How often do we dream? How long are
our dreams? What functions do dreams have? These questions
have been raised since the beginning of history.

The earliest work on dreams we know of was written in
2000 B.C. in Egypt. The Chester Beatty Papyrus, as it is
called, is really a series of books providing interpretations
of the meanings of a host of different dreams. It was thought
that dreams served a prognosticative function, and the books
were designed to provide a basis for understanding what the
future held in store for the dreamer.

Interest in dreams as portents of the future was not
limited to the Egyptians. The ancient Greeks, Romans, and
Hebrews also believed that dreams were important predictors
of future events and dream interpretation was a highly valued
skill in their cultures.

At the turn of the century, Freud (1) wrote his monumental
work, *The Interpretation of Dreams*. In it he suggested that
dreams serve the important function of preserving sleep.
Basically, Freud believed that dreams are the result of psychic
conflicts. Freud thought we have many unacceptable, instinctual wishes and desires which are normally relegated to the
unconscious during our waking lives. However, these instinctual forces strive for recognition during the night. While
sleeping, the forces of censorship which serve to keep our
unsavory wishes from consciousness are weakened as the press
for recognition and fulfillment of those wishes becomes more
immediate.

The dream appears both as a product and a resolution of
this psychic conflict between instinctual forces on the one

207

hand and the repressive forces of consciousness on the other.
The unacceptable wishes do gain representation in consciousness but in a form so convoluted and distorted that the
dreamer does not recognize their true meaning and is unaware
of their threatening nature. As a result of having the dream,
the push of the instinctual material is relieved in a symbolic
manner and the dreamer is able to continue sleeping. So for
Freud, the dream plays a dual role. First, it prevents the
destructive intrusion of unacceptable wishes into consciousness, and second, in so doing, it preserves the sleep of the
dreamer.

Freud suggested that dreams might not always fulfill this
dual function to perfection, that unconscious wishes may on
occasion invade the dream in a fashion so open and direct as
to make memory of the dream itself unacceptable to waking
consciousness. So he brought to bear the notion of repression.
He suggested that in instances where the dream material itself
is too threatening, it is expelled from consciousness or repressed when the dreamer awakens.

In Freud's formulation, waking thoughts and experience
play a minor role in the dream process. Essentially, these
experiences provide the setting or stage on which the unconscious wishes can be presented in a disguised and unobtrusive
fashion. By being interwoven with conscious, acceptable experiences, the instinctual forces are able to surround themselves with a cloak of acceptability and in so doing gain some
degree of representation in consciousness. It is for this
reason that Freud characterized dreams as the "royal road to
the unconscious." He believed that careful interpretation
of the dream would uncover hidden or "latent" content revealing
the unconscious forces at their roots. Interestingly enough,
the Iroquois, a North American Indian tribe, also believed
that dreams might serve to disguise rather than reveal the
soul's wish and at times felt it necessary to avail themselves
of the help of analysts to reveal a dream's hidden meaning.

While most of the early concern with dreams focused on
their possible function as predictors of future events and
more modern theories have been concerned with the insights
they may provide into the psyche of the dreamer, there are a
number of people who have attested to their importance as
creative or problem solving aids. For example, Robert Louis
Stevenson claimed that many of his works were embellishments
of stories presented to him in his dreams. And Fredrich
Kekule dreamed a dream which enabled him to solve the mystery
of the configuration of the atoms in the benzine molecule, a
configuration which he had puzzled over for quite some time.
His dream contained the image of a snake with its tail in its
mouth. On waking, Kekule interpreted the image to signify
the closed carbon ring of the benzine molecule.

Interestingly enough, while these notions of dream function are quite varied, they are tied together by a common, if
implicit, belief. That is, all of these notions suggest that
dreams have something to say about, or hold some importance
for gaining insight into, our waking lives.

Early, systematic studies tried to more clearly define
what the exact nature of the relationship between our dreams
and waking lives might be. For example, Poetzl (2) and Fisher
and Paul (3) showed that incidental presleep experiences could
be woven into the dream narrative. And Schrotter (4), Nachmansohn (5), and Farber and Fisher (6) demonstrated that the
content of dreams could be influenced by posthypnotic suggestion.

In addition, the numerous anecdotal accounts of incorpora-
tions of naturally occurring external and internal stimuli
(such as falling out of bed, thunder, stomachaches, and so
forth) which appeared in the early literature, led to more
systematic explorations of commerce with the environment during
sleep. For example Maury (7) had himself pinched, tickled,
and exposed to light and odors while he slept. And similarly
De Sanctis and Neyroz (8), Cubberly (9), and Max (10) explored the effects of different types of external events on
dream content. In general, these studies demonstrated that
some incorporation of external events into dreams was possible
and dreams are more readily influenced through tactile sensations than through any other sensory modality.

All of these studies and observations were interesting
and valuable first steps in exploring the relationship between
our experiences and our dreams. But it wasn't until the remarkable serendipitous discovery of rapid eye movement or REM
sleep by Eugene Aserinsky and subsequent work by Aserinsky
and Kleitman (11) and Dement and Kleitman (12) that systematic
research into the world of dreams began in earnest.

A little more than three decades ago, Aserinsky and Kleitman (11) discovered there are regular intervals during the
night when the eyes move in a conjugate fashion, much as they
do during the waking state. What is more, they and subsequent
researchers found that these eye movement periods are accompanied by distinct electroencephalogram patterns and slightly
accelerated heart and respiration rates. When subjects are
awakened during these REM periods, they are often able to recount lengthy and vivid dream sequences.

Since the initial report of these findings in 1953,
literally thousands of nights of sleep have been recorded in
many sleep laboratories throughout the world. It soon became
evident that REM periods occur in approximately ninety-minute
cycles and their duration increases as the night progresses.
Thus, the first REM period of the night might be only a few

minutes in length and the final one may last over an hour.
In short, in a six- to eight-hour night's sleep a person has
four or five REM periods occupying about twenty-two percent
of the total sleep time or approximately 105 minutes. In
addition, subjects awakened in the midst of their REM periods
recall a dream about eighty percent of the time, and in some
instances when no dream comes to mind, subjects report they
feel as if they had been dreaming but are not able to recall
any content.

The clearly developed evidence that REM periods are an
inexorable part of the sleep cycle and not random events and
that dreaming is in some way associated with REM sleep made
it possible to tackle an intriguing question. Anecdotal evidence and popular thought had given rise to the belief that
dreams are momentary, fleeting events. On the other hand,
the REM period-dreaming relationship seemed to indicate that
dreams may be regularly occurring events taking up a substantial portion of our sleeping lives.

Perhaps one of the most attractive bits of evidence suggesting that dreams are momentary, fleeting events appears
in L.F.A. Maury's book, *Le sommeil et les rêves* (7). Maury
recounts a lengthy dream he had some twenty years earlier.
The dream was set in Paris during the Reign of Terror around
1793. In the dream, Maury witnessed a number of murders and
was himself brought to trial and condemned to be guillotined
for his crimes. He was driven through the streets of Paris,
past mobs of jeering people. Arriving at the scaffold, he
slowly mounted the steps. On reaching the top, his hands were
bound behind him and he placed his head upon the block. Suddenly, he felt the blade of the guillotine separate his head
from his body.

Maury reported he awoke in extreme anxiety only to find
that the top of his bed had fallen and struck him on the neck
in just the manner the blade of the guillotine would have
struck. He speculated the dream must have been caused by
the bed hitting his neck and despite its lengthy content it
must have occurred in the brief interval between the blow and
his awakening. On the basis of this experience, Maury came
to the conclusion that the length of dreams in actual time
is extremely short with many events often being telescoped
into a relatively brief interval.

For the dream researcher, Maury's account is interesting
but not convincing. Clearly, the report of one event which
could very well have been embellished in the twenty years in-
tervening between its occurrence and the time the book was
written is tenuous at best. And the question of dream length
is an important one. If it could be shown that dream time
corresponds to actual time and if actual time dreaming can be

measured by the length of the REM period, it would be possible
to say not only that we dream four or five times during the
night, but that we spend close to two hours dreaming every
night! In short, it would be logical to infer that dreaming
itself is an inexorable part of the sleep cycle and not a
momentary, fleeting event.

Dement and Kleitman (13) set out to examine the dream
time question by awakening subjects either five or fifteen
minutes after the beginning of a REM period. They obtained
dream reports and then asked the subjects to estimate if they
had been dreaming for five or fifteen minutes. A vast majority
of their subjects' judgments of the time they had been dreaming
corresponded to the length of time they had been in the REM
period. In addition, the length of the dream narratives
themselves corresponded to the length of the REM periods from
which they were obtained.

In our laboratory, I attacked the same question in a
slightly different manner (14;15). In essence, I tried to
supply the dreamer and myself with a common reference point
in time. For this purpose, I chose a series of shocks to the
median nerve at the wrist. These low-level shocks are not
painful and it is possible to administer them without awakening the sleeping subject. The plan was a simple one. I
would administer the shocks sometime during each REM period
and awaken the subjects either thirty seconds or three minutes
after the last shock. If the stimulus were to appear in a
clearly identifiable fashion in the dream narrative, I would
ask the subject to estimate whether the shock had occurred
more nearly thirty seconds before the awakening or more nearly
three minutes before the awakening. An example of one such
instance of direct representation of the stimulus in a dream
is as follows:

> ... I started walking back here to tell you about
> it. I metcha in the hall and I told you, Hey,
> Dave, this thing here is ... I'm feeling the
> electrical impulses without the electricity going
> through. I felt it three or four times. On my
> left hand ... then I realized I was in my under-
> wear all along....

So, for example, in this instance the question was: "Did
you feel the electrical impulses more nearly thirty seconds
or more nearly three minutes before the buzzer sounded?"

As it turned out, the appearance of the stimulus could
be identified clearly in twelve instances obtained from five
subjects; ninety-two percent of the subjects' judgments (11
out of 12) placed those incidents at a time corresponding to
the time of stimulation.

The results of these and other studies indicate there is
a correspondence between dream time and actual time and
suggest that time spent dreaming can be measured by the length
of time spent in REM periods.

Commerce with the Environment during Sleep

In addition to providing some evidence for a relationship
between dream time and real time, the stimulation technique
also permitted the examination of some of the parameters of
commerce with the environment during sleep.

I found that subjects incorporated the stimulus into
their dreams in either a direct or indirect fashion approximately fifty percent of the time. But what is perhaps most
interesting are some of the other findings. While one of my
expectations was that the electrical stimulus to the wrist
would increase the bodily activity of the dreamer in the
dream, there was some evidence to suggest the stimulation
actually increased the bodily activity of *other* persons in
the dream rather than of the dreamer. If this in fact is the
case, it fits well with Freud's suggestion that the mind
"... seeks for an interpretation of them (the stimuli) which
will make the currently active sensation into a component
part of a situation ... which is consistent with sleep."

That is, there is a possibility the specific effects of
the stimulus were transposed to the other in the dream in
order to rob the stimulus of some of its significance to the
dreamer and thus permit him to continue sleeping.

In addition, there was some evidence to suggest that different individuals handle their commerce with the environment
during sleep in different ways. For example, one subject had
several stimulated dreams in which he dreamed that someone,
whom he was trying to ignore, was tugging at his sleeve to
get his attention. During a subsequent postsleep interview,
he made associative connections between the sleeve tugging
episodes and the stimulation. On the other hand, another
subject had several dreams during the stimulation condition
in which he was wired up and his thumb was moving just as it
might during the waking state in response to the stimulation.
In other words, the stimulus condition was directly and clearly
represented and central to the dream.

While none of these results can be considered definitive,
this stimulation technique, which insures responsiveness at
the level of the cortex, is a promising one for exploring the
general question of the nature of commerce with the environment

during sleep and individual differences in response to environmental experience.

There are, however, other stimulation techniques which have
been used with intriguing results. Evans and his colleagues
(16) designed a series of studies to determine whether subjects
could both receive and respond to suggestions while ostensibly
asleep. They chose suggestions that required a clearly identifiable action. For example, one suggestion was "Whenever I say
the word 'pillow' your pillow will feel uncomfortable and you
will want to move it with your hand." Another one was, "Whenever I say the word 'itch' your nose will itch until you scratch
it."

There were a number of interesting findings. First,
there were obvious individual differences among subjects.
Those subjects who were highly hypnotizable during the waking
state were the only ones who were able to respond to the suggestions. The administration of the suggestion and the cue
word to low hypnotizable subjects often resulted in arousal.
Second, the suggestion was effective only if it was administered during REM sleep and only if the cue word was administered during REM sleep. And, third, a number of subjects
who returned to the laboratory five months later were still
able to respond to the cue word. Tests during the waking
state revealed that the subjects had no knowledge or memory
of either the administration of the suggestion or cue word.

In addition to demonstrating that some sort of communication can take place with a sleeping person, this study provides insight into some of the sleep learning data. Basically,
studies by Koukkou and Lehman (17), Jus and Jus (18), and
Evans and Orchard (19) have shown that stimuli played to subjects during sleep could be recalled the next morning only
if the subjects showed signs of arousal while the stimulus
was being presented. In the study we have described above,
the subjects clearly were aware of the stimuli, could respond
to them, but could not recall them. This suggests, that while
we may assimilate complex information during sleep, we are
only able to recall those stimuli during the state in which
we learned them. Thus information incorporated during sleep
seems to be available to us only during sleep.

While this latter study involves learning a particular
response to a particular suggestion, Mario Bertini tried to
train his subjects to communicate while asleep. He trained a
number of medical students to free associate to white noise
during ten fifty-six minute sessions over a ten-consecutive-
day period. Then the subjects came to his sleep laboratory for
the night. When they were in a REM period, he would play the
white noise, hoping that he could elicit dreams by this signal. In many cases the white noise awakened the subjects,

but there were some instances where they produced verbaliza-
tions, although once again they were generally unable to recall them on waking in the morning. In some cases, on hearing
a playback of their reports, subjects expressed astonishment
at what they heard.

For example, one subject, who was able to recall a dream
he had previously reported during the night, said that his
feelings had been neutral. The main theme consisted of a
"trivial" examination where the teacher was present. However,
on listening to the recording of the dream report during the
night, both the subject and the experimenter were struck by
the strong feelings expressed. There was also the striking
realization that the teacher was actually the subject's fiancée,
Corinna. In fact, by listening to his dream recorded at the
time of its occurrence the subject became aware of his general
feeling of being judged by Corinna.

This example is interesting and instructive for two reasons.
First, it suggests to us in a rather dramatic way how dreams may
reflect and at times provide insight into our feelings. Second,
it shows how waking recollections of our dreams may be something
less than the dream experience itself. Whether this is the result of the translation of a primarily visual and ephemeral experience into a verbal medium or the result of defenses thrown
up at the time of waking is certainly an open question.

Presleep Experiences and Dreams

Some years ago, I was doing a study involving multiple
awakenings during the course of the night. I wasn't concerned
with dream content but wished to keep the subjects up for a
short period of time after each awakening. To do this, I
decided to have subjects relate their dreams.

The first subject was going to an adoption agency directly
from the laboratory to pick up his second adopted child. That
night he had the following dreams:

> a) Yes. We had taken the horses out to round
> up the cows. No! no! Scratch that. I know what
> it was. Er, another fella and I were out collecting
> semen from this bull for artificial insemination.
> That's what it was.

> b) Well we were looking at tricycles. Er, it
> seems as if we were looking at some special kind
> of tricycle, er, maybe it was one of those tractor
> peddle types.

The second subject had just been to a funeral of a friend of his who had been killed in a car crash. He had the following dream:

> Oh yeh. It just. I dreamt that I was, I was watching some people. They were all standing around in front of this church. It was, I think it was on a Sunday. And I remember everybody was all dressed up and everything. But there was this one man and I think, I think what he did was, he was laying there on purpose but he was laying between two, two cars. Two parked cars by the side of the road and he had blood smeared all over him and his clothes were all torn up and everything and um ... and when the people came by, I think he was just laying there to see what their reactions were. And um, I can't remember if anybody asked him to come to church so they could help him or if anybody asked if he was ... um ... hurt or anything. I'm trying to think, like, let me think just a second. And he said, er, oh! He asked them what kind of church this, it was, but they didn't say anything to him and that's all, that's all I can remember.

These dreams seem to clearly reflect important events occurring in each of the dreamers' lives. The dreams of the first subject are apparently related to conception and children and the dream of the second subject is evidently related to his friend's fatal car accident and the ensuing funeral.

Yet, interestingly enough, both of these subjects spontaneously remarked on these dreams in the morning, and both wondered aloud about their possible meanings. Here we apparently have instances of dream material which is disguised only by virtue of the dreamers' inability or lack of desire to make connections between their dreams and their waking experiences.

In order to better understand what the nature of the relationship between dreams and the residual psychological business of the day might be, my colleagues, Herman Witkin, Don Goodenough, Helen Lewis, Harvey Cohen, Arthur Shapiro, and I (20) decided to provide our subjects with presleep experiences which could serve as tracers through the dreams of the night.

We used four films as our presleep stimuli. Two neutral films were travelogues, one of the far western United States and the other of London. The other two films were stressful films. One involved the birth of a baby with the aid of a Malstrom Vacuum Extractor and the other was an anthropological

film of a subincision rite. The subjects slept in our laboratory one night a week for five weeks, with the first night
serving as an adaptation night. On the experimental nights,
subjects would see one of the four films before going to
sleep.

As I mentioned, the birth film depicted the birth of a
baby with the aid of a Malstrom Vacuum extractor. Among the
scenes the subjects saw was the insertion of the cup of the
extractor into the vagina, the rhythmic pulling on the wire
attached to the cup in time with the contractions, the
episiotomy, and the sudden appearance of the baby. After
this film, one subject had the following dream:

>   At the moment you woke me up I was flying around
>   in the airplane looking out, sort of, like looking
>   out well, not through a window exactly, looking out
>   through a, a like a hole. Well anyhow I could see
>   part of the airplane where the wing is attached,
>   the body of the plane. And just above me and to my
>   left was a hole, and through the hole was protruding
>   a coil of wire, and there was a man holding a ...
>   the end of the wire ... big wire, he had his
>   finger through the end of it. One loop at the end
>   of it pulling it, it was attached ... the other
>   part of the wire was attached to a door, and when
>   he pulled the wire, the door would go up and down
>   and the wire ... his hand would pull the wire and
>   would cause him, the door would go up, he'd let
>   it go back in, the door would go down, and uh, it
>   was sort of a troop carrier plane, people, para-
>   chutists, jumping out of the airplane.

So in this dream, we have an instance of a rather clear
representation of some of the images from the film along with
the symbolic representation of the birth by the people jumping
out of the plane.

The subincision film depicted a rite of passage of the
Arunta, an Australian tribe. The rite involved the cutting
of the penis from the tip to the scrotal sack with a sharp
stone. The wound was cauterized over an open fire.

After seeing this film, another subject had a dream about
a rooster, an easily inferred symbol of the male phallus:

>   One segment of the dream quite ironically
>   dealt with the fact that I walked with my grand-
>   mother into a pet shop and wound up buying a roos-
>   ter. My grandmother was going to buy the rooster.
>   One of those multicolored things. And of course
>   I was opposed to on the grounds only of course I

said, 'Well, they're very hard to raise, they're
dirty,' and so forth and so on. She says 'Yes'
but she says 'look how alert this thing is, they're
very smart looking, you know multicolored thing.'
Well we wound up buying it, and uh, plus they
bagged it like they would a dead chicken. Uh, we
finally got this thing into the bag and we waited
a few moments and it was out of the bag. He was
very ornery.... When he was put in a bag, he, uh,
broke out of the bag, and now another party came
along and picked him up in the broken bag and all,
and put him in another bag because, uh, you know,
uh, just, uh, in other words, he was just bouncing,
trying to get out of this bag.

In a subsequent interview, the subject was able to make
a connection between the dream and early memories. He recalled that he used to go to a chicken market with his grandmother. "Usually they would have men to pull out [from the
coops] the chickens," he said, "and the scales would have
pieces of string on to tie the wings or legs and weigh the
chicken. Well, this didn't happen with my grandmother. She
had to go and pull the chicken outa the coop and feel it or,
in the event he would pull it out, she had to feel it before
this man was allowed to weigh it." When asked if he knew
what she was feeling for, he answered, "No, she would say
in Italian, 'la ozza,' which is the neck, or the feedbag in
the neck. But she was feeling down around the stomach, so, uh,
she was feeling for something else. Because I don't know
whether they feel down that position where the chicken's eggs
are, which is right about here. She would feel here and tell
me it was the chicken's neck. Maybe she was afraid she'd
have to go into detail about the boy and girl chicken, I don't
know." And then he laughed.

Here the phallic theme of the subincision film not only
finds its way into the dream, the sexual significance of the
rooster is clearly identified by the subject's associations
to his early childhood experiences.

These are but a couple of examples of how the presleep
charged films found their way into the dreams of our subjects. As with the stimuli presented during sleep, it became
clear that each person had a particular way of handling these
waking experiences in their sleeping lives.

There was also another finding of interest in this study.
In addition to alteration of dream content, we discovered
that the mood accompanying dreams following the charged films
was altered. In general, there was a decrease in social affec-
tion and an increase in anxiety in these dreams. Basically,

the mood in the dreams reflected the waking mood after seeing the film.

A companion study on uninterrupted sleep done by Fred Baekeland, Richard Lasky, and me (21), demonstrated that after viewing the subincision film, subjects had more spontaneous awakenings during REM periods than they did after viewing a neutral film. It seems reasonable to speculate that the anxious emotions connected with the REM period dreams aroused the sleeping subjects.

From these and other similar studies, it is apparent that dreams reflect and can be altered by waking experience, and that dream mood is to some extent a reflection of waking affect. In addition, it is clear that dreams are not always the guardians of sleep, but rather if they are sufficiently charged with emotion they may well awaken the dreamer.

The fact that dream content can and does change as a result of day to day experiences raises the interesting question of whether or not dreams play some role in dealing with these contemporary experiences.

Indeed, partly as a response to the burgeoning information about dreams and the need to integrate it in some fashion, a number of new theories of dream function have recently been advanced. One such theory is known as the compensation hypothesis. Proponents of this notion suggest that dreams in some way compensate for or fill a gap in waking experience. For example, one experimenter found that people who were kept in social isolation for a period of time before going to sleep had an increase in social content in their dreams, presumably compensating for the lack of social interaction during their waking hours.

Another theory, often referred to as the mastery hypothesis suggests our dreams help us to master or handle problems or psychologically distressing situations that confront us from time to time during our waking lives. Although the process by which mastery is supposed to occur is not clearly spelled out, some theorists suggest dreams integrate the disturbing material within memory systems that have in the past provided satisfactory solutions for dealing with similar difficulties.

In order to investigate this notion, Joseph De Koninck and I (22) showed subjects a disturbing, industrial accident film before they went to sleep and again when they woke up in the morning. In the film, three separate accidents are depicted: the tip of a worker's finger is cut off, then half of another worker's finger is cut off, and finally a third worker is killed by a board shot from a circular saw. He is shown dying on the floor, impaled by the board.

We reasoned that if the mastery hypothesis had validity, the subjects who dream about the film would be more likely to "master" its disturbing elements and consequently would be less distressed on seeing the film for the second time. During the course of two nights, we collected dreams from our subjects and found some of them did indeed have direct incorporation of elements from the film. Here are some excerpts from one such dream:

> There were about six different men chasing me and they had knives and they were trying to stab me.... Through the course of events I managed to get some knives I think by them throwing them at me.... We cut each other a couple of times.... I was washing blood off my face and the wounds when I washed them off still had blood coming, sort of seeping through the skin.... And then I was going to a show with my friend and my wife and my daughter....

In this dream, elements from the film such as knives, cuts, and blood are clearly and openly represented. In fact, it is likely the context in which these elements were seen (that is, in a film) is itself represented by the reference, "going to a show." To our surprise, however, dreamers who had such direct representations of the film in their dreams were more disturbed at the second viewing of the film than the subjects who had dreams with no apparent reference to the film.

Interestingly enough, there was a parallel in the response of people who dreamed about the film and another group of people who saw the film twice, with only a waking interval between the two films. Some of these people from this latter group, who obviously had a chance to think about the film, were also more distressed on seeing it the second time. One possible way of explaining this parallel between the responses of the sleeping subjects who dreamed about the film and the waking subjects who thought about it is that dreams function in a manner similar to waking thoughts. In other words, rather than representing a hidden network of unconscious wishes, dreams may be a reflection of prominent concerns, emotions, and wishes that are part and parcel of our daily lives.

This viewpoint is consistent with the results of a number of studies in addition to the ones we have just discussed which demonstrate that presleep experiences find their way directly into dreams. In fact, instead of thinking of dreams as the royal road to the unconscious, it may be more apt to think of them as indices of our intellectual and emotional states.

During the course of our daily lives, we have contact with numerous people and many events are taking place. Because of waking demands and the need to function efficiently in our society, we have little time to reflect on a large portion of these waking experiences. Often, in fact, we have to push aside events which may be of some importance to us. What better time for these concerns to gain some of our attention than when we are sleeping. At this time, more or less unhampered by intrusions from the outside world, we can devote ourselves to matters that have been put aside earlier. Probably, the concerns which find their way into dreams range from the highly charged or emotionally important events to relatively mundane matters, with the former taking precedence over the latter.

This view is not inconsistent with the fact that our dreams are sometimes disjointed, surrealistic, or even bizarre. It seems reasonable to suppose that when sleeping, our thought processes are less controlled than they are during the waking state. Under these conditions, many elements from our waking lives may run together either because of their similarity or their proximity of occurrence in time.

Of course, the question of what function dreams may play in dealing with contemporary experiences is still an open one. Recently, Janet Wright and I (23) advanced a notion which suggests that dreams may in fact serve variously the function of helping to master stressful experiences as well as helping to avoid them (22).

Simply put, we hypothesized that when we dream of stressful waking experiences we are in fact trying to come to grips with them. We speculated that this process of mastery insofar as it calls up the stressful experience and the associated affect into the dream is itself potentially disruptive.

When the disruption becomes too great, the dreamer resorts to avoidance dreams. That is, he or she "turns off" the disruptive dreams by replacing them with pleasant ones. Avoidance dreams may take place within the same night as disruptive dreams or on subsequent nights.

Our belief is that this process of oscillation between dreams concerning the stressful event and avoidance dreams continues until some sort of resolution of the stress is obtained by the dreamer. In short, we are postulating that dreams are just one more weapon in the arsenal of weapons we enlist to help us to cope with some of the more difficult aspects of our daily lives.

References

1. Freud, S. (1953). *The Interpretation of Dreams.* Standard ed. London: Hogarth Press.

   A monumental work which provided the impetus for much of the experimental work on dreams.

2. Poetzl, O. (1962). "The Relationships between Experimentally Induced Dream Images and Indirect Vision." *Psychological Issues, 2,* 1-46.

3. Fisher, C., and Paul, I.H. (1959). "Subliminal Visual Stimulation and the Dream." *Journal of the American Psychoanalytic Association, 7,* 35-83.

4. Schrotter, K. (1951). "Experimental Dreams." In D. Rappaport (Ed.), *Organization and Pathology of Thought* (pp. 249-256). New York: Columbia University Press.

5. Nachmansohn, M. (1951). "Concerning Experimentally Produced Dreams." In D. Rappaport (Ed.), *Organization and Pathology of Thought* (pp. 256-287). New York: Columbia University Press.

6. Farber, L.H., and Fisher, C. (1943). "An Experimental Approach to Dream Psychology through the Use of Hypnosis." *Psychoanalytic Quarterly, 12,* 202-216.

7. Maury, L.F.A. (1861). *Le sommeil et les rêves.* Paris.

8. De Sanctis, S., and Neyroz, U. (1902). "Experimental Investigation Concerning the Depth of Sleep." *Psychological Review, 9,* 254-282.

9. Cubberly, A. (1923). "The Effects of Tensions of the Body Surface upon the Normal Dream." *British Journal of Psychology, 13,* 243-265.

10. Max, L.W. (1935). "An Experimental Study of the Motor Theory of Consciousness. III: Action-current Responses in Deaf-Mutes during Sleep, Sensory Stimulation and Dreams." *Journal of Comparative Psychology, 19,* 469-487.

11. Aserinsky, E., and Kleitman, N. (1953). "Regularly Occurring Periods of Eye Motility and Concomitant Phenomena during Sleep." *Science, 118,* 273-274.

12. Dement, W., and Kleitman, N. (1955). "The Relation of
     Eye Movements during Sleep to Dream Activity: An Ob-
     jective Method for the Study of Dreaming." *Journal of
     Experimental Psychology*, *53*, 339-346.

13. Dement, W., and Kleitman, N. (1957). "Cyclic Variations
     in EEG during Sleep and Their Relation to Eye Movements
     Body Motility, and Dreaming." *Electroencephalography
     and Clinical Neurophysiology*, *9*, 673-690.

14. Koulack, D. (1968). "Dream Time and Real Time." *Psycho-
     nomic Science*, *11*, 202.

15. Koulack, D. (1969). "Effects of Somatosensory Stimula-
     tion on Dream Content." *Archives of General Psychiatry*
     20, 718-725.

     This study explores the effects of an electrical stimu-
     lus to the wrist on dream content. It shows the differ-
     ent types of responses that individuals may make in their
     dreams to an external stimulus presented during sleep.
     The technique used insures registration of the stimulus
     at the level of the cortex.

16. Evans, F.J.; Gustafson, L.A.; O'Connell, D.N.; Orne, M.T.
     and Shor, R.E. (1970). "Verbally Induced Behavioral
     Responses during Sleep." *The Journal of Nervous and
     Mental Disease*, *150*, 171-187.

17. Koukkou, M., and Lehmann, D. (1968). "EEG and Memory
     Storage in Sleep Experiments with Humans." *Electro-
     encephalography and Clinical Neurophysiology*, *25*, 455-
     462.

18. Jus, K., and Jus, A. (1972). "Experimental Studies on
     Memory Disturbances in Humans in Pathological and
     Physiological Conditions." *International Journal of
     Psychobiology*, *2*, 205-218.

19. Evans, F.J., and Orchard, W. (1969). "Sleep Learning:
     The Successful Waking Recall of Material Presented
     during Sleep." *Psychophysiology*, *6*, 269.

20. Goodenough, D.R.; Witkin, H.A.; Koulack, D.; and Cohen,
     H. (1975). "The Effects of Stress Films on Dream Affect
     and on Respiration and Eye-Movement Activity during
     Rapid-Eye-Movement Sleep." *Psychophysiology*, *12*, 313-
     320.

21. Baekeland, F.; Koulack, D.; and Lasky, R. (1968). "Effects of a Stressful Presleep Experience on Electroencephalograph-recorded Sleep." *Psychophysiology*, *4*, 436-443.

22. De Koninck, J.M., and Koulack, D. (1975). "Dream Content and Adaptation to a Stressful Situation." *Journal of Abnormal Psychology*, *84*, 250-260.

23. Koulack, D. "Dreams and Waking Thoughts." Paper presented at a symposium, "Cognitive Psychology and Dreaming," at a meeting of the Eastern Psychological Association at Boston, Mass., March 21-24, 1985.

Bibliography

Aarons, L. (1976). "Sleep Assisted Instruction." *Psychological Bulletin*, *83*, 1-40.

An overview of the literature on the ability to learn during sleep.

Cartwright, R.; Bernick, N.; Borowitz, G.; and Kling, A. (1969). "Effect of an Erotic Movie on the Sleep and Dreams of Young Men." *Archives of General Psychiatry*, *20*, 262-271.

This is a study of dream formation. It attempts to answer the question "Where do dreams come from and what are their relations to waking perceptions?"

Dallet, J. (1973). "Theories of Dream Function." *Psychological Bulletin*, *6*, 408-416.

A review of some of the more prominent theories of dream function.

Koulack, D. (1983). "Information Processing during Sleep." In W.P. Koella (Ed.), *Sleep 1982* (pp. 46-62). Basel: Karger.

A number of papers concerning the types and nature of transformation of information from our waking states into sleep.

Koulac, D.; Prevost, E.; and De Koninck, J. (1985). "Sleep, Dreaming and Adaptation to a Stressful Intellectual Activity." *Sleep*, *8*(3), 244-253.

This study examines the effects of a preschool experience on both dream content and subsequent waking mood. It examines the efficacy of both the compensation and mastery hypothesis of dream function.

Rados, R., and Cartwright, R.D. (1982). "Where Do Dreams Come From? A Comparison of Presleep and REM Sleep Thematic Content." *Journal of Abnormal Psychology, 91*, 433-436.

A study of the relationship between waking thought and dream content.

Sirois-Berliss, M., and De Koninck, J. (1982). "Menstrual Stress and Dreams: Adaptation or Interference." *The Psychiatric Journal of the University of Ottawa, 7*, 78-86.

A study of the relationship between dream content and menstrual stress.

SECTION B
COGNITIVELY BASED THEORETICAL
CONSIDERATIONS OF DREAMING

Chapter 8
DREAMS AND SELF-KNOWLEDGE

Don Kuiken

Most people would attest that dreams are not merely nocturnal
reruns of waking events. Connections between dreams and
waking are typically veiled and indirect. Fragments of familiar and unfamiliar events coalesce to create images which are
at once intimate and obtuse. Even the best systematic studies
(e.g., Cohen & Cox [1]) emphasize that, although there is
detectable correspondence between waking and dreaming, the
factors shaping and limiting that relationship are unclear.
Because the basic relationship between waking activities
and dreams is ambiguous, it may seem premature to discuss
dreams and self-knowledge. However, recent developments
suggest that dreams mirror our *conceptions* of our actions
and feelings rather than what we *actually* do and feel, significantly changing the focus of study (2). The goal of the
present chapter is to provide a formulation of the relationship between dreams and self-knowledge which a) clarifies
some prior discussions of this relationship and b) reflects
the recent change in focus. Perhaps by considering previous
attempts in relation to current directions, we can appreciate
the persistent problems that researchers must face and solve.
   A pervasive hypothesis in modern studies of dreams is
that dreams provide, in Jones' (3) phrase, "self-perception
in depth." In some way, dreams provide hints of a personal
reality typically unknown--a personal reality which contrasts
with everyday self-perception. It is incumbent on dream researchers to clarify in exactly what ways dreams could possibly influence "self-perception in depth" and, then, establish
empirically whether they actually do so. The history of this
enterprise demonstrates that neither the theoretical nor the
empirical task is easy.

Self-Reference in Dreams

If dreams reflect our conceptions of ourselves, these
conceptions derive from a form of consciousness that contrasts
with waking self-reflection. During waking, self-reflection
is likely to include at least periodic monitoring of how we
are making inferences and drawing conclusions. In contrast,
during dreaming, we typically do not monitor our mental acts
in this way. One of the distinctive characteristics of dreaming may be this decline in our awareness of what we are doing
(i.e., dreaming) as we do it (4).

Regardless of the form of self-reflection from which they
derive, dreams are consistently self-referential. Snyder (5)
reported that the most frequently occurring character in
dreams is the dreamer, who appears in about 95% of REM dreams.
Furthermore, Foulkes (6) found that representation of dreamer
feelings and dreamer actions was more common in REM reports
than in NREM reports. Thus, dreams--at least adult dreams--
consistently include a character who is physically identifiable
as continuous with the dreamer's waking self.

That dreams typically depict the physical identity of the
dreamer does not necessarily mean that the dream is about the
dreamer's actions and feelings. The fusions and juxtapositions
that form the dream may present the dreamer as the agent for
actions and feelings, which in actuality are attributable to
others. However, frequently the dream *is* about the dreamer's
own actions and feelings. Foulkes (7) found evidence that
explicit representation of the dreamer as the agent for actions
and feelings attributable to the dreamer is a developmental
accomplishment. Specifically, he found that, for children
between three and five years of age, dreams largely lacked
self-reference. For children between five and seven years
of age, dreamer self-reference was still infrequent, and
dreamer waking activities correlated with the activities of
non-self characters in their dreams. Finally, for children
between seven and nine years of age, dreams included representation of an active and frequently affectively involved
self character whose activites correlated with dreamer waking
activities. These developmental data indicate that, beginning
at about seven years of age, dreaming self-reference is continuous not only with the physical self but also with the
active self during waking.

Dreams are not simply images of the dreamer's contemporary
activites and feelings. There is evidence that dreams include
people, places, objects, and events extending from the present
to the remote past. First, Cohen and Cox (1) found that an
experimentally induced predicament during the day was subtly

but reliably echoed in the dreams of the following night. Second, Cartwright, Bernick, Borowitz, and Kling (8) found that maximum incorporation of elements from an emotionally engaging presleep event occurred in dreams during the second night following the event, rather than during the night immediately following the event. Third, Verdone (9) found that dreamers rated dream elements as most commonly being from events that occurred during the week preceding the dream. He also found that dreamers rated the oldest REM dream element as most commonly being from events that had occurred about 1-2 years earlier. It was less common—but not infrequent—for the oldest element to come from events more than five years before. Although the preceding studies are suggestive rather than definitive, dreams do seem to echo of things past; they commonly draw from a repertoire of both recent and remote personal memories.

Even though recent and remote personal memories are raw material for dreams, the hypothesis that dreams allow "perceptiveness in depth" requires that we know more about the attributes of these personal memories and about how the dream transforms them. From what does the "depth" in this hypothesis derive? Are the memories that infiltrate the dream personally significant? Does their transformation in the dream or their recall during reflection on the dream affect self-knowledge? To provide satisfactory answers to these questions, it is necessary to be as precise as possible about what is meant by "significant memory" and by "self-knowledge." An articulation of these concepts may be based on recent theory and research on memory.

Significant Memories and Affective Scripts

Contemporary theories of memory describe the processes by which memories are elaborated on and reorganized rather than merely retrieved or recalled. Such conceptions of memory reconstruction are appropriate in the present context because memories are obviously elaborated on and reorganized to produce that nocturnal concoction we call a dream. Also, some contemporary theories of memory describe the processes by which action episodes are organized in memory. This may be useful in the present context because research indicates that dreams, especially REM dreams, typically have an episodic structure in which dream events initiate dream actions and in which those actions cause certain dream consequences (10).

228 Dreams and Self-Knowledge

One recent theory about memory for such causally linked events is script theory (11;12). Script theory suggests that people categorize events in their lives according to resemblances between the ordered sequence of actions in those events To demonstrate, consider the following scenario:

> A child is asked by his teacher to recite an assigned poem from memory. He does so to the best of his ability, and his teacher praises his performance mildly.

Imagine that a later interaction occurs as follows:

> The child is asked to write a portion of the multiplication table on the blackboard. He does so, and his teacher encourages him to continue his diligent study.

This child may categorize the first event with the second because of the similarity of his own actions in the two events (i.e., demonstrating his academic skills), because of the similarity of the teacher's actions in the two events (i.e., requesting that the child perform and, later, evaluating his presentation), and because of the similarity of the action sequence (request, demonstration, evaluation). The mental structure that classifies events at this concrete level is called a script.

With increased experience, a person may develop more abstract categories of events. At higher levels of abstraction, instances of a category may show only a loose resemblance between the characters and settings, although there is still similarity between the actions and their sequence. Imagine the same child in the following interaction:

> One evening a parent asks the child to demonstrate his multiplication skills. After the child does so, he receives some praise and is encouraged to correct his errors.

Despite the dissimilar setting and change of characters, the child might categorize this event with those described earlier because of the similarity of his actions, because of the similarity of his parent's and his teacher's actions, and because of the similarity of the action sequence.

At the highest levels of abstraction, instances of a category are identifiable by virtue of their shared goal type (e.g., demonstrating achievement) and goal conditions (e.g., uncertain success). To continue our example, the child's category might be expanded to include the following event:

> During conversation, the child tries to show a friend the extent of his movie knowledge. The

friend asks questions and shows interest but challenges some of the child's claims about movies.

Note that neither the characters, settings, nor specific
actions need be similar at this level of abstraction. This
is consistent with evidence from taxonomic studies indicating
that goal types and goal properties take precedence over
other attributes in the perception of categories of social
events (13).

Tomkins (14) has extended script conceptions by suggesting
that, in addition to goal types and goal conditions, affect
associated with goal conditions may additionally determine
some script categories. He described several attributes of
affective events which combine with goals and goal conditions
to determine their categorization with other affective events:
a) the most dense, i.e., the most intense and enduring, affect;
b) the sharpest gradients of affective change; c) the most
frequently repeated sequences of such dense and changing affect. Tomkins, in effect, specifies that relevant actions in
some script sequences include the actions expressive of affect
(e.g., frowning) and the restraints on such expression (e.g.,
inhibiting angry outbursts). Events classifiable by reference
to goal types, goal conditions, and these affective qualities
may be called personally significant events and memories for
such events personally significant memories. The cognitive
structures organizing personally significant memories may be
called affective scripts.

The child in our example will form an affective script
only if particular goals, goal conditions, and expressive
actions are associated with each event in the category. For
example, consider this elaborated version of one of the relevant events:

> A child is asked by his teacher to recite an as-
> signed poem from memory. He looks down, frowns,
> and immediately feels apprehensive about the im-
> pending evaluation. He recites the poem to the
> best of his ability, frowning nervously with each
> groping hesitation. His teacher mildly praises
> his performance. The child becomes irritated with
> the evaluative ambiguity of the teacher's reaction
> and kicks the leg of his chair impatiently.

If the child's other experiences include similar attempts to
demonstrate achievement, similarly uncertain success, and a
similar sequence of apprehension and irritation, the abstract
representation of those events will be called an affective
script.

The activation of scripts by events having relevant goal
types and goal conditions facilitates reproduction of memories

which are exemplary instances of the general script category.
Reproduction of an exemplary memory involves the combination
of elements from a specific remembered event with probable
elements inferred from script knowledge (15). By implication,
activation of affective scripts will prompt recall of exemplary instances of a class of events with similar goal types,
goal conditions, and affective qualities. For example, activation of the child's achievement/uncertain success, apprehen-
sion/impatience script will prompt his recall of personally
significant memories in which similar goal properties and
expressive actions are exemplified. There is some evidence
that an affective state does enhance recall for material associated with similar affective states (16;17;18), as required
for this hypothesis. However, the exact role of expressive
actions in this process has not been studied.

The recall of exemplary personally significant memories
is a pivotal feature of self-knowledge. The exemplary memories
available when affective scripts are activated are probably
what most people, with some justification (19;20), regard as
self-knowledge. Furthermore, recall of exemplary personally
significant memories may be directly related to dreams. To
see how this may be so, imagine the child, now a young adult,
who reports the following dream:

> I was watching several dancers who were demonstrating
> their skills to a crowd. The dancers were all very
> tall, and their performance was an awkward, off-
> balance dance by giants. After they stopped, I
> told one of them that their performance would be
> better if they included some smaller dancers with
> more finesse. There was no reaction. He looked
> at me as though he had heard me but was indifferent.

Imagine further that the dreamer, while reflecting on this
dream, recalls the following experience:

> Two days ago I was discussing some ideas about
> philosophy with a group of intellectual friends
> who knew the background to some of the relevant
> material better than I did. I suggested that I
> had some ideas which usefully extended the material
> that they were familiar with. I was given a patient
> hearing, but I had the distinct impression that it
> was merely indulgence.

Continued reflection results in recall of the following memory
as well:

> Two weeks ago, I told my basketball teammates that
> I wanted to play in a different position. I was
> sure that I could contribute more in the new

> position. The response was mild praise for my
> play in the old position but no change in the posi-
> tion I was expected to play.

Finally, the dreamer recalls a more remote event:

> For some reason, the dream also reminds me of a
> time when, as a fourth grader, I was demonstrating
> my knowledge of multiplication to my father. He
> said he was satisfied, but he also talked about
> what I needed to do to improve.

This idealized example suggests that the dream reminded the
dreamer of a series of memories with similar goal properties
and affective qualities--as though the dream and the memories
were instantiations of a single affective script.

Do dreams typically remind people of such coherent families
of personally significant memories? Does this tendency depend
upon how the dream fused and juxtaposed such memories? How
might we study these possibilities? One way to begin examination of these questions is to compare the present formulation
with Freud's influential theory of dream formation. Freud and
his successors attempted to identify recurrent motivationally
and affectively significant memories which a) shape perception
and interpretation of new experiences, including motivationally
and affectively similar presleep events, and b) combine with
the memory for the relevant presleep event to produce the
dream. There are several noteworthy parallels with the affective script formulation described above.

Significant Memories and Dream Work Mechanisms

Despite declining confidence in psychoanalytic theory,
especially its drive-discharge components, Freud's (21) classic
study of dream formation continues to be an important point
of departure in dream psychology. One major tenet of Freud's
model is that the memories of which a dream is formed have a
similar motivational and affective "tenor." He hypothesized
that, when presleep events elicit certain motives and affects
and those motives and affects remain activated during the
night, memories having similar motivational and affective
qualities are combined with the memory of the presleep event
to produce the dream. Freud's most thorough analyses of
associations to dreams revealed not just one or two but a
family of motivationally and affectively similar memories
from which the dream was formed. For example, analysis of

memories associated with his own "Irma's Injection" dream revealed several memories that converged on one theme: self-
justification and revenge.

The results of his analysis are analogous to the reminis-
cences during reflection on the "awkward dance dream" in the
example described earlier. In that example, the dream reminded
the dreamer of several memories with the same theme: achievement and uncertain success. This analogy suggests that
Freud's hypothesis about the memories of which the dream is
formed may be restated in the language of script theory. The
family of motivationally and affectively similar memories
identified by Freud are equivalent to instances of a class
of memories organized by an affective script. If an affective
script is activated by presleep events with the goal properties
and affective qualities that identify the script, and, if that
script remains activated during sleep, script instantiating
memories will be combined to form the dream.

Hoelscher, Klinger, and Barta (22) have presented data
which fairly directly test the hypothesis that activation of
an affective script during dreaming sleep elicits script
related memory elements. They asked individuals to identify
personal goals to which they were highly committed. The pursuit of these goals was continuing rather than momentary in
peoples' lives, so, they might be expected to have a repertoire of memories about recurrent attempts to attain these
goals. During sleep, but without inducing arousal, Hoelscher
et al. presented audio recordings of words or phrases descriptive of the goals to which the individual was highly committed.
During REM sleep, but not during NREM sleep, these words or
phrases were more likely to prompt dream images with goal related content than were words or phrases describing goals to
which another individual was highly committed. If continued
commitment to a goal is interpreted as evidence of an affective script, the Hoelscher et al. results indicate that activation of affective scripts during REM sleep prompts dreams
in which script instantiating memories are involved.

The Hoelscher et al. data are consistent with the notion
that activation of a script during sleep influences dreaming.
The restatement of Freud's hypothesis also suggests that activation of an affective script prior to sleep will transfer
into the sleep of the subsequent night and affect dreaming.
Kuiken, Rindlisbacher, and Nielsen (23) presented data which
fairly directly test this notion. They presented presleep
films either with instructions designed to encourage attention
to affective reactions during the films or with instructions
designed to encourage objective evaluation of the films.
When the instructions directed attention to affective reactions, presumably activating relevant scripts, subsequent

dreams were a) more likely to include affective reactions similar to those experienced during the films and b) less likely to include specific characters, scenes, and non-expressive actions from the films. These results are consistent with what would be expected if an activated affective script elicited a family of script instantiating memories. That is, the affect common to each instantiation of the script would be incorproated into the dream, and the disparate characters, scenes, and non-expressive actions from the several instantiations would be combined to obscure reference to any particular memory, including memory for the presleep films themselves. The Kuiken et al. data are susceptible to alternative interpretation, but they are compatible with the hypothesis that affective scripts were activated by the presleep films and remained activated during dreaming sleep.

There is also evidence (24) that peoples' descriptions of persistent and continuing goals, as indicated by self-report personality tests, correlate positively with judges' ratings of these same goals in dream content. These correlations are approximately as large as those typically obtained in personality research involving global trait measures, suggesting that more specific procedures would provide more compelling evidence. Specifically, there is evidence that unless a trait is significant to an individual, self-reported levels on that trait are poor predictors of thoughts or activities in other situations (25). Analogously, unless an individual has an affective script with a corresponding array of affectively significant memories related to pursuit of a particular goal, those goal properties are unlikely to be manifest in the dream. Research in which affective scripts are more precisely identified (cf. Hoelscher et al. [22]) may clarify this issue.

Freud's theory of dream formation is more than an hypothesis about the motivational and affective similarity of the memories of which the dream is formed. Perhaps of equal importance is that Freud described in detail how elements from a family of motivationally and affectively similar memories are selected and combined to create the dream. An important characteristic of this combinatory process, as Freud saw it, is that complete memories are not typically incorporated into the dream. Instead, elements from those memories, perhaps isolated objects, actions, or persons, are found in the manifest dream. These memory elements are combined and transformed by dream work mechanisms to produce the manifest dream.

Condensation is the first of two major dream work mechanisms. In condensation, either a) the features of several different memory elements are combined to form a single composite image or b) a single memory element, possessing features

in common with several different memory elements, is included
as a collective dream image. For example, the awkward dancer
to whom the dreamer speaks might condense an adult view of a
basketball teammate with a childhood view of a parent, e.g.,
with the facial features of the teammate, the greying hair
of the parent, and the relative height of both. Displacement
is the second major dream work mechanism. In displacement,
motivationally and affectively insignificant elements of significant memories are incorporated into the manifest dream.
For example, the indifference of the dancer in the dream may
be a displacement of the ambivalent evaluation by the father
in an associated memory, with affectively neutral indifference
substituting for affectively significant evaluation.

   The dream work mechanisms described by Freud resemble the
abstractive processes that characterize the development of
affective scripts. Recent studies of concept learning (26)
suggest that, when a person does not know the rule that determines whether an event belongs to a category, the strategy
used is to respond on the basis of similarity of the to-be-
categorized event to known exemplars in memory. It is possible
to consider dream formation as a process by which memories for
recent events are compared with exemplars of classes of personally significant memories. In this view, Freud's dream
work mechanisms are the processes by which features of a personally significant presleep event are compared with features
of exemplary instantiations of a relevant affective script
(see Palombo [27] for a similar conception of the dream work
mechanisms).

   Condensation is a process by which memory elements are
compared and matched. More specifically, when the compared
elements are similar in some respect, they are fused into a
single image or jointly represented by a collective image.
Since affective scripts organize memories for events with
similar goal properties and affective qualities, the comparison and fusion process does not significantly alter the representation of these properties in the dream. On the other
hand, the characters, settings, and non-expressive actions
of script instantiating memories are not the identifying
features of that class of memories. Therefore, they will
coalesce into condensed representations that transform features
of the original memories. For example, the awkward dancer is
a fusion of the attributes of a basketball teammate and a
parent. These memory elements are similar in that a) the
adult view of the teammate and the child view of the parent
are of figures taller than the dreamer and b) the two figures
fill the same roles as indifferent evaluators of the dreamer in
instantiations of the hypothetical affective script. Considered
in terms of their physical features alone, or considered in

terms of the role categories that are salient during waking, this categorization of figures might seem overgeneralized. Nonetheless, the fusion of basketball teammate and parent provides insight into the equivalences determined by affective scripts during dreaming.

Displacement also may be given an articulation that reveals the process of memory comparison during dreaming. Script theory, especially as presented by Schank (11), proposes that, when an event activates a relevant script, script based expectations influence interpretation of ensuing events. When script expectations fail, the anomalous event is remembered with a specific notation about the deviation from expectations. Hypothetically, the event that deviates from expectations is remembered and included as a script instantiating memory until a similar event including a comparable deviation from expectations occurs. At that point, a new script might be formed to organize this new class of events.

Continuing with the assumption that dreaming reflects the comparison of personally significant events with instantiations of an affective script, displacement may be regarded as a dream indication of mismatches between aspects of a presleep event and the affective script which most nearly represents it. This might occur when the presleep event disconfirms script expectations. When script exemplars and script disconfirming anomalies are both activated and combined to form a dream, the result may be that anomalous memory elements from one memory are substituted for exemplary memory elements from another memory. For example, the awkward dancer to whom the dreamer speaks appears to include the indifference of the friends in the "intellectual friends" memory rather than the ambivalent but explicit evaluation by the father in the "parental evaluation" memory. If ambivalent evaluation characterizes the exemplary instances on which the script category was based, then the indifference is an anomalous element which substitutes for an exemplary one to form the dream image. Thus, particularly when the anomalies involve goal properties that identify the affective script, the anomalous substitutions are displacements from the core of the dream, much as Freud hypothesized.

The script theoretic restatement of Freud's dream theory suggests that, because a) dreams include memory elements rather than intact memories and b) these elements are selected and combined through dream work mechanisms, dreams hint at but do not directly reveal the memories of which they are formed. What amazes the unsympathetic observer is that, despite these obscuring factors, Freud believed that it is possible to retrace associative connections from the manifest dream to the original memories of which the dream is formed. He argued

that the dream work could to some degree be reversed in free
associations to the dream. Thus, a dream element which is a
product of condensation should elicit associations that include
the several memory elements which it condenses. For example,
the awkward dancer to whom the dreamer speaks should elicit
the basketball teammate and the parent as associations. Also,
an insignificant dream element which is a product of displacement should elicit the original significant element. For
example, the indifferent dancer in the dream might elicit the
ambivalent father as an association.

Freud was at his empirical best in some of his examples
of dream and dream association analysis. He was sufficiently
precise to enable Foulkes (28) to develop procedures for
assessing the dream work mechanisms. Foulkes' explication
enables description of the associative structures that define
condensation and displacement in terms of the mathematical
formalizations of digraph theory. Thus, despite frequent
criticisms of ambiguity in psychoanalytic dream theory, dream
work mechanisms are precisely defined. These precise definitions enable examination of psychoanalytic hypotheses about
how elements from motivationally and affectively similar
memories are selected and combined to form dreams. With some
modification, they may be used to test the analogous script
theoretic formulations.

From Association to Amplification

There is reason for caution before proceeding with investigation of the dream work hypotheses. The dream work
hypotheses and free associative procedures apply to elements
from the dream and to elements from the memories from which
the dream is constructed. Freud was not explicitly concerned
with the dream as a story-like narrative in which (usually)
the dreamer interacts with other characters in a complexly
structured narrative. He attributed the story-like coherence
of dreams to the rationalizing influences that emerged upon
awakening—what he referred to as secondary elaboration. That
the psychoanalytic analyses ignore the narrative properties
of dreams is also evident in the procedures developed by
Foulkes (28). As he acknowledged, his analyses apply to low-
order semantic units in the dream report and in dream associations, roughly, sentences.

Such an analysis of the predicative concepts (verbs, ad-
verbs, adjectives, connectives) and arguments (agents, objects,
and goals) combined into propositions is referred to as a

microstructural analysis (29). Macrostructural analyses, in contrast, address sequences of propositions linked by temporal, enabling, or causal relations, such as constitute a story narrative. While microstructural analyses may have their place in studies of dreams and self-knowledge, their relation to macrostructural analyses should be kept in perspective. Since dreams do manifest macrostructural properties, the study of dreams at that level of complexity is also appropriate.

Jung (30) was among those dynamic psychologists to argue that the dream often takes the form of a story. The story form that he described includes the elements of tragic drama: a) exposition, i.e., the setting, characters, time, etc., b) plot, i.e., how the characters engage each other in ways that lead to conflict or tension, c) crisis or peripeteia, i.e., the culmination, turning point, or high point of plot development, and d) lysis or catastrophe, i.e., the resolution of the dramatic action. As Jung acknowledged, dream stories are often fragmented or incomplete versions of this pattern, but sometimes rather complete dramas are enacted on the internal stage.

As a result of his macrostructural approach to the dream, Jung departed from Freud's free associative procedures to develop a dream reflection technique he called amplification. Amplification (see Mattoon [31], for a reasonably clear explication of this concept) is a directed form of reflection in which analogues to the dream narrative are sought in episodes from the dreamer's life and in the culture's repository of myths, fairy tales, and literature. In addition to associations to elements within the dream, Jung sought parallels to the complexly structured narrative features of the dream. In his view, the "basketball" memory, the "intellectual friends" memory, and the "parental evaluation" memory are personal amplifications of the "awkward dancer" dream.

In the language of Schank's (11) version of script theory, the dream is a reminder of memories which are instantiations of affective scripts. As a description of reminding, the script analysis of dream and memory narratives may provide a more precise account of the processes involved in Jung's technique for dream analysis. Jung (30) did not abandon Freud's dream work mechanisms, and it is worthwhile to make explicit how those mechanisms may affect the form of the dream narrative. To see this clearly, it is necessary to consider which elements within the dream and an associated personal memory are analogous. For example, the dancer addressed by the dreamer in the "awkward dancer" dream is analogous to the intellectual friends addressed in the "intellectual friends" memory. This is determined by their identical positions as the objects of

the dreamer's attempts to persuade in the two narratives. By
using available methods for describing analogous positions
within narratives about action sequences (cf. Stein & Glenn
[32]), it is possible to consider the intellectual friends
as an association to the dancer. By applying Foulkes' (28)
microstructural procedures to this and other such associations,
it may be possible to trace the transformation of analogous
elements in script instantiating memories which form the dream.
This form of analysis sets useful restrictions on the free
associations regarded as relevant to dream formation. It
also specifies that condensation is a mechanism by which
analogous narrative elements from instantiations of an affective script are compared and either superimposed or selected
for inclusion in the dream. Displacement is similarly specified as the mechanism by which analogous narrative elements
from instantiations of an affective script are compared, such
that anomalous elements displace exemplary elements. As an
account of the memory transformations that form the dream,
script theory could be enhanced by incorporation of such
mechanisms and procedures.

Dreaming and Memory for Significant Events

The proposition that dream formation involves the comparison of personally significant presleep events with instantiations of an affective script suggests that dreaming is a
part of the abstractive process that forms affective scripts.
It follows fairly directly that an event categorized with
others during affective script development will more likely
be reproduced when that script is activated again. Thus, the
script model naturally prompts inquiry into the question of
whether dreaming enhances recall for personally significant
events. This question was not anticipated by Freud. The
psychoanalytic theory of dream formation is primarily a theory
of how memories for motivationally and affectively significant
events subtly penetrate the dream. Rather than influencing
memory, Freud hypothesized that the coalescence of recent and
remote memory elements in the dream provides surreptitious
gratification of wishes in order to protect sleep. However,
a number of Freud's successors argued that dreaming has functions independent of drive discharge. For example, Lowy (33)
hypothesized that dreaming related recent memories to earlier
but motivationally and affectively similar memories, making
the latter more readily available for recall. Dream researchers
have examined a comparable hypothesis during the last several
years.

There is now fairly good evidence--especially from studies
of animals--that memory for events occurring prior to sleep is
greater when tested after NREM sleep is interrupted than when
tested after REM sleep is interrupted. The evidence from
human studies is far more equivocal, but it does point to a
memory facilitative effect for REM sleep when the remembered
event is personally involving and affectively arousing (34).
For example, in a study by Greiser, Greenberg, and Harrison
(35), high ego-strength participants attempted to solve anagrams preselected to ensure that about half of them could be
solved in the time allowed. To make the task affectively
engaging, participants were informed that the task assessed
intelligence. Relative to NREM deprivation, REM deprivation
disrupted recall of failed (affectively negative) anagrams.

Cartwright, Lloyd, Butters, Weiner, McCarthy, and Hancock (36) directly studied the recall of personally significant material. Participants completed two tasks, one in which
they assessed whether selected adjectives were self-descriptive
and another in which they assessed whether the adjectives
described themselves as they would like to be. They were
tested for recall of the adjectives after one hour and after
seven hours, and recalled words were divided into old words
(i.e., words recalled on both tests) and new words (i.e.,
words recalled on the delayed test only). The REM deprived
participants recalled fewer adjectives than participants only
partially REM deprived, conceptually replicating the Greiser
et al. study (35). Equally interesting is that the two groups
differed in the kinds of adjectives remembered. The new words
recalled by REM deprived participants tended to be negative,
introspective self-descriptors, whereas the new words recalled
by partially REM deprived participants tended to be positive,
achievement and interaction related self-descriptors. These
data suggest that memory for the presleep event was reproduced
differently when participants were allowed more dreaming sleep.
Perhaps activation of relevant affective scripts during
dreaming facilitated memory reorganization, such that subsequent recall was selective for different self-descriptive
adjectives.

Generally, the preceding research is consistent with the
notion that REM sleep enables continued reorganization of
memories for personally significant events. However, the research to date does not differentiate the physiological effects
of REM sleep on memory from the psychological effects of dreaming on memory. Research on dreaming per se is necessary to
clarify this issue. For example, to determine whether the
Cartwright, Lloyd, et al. (36) results are due to activation
of affective scripts, the methods used by Hoelscher et al. (22)
to influence which scripts are activated would enable differentiation of the physiological from the psychological effects.

It should also be possible to examine the relation between the form that dreams take and memory for personally significant presleep events. If condensation is the matching of analogous elements from presleep memories and script instantiating memories, indices of condensation, such as developed by Foulkes (28), may be expected to increase to the extent that the presleep memory is assimilable within existing script organization. If displacement, on the other hand, is the substitution of anomalous elements from presleep memories for exemplary elements from script instantiating memories, then indices of displacement may be expected to decrease as the recent memory becomes increasingly collated with similar memories. Finally, increases in condensation and decreases in displacement should predict accuracy of recall for aspects of the recent event if dreaming is indeed a psychological process which enhances memory. Such research might provide more systematic evidence than was offered by Palombo (27) in his theoretically similar approach.

The preceding analysis suggests that dreaming enhances memory for personally significant events when activation of relevant scripts occurs during REM sleep. This formulation is similar to that offered by Spear and Gordon (37), according to whom, activation of relevant memory structures has effects that linger for hours. This is long enough for significant presleep events to influence activation of relevant affective scripts during subsequent sleep and affect dream content. It is long enough for dreams within a night to manifest thematic continuity (see review in Schwartz, Weinstein, and Arkin [38]). It is also long enough for activation of an affective script to transfer from dreaming sleep to test situations on the following day, which may account for the effects of REM sleep on recall of presleep events relevant to the activated affective script. One further implication is that, if activation of an affective script transfers into waking during the subsequent day, then instantiations of the affective script, other than the script activating presleep event, also should be more readily reproduced. If such a repertoire of memories is more readily available, this constitutes a subtle but important change in self-knowledge.

Dream Reflection and Self-Knowledge

The discussion so far suggests that dreams combine elements from recent and remote personally significant memories, that dreaming is the implicit comparison of presleep memories

with exemplary instances of a class of such memories, and that
dreaming influences the waking availability of presleep events
which match exemplary instances of such memory classes. These
hypotheses about dream formation and dream function have certain implications for the effects of reflection on dreams
during waking, and they help clarify dreams' potential contribution to self-knowledge. Insight-oriented therapies
differ in their hypotheses about a) the conditions which are
optimal for dream reflection and b) the specific effects of
dream reflection. However, there has been little systematic
research on the processes or consequences of dream reflection.
The differences between free association to dreams, dream interpretation, psychodramatic enactment of dreams, etc., are
not sufficiently understood to comparatively evaluate techniques of dream use. There may be merit, however, in considering some general issues not associated with particular
techniques.

Many techniques for dream reflection involve procedures
by which the dreamer's attention is redirected toward the
goal properties and affective qualities of actions in the
dream narrative. For example, dream dramatization (39) involves enactment of dream actions by the dreamer, with attention to accompanying wants and feelings. Perhaps this process
accentuates and clarifies goal properties and affective qualities that are characteristic of a class of personally significant memories. For this to occur, the goal properties and
affective qualities characteristic of affective scripts activated during sleep must be evident to the person reflecting
on his or her dreams. Is the dream enactor merely elaborating
dream narratives by inferring appropriate goal properties and
affective qualities, or is the dream enactor accurately perceiving those properties and qualities as features of the
original dream experience?

Freud's observations of dream associations suggested that
the goal properties and affective qualities of dreams are not
readily discerned by the dreamer. He hypothesized that displacement was the dream "censor," substituting insignificant
for significant memory elements and thereby reducing the
likelihood of direct representation of disturbing goal related
memory elements in the dream. He also suggested that dream
affect was inhibited, although not distorted, for purposes
of pscyhological defense. Consequently, during dream reflection, Freud supplemented dreamer free association with therapist interpretations, i.e., hypotheses about the goal properties
and affective qualities hinted at by the dream.

Freud's hypothesis about distortion of goal properties
during dream formation is closely related to his particular
concern with psychosexual motives, which, in his drive-discharge

theory, were more basic than other motives. However, if we assume that personally significant motives or goals are of a more mundane variety, involving affiliation, achievement, etc., then there is evidence that goal types *are* directly manifest in dream content. Domino (24) found reliabilities for rating general goal types in dreams ranging from .53 to .81, indicating that goals are salient enough in dream activities for judges to detect them consistently. It is reasonable to suspect that familiarity with specific dream actions enables dreamers to even more readily discern the goal properties of their own dreams.

The discernibility of dream affect during dream reflection is perhaps more problematic than the discernibility of goal properties. Freud's hypothesis about inhibition of affect in dreams is, at first glance, consistent with the reported infrequency of explicit affect in dream reports. However, methodological issues obscure the significance of Snyder's (5) oft-quoted finding that no more than 35% of dream reports include explicit descriptions of affect. First, the failure to explicitly recall affect is a common feature of recall for story-like narratives (40). Second, compared to visual and auditory imagery, feeling qualities may be less salient and, when subtle, difficult to describe. Finally, although little affect is spontaneously reported in dreams, considerable affect does emerge when the dream becomes the object of continued contemplation. In the latter circumstance, there is even evidence of greater affective arousal than during recall of waking visual imagery (41;42). This suggests that spontaneous reports of affect are poor criteria for detection of dreams' affective qualities and that concentrated attention is required to discriminate and describe affective qualities in the dream. Although it is necessary to be cautious about *post hoc* inferences of affective qualities appropriate for the recalled dream imagery, it is likely that explicit requests for the dreamer to attend to and describe affective qualities will indicate that affective qualities are more evident than previously assumed.

Another factor influencing the effects of dream reflection may be whether the dream occurs during a period of sleep in which goal properties and affective qualities are salient and in which an array of recent and remote memories is activated. There is evidence that dream reports elicited upon arousal from late night REM periods are more dream-like (i.e., vivid, emotional, and dramatically elaborated) than dreams from early night awakenings (43). There is also evidence that late night dreams include elements from more remote memories than early night dreams (9). If greater dramatic elaboration is associated with the linkage of scripted action sequences, if greater

emotion reflects activation of affective scripts, and if
greater bizarreness reflects the influence of dream work upon
an array of script instantiating memories, perhaps an appropriate conclusion is that late night dreams are more likely
to be constructed from a temporally broad array of affective
script instantiating memories than early night dreams. If
so, perhaps reflection on such dreams will result in recall
of an equally broad array of recent and remote personally
significant memories.

Even though time of night may enable rough identification
of dreams that elicit a broad array of personally significant
memories, it should be possible to more precisely identify
such dreams—independently of whether they occur early or late
in the night. Recall that dreaming reflects the continuing
process of abstraction from instances of personally significant events to create categories of such events and facilitate memory for such events. Recall also that condensation
is the comparison of features of script instantiating memories
to produce dream images that combine shared features of the
seemingly heterogeneous characters, scenes, and non-expressive
actions in script instantiating memories. It follows that a
dream formed by condensation in the absence of displacement
might be an exemplar for an affective script—an exemplar that
encapsulates a greater portion of the similarities among the
relevant memories than any of the waking memories, constrained
by reality, possibly could. A condensation dream might be an
optimal exemplar even though many of the fused elements have
never been experienced during waking. If so, it would justify
claims that dreams should not always be treated as though they
are understandable only by reference to the memories from
which they are formed (cf. Hillman [44]). Instead, condensation dreams may be understood as optimal exemplifications of
particular affective scripts.

If it were possible to identify dreams that are especially
high in condensation and low in displacement, these dreams
might prove useful for waking reflection because of their relatively direct connection with an array of instantiations of an
affective script. Reflection on a condensation dream should
increase the likelihood of recall for events with similar goal
properties and affective qualities, including the memories
that combined to form the dream. In contrast, for dreams which
are high in displacement, anomalous memory elements may elicit
competing associations and more disparate memories.

Condensation dreams may be useful vehicles for self-reflection for other reasons, too. First, condensation dreams
may exemplify the goal related actions and feelings that an
individual is psychologically prepared to interpret and understand. This follows from the proposition that condensation

dreams are exemplary instantiations of affective scripts,
i.e., instantiations of those memory structures an individual
uses to interpret script related events during waking. The
condensed images provide instances of the types of persons,
actions, and feelings that are expected and inferred when
relevant affective scripts are activated during waking. This
aspect of dream significance has been discussed most clearly
by investigators in the existential-phenomenological tradition,
such as Boss (45). Second, condensation dreams may be especially apt metaphors for referring to personal memories that
also instantiate the relevant affective script. That the
dream formation process did not "intend" these images as metaphors, as suggested by Fromm (46), is irrelevant to the proposition that condensation dream images may be especially apt
metaphors for revealing the goal conditions and depth of feeling associated with script instantiating memories. In the
present view, condensation dreams may allow a deepened emotional reliving of these personal memories; they may facilitate
the vivid and affective recall repeatedly emphasized in
therapies that utilize some form of catharsis. Perhaps this
is why Cartwright, Tipton, and Wicklund (47) found that enhanced recall of dreams in the sleep laboratory was associated
with increased feeling expression during subsequent psychotherapy.

    To identify condensation dreams, it may be useful to con-
sider other perspectives in which extraordinary dreams are
distinguished from mundane dreams. For example, Jung (30)
differentiated personal from archetypal dreams and suggested
that archetypal dreams include the same symbolic and narrative forms that are found in myths, e.g., character metamorphoses, hero journeys, etc. Perhaps archetypal dreams are
equivalent to condensation dreams. Consider, for example,
that dreams rated as extraordinary by the dreamer are like
myths in that they are more likely to include character
metamorphoses, e.g., a human figure assuming animal characteristics, than are mundane dreams (48). Metamorphoses suggest incompletely superimposed memory elements and may be
internal evidence that the dream is a condensation dream.
Other indicators of condensation dreams are required because
metamorphoses rarely occur in dreams, but perhaps they, too,
may be found among the anomalies that occur in some--but hardly
all--of our dreams (49).

    Equating myth-like dreams with condensation dreams would
be compatible with Jung's idea that archetypal dreaming effects personality reorganization, if by that it was understood
that reorganization involved formation of more inclusive memory
structures during dreaming. It would also be compatible with
Jung's hypothesis that reflection on myth-like dreams evokes

the deepest of human concerns, if by that it was understood
that a rich array of personally significant memories is evoked.
While not entirely faithful to Jung's notions, these reformu-
lations provide analogous hypotheses about the role of dreams
in self-knowledge. They are not burdened by the generally
discredited conception of a collective unconscious, and they
are amenable to systematic study.

Conclusion

A considerable portion of the preceding review is speculative, although an attempt has been made a) to propose nothing
that was clearly contradicted by existing data and b) to build
upon earlier studies of dreams and self-knowledge. The literature covered might have been more inclusive but only by omitting descriptions of directions that current research is
taking and that future research might take. If a balance of
review and theory is evident, the author's goals will have
been attained. Such a balance would confirm that contemporary
dream psychology is usefully linked to a dynamic tradition in
which self-knowledge is intimately related to the dream and to
a psychological tradition that may enable us to see the dream
as a cognitive accomplishment. Selecting what is best from
these traditions enables both richer and more precise research
strategies.

References

1. Cohen, D.B., and Cox, C. (1975). "Neuroticism in the
Sleep Laboratory: Implications for Representational and
Adaptive Properties of Dreaming." *Journal of Abnormal
Psychology*, *84*, 91-108.

2. Foulkes, D. (1985). *Dreaming: A Cognitive-Psychological
Analysis*. New York: Lawrence Erlbaum.

   A cautious and thorough statement of how dreams may reveal aspects of cognitive processes that are not similarly
   revealed during nondreaming mentation. Well grounded in
   prior empirical studies, describes the possibilities for
   research into how dreams reflect our conceptions of ourselves and others. A valuable discussion of recent dream
   research.

3. Jones, R.M. (1970). *The New Psychology of Dreaming.*
    New York: Grune & Stratton.

    Provides an introduction to a variety of theories of
    dream interpretation and theories of dream formation and
    function, with some attention to how dreams provide "self-
    perception in depth." Limited and somewhat dated dis-
    cussion of empirical studies.

4. Rechtschaffen, A. (1978). "The Single-Mindedness and
    Isolation of Dreams." *Sleep, 1,* 97-109.

5. Snyder, D. (1970). "The Phenomenology of Dreaming." In
    H. Madow and L.H. Snow (Eds.), *The Psychodynamic Impli-
    cations of the Physiological Studies of Dreams* (pp.
    124-151). Springfield, Ill.: Charles C. Thomas.

6. Foulkes, D. (1962). "Dream Reports from Different Stages
    of Sleep." *Journal of Abnormal and Social Psychology,
    65,* 14-25.

7. Foulkes, D. (1982). *Childrens' Dreams: Longitudinal
    Studies.* New York: John Wiley & Sons.

8. Cartwright, R.D.; Bernick, N.; Borowitz, G.; and Kling,
    A. (1969). "Effects of an Erotic Movie on the Sleep
    and Dreams of Young Men." *Archives of General Psychol-
    ogy, 20,* 263-271.

9. Verdone, P. (1965). "Temporal Reference of Manifest
    Dream Content." *Perceptual and Motor Skills, 20,*
    1253-1268.

10. Nielsen, T.; Kuiken, A.; Moffit, A.; Hoffman, R.; and
    Wells, R. (1983). "Comparison of the Story Structure
    of Stage REM and Stage 2 Mentation Reports." *Sleep
    Research, 12,* 181.

11. Schank, R.C. (1982). *Dynamic Memory.* Cambridge: Cam-
    bridge University Press.

12. Schank, R.C., and Abelson, R. (1977). *Scripts, Plans,
    Goals, and Understanding.* Hillsdale, N.J.: Lawrence
    Erlbaum.

13. Forgas, J.P. (1981). "Affective Elements in Episode
    Cognition." In J.P. Forgas (Ed.), *Social Cognition:
    Perspectives on Everyday Understanding* (pp. 165-180).
    New York: Academic Press.

14. Tomkins, S.S. (1979). "Script Theory: Differential Mag-
    nification Effects." In H.E. Howland and R.A. Dienst-
    bier (Eds.), *Nebraska Symposium on Motivation 1978:
    Human Emotion (Vol. 26)* (pp. 201-236). Lincoln, Neb.:
    University of Nebraska Press.

15. Alba, J.W., and Hasher, L. (1983). "Is Memory Schematic?"
    Psychological Bulletin, 93, 203-231.

16. Bower, G. (1981). "Emotional Mood and Memory." *American
    Psychologist, 36,* 129-148.

17. Leight, K.A., and Ellis, H.C. (1981). "Emotional Mood
    States, Strategies and State Dependency in Memory."
    Journal of Verbal Learning and Verbal Behavior, 20,
    251-266.

18. Teasdale, J.P., and Fogarty, S.J. (1979). "Differential
    Effects of Induced Mood on Retrieval of Pleasant and
    Unpleasant Events from Episodic Memory." *Journal of
    Abnormal Psychology, 88,* 248-257.

19. Andersen, S.M. (1984). "Self-knowledge and Social In-
    ference: II. The Diagnosticity of Cognitive/Affective
    and Behavioral Data." *Journal of Personality and
    Social Psychology, 46,* 294-307.

20. Andersen, S.M., and Ross, L. (1984). "Self-knowledge and
    Social Inference: I. The Impact of Cognitive/Affective
    and Behavioral Data." *Journal of Personality and Social
    Psychology, 46,* 280-293.

21. Freud, S. (1953). *The Interpretation of Dreams* (1900).
    In J. Strachey (Ed.), *Standard Edition of the Complete
    Works of Sigmund Freud (Vol. 4).* London: Hogarth Press.

    A classic work on dreams that describes how memories
    are related to dreams, how the dream work mechanisms
    transform memory material to produce dreams, and how
    dreams preserve sleep by providing hallucinatory gratifi-
    cation of wishes. Deserving of study by anyone consider-
    ing how dreams subtly reveal and conceal their origins.

22. Hoelscher, T.; Klinger, E.; and Barta, S.G. (1981). "In-
    corporation of Concern- and Nonconcern-related Verbal
    Stimuli into Dream Content." *Journal of Abnormal
    Psychology, 90,* 88-91.

23. Kuiken, D.; Rindlisbacher, P.; and Nielsen, T. (1984).
     "Feeling Expression and the Incorporation of Presleep
     Events into Dreams." *Sleep Research, 13,* 109.

24. Domino, G. (1976). "Compensatory Aspects of Dreams: An
     Empirical Test of Jung's Theory." *Journal of Personality
     and Social Psychology, 34,* 658–662.

25. Bem, D.J., and Allen, A. (1974). "On Predicting Some of
     the People Some of the Time: The Search for Cross-
     situational Consistencies in Behavior." *Psychological
     Review, 81,* 506–520.

26. Medin, D.L., and Smith, E.E. (1984). "Concepts and Con-
     cept Formation." In M.R. Rosenberg and L.W. Porter
     (Eds.), *Annual Review of Psychology (Vol. 35)* (pp. 113–
     138). Palo Alto, Calif.: Annual Reviews.

27. Palombo, S.R. (1978). *Dreaming and Memory: A New Infor-
     mation Processing Model.* New York: Basic Books.

     One of several recent theories of how dreaming affects
     long-term memory for personally significant events.
     Relies mostly upon anecdotal evidence to clarify and
     substantiate hypotheses about how dream work changes
     memory organization.

28. Foulkes, D. (1978). *A Grammar of Dreams.* New York:
     Basic Books.

29. Kintsch, W., and van Dijk, T.A. (1978). "Toward a
     Model of Text Comprehension and Production." *Psycho-
     logical Review, 85,* 363–394.

30. Jung, C.G. (1974). *Dreams.* (R.F.C. Hull, Trans.)
     Princeton: Princeton University Press.

     A useful collection of Jung's otherwise scattered
     essays on dreams, including his description of archetypal
     and personal dream meanings, his theory of the origins
     of archetypal dream images in the collective unconscious,
     and case material showing the progression of dream images
     that accompanies personality development. At times com-
     pelling, at times obtuse, reveals the many-sidedness of
     dreams' relation to personality development.

31. Mattoon, M.A. (1984). *Understanding Dreams.* Dallas, Tex.:
     Spring Publications.

32. Stein, N.L., and Glenn, C.G. (1979). "An Analysis of Story Comprehension." In R.O. Freedle (Ed.), *New Directions in Discourse Processing (Vol. 2)* (pp. 113-155). Norwood, N.J.: Ablex.

33. Lowy, S. (1942). *Foundations of Dream Interpretation.* London: Kegan Paul, Trench, and Trubner.

34. McGrath, M.J., and Cohen, D.B. (1978). "REM Sleep Facilitation of Adaptive Waking Behavior: A Review of the Literature." *Psychological Bulletin, 85,* 24-57.

35. Greiser, C.; Greenberg, R.; and Harrison, R.H. (1972). "The Adaptive Function of Sleep: The Differential Function of Sleep and Dreaming on Recall." *Journal of Abnormal Psychology, 80,* 280-286.

36. Cartwright, R.D.; Lloyd, S.; Butters, L.; Weiner, L.; McCarthy, L.; and Hancock, J. (1975). "The Effects of REM Time on What Is Recalled." *Psychophysiology, 12,* 149-159.

37. Spear, N.E., and Gordon, W.C. (1981). "Sleep, Dreaming and Retrieval of Memories." In W. Fishbein (Ed.), *Sleep, Dreams, and Memory* (pp. 188-203). New York: Spectrum.

38. Schwartz, D.G.; Weinstein, L.N.; and Arkin, A.M. (1978). "Qualitative Aspects of Sleep Mentation." In A.M. Arkin, J.S. Antrobus, and S.J. Ellman (Eds.), *The Mind in Sleep: Psychology and Psychobiology* (pp. 143-241). Hillsdale, N.J.: Lawrence Erlbaum.

39. Perls, F.S. (1969). *Gestalt Therapy Verbatim.* Lafayette, Calif.: Real People Press.

40. Mandler, J.M., and Johnson, N.S. (1977). "Remembrance of Things Parsed: Story Structure and Recall." *Cognitive Psychology, 9,* 111-191.

41. Morishige, H., and Reyher, J. (1975). "Alpha Rhythm during Three Conditions of Visual Imagery and Emergent Uncovering Psychotherapy: The Critical Role of Anxiety." *Journal of Abnormal Psychology, 84,* 531-538.

42. Reyher, J., and Morishige, H. (1969). "Electroencephalogram and Rapid Eye Movements during Free Imagery and Dream Recall." *Journal of Abnormal Psychology, 74,* 576-582.

43. Pivik, T., and Foulkes, D. (1968). "NREM Mentation: Relation to Personality, Orientation Time, and Time of Night." *Journal of Consulting and Clinical Psychology*, *37*, 144-151.

44. Hillman, J. (1978). *The Dream and the Underworld*. New York: Harper & Row.

45. Boss, M. (1958). *The Analysis of Dreams*. New York: Philosophical Library.

   Working within the existential-phenomenological tradition, develops a case for conceiving dreams as reflective of our conceptions of ourselves in relation to others and the world. Emphasizes explication of implicit meanings in the dream experience.

46. Fromm, E. (1951). *The Forgotten Language*. New York: Grove Press.

47. Cartwright, R.D.; Tipton, L.W.; and Wicklund, J. (1980). "Focusing on Dreams." *Archives of General Psychiatry*, *37*, 275-277.

48. Kuiken, D.; Nielsen, T.; Thomas, S.; and McTaggart, D. (1983). "Comparison of the Story Structure of Myths, Extraordinary Dreams, and Mundane Dreams." *Sleep Research*, *12*, 196.

49. Hunt, H.; Ogilvie, R.; Belicki, K.; Belicki, D.; and Atalick, E. (1982). "Forms of Dreaming." *Perceptual and Motor Skills*, *54*, 559-633.

Chapter 9
TOWARD A COGNITIVE PSYCHOLOGY OF DREAMS

Harry T. Hunt

Cognitive Psychology and the Meaning of Dreams

Dreaming, whatever else it may be, is surely a cognitive process, and we will fail to address the phenomenon of dreaming unless we try to understand something of its cognitive or mental genesis. More specifically, the classical concern with whether and how dreams might have symbolic meanings that are open to interpretation requires a cognitive psychology of dreaming. Indeed, as we learn something of how the dream is constructed, specific approaches to dream interpretation (as well as the very idea of dreams having meaning) will become either more or less plausible.

For instance, Freud's (1) method of free association disassembles the "manifest" dream into separate elements, so that the largely verbal free associations to these elements will branch out and reconstitute the "latent" pathways by which the dream was formed. Thus, Freud felt that the dynamic, personal meanings being simultaneously disguised and expressed by the "dream work" would be revealed. It is not *accidental* to this method that Freud believed *all* dreams to be formed from background verbal-propositional thoughts. These thoughts were not permitted direct awareness due to the limiting conditions of sleep and so had to be translated into a more "primitive" visual mode of expression. So, for Freud and more recently for the cognitive psychology of David Foulkes (2) the beginning of all dream formation is verbal, with a secondary visual surface that is to be unravelled by a method of interpretation that reverses the postulated formation process. Freud's method of interpretation assumes that dreaming is a specific kind of cognitive process.

I would like to thank Kate Ruzycki for her careful and humorous editorial assistance.

On the other hand, for Jung (3), and more recently for
James Hillman (4), dream interpretation is not seen as unravelling or reversing the pathways of dream formation, but
instead aims to *finish* the dream through a set of techniques
usually defined as "amplification." Thus the dream might be
paraphrased to show its general metaphoric structure or connected to the cross-culturally common "archetypal" themes of
mythology. For Jung and Hillman dream formation is a positive,
abstract form of thought that conveys self-insight through a
visual-imaginal or "presentational" cognitive mode. Here
interpretation *completes* the dreaming process by rephrasing
it in a verbal-representational mode, and so bringing home
its potentially creative insights. No unravelling or reversing
of an actual process of dream formation is involved. The key
lies in a view of visual imagination and metaphor as an abstract cognitive faculty in its own right.

More academic research-oriented approaches to dreaming
have always been skeptical of attributing symbolic or metaphoric meanings to dreams. Hobson and McCarley's (5) activation-synthesis model of dream formation, for instance, points
to the basis of the REM state in phasic discharge processes in
the pontine formation of the brainstem--common to all mammals.
They and other physiologists argue that what both Freud and
Jung (for different reasons) took as symbolic features of
dreaming--especially its bizarre, constantly shifting quali-
ties--are the product of a non-psychological, more or less
random discharge process in the brainstem. The presence of
inhibited muscle movements in REMing animals (see below)
would mean that dreaming is not a form of thinking at all.
Since most psychologists believe that animals, while capable
of association learning, are not capable of the sort of recombinatory novelty that is basic to human symbolism, dreaming
in itself would not be a meaningful symbolic expression. It
would "work" as such only to the extent that our cognitive
elaborations of randomly activated neuronal subsystems might
offer a fresh perspective on life experiences. But whatever
we learned from dream interpretation would have nothing essential to do with what dreaming was about as a process. (Thus
we are led toward the ever popular mechanical randomness model
of human creativity so current in Artifical Intelligence
circles.)

It is true that interpretation--by whatever method and
according to whatever view of dreaming--comes *after* the dream.
Empirically, it is superimposed over the dream. Most certainly
dreams can thereby be *turned into* symbols, but the real question for a cognitive psychology of dreams is whether there
are empirically demonstrable features within dream experience
which show the operation of symbolic-creative processes--and

if so, whether these processes are verbal-representational, visual-metaphoric, or both. Thus we see the need for a cognitive perspective on dreams with respect to their most basic source of historical interest: symbolic meaning and its genesis.

However, the apparent exoticness of much dreaming, and its apparent close relation to waking altered states of consciousness, make it hard to relate to the sort of cognitive psychology currently being held up by some as the discipline needed to make sense of dreams. Indeed, experimental-cognitive psychology, with its bias against phenomenology and its concentration on language, is far too narrow to provide a satisfying account of the varieties of dreams. *If* dreaming, especially in its creative-bizarre forms, is mainly visual-spatial and metaphoric, then its exploration necessarily becomes a contribution to the heterodox organismic-holistic psychologies of imagination, metaphor, and aesthetics associated with Werner and Kaplan (6) and Rudolph Arnheim (7). Indeed, this was the thrust of Calvin Hall's original call for a cognitive psychology of dreaming in the 1950s (8).

Is dreaming, by definition, a form of thinking--a symbolic imagination unique to man (older children and adults)? Or is it a species-specific constructed "life space"--contingent only on the cortical activation of the REM state? If the latter, then only with man would come the added potential for a partial or complete transformation by symbolic processes. Different views on how to understand dreaming in terms of cognition (and possibly even vice versa) seem to depend on the position taken by the investigator on a number of different but potentially related dimensions.

Theories of Cognition

For Edelson (9), as extended by Foulkes (2), language, with its representational, propositional "deep structure," is the ultimate source for all specifically human cognition. So dreaming, to the extent that it involves symbolic cognition, becomes merely a visual or "presentational" paraphrase of language. Thus, features of speech production will ultimately account for the visual "surface array" of dreaming. The cognitive psychology of dreams becomes a kind of psycholinguistics. At the other extreme, Werner and Kaplan (6) and Arnheim (7) see the creative core of the human symbolic capacity as based on visual-spatial imagination and imagery based metaphor, with language primarily being its communicative form of expression. In this view, dreams and related alterations in "rational"

consciousness are especially important because they offer a
more direct access to the nature of thought than any currently
available in cognitive research. Of course, the existence of
"dual code" approaches, postulating more or less separate
verbal-propositional and visual-spatial symbolic faculties
that interact in emergent, creative ways, might be consistent
with the existence of distinct types and varieties of dream
symbolism. Some dreams may rest mainly on linguistic intelligence, some on visual imagination, and some on both.

*Features of the Dream that Show Symbolic-Recombinatory
   Thought*

On the one hand, the story-like, dramatic cohesion of
dreams may be taken as the core of the creative dream process.
On the other hand, some investigators, and most clinically
based approaches to dream interpretation, have been more im-
pressed by predominantly visual forms of dream bizarreness.
These may actually seem to disrupt the dream narrative but com
imbued with the unexpected transformations and recombinations
basic to symbolic thought.

The Nature of Imagery

Dreaming may be understood as *necessarily* a form of
imagination (since your eyes are closed and you still seem
to be seeing and hearing things). If so, *all* dreaming would
be symbolic and abstract and beyond the capabilities of organisms lacking creative imagination. Or, the capacity for
mental imagery as such may be seen as part of *perception* and
so not in itself requiring a true symbolic capacity.
(Accordingly, dream bizarreness might show *that*.)

The Nature of Consciousness

Some psychologists see consciousness as essentially and
criterially human (with possible exceptions for dolphins and
higher apes) and so based on a capacity for self-consciousness, "self-reference," or "reflexivity." Accordingly, only
organisms with the capacity to turn around on their own perceptual and affective processes--what George Herbert Mead (10)
called "taking the role of the other"--could dream. Alterna-
tively other psychologists insist that there are different

levels of "consciousness." The first is an immediate sentience present by definition in all motile creatures with
aroused nervous systems--and which could form the basis of
all dreaming to the extent that dreaming results automatically
from the activated cortex of the REM state.

The Nature of Dream Bizarreness and Altered States of Consciousness

Dream bizarreness, or what might be called "hallucinatory"
features of dreaming, is sometimes seen as a non-cognitive
disruption in the narrative core of dream experience--directly
caused by the phasic discharge activities of the pontine
formation responsible for initiating REM sleep. Or, dream
bizarreness, and closely related states of consciousness in
waking associated with psychedelic drugs and deep meditation,
may be taken as a uniquely direct manifestation of the processes
involved in metaphor and imagination.

Methodology for the Study of Dreams

Possibly in no other area of psychological study is the
contrast between laboratory-experimental methods (for the
study of psychophysiology and content norms of recalled
dreams) and phenomenology (of special types, cases, and meanings) so striking--or the need for their creative synthesis
more obvious.

Indeed, any attempt at a cognitive psychology of dreams
will tap directly into the major debates of the human sciences.
While positions taken on any of the above dimensions tend to
determine what investigators "see" when they look at dreams,
each position has also managed to generate new and unexpected
empirical findings. If, as it seems, we have strong evidence
favoring *both* poles of these alternatives, then we will want
a cognitive psychology of dreaming that is correspondingly
eclectic and multiple--but that has not proven so easy.

The Dream as a Linguistic Narrative-- Absent in Young Children and Lower Mammals: The Contribution of David Foulkes

In recent years David Foulkes has worked prodigiously to
develop a cognitive psychology of dreaming as psycholinguistic

skill. The great strength of such an approach is, of course, that most dreaming involves an internally generated story, and it is this side of the phenomenon that Foulkes makes central. He points to a potential separation of the processes of dreaming from the physiology of the REM state, arguing that a cognitive theory of dreams can largely dispense with psychophysiological studies of REM sleep. The striking correlations between dream bizarreness ratings (5;11) and phasic REM events are used by Foulkes to dismiss dream bizarreness as "peripherally induced aberrations in the central organization of dreaming" (12, p. 358). Bizarreness in dreams is held to be akin to "errors" in speech production—even though such phenomena are the traditional source of clinical and personal impressions that dreams involve symbolic metaphor.

A fascinating consequence of his view is that dreams would be absent in very young children and lower animals, since they would lack the necessary linguistic and self-referential capacities to construct the imaginative scenarios of dreaming. Their REM periods, with respect to experience would be "empty" (13;14). Indeed this might appear to solve one of the dilemmas of REM psychophysiology—that the early neonatal and later fetal period seems to be spent predominantly in the REM state. Now, any account of neonatal and fetal *dreams* must be purely speculative. (Although it is worth noting that the most recent tendency in developmental psychology has been to push back, further and further toward birth, the sorts of perceptual, affective, and cognitive sensibilities that Piaget assumed took months and even years to appear.) If we can rule out infant dreams by definition, then we are let off worrying about what they might "be" or "be for." Yet perhaps that is a question that should remain open rather than closed.

Before proceeding, it is worth being clear on two points: first, I do not know whether animals and infants dream. So far there is no way to even gather evidence bearing on such a question. It remains necessarily inferential, either way. But it is a truly heuristic question in the sense of being a useful litmus test of competing cognitive theories of dreams. It will force us and help us to think through the complex relations between immediate awareness and self-consciousness on the one hand, and perception and imagination on the other. Second, it is my personal conviction that Foulkes' cognitive theory of dreams is as narrow and prematurely restricted as his experimental data are unique, fascinating, and exciting. We will look more closely at this potentially poor fit between theory and data, but it is worth noting that any student of this area must begin with the recent empirical findings of Foulkes and his colleagues. The problem comes with trying to reconcile Foulkes' material with the equally rich but very

different traditions of dream phenomenology and dream interpre-
tation--which since Freud and Jung have centered on the bizarre
and visually fantastic side of dreaming as the core of dream
symbolism--however difficult such phenomena may be for current
cognitive orthodoxy. Perhaps here dream psychology might do
something for cognitive theory, rather than just the other way
around!

In the only sleep laboratory longitudinal studies ever
done with young children (12;13), Foulkes found that three-
to five-year-olds described content from only 27% of REM
awakenings and that these reports were surprisingly simple:
single, static images, without narrative transformation or
dynamic movement, without affect or presence of self. Their
content was often of animals (38% of recalled episodes) and
tended toward themes of tiredness or sleep (25% of dream reports). Foulkes relates this apparently gradual development
of childhood dreaming to Piagetian views of waking cognitive
development--citing similar stages in tests of voluntarily
generated imagery, moving from the static to the gradually
kinematic (notwithstanding the fact that dreams are not voluntarily generated images of the sort studied by Piaget). Foulkes
reports that the early occurrence of these simple dreams and
the rate of their progression toward narratively complex dreams
were significantly correlated with tests of visual-spatial
skills, specifically, embedded figures and block designs.
The lack of correlation with the child's verbal and recall
abilities certainly does not support any simple interpretation
in terms of memory or confabulation. In other words, these
dreams really do seem to occur at these ages. But, as an
aside, it would seem that such findings actually support a
spatial-metaphoric view of dream formation--not one related
to speech production per se. Foulkes cites several studies
showing loss of dreaming (or dream recall?) with aphasia,
arguing that anything impairing the "inner speech" process
which generates the narrative core of dreaming must eliminate
the phenomenon. However, Foulkes' view that the deep structure of dreaming is left hemisphere linguistic, with the supposedly visual "surface" of dreams being lost with right
hemisphere damage, has been contradicted by more systematic
study of the effects on dreaming of various forms of brain
damage (15).

Foulkes (13;14) does provide some fascinating case study
evidence suggesting that deficit or lack of development in
the spatial analytic and recombinatory capacity measured by
embedded figures and block design tests was associated with
an absence of the narrative story component of dreaming (in
fourteen-year-old twins with otherwise normal cognitive
development). Severe impairment in the capacity for imaginal

spatial rotation in two subjects (as measured by deficits in
the ability to match pictured geometric forms to correct test
forms presented at different angles of possible three dimen-
sional rotation) still allowed the subjects to report complex
narrative dreams, but without any specific visualized detail.
Whether these findings pertain to all dreaming per se or only
to a symbolic elaboration of the dreaming process remains to
be determined.

But the real problem with respect to Foulkes' child studies
is how we are now to regard the many anecdotal and clinical
reports of explicit narrative dream recall in the second and
third years, parental reports of telltale confusions in
awakening children in the first and second years, or the
powerful anxiety dreams of some very young children. I do
not think we can follow Foulkes' outright rejection of all data
that aren't laboratory based, especially since--whatever the
respective strengths and weaknesses of experimental versus
observational methods--his reports were in all probability
destined for instant oblivion without laboratory intervention,
whereas it was the anecdotal reports that actually intruded
on their observers. We need a cognitive account that includes
both sets of material and that avoids theoretical and methodological straightjackets, however "tightly" appealing.

Which brings us to a crux of the matter: whether the basic
processes of dreaming are more like perception--and so potentially available to any creature in the REM state--or more
like creative imagination--and so *by definition* beyond infants
and animals. Once again, Foulkes and his colleagues have a
fascinating study of partially blind subjects (16). They
argue that the visually precise dreams of settings encountered
only *after* their subjects' blindness show that we dream not
as we see but as we *imagine*. Surely this *can* be true, but it
ignores the equally "hard" but contrary data of Roffwarg et
al. (17) on the carry-over of distorting prism effects into
dreaming and also Herman et al.'s (18) work on the similarity
between rapid eye movements during activated sleep and waking
scanning patterns in *darkened* surroundings. In other words,
the eye movements of dreaming are functionally related to
those of waking perception.

Foulkes says, "Literally, of course, conditions of sleep
make it impossible for dreaming to be any kind of perception.
Dreaming is a mental-imaginal process: it can be nothing
else" (13, p. 281). So, if your eyes are closed, it can't be
perception! That only follows on a narrow "copy" model of
perception. It makes no sense at all if we concede any constructive aspect to perceptual activity. On this latter view,
if the brain is working in the REM state more or less as it
does when awake, which seems to be the case, then the "life

world" of such a creature would have to be reconstituted in more or less the same way. Further, there is reason to suggest that reproductive imagery itself is closer to perception than to symbolic imagination, in that it reuses and reactivates the schemata or patterns of perception. Ulric Neisser (19), for instance, separates the capacity for imagery *from* creative imagination, suggesting that imagery is a "detachment" of perceptual schemata from perception-action cycles in service of the sorts of memory and anticipation that are part of the learning abilities in all mammals.

So, if animals exhibit REM, they can dream--dreams that would presumably reproduce their species-specific life world, but not creatively reorganize or recombine it. The squirrel's dream tree is then no more symbolic than its waking tree. It presumably dreams in the motorically organized, sequential "stories" of its waking life, just as we do. And we can add that if lower animals do dream (as the inner side of their capacities for recall and anticipation) then they *would* lack the self-referential abstract attitude needed to *recall* those dreams--which fits both with the typical lack of recall in children ages three to five and the occasional anomalous breakthroughs of highly vivid dreams at these same ages and younger.

I would suggest that it is dream recall that is like pulling an embedded figure (the rapidly receding dream) out of the complex array of one's situation on awakening. In his younger laboratory subjects Foulkes may actually be picking up not this perception-imagery core of dreaming, but the first *symbolic* transformations of that core. The child's nascent symbolic capacity would impinge on and transform the more basic but inherently forgettable dream reproduction of the forms of waking experience. Foulkes may be measuring not dreaming per se but the meshing of the child's developing capacity for abstract recall with the steps by which dreaming (and waking) cognition actually becomes symbolic. Dream reports of self-representation of one's own sleeping state and anthropomorphic identifications with animals, along with the lagging of the imagery of self-representation behind that of others, all fit with accounts of general *symbolic* development.

Further support for this re-interpretation of Foulkes' work comes from the surprising predominance of realistic, true-to-daily-life dreams in adult sleep laboratory subjects-- dreams which are otherwise readily forgotten. Dorus, Dorus, and Rechtschaffen (20) found that 66% of their laboratory dream samples were rated by judges as either having occurred in a similar manner in the subjects' waking life or entirely plausible therein. Snyder (21) upset other traditional applecarts by showing that 90% of his trained laboratory subjects

could recall spoken content from their dreams, and 60% could
quote it. Dream speech was generally ordinary and undistorted
while 70% of the dreams showed original and generally adequate
cognitive reflection on ongoing dream circumstances and implications. (As an aside, it is worth noting that the prevalence of dream-appropriate speech and reflective thought in
dreams contradicts both Foulkes and Freud on the idea that
dream formation necessarily uses up or suppresses verbal
thought. So much for the simple solutions.) In other words,
dreaming, in the first instance, reduplicates our waking world
We can do in it more or less what we can do when we are awake--
a point made long ago in the phenomenological approach to
dreams of Medard Boss (22). Such realistic dreams may be the
human form of the species-specific dreamscapes I am positing
for all REMing creatures. A childhood development of an abstract self-referential capacity would be more naturally
attuned to the recall of correspondingly abstract symbolic
forms of dreaming, *but* eventually it would help even these
realistic mundane dreams through the recall barrier of the
REM state--a barrier which even the most direct laboratory
intrusions cannot completely eliminate.

Another crucial point for our discussion lies in the
definition of consciousness in cognitive psychology. Foulkes
believes that defining consciousness in terms of organismic
responsiveness is ultimately *uninteresting* and that conscious
awareness must entail multiple levels of information process-
ing--which he defines as "internal self-reference" or the
ability "to process the fact that we are processing" (14, p.
329). If so, then of course *by definition* the REM period of
creatures lacking self-reference will be "empty." However,
most recent discussions of human consciousness (23) and animal
awareness (24) have tried to distinguish at least three
levels: immediately given sentience, as indexed by specific
motor responsiveness; the capacity to image in the absence of
concurrent stimulation, indexed by the response delays in
anticipation and by various forms of learning; and the self-
referential capacity first found in higher primates and dolphins, uniquely developed in man, and indexed by novelty and
fantasy, or by what Neisser terms "schematic rearrangement."
The first two levels would allow animal dreaming. And if such
dreaming in lower animals and infants reactivates perceptual
activity, there is no reason to believe they are conscious of
that *experience* in anything like the introspective fashion
that opens out with the full development of human intelligence.
Of course, we have all been taught to wield Occam's razor on
the whole issue of animal awareness. But there are more and
more dissenting voices, and we need to consider the corresponding dilemma of theoretical parsimony in trying to explain how

creatures with an activated cortex, organized sequences of
inhibited outward behavior (which can be surgically disinhibi-
ted), and "scanning" eye movements are, nonetheless, not experiencing anything.

Which of course brings me, for good or ill, to my own
many years of playing Jane Goodall in the privacy of my own
study with the REM states of my golden retriever, Bill. All
of you who have pets have seen the phenomenon. Bill's eyes
start moving rapidly under his lids, he twitches, groans,
growls, wags his tail, makes drinking sounds, and shows the
incipient rapid paw movements (RPM) of ostensible walking and
running. One of the pioneers of research on the REM state,
Michel Jouvet, was the first to show that the surgical disinhibition of REM state muscle paralysis in cats resulted in
complex behaviors which he and others interpret as the acting
out of dreaming. Morrison (25) has recently called into
question Jouvet's direct oneiric interpretation by showing
that, depending on the placing of the experimental lesion
around the pontine formation, these REM behaviors can appear
as isolated, stereotyped reflexes, which can erupt during
wakefulness as well. He interprets the surgical disinhibition
of REM movements and the resulting increase in motoric activity when awake as showing a *common* disruption of the orienting
response to novel stimuli—which he locates in the brainstem
and sees as working in essentially the same way, whether the
creature is awake and responding to outward stimulation or
in REM sleep and responding to internal phasic activations.
However, as to whether the normally inhibited REM movements
in dogs and cats show *dreaming*, I can only point to the
natural *ordering* and *pacing* of diverse incipient movements
in my dog—*and* the occurrence of more drinking sounds if I
forget his water (in apparent mimicking of Freud on wish fulfillment), his responsiveness to reassuring vocalizations
during signs of REM distress, but without any behavioral sign
of arousal, *and* the one memorable time when he started fully
awake in the midst of an unusually intense anxiety REM and
looked with an all-too-brief surprise and ostensible puzzlement
at his surroundings. Parsimony calls this dreaming.

The core of the dream process is unique. It is not
exactly a perception, not *exactly* a functional image, and not
exactly an hallucination. I would suggest it is the reconsti-
tution of the typical life world of the REMing creature—which
is very far from presupposing self-reference or symbolic
imagination. But note the irony here too. For the reason we
study dreaming is for its symbolic imaginative transformations
and their potential development—not for the part that recon-
stitutes everyday life, and rightly so.

Foulkes' childhood studies do trace the development of
this symbolic-imaginative line of dreaming. But his assimila-
tion of dreaming to current "cognitive science" has slipped
steeply down one side of traditional Cartesian dualism. We
cannot afford to see dreaming only through the prism of language. Rather, its metaphoric and visually fantastic properties lead us to the more organismic approaches of Werner and
Kaplan (6) and Arnheim (7), which are naturally attuned to
the phenomenologies of image and metaphor and to the notion
that the symbolic capacity is ultimately of the senses and
their recombinatory reuse. This brings us to the varieties
of dream bizarreness and to the question of whether they are
to be understood, with Foulkes, as peripheral and primitive
disruptions of dreaming, or as the very fabric of symbolic
cognition.

Dream Bizarreness as Visual-Spatial Thinking
and Creative Metaphor

My own empirical work with dreams began with the systematic study of the varieties of dream bizarreness--of what
it is about dreams that *can* make them different from everyday
waking experience in terms of perception, thinking, memory,
volition, and interpersonal relations (26). These transformations are generally highly similar to the wide range of
so-called "altered states of consciousness," so that the same
debate between theories of abstract metaphor and theories of
primitive regression applies to both.

The most striking form of dream bizarreness consists in
unlikely or impossible events intruding on an otherwise generally plausible dream setting. These intrusions were almost
always visual, and occurred in 47% of home recalled dreams
(27% if we restrict the ratings to events that are virtually
impossible in ordinary waking life--like seeing a leopard
walking down a city street, etc.). Unlikely or impossible
somatic perceptions and auditory perceptions occurred in 10%
and 14% respectively. If subjects were asked to report their
most fantastic "dream-like" dream, these visual, somatic, and
auditory "bizarre intrusion" scores jumped to 86%, 43%, and
26%. A related category for transformations in perceptual
form (similar to the spontaneous changes in color, size,
distance, and shape occurring with psychedelic drugs and including geometric or mandala patterns of the sort considered
important in religious visions by Jung) was relatively infrequent in ordinary dream samples (13%), but climbed to 43%

for the "most fantastic" sample. These were almost entirely
visual, and in general, the major "positive" forms of dream
bizarreness do seem to be predominantly visual. This perhaps
explains the traditional false impression that all dreaming
is basically visual--since it is first and foremost the bizarreness of their dreams that calls peoples' attention to them.

The other striking characteristic of dream experience
consisted in lacuna or deficits in verbal intelligence or
narrative cohesion: abrupt shifts in scene (20% of home recall
dreams), confusions and inadequacies in reasoning about ongoing dream events (41%), problems of recall within the dream
about preceding dream events (15%); and difficulties in recalling parts of the dream after awakening (30%). But these
categories of confusion do not go up to the same degree as
bizarre perceptions if we ask subjects to give us their most
fantastic dreams. Finally, it is interesting that supposedly
classical staples of dreams like encountering "bizarre personi-
fications" (monsters, terrifying animals, mythic figures, etc.)
and changes in dreamer identity were infrequent in ordinary
dream recall (4% and 3% respectively)--increasing only to 34%
and 17% in the "most fantastic" sample. Again it is important
to note, even with this very detailed attempt to categorize
all forms of dream bizarreness, including barely noticeable
slippages of thought and memory, that 30% of home and laboratory dreams lack *any* feature that would distinguish them from
stories told about one's everyday waking life.

So what makes dreams bizarre is a relative lack in verbal
continuity and the positive intrusion of anomalous visually
perceived events. How might this fit with the view that such
intrusions show an abstract metaphoric or symbolic capacity--
a capacity possibly of the right hemisphere in contrast to
the left hemisphere narrative features emphasized by Foulkes?
Several empirical studies have found significant correlations
between bizarreness in dreams and measures of creativity--and
in a recent study with Theresa Casteels, we found a measure
of visual-metaphoric thought (the physiognomic cues test) to
be a better predictor of bizarreness than a verbal word association measure. Theoretically the organismic-holistic approach to cognition associated with Werner and Kaplan (6),
Arnheim (7), and Ulric Neisser (19) views human symbolism as
resting on a capacity to "turn-around on" and "disassemble"
the basic patterns or schemata of perception and recombine
them in novel, creative ways. These theories tend to separate
the basic operations of thought from language, as their major
means of functional expression. Accordingly, the intrusion
of unlikely visual content into the dream setting and the
occasional presence of what Freud called "condensation" in
the dream--where normally separate elements are fused together

in one percept--show, perhaps uniquely, just the sort of unusual juxtaposition and recombination basic to all symbolic
cognition. The paucity of auditory and verbal anomalies in
contrast to these visual transformations is striking. Indeed,
the more psychedelic changes in size and shape and occasional
geometric designs would illustrate the sort of geometric-
abstract imagery and imagery manipulations basic to Rudolph
Arnheim's approach to visual thinking in the arts. If we
share the assumption common to clinical neurology and much
of psychiatry that anomalies of consciousness show the normally
"masked" and necessarily unconscious phases of cognitive operations, then we have to conclude that the predominance of
visual bizarreness in dreams shows the underlying processes
of creative thought in dreams. The predominant source of
this creative-recombinatory activity in dreaming (and perhaps
waking) is visual-spatial rather than linguistic.

The neurologist Norman Geschwind (27) suggested that
human symbolic capabilities were based on the emergent capacity
for direct, synaesthetically based, cross-modal translation
between patterns of the different senses, in terms of their
structural possibilities and independent of subcortical reward-
punishment contingencies that control the non-recombinatory
forms of associational learning in lower animals. Extrapolating
from his suggestion we can see how such a cross-modal translation capacity could account for human creative-recombinatory
thinking. Since the qualities of the different senses are
both similar and different in structure and rhythm, their
inter-translation, ultimately occurring for its own sake in
terms of structural possibilities, would generate the sort of
novelty long held criterial to human intelligence. In addition, I would suggest that it is the cross-modal translation
between visual and tactile-motor patterns that constitutes
the core of "thinking," which is, at various phases of its
operation, more or less independent of the sorts of verbal-
auditory cross-modal translations that would allow language.

Interestingly, some of the most bizarre forms of dream
content seem to be based directly on this sort of translation
between visual and somatic patterns. In several instances
bizarre visual effects can be experimentally "driven" by unusual tactile stimulation--thereby possibly illustrating something of the normally hidden processes of metaphor formation.
Herbert Silberer (28), one of the early pioneers of dream
studies, was struck by the way that external or internal
somatic states could be turned into visualized dream events.
He termed these "somatic autosymbols"--self-referential visual
depictions of physiological and muscular conditions. There
has long been speculation on whether certain kinds of visual-
somatic bizarreness in dreams might be medically diagnostic.

A brief example comes from one of my own experiences in which a feverish flu-like condition, associated with rapid involuntary tremors in my lower limbs, was translated into a dream of an approaching rattlesnake--with its uplifted head oscillating at the same rate as my shaking leg muscles. When with great effort I managed to interrupt its steady advance by pushing a chair in front of it, I immediately awakened with the fever gone. The snake was in some sense symbolic or metaphoric, since the illness did advance suddenly and unexpectedly, like a deadly snake, leading immediately to the sleep onset during which the dream occurred. Tore Nielsen and Don Kuiken (29) report what may be a similar artificial driving of our metaphoric ability to "embody" in visual structure various kinesthetic-tactile "postures." They describe a recent study in which dreaming subjects with a blood pressure cuff on one leg described highly unusual types of flying, falling, and dancing dreams, very similar to the dreams of patients with damage to the vestibular or balance-coordination region of the nervous system.

Another place where visually bizarre dreams are closely linked to similar somatic sensations and hallucinations within the dream, and of obvious metaphoric significance, is in the dreams of some acute schizophrenics (30). These dreams show a striking sense of uncanniness and cosmic import and extreme, often morbid, sexuality and aggression, with the latter involving peculiar body-image distortions, mutilations, and dismemberment. These dreams of somatic dismemberment and internal mutilation are very similar to waking somatic complaints in these patients. A number of psychiatrists have interpreted the latter as evidence of impacted or defensively concrete metaphorical thinking (31)--and when these implicit self-referential depictions are finally faced by the patient, we see a manifestation of the unusual creativity that has sometimes been detected with experimental measures in hospitalized schizophrenics. The importance of visionary dismemberment experiences in tribal shamanism may also suggest that the visualization and ultimately the "saying" of such incipient metaphoric expressions are part of mythological and imaginal thinking and so at the core of culture. Although most cognitive psychologists view such phenomena as merely a regressive disorganization rather than as a positive revelation of the processes of metaphor, many psychiatrists and psychoanalysts have come to understand acute schizophrenia as a massive problem solving crisis ("thought attack") that bears some relation to creative cultural and religious mentation. This would be true whether the immediate pressure on the metaphoric capacity was "caused" by genetics and biochemistry or by personal and sociocultural crisis.

If recombinatory thought rests on a turning around on and disassembling of the *perceptual* schemata and if this turning around operates by means of cross-modal translations and re-translations (especially between the structures of touch and vision), then highly intensified, desperately driven thinking about matters that are "encompassing" *should* a) be hallucinatory, i.e., appear directly in the perceptual forms being reused, b) involve the dislocation and sensed collapse of perception and affect along the lines of their own structural patterns and unfolding, and c) feel metaphorically or physically like torture and dismemberment. The latter would be produced by what Hillman (4) sees as the inherent and necessary destructiveness of creative thought--especially, we can add, if such thought is mediated by tactile-gestural embodiment. By definition, creative thought shatters the previous assumptions of an individual (and society) and to the extent that thinking ultimately rests on and reuses the senses, that shattering may be directly and painfully felt.

A further indication that it is dream bizarreness which shows creative cognitive symbolism most directly, along with the first hint that there may be distinct types of dreaming (each with its roots in different forms of imagination), comes from looking at the personal dreams of Freud (1) and Jung (3). It seems significant that in these famous instances where dreams were especially cultivated as a means of symbolic self-reflection, bizarreness is heightened in comparison to normative recall samples (26). There have long been indications that serious interest in ones' dreams will change them in the direction of the interpretive method being used. It is as if the dreaming process itself can be modified from within so as to "answer" the kind of questions asked of it. True to his theory of the senseless hodge-podge of the "manifest" dream and the necessity of finding a disguised latent meaning through verbal free association, Freud's own dreams were unusually confused in cognition and memory and were lacking in verbal continuity, with unlikely but not highly bizarre visual intrusions. These unlikely visualizations came predominantly from his own recent past experience and only made sense through the related memories to which his free association would lead him. Jung, on the other hand, had appropriately Jungian dreams--with comparatively little cognitive or verbal confusion and strikingly "archetypal" and uncanny visualizations of mythic figures, fantastic settings, and psychedelic transformations of size, shape, and geometric structure. So it is hardly surprising that for Jung dreams were clear and undisguised creative expressions of a deep visual-imaginal intelligence, and that interpretation was not the unravelling of a superficial surface array, but a finishing or "dreaming on" of what the dream had already "said" in non-verbal metaphor.

Given the complexity of a symbolic intelligence based on translations back and forth among visual, tactile-kinesthetic, and verbal-auditory patterns, it certainly seems plausible that dream formation could take very different forms to the extent that it becomes symbolic--being predominantly visual-tactile and metaphoric in some instances and verbal-associational or linguistic in others. This impression is strengthened by the existence of what could be termed a "second order" of dreaming, in which the *entirety* of the dream setting and its activities are transformed by creative symbolic imagination. This contrasts with the periodic intrusions and confusions which we have been discussing up to now. For instance, there are occasional reports of dreams of great narrative and dramatic complexity and originality, but with no necessary visual-spatial bizarreness. These might make excellent short stories and indeed Robert Louis Stevenson is one of several well-known writers who asserted that they originally "dreamt" their best stories. There are also relatively infrequent but striking narrative-propositional dream anomalies that certainly resist classification in terms of "confusions." Here we would include an "inner voice" narrating the dream (often ahead of unfolding events) or elaborate memories that turn out to be false on awakening. While it would be cumbersome indeed to give such narrative-propositional phenomena a visual-spatial or imagery explanation, the opposite is the case with certain equally rare dreams of utterly fantastic, unearthly settings--such as the elaborate visualizations in some of Jung's dreams or the dreams of the writer H.P. Lovecraft. Here are striking descriptions of visual-spatial imagination taking over the entirety of the dreaming process. Perhaps within more ordinary dreaming it is verbal intelligence that contributes most to the dream narrative and visual-spatial imagery that contributes to dream bizarreness. There is also clear indication that verbal and visual-spatial intelligence can interact in complex ways, i.e., highly bizarre dream events can determine the subsequent story, while seemingly incongruous dream elements may turn out to be linked by verbal puns.

The major barrier to understanding visual-spatial forms of dream bizarreness as abstract metaphor has been their close statistical association with the phasic arousal bursts of the REM state (5;11). Since the latter are widely believed to come from the primitive pontine formation of the brainstem and are common to all REMing mammals, they are usually regarded as "non-cognitive." However, studies by my colleagues and me at Brock (32) and by Moffitt (33) have shown that dream bizarreness is also correlated with heightened alpha rhythms within REM state EEG--which can in turn be regarded as indicative of cognitive mentation in the dream. If Morrison (25) is

right and REM phasic activations are linked to the orientation reflex, it would make sense that in *man* they will be involved in cognitive novelty and creativity--which most definitions of human intelligence make criterial and which thereby
becomes as salient to us as unexpected events in the environment of lower animals, both eliciting the orientation response.
Foulkes (12) summarizes evidence suggesting that through
childhood REM sleep gets progressively more impervious to
unexpected external stimulation. If he were correct that in-
trusive bizarre events are "errors" in dream production due to
"peripherally induced aberrations," then they should decline
with development--just as children learn to block out external
intrusions, they would gradually block out internal intrusions.
But Foulkes' own data show that dream bizarreness develops
progressively in extent and quality and in a way fully consistent with the parallel waking development of visual and metaphoric imagination. Indeed, recent research on phasic activity
seems to imply the possibility of an antecedent cortical involvement or even initiation. There has been much speculation
in recent years about complex loops between cortex and brain-
stem--which, again, makes a lot less sense if the brainstem
processes of the REM state are part of the physiology of the
orientation response to novel stimuli in wakefulness as well.
With the psychophysiology of dream bizarreness still very much
open, psychologists must look to the phenomenon itself. As we
have seen, dream bizarreness shows the unmistakable presence of
abstract symbolic operations in its very fabric.

Lucid Dreams and Their Relation to
Dream Bizarreness: A Test Case for an
Organismic-Holistic Cognitive
Psychology of Dreaming

     Lucid and control dreams are another type of "second
order" cognitive transformation of dreaming. Lucid dreams
are dreams in which you know that you are dreaming while the
dream is going on and manage to retain that awareness. They
often include deliberate "magical" transformations and control
of dream content, such as voluntary flying. Most subjects
find such dreams uniquely exciting and intriguing. Following
the pioneer study by Green (34), lucid dreams have become the
focus of considerable research interest.
     This has been greeted with a certain amount of suspicion
by the more traditional psychophysiological, cognitive, *and*
clinical approaches to dreams. What Green (34) referred to

as the "perceptual realism" of lucid dreams—the relative
absence of those visual-spatial transformations that are
direct indicators of symbolism in dream formation—has made
it seem that lucidity and dream control might interfere with
the self-reflective "function" of such dream symbolism. Correspondingly, those committed to the idea that "true" dreaming
is "singleminded" (cognitively narrowed and isolated by the
restrictions of the REM state) and deficient in verbal-
reflective capacities have tended to treat lucid dreams as
the trivial exception that proves the rule. In this view
lucid dreaming is a sort of mental and verbal "waking up"
within the dream that bears no essential relation to the
underlying processes of dream formation. On the contrary,
we will see that lucidity involves a natural *transformation*
of the dreaming process closely related to meditation and
bearing a complex relation to dream bizarreness—thereby
casting a crucial light on the genesis of non-lucid forms of
bizarreness as well. The key to such an understanding rests
with a shift away from the more narrow cognitive psychology
of verbal intelligence toward the organismic tradition and
its natural attunement to metaphoric and visual-spatial
processes.

The view that lucid dreams entail a sort of waking up in
the dream—or an approximation to our waking cognitive
capacity—is contradicted by the prevalence of "dream-like"
confusions in thinking and memory in even very experienced
lucid dreamers. Indeed, the experience of lucidity is clearly
different from the mere intellectual awareness that one is
dreaming. The experience is as distinct from 90% of waking
experience as it is from 90% of dreaming, and is very much
like the attitude sought in long-term meditation. Both advanced meditation and fully established dream lucidity show
the same development of a special and difficult to attain
attitude of detached receptivity and its tenuous balance with
our more "singleminded" and everyday practical involvements—
whether dreamt or awake. Lucid dreams are thus a spontaneous
form of the state of mind *sought* within so-called "insight"
or "mindfulness" meditative traditions—with the same subjective sense of release, exhilaration, and cognitive clarity.
What Green (34) described as the "perceptual realism" of lucid
dreams—their vivid sense of perceptual texture and immediacy—
is the opposite of the true-to-daily life, mundane qualities
of most dreams, as described by Dorus, Dorus, and Rechtschaffen (20). Rather it shows an approximation to what Maslow
termed "peak experience." It is worth noting that Deikman
(35) conceptualized the attitude common to many altered states
of consciousness, and exemplified best by meditation, as a
shift to a detached, purely observing "receptivity." This

involves the suppression or inhibition of ordinary verbal intelligence and "inner speech." Meditation is not so much a
cessation of thinking per se, as a shift to the aesthetic-
expressive properties of non-verbal metaphor, and we find a
similar process occurring with very experienced lucid dreamers.

Of course, the best evidence for this equation of the
state of mind in lucid dreams with meditation, previously
suggested by Goleman (36) and Sparrow (37), is the cultivation
of such dreams within traditional Tibetan Buddhist meditation
practice, as the form of meditation naturally available during
dreams. In a study with Barbara McLeod, we found significantly
elevated control dreams, more lucidity, and significantly
less nonlucid dreaming in a group of 18 long-term meditators
(an average of 5.1 years of practice) compared to a control
group with very good dream recall. We also found a strong
correlation of lucid and control dreams with years of meditative practice. Another study, with Roc Villeneuve, found a
significant association between subjective estimates of frequency of control dreams and intensity of response to a technique of contemplative meditation taught to subjects as part
of the experiment. Since, in the study with long-term meditators there was no association at all between degree of lucidity
and deliberate attempts to change one's dreaming toward
lucidity, it may well be that lucid and control dreams develop
automatically as the result of long-term meditation. We were
especially interested to find that some of our subjects were
not sure themselves how to categorize their highly unusual
dreams (see below). They sometimes could not tell whether
they had awakened and were spontaneously meditating or whether
they were asleep and having what we had defined for them as a
"lucid dream."

We also found a complex interaction between the degree of
lucidity and forms of dream bizarreness. In our first laboratory studies at Brock, with Bob Ogilvie and Paul Tyson (32),
we found what others have noted, that lucid dreams were relatively realistic and true to daily life in thematic content.
It is the prelucid dreams, where subjects are *unsure* whether
or not they are actually dreaming, that are highly bizarre
compared to normative laboratory samples--showing elevations
in the sort of visual intrusions of unlikely content, abrupt
scene shifts, and confusions of thinking and memory discussed
above. So far, this supports the idea of a possible antithesis
between lucidity and symbolism--except that prelucid dreams
move easily into full lucidity and there is evidence that both
bizarreness and lucidity are related to visual-spatial imaginative abilities. Both dream bizarreness and lucid dreaming are
associated with measures of creativity, and Snyder and Gackenbach (38) report significant associations between lucidity and

test measures of visual-spatial rotational ability of the sort
found by Foulkes to be necessary for the visualized side of
dreaming. So it makes more sense to see lucidity as a natural
development of the dream process rather than as some special
hybrid. These associations suggest that bizarreness-symboliza-
tion and the continuum of lucid dreaming make use of the same
background cognitive processes and thus come into competition.
They would develop together up to some point (prelucid dreams
as highly bizarre) but the push into full lucidity would sub-
ordinate or use up the processes that would otherwise construct the more fantastic forms of symbolism (and vice versa).
In other words, in the higher development of dreaming, you
would typically end up either with dreams like those of Jung
and Freud or the sort of lucid and control dreams described
by Green (34).

    And so it often seems. Some individual subjects do report
that symbolic and lucid dreams seem to be alternatives; they
dream one way or the other. But there has also long been
anecdotal evidence that unusually developed and stabilized
levels of lucidity can be associated with strikingly spiritual
or archetypal forms of dream content. Indeed, the *lucid*
dreams of our long-term meditators showed a level of dream
bizarreness of a kind that I had not encountered before in
any previous study, on a par with the sort of psychedelic/
archetypal dreams described by Jung. These included flying
and floating, descriptions of geometric imagery, encounters
with mythological beings, and the white light or luminosity
experiences described in classical mysticism--all with corresponding feelings of special portent and meaning. These are
just the sorts of transformations of consciousness also found
with long-term meditative practice within wakefulness. Indeed,
the presence of these unusual categories of dream bizarreness
was significantly correlated with both years of meditational
practice and frequency of lucidity. Thus dream lucidity would
eventually operate on dream consciousness in the same ways
that the receptive attitude of meditation operates on waking
consciousness.

    Before showing how all this might work in cognitive terms
I should mention a further implication of this linkage of
dream lucidity and meditation. The sustained self-reference
for its own sake that is involved in meditation/lucidity makes
for a powerful *transformation* of cognition. It changes consciousness in the very breath that consciousness is observed.
Accordingly, widespread suggestions that we can use lucid
dreams to study the processes of ordinary dreaming suffer from
an inherent indeterminancy. It will not be clear whether
lucid dream observations have really located a supposed
feature of all dreaming or whether such effects are part of

the transformation created by lucidity and incipient lucidity. Consider, for instance, Gackenbach et al.'s (39) fascinating finding showing a tendency for lucid dreamers to have unusually good physical balance in test situations involving vestibular disruption and disorientation. These findings, along with the very existence of flying and falling dreams, could be understood in terms of the general disruption of vestibular function that has been taken as inherent to REM physiology. If so, persons who have good balance in conditions that cause dizziness could better overcome the natural delirium of REMing and become lucid. Others, however, like Green (34), have related flying and falling dreams to the dimension of lucidity, suggesting that such dreams are based in the *double* awareness of a *dreamt* and an *actual* body position. This would be the same sort of double awareness basic to lucid dreams and meditation, where the individual is both in a situation and outside it, looking on at the same time. In flying dreams the double tactile-kinesthetic sensitivity to the dreamt body and the real sleeping position would be directly translated into visual imagination and "reconciled" in the form of the flying, falling, or floating experience.

Along these lines Swartz and Seginer (40) reported a significant correlation between the Hood scale of spontaneous mystical and peak experience and a test of physical balance and coordination (pin the tail on the donkey). In the study with Roc Villeneuve, we not only replicated that, but also found associations among lucid/control dreams, experimental meditation, and physical balance. In other words, Gackenbach's "balance" factor is not specific to dreaming or lucid dreaming, but is more generally related to the waking experiences that are most like lucidity. Indeed, if imaginal cognitive ability is based on a cross-modal translation between the patterns of vision and tactile-kinesthetic schemata, we would expect that its most intense expressions would be physically disorienting (since imagery reuses perceptual patterns) *and* that physical/ cognitive "balance" would be more likely to lead toward metaphoric "insights" that integrate rather than disrupt.

Now comes the point to try to say more about what *kind* of cognitive intelligence is involved in the attitude common to dream lucidity and meditation and *how* it would change symbolic consciousness. If we follow George Herbert Mead (10), human intelligence is based on a capacity for self-reference or "taking the role of the other" that operates on the model of an inner imaginative conversation. Whether we are dealing with language, imagery, or gesture, it is in the form of an inner dialogue, and there is reason to think that this self-reference is what gives rise to language, rather than the other way around. All dialogues alternate between two roles:

first an active sending role, in which our reflective capacities are subordinated to maintaining and guiding active articulation. The consequence is a practical narrowing of focus (involved for instance in speaking and writing) and a relative loss of the overall sense of context or perspective. So that, as Mead points out, we only see the full significance of what we have said or done later in our more detached or reflective moments. Correspondingly, there *is* also a more receiving, receptive, or "listening" role. A broader sense of context does come with receiving rather than sending, precisely because our "taking the role of the other" is not subordinated to the ongoing demands of organizing and reorganizing a communication. It is interesting to recall that Deikman (35) characterized all altered states as involving a shift to a mode of pure receptivity--a "taking the role of the other" in Mead's sense but for its own sake and independent of practical uses of intelligence.

We also need a distinction here--almost totally neglected within current experimental cognition--between representational symbolism, best illustrated by language, and the presentational forms of symbolism that predominate in the expressive arts. In representational processes the connection between symbolic vehicle and referent is relatively fixed, arbitrary, and automatized, and the properties of the medium itself are generally ignored. In the presentational side of symbolism, meaning rests in the directly felt qualities and rhythm of the expressive medium--to the point where material in the visual arts and music and certain imageries in altered states of consciousness resist any full or complete narrative formulation. It is important to note that the relation between presentational and representational modes on the one hand, and the receptive and active sending roles on the other, is not independent, but skewed. Presentational meanings are *not* fixed and automatized, but polyvalent and multiple. Thus they depend on a full and contemplative *experiencing* that necessarily entails Deikman's (35) receptive mode or observing self as its predominant attitude. Presentational meanings open out toward the sensed totality or context of any situation--which in a reflective, recombinatory system like the human mind *is* necessarily open and uncompleteable. We are always open to suddenly "seeing" a new significance to past situations that we have lived through and new levels of meaning in a work of art or a dream.

Putting this all together, we can say that lucidity shows the predominance of the broader sense of context of the receiving role, but operating within presentational forms, while dream bizarreness constitutes a visual, presentational expression of the active sending role. Our evidence comparing

the lucid dreams of meditators with more typical lucid, prelucid, and nonlucid dreaming suggests that in the *potential*
development of dreaming these two attitudes alternate like a
conversation between two partners--in a developing spiral between "listening" and "speaking" that may take many years to
unfold. First, bizarreness comes forward as the novel, creative meaning of dream symbolism, but that in turn leads to a
switch to the receptive or receiving role in the form of full
lucidity and a temporary suppression of such active expressions.
But with the full meditation-like stabilization of lucidity,
forms of symbolization come forward again that are progressively more abstract and all encompassing in meaning.

  We can also gain a better understanding of *how* the attitude of lucidity could result in the direct release of presentational forms like complex synaesthesias, geometric-mandala
patterns, and white light experiences: the shift to a receptive role would operate as in any real external conversation,
where if we exaggerate the listening role, refusing to actively
communicate in a situation where some sort of conversation
must occur, then the "other" is forced to reveal more and more
of his or her nature and capabilities. This is exactly what
seems to happen in meditation, with the "other" being the active expressive potential of one's own mind. The resulting
alterations in consciousness offer a unique access to various
processes *postulated* by organismic cognitive psychology. For
instance, geometric-mandala patterns and synaesthesias would
be the direct manifestation, respectively, of Arnheim's notion
of the abstract geometric imagery at the basis of all conceptual thought and of Geschwind's view of the cross-modal translation capacity between patterns of the different senses that
he made central to all symbolization. Both mandala and white
light patterns could be understood as "abstract" or "complex"
synaesthesias, since to the extent that the resulting state
becomes metaphoric and meaningful, the individual seems to
report a felt fusion or mergence of body percept with visual
form. The more structurally simple or "disassembled" these
visual forms are, the more potentially abstract their felt
meaning--culminating in the active expression of luminosity
or empty space experiences, where the most preliminary stage
of vision (light) is "embodied" and sensed as the underlying
unity of existence. On the above model we could say that this
is the closest that "form" can come (as in a conversation) to
the openness of mind itself.

Conclusions

Dream studies can illustrate the more general processes
of all symbolic cognition. But it is not so much that dreaming
needs cognitive psychology as that cognitive psychology needs
dreams and related imaginal phenomena if it is to overcome
the kind of narrowness endemic in current "cognitive science"
(41). More specifically, certain processes postulated by
organismic-holistic psychologists like Werner and Kaplan,
Arnheim, Mead, Geschwind, and Neisser may be seen best where
verbal-representational intelligence is minimized and symbolism
operates directly in presentational forms.

While dreaming clearly has its narrative story side, requiring explanation in terms of linguistic intelligence, it
also has its bizarre and fantastic visual-spatial side—which
both needs and will help to create a cognitive psychology of
metaphor and imagination. Certainly, if the sort of heightened
form of self-reflectiveness involved in highly developed lucid
dreaming (Deikman's nonverbal receptive attitude) leads to
such extreme forms of metaphoric expression, we can postulate
a similar process underlying ordinary levels of dream bizarreness. Thus, more typical forms of dream bizarreness would be
created by an implicit or "masked" level of the same self-
referential capacity that seems to be crucial in all symbolic
intelligence. If so, they are certainly not to be understood
as extraneous disruptions of cognition.

Dream bizarreness is unintelligible without a cognitive
psychology of symbolic imagination. And so it becomes inherently plausible that dreams could have meanings within
their very fabric that call for interpretation and explication. The same is true of the expressive arts—which makes
the point best that some dreams and types of dreams are truly
asking to be interpreted. Psychology as heterodox science
encourages us toward this undertaking, but then leaves us to
go forward on our own. There is no scientific method, thank
goodness, for the development of understanding and awareness.

References

1. Freud, S. (1965). *The Interpretation of Dreams*. New
      York: Avon. Original work published in 1900.

   The classic work. All roads begin from Freud's complex
   integration of dream interpretation, dream formation, and

theory of dreaming as a causal process, based largely on
his own dreams.

2. Foulkes, D. (1978). *A Grammar of Dreams.* New York: Basic
    Books.

    Argues that the psychology of language provides the key
    to dreaming. In part a translation of Freud's approach
    into orthodox cognitive terminology.

3. Jung, C.G. (1961). *Memories, Dreams, Reflections.* New
    York: Pantheon Books.

    The major alternative to Freud's treatment of dreams
    and probably the most revealing and personal autobiography
    ever written by a psychologist.

4. Hillman, J. (1979). *The Dream and the Underworld.* New
    York: Harper & Row.

    Imaginatively elaborates Jung's approach to dreams
    based on the imagery of a nightly descent to the mytho-
    logical underworld of the Greeks.

5. McCarley, R. (1983). "REM Dreams, REM Sleep and Their
    Isomorphisms." In M. Chase and E. Weitzman (Eds.),
    Sleep Disorders: Basic and Clinical Research (pp. 363-
    392). New York: Spectrum Medical and Scientific Books.

    Hobson and McCarley's controversial integration of the
    psychology and physiology of dreams, by making the latter
    the cause and the former the effect.

6. Werner, H., and Kaplan, B. (1963). *Symbol Formation.*
    New York: Wiley.

    Sees all symbol formation as an organismic process
    based on the expressive (physiognomic) properties of the
    senses.

7. Arnheim, R. (1969). *Visual Thinking.* Berkeley: University
    of California Press.

    Shows how all abstract cognition may be based on the
    geometric-dynamic properties of visual imagery. Develops
    a gestalt psychology of aesthetics and then extends it
    back into the rest of cognition.

8. Hall, C. (1953). "A Cognitive Theory of Dream Symbols."
    Journal of General Psychology, 48, 169-186.

    The original call for a cognitive psychology of dreams,

citing the importance of approaches to metaphor and creative imagery for understanding dreaming.

9. Edelson, M. (1972). "Language and Dreams: The Interpretation of Dreams Revisited." *Psychoanalytic Study of the Child*, *27*, 203-282.

    Relates dreaming to theories of language, inner speech, and aphasia. A major influence on Foulkes.

10. Mead, G.H. (1934). *Mind, Self, Society*. Chicago: University of Chicago Press.

    Shows how all symbolic activity rests on the forms of social communication, with thinking as an imaginal conversation based on "taking the role of the other."

11. Ogilvie, R.D.; Hunt, H.T.; Sawicki, C.; and Samahalskyi, J. (1982). "Psychological Correlates of Spontaneous Middle Ear Muscle Activity during Sleep." *Sleep*, *5*, 11-27.

12. Foulkes, D. (1983). "Dream Ontogeny and Dream Psychophysiology." In M. Chase and E. Weitzman (Eds.), *Sleep Disorders: Basic and Clinical Research* (pp. 347-362). New York: Spectrum Medical and Scientific Books.

    Summarizes his research showing an apparent lack of dreaming in very young children and the link between its development and waking cognitive abilities.

13. Foulkes, D. (1982). *Children's Dreams: Longitudinal Studies*. New York: John Wiley.

    Presents detailed findings on children's dream recall. Tries to show that all dreaming requires an abstract imaginative capability.

14. Foulkes, D. (1983). "Cognitive Processes during Sleep: Evolutionary Aspects." In A. Mayes (Ed.), *Sleep Mechanisms and Functions in Humans and Animals--An Evolutionary Perspective* (pp. 313-337). Berkshire, England: Van Nostrand Reinhold.

    Extends his cognitive approach to the possibility of dreaming in lower animals and dismisses it, perhaps too quickly.

15. Schanfald, D.; Pearlman, C.; and Greenberg, R. (in press). "The Capacity of Stroke Patients to Report Dreams." *Cortex*, *21*.

    Contradicting Foulkes, shows that aphasia does not eliminate dreaming.

16. Kerr, N.; Foulkes, D.; and Schmidt, M. (1982). "The Structure of Laboratory Dream Reports in Blinded and Sighted Subjects." *Journal of Nervous and Mental Disease*, *170*, 286-294.

    Uses dreaming in partially blinded subjects to argue that dreaming is more like imagination than perception.

17. Roffwarg, H.; Herman, S.; Bowe-Anders, C.; and Tauber, G. (1978). "The Effects of Sustained Alterations of Waking Visual Input on Dream Content." In A. Arkin, S. Antrobus, and S. Ellman (Eds.), *The Mind in Sleep: Psychology and Psychophysiology* (pp. 295-349). Hillsdale, N.J.: Erlbaum.

    The carry-over into the dream of distorting prism effects shows that dreaming can also function like perception.

18. Herman, J.; Barker, D.; and Roffwarg, H. (1983). "Similarity of Eye Movement Characteristics in REM Sleep and the Awake State." *Psychophysiology*, *20*, 537-543.

19. Neisser, U. (1976). *Cognition and Reality*. San Francisco: Freeman.

    A basic work in current cognitive psychology, with close ties to earlier organismic and gestalt approaches.

20. Dorus, E.; Dorus, W.; and Rechtschaffen, A. (1971). "The Incidence of Novelty in Dreams." *Archives of General Psychiatry*, *25*, 364-368.

    Demonstrates just how mundane and true-to-daily-life dreams can be.

21. Snyder, F. (1970). "The Phenomenology of Dreaming." In L. Madow and L. Snow (Eds.), *The Psychodynamic Implications of the Physiological Studies on Dreams* (pp. 124-151). Springfield, Ill.: C. Thomas.

Shows that dreams may contain complex speech and re-flective thought. Contradicts both Freud's and Foulkes' assumptions about dream formation.

22. Boss, M. (1958). *The Analysis of Dreams*. New York: Philosophical Library.

The classic work on dream phenomenology, showing that dreams can include all the existential dimensions of waking experience. Offers a strong critique of both Freud and Jung.

23. Natsoulas, J. (1983). "Concepts of Consciousness." *Journal of Mind and Behavior*, 4, 13-59.

Shows the multiplicity of concepts of consciousness in psychology and the necessity of distinguishing between the very different cognitive levels involved.

24. Griffin, D. (1978). "Prospects for a Cognitive Ethology." *Behavioral and Brain Sciences*, 4, 527-629.

25. Morrison, A. (1983). "Paradoxical Sleep and Alert Wake-fulness: Variation on a Theme." In M. Chase and B. Weitzman (Eds.), *Sleep Disorders: Basic and Clinical Research* (pp. 95-122). New York: Spectrum Medical & Scientific Publishers.

Shows again how close the brain in REM sleep is to its functioning in alert wakefulness and relates both to the orientation response to novelty.

26. Hunt, H.T. (1982). "Forms of Dreaming." *Perceptual and Motor Skills*, 54, 559-633.

A more detailed treatment of the approach to dreams covered in this chapter.

27. Geschwind, N. (1965). "Disconnexion Syndromes in Animals and Man." *Brain*, 88, 237-294, 585-644.

Shows how abstract symbolic intelligence might result from cross-modal translation between the patterns of the different perceptual senses. Offers important evidence for an organismic cognitive psychology.

28. Silberer, H. (1951). "Report on a Method of Eliciting and Observing Certain Symbolic Hallucination-Phenomena."

In D. Rapaport (Ed.), *Organization and Pathology of Thought* (pp. 195–207). New York: Columbia University Press.

These pioneering observations of his own dreams at sleep onset were of interest to both Freud and Jung and offer important clues to the formation of metaphor.

29. Nielsen, T., and Kuiken, D. (1985). "Kinesthetic Sensation and Dreaming." Paper presented at the Lucid Dream Preconvention Symposium, Association for the Study of Dreams, Charlottesville, Va.

30. Carrington, R. (1972). "Dreams and Schizophrenia." *Archives of General Psychiatry*, *26*, 343–350.

31. Searles, H. (1965). "The Differentiation between Concrete and Metaphorical Thinking in the Recovering Schizophrenic Patient." In H. Searles (Ed.), *Collected Papers on Schizophrenia and Related Subjects* (pp. 560–583). New York: International University Press.

Shows how somatic hallucinations in schizophrenia (very similar to Carrington's dream reports) can be understood as frozen or defensively impacted metaphors that offer a self-referential depiction of the patient's life circumstances.

32. Ogilvie, R.D.; Hunt, H.T.; Tyson, P.D.; Lucescu, M.L.; and Jenkins, D.B. (1982). "Lucid Dreaming and Alpha Activity: A Preliminary Report." *Perceptual and Motor Skills*, *55*, 795–808.

Shows how highly bizarre prelucid dreams have the same sort of EEG alpha enhancement associated with meditation.

33. Moffitt, A.; Hoffman, R.; Wells, R.; Armitage, R.; and Shearer, J. (March 1985). "Dream Psychology and Psychophysiology." Paper presented at the symposium on Cognitive Psychology and Dreaming, Eastern Psychological Assoc., Boston.

34. Green, C. (1968). *Lucid Dreams*. London: Hamish Hamilton.

The classic work on the phenomenology and classification of lucid dreams and related states.

35. Deikman, A. (1982). *The Observing Self*. Boston: Beacon Press.

36. Goleman, D. (1971). "Meditation as Meta-therapy: Hypotheses Toward a Proposed Fifth State of Consciousness." *Journal of Transpersonal Psychology*, 3, 1-25.

    Probably the first discussion in western psychology of the psychological identity of lucid dreams and meditative states.

37. Sparrow, G.S. (1976). *Lucid Dreaming: The Dawning of the Clear Light*. Virginia Beach: A.R.E. Press.

38. Snyder, T.J., and Gackenbach, J.I. (in press). "Individual Differences Associated with Lucid Dreaming." In J.I. Gackenbach and S. LaBerge (Eds.), *Lucid Dreaming: New Research on Consciousness during Dreams*. New York: Plenum.

39. Gackenbach, J.I.; Snyder, T.J.; Rokes, L.M.; and Sachau, D. (in press). "Lucid Frequency in Relation to Vestibular Sensitivity as Measured by Caloric Stimulation." *The Journal of Mind and Behavior: Cognition and Dream Research* (special issue).

40. Swartz, P., and Seginer, L. (1981). "Response to Body Rotation and Tendency to Mystical Experience." *Perceptual and Motor Skills*, 53, 638-683.

    Presents fascinating evidence that people who have mystical experience also have good physical balance and orientation. Closely related to similar findings on lucid dreamers.

41. Foulkes, D. (1985). *Dreaming: A Cognitive-Psychological Analysis*. Hillsdale, N.J.: Erlbaum.

    Since the writing of this chapter Foulkes has published a major synthesis of his "cognitive science" of dreams. He now likewise cites "supramodal" interactions in dream formation, which remains, however, chiefly a one way passage from diffusely activated semantic memory via narrative structures to a visual surface array, with bizarreness as error. The price of fitting the dream *to* currently fashionable cognitive theory includes missing the multi-directional, cross-modal interactions of dream formation, the metaphoric basis of dream bizarreness, and the entire phenomenological-clinical tradition of dream observations.

Chapter 10
TRANSCENDENTAL CONSCIOUSNESS:
A FOURTH STATE OF CONSCIOUSNESS
BEYOND SLEEP, DREAMING, AND WAKING

*Charles N. Alexander, Robert W. Cranson,
Robert W. Boyer, and David W. Orme-Johnson*

The purpose of this chapter is to introduce a fourth major
state of consciousness--transcendental consciousness--to
distinguish it from the states of deep sleep, dreaming, including lucid dreaming, and waking, and to suggest its role
in a model of human development to higher states of consciousness.

Introduction

Psychophysiologists have identified three major states
of consciousness--waking, dreaming, and sleeping (1). During
the past 15 years, a large body of further research (2;3) has
indicated that during practice of the Transcendental Meditation (TM) technique, a fourth state of consciousness referred
to as transcendental consciousness (TC) is produced (4;5).
Researchers have described this as a state in which all mental
activity is transcended and the experiencer directly experiences
content-free or pure consciousness without thoughts or any
localized boundaries of awareness. In ordinary waking awareness, the observer is separate from the object of observation.
In transcendental consciousness the observer, the objects of
observation, and the process of observation are said to become
unified in one wholeness of pure self-awareness. The following
is a report of an experience of transcendental consciousness,
given by a subject:

> During the TM technique my mind settles down,
> thoughts become less and then suddenly all thought
> activity ceases and I slip into an unbounded ocean
> of awareness which is pure, quiet, unexcited and

infinitely extended beyond space and time. Simultaneously my body settles down, breathing becomes
less and I feel relaxed.

Recent studies have indicated that periods in which subjects reported experiencing transcendental consciousness
during practice of the TM technique by pressing a button are
highly correlated with enhanced alpha and theta EEG coherence,
suggestive of high alertness, and with periods of respiratory
suspension or extremely light breathing, decreased heart rate,
decreased metabolic rate, hormonal changes, stable phasic GSR,
and heightened basal GSR indicative of physiological quiescence (4;5;7). Table 13 summarizes these correlates and others
associated with transcendental consciousness.

Transcendental Consciousness in the
Context of Higher States of Consciousness

The experience of the fourth state of consciousness has
been described and its physiological correlates have been
predicted by the Vedic psychology of Maharishi Mahesh Yogi.
This comprehensive psychological theory and technology of
human development is based on the ancient classical science
of the Veda which emphasizes the subjective approach to gaining
knowledge, as well as the objective approach of modern science (8-11). Vedic psychology describes transcendental consciousness as an unbounded, unified field of consciousness or
unified field of natural law at the source of both subjective
and objective existence.[1] All thoughts and feelings are said
to be fluctuations or excitations of this underlying field of
consciousness.

Vedic psychology proposes that repeated experience of
transcendental consciousness through the Maharishi Technology
of the Unified Field (MTUF), which includes the Transcendental
Meditation (TM) and TM-Sidhi techniques, in alternation with
daily activity fosters growth of higher states of consciousness beyond the ordinary endpoint of adult development.[2]

The MTUF is held to promote neutralization of accumulated
stress in the nervous system and refine mental and physiological
functioning, giving rise to a new style of functioning that is
capable of sustaining transcendental consciousness along with
the three ordinary states of consciousness. In this experience,
called witnessing, transcendental consciousness becomes a
silent, uninvolved witness to mental processes. Development
of a permanent style of physiological functioning that spon-

taneously maintains witnessing at all times during waking,
dreaming, and deep sleep defines the fifth state of consciousness, termed cosmic consciousness, a state of inner peace and
self-realization in which individual awareness remains permanently identified with the unbounded silence of pure consciousness. If transcendental consciousness is a unique state
of consciousness which is the foundation of higher states of
consciousness, it should be clearly distinguishable from the
ordinary states of sleeping, dreaming, and waking.

Transcendental Consciousness Distinguished
from Deep Sleep

Psychophysiological research indicates that transcendental
consciousness can be distinguished from deep sleep on a number
of dimensions, as shown in Table 13.

These two states differ markedly on the subjective dimension of awareness. Deep sleep is characterized by complete
absence of awareness, no awareness of the self or the environment. In contrast, transcendental consciousness is experienced
as a state of heightened inner wakefulness. In this state the
individual is clearly alert and able to respond to outward
stimuli when necessary (4). If left undisturbed in transcendental consciousness, the individual is not aware of any
thoughts, feelings, or images, but of consciousness itself,
experienced as a state of complete contentment or inner
bliss (8-11). In deep sleep, the arousal threshold for responding to a stimulus is higher than in stage 1 sleep but
lower than dreaming (1;12;13), whereas in transcendental consciousness the threshold appears to be very low--virtually the
same as in the waking state (4). The individual's EEG readily
responds to outside click stimuli during TM practice (4;14).

During deep sleep the electroencephalographic pattern is
characterized by a preponderance of delta in the spectral
power, and there is little or no EEG coherence, correlation,
or synchrony within and among the different regions of the
brain (1;11;14-16).[3] In the state of transcendental consciousness during TM practice, high amplitude alpha and theta spindles
predominate in the EEG pattern with beta spindles being observed as well as EEG synchrony (16). During these periods
an apparently unique phenomenon occurs--marked EEG coherence
in alpha, theta, and sometimes beta frequencies appears within
and between left and right hemispheres, especially in the
frontal and central regions. This result has been interpreted
as evidence of a very orderly "macroscopic" neurophysiological

integration which supports the wholeness of awareness experienced in transcendental consciousness (7;16-21). High
coherence probably reflects uninterrupted volume conductance
of the EEG from a common generator to scalp areas where it is
measured. The "low noise" condition of the nervous system
achieved during transcendental consciousness may facilitate
this uninterrupted conductance.

During deep sleep some slow eye movements occur, followed
by immobility; during TM eye movements are about the same as
during relaxed waking with eyes closed (4).

Generally, brainstem auditory evoked potentials remain
unchanged during deep sleep, dreaming, or waking. During TM,
in comparison to relaxation with eyes closed, there may be
changes in the pattern of brainstem auditory potentials suggestive of enhanced processing of auditory information (22).
Further, during sleep and dreaming there is marked attenuation
of the cognitive components of the auditory evoked potential.
In advanced mediators during rest and TM, there is actually a
shorter latency of the N1 cognitive component of the auditory
potential than in controls, suggesting improved efficiency of
information transfer in the brain through the practice of
TM (23-25).

During deep sleep, breathing is less variable than during
dreaming or waking, and takes on a monotonous rate. Frequency
is lower with larger tidal volume, and there is a slight decrease in minute ventilation (1). During transcendental consciousness breathing appears to be very light, minute ventilation decreases substantially, and in some subjects there are
complete suspensions of breath (4;15;26-28). Respiration
during deep sleep and in waking is generally understood to be
driven by neural response to CO_2 concentration in the lungs;
however, in the case of severe oxygen deprivation or in "apneustic" breathing, the neural regulation of breathing is
driven by amount of oxygen in the bloodstream (2;3). In apneustic breathing there is prolonged, slow inspiration. Kesterson (27) found the breath suspensions of his subjects during
TM appeared to be similar in this respect. He found a reduction
of sensitivity to CO_2 and increased sensitivity to O_2 resulting
in very light breathing, prolonged inspiration, and lowered
respiratory quotient. Kesterson observed that if the subjects
actually had been experiencing O_2 deprivation (or apneustic
breathing) an *increase* rather than a decrease in respiratory
quotient (RQ) would have been found. Hence, he concluded that
TC appears to be a naturally balanced hypometabolic state.

It should be noted that there may be stages, or periodi-
cities, during TM practice. Subjects typically do not experience transcendental consciousness throughout the whole
period of TM practice. Periods of TC, however, do appear to

Table 13

Comparison of Four States of Consciousness on Various
Psychophysiological Dimensions

DIMENSION	DEEP SLEEP	DREAMING	WAKING	TRANSCENDENTAL CONSCIOUSNESS
Awareness Dimension	No Awareness	Illusory Awareness	Awareness of Percepts, thoughts	Pure Awareness
Response Threshold	High	Highest	Nil	Nil
EEG Pattern	In stage 2, 12–14 Hz spindles and K complexes. In stage 3 & 4 at least 50% delta waves.	Low voltage desynchronized sawtooth waves (Stage 1 REM). In stage 2, 12–14 Hz spindles and K complexes.	Low voltage mixed frequency and/or alpha (9–11 cps.–eyes closed). Alpha decreases and some beta occurs with concentration.	Predominance of high alpha and theta with synchronous alpha, theta, and beta spindles occurring.
EEG Coherence	Low to Nil	Low to Nil	Intermediate	High
Eye movements	First slow eye movements (several seconds each), then rolled up and immobile.	Episodic rapid eye movements (REMs).	Some rapid eye movements, eye blinks, various movements.	No apparent change from relaxed waking, eyes closed.
Auditory Evoked Potential (brainstem component)	Stable brainstem auditory evoked potential.	Stable brainstem auditory evoked potential.	Stable brainstem auditory evoked potential.	Changes in brainstem auditory evoked potential suggestive of improved auditory processing.
Auditory Evoked Potential (cognitive component)	Marked attenuation of cognitive component of auditory potential.	Marked attenuation of cognitive component of auditory potential.	"Normal" presence of cognitive component of auditory evoked potential.	Shorter latency of N1 cognitive component (associated with selective attention) in mediators during rest and TM.
Amplitude of Paired H-reflex	Paired H-reflex recovery reduced.	Tonically inhibited during REM sleep.	Generally higher; positive relationship between degree of alpha in EEG and reflex amplitude.	Response amplitude positively correlated with clarity of transcending.
Galvanic Skin Response (GSR)	Increases gradually throughout the night to about twice the level of waking.	Increases gradually throughout the night to about twice the level of waking.	Baseline level.	Increases rapidly (10–20 min.) to about twice the level of waking. Less variable than during sleep or dreaming.

Breathing Pattern	Steady, shallow	Erratic and highly variable. Fluctuates widely above and below wakefulness. Average value higher by 1-2 breaths/min. over deep sleep.	Changes according to the activity.	...very light with suspensions observed in some people. Wallace found significant decrease—mean decrease of 3/min. compared to relaxed waking.
Minute Ventilation	Slight decrease in minute ventilation.	Minute ventilation approaches waking state.	Varies widely with activity level.	Significant decrease from relaxed waking.
Metabolism (O_2 content of arterial blood)	Slight reduction (less than 5%) from waking.	Slight reduction (less than 5%) from waking.	Baseline level.	20-28% reduction from waking.
Metabolism (CO_2 content of arterial blood)	Production decreases (10 to 20%).	Variable, ranging from level of sleep to level of wakefulness.	Marked decline (85%) in CO_2 elimination during relaxed waking.	CO_2 elimination entirely ceases and CO_2 uptake actually observed.
Red cell metabolism	No significant reduction.	No significant reduction.	Baseline level.	23% reduction.
Heart rate (counts per minute)	Falls to lowest level in circadian cycle.	Erratic. Usually about 5% increase above sleep.	Changes according to activity.	Decreases significantly with a mean decrease of about 5 beats per minute.
Plasma cortisol (stress hormone)	Slight decrease.	Slight decrease.	Baseline level.	Reduced significantly compared to sleep, dreaming, and waking.
Plasma lactate	Not known at present.	Not known at present.	Increases gradually throughout the night.	Decreases significantly from waking.
Plasma prolactin	Increases gradually throughout the night.	Increases gradually throughout the night.	Baseline level.	Increases significantly at the end of period of TM and afterward.
Plasma Phenylalanine	Decreases slightly.	Decreases slightly.	Baseline level.	Increases significantly from waking.
Plasma TSH	Unchanged.	Unchanged.	Unchanged.	Decreases significantly from waking.
Serotonergic activity	Peaks during night sleep cycle.	Increases in serotonergic activity may increase REM sleep.	Increased serotonergic activity may be associated with relaxed waking state.	Serotonergic activity is higher during TM than during relaxed waking.
Plasma Arginine Vasopressin (AVP)	No significant change.	No significant change.	Baseline level.	Secretion increases to 2.6-7.1 times level of relaxed waking.

be characterized by more intensified changes in the same
parameters that tend to change throughout the TM session,
such as respiratory decline (28).

Jevning et al. (29) found a 23% decrease in whole blood
metabolism during TM, whereas during sleep there was no significant decrease. In another study (30) Jevning, Wilson, and
Guich found a 20-28% reduction of oxygen content of forearm
arterial blood, with no compensatory increase in CO_2 concentration. Therefore, they inferred that this is a natural
hypometabolic state. During sleep and dreaming there is a
decrease of only 5% or less in oxygen content (1).

Plasma cortisol, a major stress hormone, decreases substantially during TM in contrast to deep sleep, and the decrease is rapid (4;31;32). Plasma lactate concentration also
decreases compared with relaxed waking state (4). The reductions in cortisol and plasma lactate have been taken to indicate a neutralization of physiological stress during TM (4;31).

Jevning et al. (33) found that thyroid stimulating hormone
(TSH) increased during TM but remained unchanged in deep sleep.
They also found that practitioners of TM had lower basal
levels of TSH than non-practitioners (33). They concluded
that the set point for TSH is at a much lower level in subjects
who regularly experience transcendental consciousness through
TM than in non-practitioners, indicating more efficient control of the thyroid gland and metabolism. This conclusion is
supported by a longitudinal study showing reduction of TSH and
other endocrine changes in advanced TM practitioners (34).

Jerving, Wilson, and Vanderlaan (35) found that plasma
prolactin increased significantly at the end of TM practice
or during the post-TM period. By comparison, the authors
noted that increased prolactin secretion accompanies sleep
and immediately wanes upon awakening. They therefore concluded that the underlying processes involved during TM are
different from those activated in sleep.

Basal galvanic skin resistance (GSR), a measure of relaxation, increases rapidly during TM to about double the average
in waking (4), whereas in sleep there is a very gradual increase during the entire night to about the same level (1).

Basal GSR becomes especially elevated and phasic GSR more
stable during self-reported periods of transcendental consciousness (4;36;37). Phasic or spontaneous GSR becomes more
stable during TM, whereas deep sleep may contain GSR "storm"
periods of lability (37-39).

Van Boxtel (40) reported that motor neuron recovery as
modulated by the central nervous system is low during sleep,
tonically inhibited during dreaming, and greater in amplitude
with increasing alpha in waking. Haynes et al. (14) found
that paired H-reflex recovery was greater during TM than rest

at 200 milliseconds' delay, and was positively correlated with
clear experiences of transcendental consciousness. H-reflex
recovery has been shown to be further enhanced through practice of the advance TM-Sidhi program (41).

Several researchers have challenged the finding that there
is a unique, fourth state of consciousness which occurs
during TM. Pagano et al. (42) contended that metabolic
changes observed during TM practice were due to unsuspected
periods of sleep, based on their interpretation of EEG recordings. Since Pagano's study, a total of ten studies (43)
have been conducted in which EEG recordings were analyzed for
the amount of time spent in sleep. None of the studies reported any deep (stage 3-4) sleep during TM. The studies found
on the average 16% stage 1 sleep, or drowsiness, and only 3%
stage 2 sleep. The four studies (29;30;44;45) which investigated the relationship between stage 1 sleep and reductions in
blood cell metabolism showed that they were uncorrelated. Thus,
it is highly unlikely that the metabolic changes observed during
TM can be attributed to sleep and seem rather to be generally
associated with a distinctive state of restful alertness.

Transcendental Consciousness Distinguished
from Dreaming

The dreaming state is subjectively characterized by illusory perception of the self and the environment and their
interaction. Typically, the dreamer's awareness is completely
identified with a dream self as it appears in the dream, or
with other dream content. Bizarreness and irrationality of
mental content often characterize the dream state. The dreamer
is typically not conscious of the fact that he had previously
been awake nor that his current dreams are illusory (46).
Clearly, such a state is in marked contrast to experience of
the content-free wakeful state of transcendental consciousness.

The response threshold during dreaming is higher than in
deep sleep (4;13) and hence quite distinct from the low
threshold associated with transcendental consciousness.

Dreaming occurs primarily during stage 1 D-sleep and sometimes during stage 2 sleep. It is accompanied by rapid eye
movements (REMs), slowly drifting eye movements (SEMs), decreased muscle tone, and EEG activity in the form of low
voltage mixed frequency, or high amplitude slow waves called
"K-complexes," 12-14 Hz rhythms called "sleep spindles"
(stage 2 sleep) (1;13;47). Coherence of power between different parts of the brain is sparse or nil (1).

Table 13 shows the EEG pattern associated with transcendental consciousness is completely different from the EEG pattern during dreaming. In addition, during TM there are few eye movements (4;13).

During dreaming, respiration is more variable and shows a smaller decrease in minute ventilation than in deep sleep. The pattern of respiration during dreaming is more akin to the level of waking respiration than to deep sleep (1;12) and hence differs more from transcendental consciousness than from the pattern observed in sleep.

During dreaming blood concentration levels of the hormones previously described (except for prolactin), are similar to those observed in deep sleep and hence different from those occurring during TM.

As in sleep, the overall GSR level rises slowly during dreaming, though it is more variable (1). By contrast, during TM GSR rises more rapidly and is less variable.

Dreaming appears to serve the function of releasing physiological and emotional stress to normalize physiological and mental functioning (1;12;14). The addition of TM to the daily routine appears to permit efficient neutralization of more or deeper abnormalities of functioning than can be released through dreaming or sleep alone (28;31;32;39). Further, transcendental consciousness serves not only to restore, but directly promote positive improvements in physiological and psychological functioning (6;7;14;20;34;41). As we shall discuss later, the repeated experience of transcendental consciousness may promote development of the nervous system beyond the restrictions imposed by the waking, dreaming, and sleep states to a full expression of human potential.

Transcendental Consciousness Distinguished
from Waking

As typically experienced, the waking state is predominately characterized by a continuous flow of thoughts, perceptions, feelings, and actions (48). There is no awareness, however, of the mind's silent, transcendental basis in pure awareness, the unified field of natural law. Consequently, the individual's awareness is as if cut off from the ultimate reality of the union of objective and subjective existence, which is said to be directly appreciated in the state of transcendental consciousness.

In contrast with deep sleep, the waking state of consciousness expresses some degree of conscious awareness, but is

highly constrained by the very structure of experience. According to Vedic psychology, consciousness in the waking state
is fragmented into its partial aspects of knower, known, and
process of knowing. The knower, self, or individual psyche is
experienced as localized in time and space and subject to
constant change. This is why Vedic psychology refers to the
status of the self experienced in the normal waking state as
the "small self," in contrast to the "Self" experienced as an
unbounded or cosmic psyche during transcendental consciousness (8;9).

In the waking state, the knower can know himself only indirectly through the "process of knowing"--through the excited
levels of perceiving, thinking, and feeling. The localized
self is identified with and reflected upon cognitive structures related to body image, personal ability, values, past
experiences, social position, and other components that define
the individual in the social world in which he or she is embedded (46).

In contrast, Vedic psychology identifies transcendental
consciousness as well as the higher states of consciousness
as having the property of *self-referral*. Self-referral is
not the same, however, as the self-reflective thinking characteristic of the adult waking state. Self-referral means
that the inner self is fully awake to its true nature as the
transcendental Self at the source of thought. It is a state
of pure conscious*ness*, as opposed to being *conscious of* something other than itself. In the self-referral state, awareness *curves back* onto itself and knows itself directly as the
unified field of pure consciousness. Regardless of how re-
cursive and complex self-reflective thought becomes, the self-
referral state remains completely simple, the silent witness,
uninvolved with the active social self.

The waking state is often characterized by a state of high
arousal, and by a low response threshold to stimuli in contrast
to deep sleep and dreaming. In transcendental consciousness
the subject is also fully aware, with a low response threshold,
yet is simultaneously in a state of very low somatic arousal as
evidenced by metabolic rate. This suggests that bodily arousal
and degree of mental awareness can be potentially orthogonal
dimensions. In transcendental consciousness, awareness is
heightened though settled and arousal is low; in sleep, awareness and arousal are both low; in dreaming, some indices of
arousal are high, but awareness is low; in waking, both awareness and arousal vary.

In the waking state, the EEG pattern is generally characterized by mixed frequency, low amplitude EEG. Depending on
the degree of mental exertion, alpha and alpha spindles tend
to decrease; during relaxation they increase (4;7).

During transcendental consciousness, the EEG typically shows the presence of high amplitude from all areas of the scalp (7;19;20;21) that is more coherent than in a resting-with-eyes closed condition.

There is less respiration during transcendental consciousness than during ordinary waking or even relaxed waking with the eyes closed. In a series of studies Farrow and Hebert (15) discovered significantly more periods of apparent respiratory suspension lasting 10 to 60 seconds during TM than during relaxation sessions in control subjects. There was also a very high correlation between periods of respiratory suspension and subsequent signalling by subjects of a completed TC episode Badawi et al. (21) also found substantially more periods of apparent respiratory suspension in those practicing TM than in relaxation controls. More recently Kesterson (27) found decreased minute ventilation during TM, compared with eyes-closed waking, and respiratory suspensions in some subjects during TM.

Metabolism also appears to decrease during transcendental consciousness, compared with eyes-closed waking state. Significantly greater declines were observed during TM of forearm oxyg consumption, respiratory quotient (CRQ), red cell metabolism, a plasma lactate concentration (24;30;44;45).

One finding of particular interest appears in Jevning, Wilson, and Guich (30). They discovered that when forearm O_2 consumption declined during TM, CO_2 elimination ceased and there was actually a unique net forearm *uptake* of CO_2 and therefore a *negative* RQ during TM. The experimenter concluded that the results "imply major importance of behavior in the control of metabolism and need for expansion of the repertoire of metabolic pathways currently understood in human physiology" (30).

In several studies (31;32;49) plasma cortisol, a stress-related hormone, decreased significantly during TM compared to relaxed waking state. Plasma phenylalanine concentration increased during TM compared to relaxed waking (50) as did plasma prolactin (30). O'Halloran et al. (51) found increased arginine vasopression (AVP) secretion during the TM technique compared to relaxed waking state. Potentiation of AVP may mediate reported effects of TM on learning, memory, and psychotherapeutic processes. Several studies reported marked increases in GSR during TM compared to relaxed waking, suggesting that a deeper state of rest was achieved during TM (36;37;52).

Also, serotonergic activity appears to be higher in TM than during eyes closed relaxation (53;54). Increased serotonin turnover has been associated with mollifying the effects of stress and enhancing positive mood state (55), as well as with central nervous system modulation of alertness level. Serotonin turnover generally peaks during the late night or

early morning sleep cycle and is at its lowest ebb during
waking state in the pre-afternoon (56). A recent research
study has located high concentrations of an as yet unidentified
biochemical in the urine of advanced TM practitioners which
may be a candidate for a naturally occurring antidepressant
agent (57).

One review study (58) argued that meditation-induced
transcendental consciousness did not produce lower somatic
arousal than simple eyes-closed rest in the waking state.
This contention was responded to in a study by Orme-Johnson
and Dillbeck (28) which, using a more detailed and quantitative
meta-analysis, showed that TM does reduce somatic arousal more
than simple eyes-closed rest; in fact, the statistical effect
size was more than twice as large during TM than during rest
on basal GSR, oxygen consumption, respiration rate, and plasma
lactate. Of even greater practical importance is whether
these physiological changes translate into enduring effects
after the practice. If simple relaxation reduces somatic
arousal to the same degree as transcendental consciousness
during TM, then the long-term effects of relaxation on stress
reduction should presumably be equivalent.

A recently completed, exhaustive, quantitative meta-
analysis (59) of over 100 studies indicated that the TM program was not only significantly more effective than other relaxation procedures in reducing trait anxiety (a measure of
chronic stress level), but also was more effective than other
available practices of meditation.[4]

In summary then, a large body of research suggests that
transcendental consciousness as induced by the TM technique is
fundamentally different from the waking state on dimensions
of awareness, arousal, EEG, evoked potentials, paired H-
reflex, breathing patterns, metabolism, blood chemistry, and
GSR. Such differences are maintained even when transcendental
consciousness is compared to simple or stylized relaxation.
Also, the long-term effects of the regular experience of
transcendental consciousness during TM on reduction of stress
appear to be more pronounced and enduring.

Transcendental Consciousness Distinguished
from Lucid Dreaming

Lucid dreaming, or lucidity, is generally defined as dreaming while knowing one is dreaming (60). It is reported to
combine the self-reflective awareness (71), volitional discriminative and memory processes of the waking state with the

illusory imagery associated with the dream state, but to be
different from either of those states. Interrupted sleep
studies indicate spontaneous lucid dreaming occurs most often
in the final hours of night sleep in a REM period and is
associated with patterns of electrophysiological arousal (46;
61). The onset of lucidity is accompanied by increases in
eye movement, heart rate, respiration, and skin potential,
and all of these measures decrease shortly after the onset (61).
    During lucid dreaming the subject recognizes and thinks
about the fact that he is dreaming, has pleasant feelings of
increased psychological balance, reduced identification with
dream egos (46;61), increased control of dream events (46;61),
and the ability to execute motor responses while dreaming
(46;61). The lucid dreamer also has active decision-making
capacities similar to the waking state, increased external
origin of achievement motivation in the dream (62), and
usually increased perceived intensity of audition, sometimes
with increases in other sensory content (61). The following
is an account of a lucid dream given by a university student
(63):

> A horse I'm responsible for is missing with no
> trace of evidence. A vast jungle exists on the
> edge of a field and I know the animal is lost some-
> where in the expanse. I begin a search for the
> horse. I cannot capture one of the other horses to
> ride and search for the lost animal. I become aware
> that I am dreaming; I tell myself, and am aware of
> the fact that I must play this dream through, but
> I am pleased that it is merely a dream, and that
> the horse is really safe and well, not injured or
> lost somewhere out of sight, since I must play
> the dream out.

    In this section similarities and differences between lucid
dreaming and transcendental consciousness or witnessing—the
maintenance of transcendental consciousness during dreaming—
will be discussed. Subsequently, similarities between the
de-identification process LaBerge (47) describes as an aspect
of lucid dreaming and our speculations on further de-embedding
of levels of mental processes in the development of higher
states of consciousness will also be considered.
    The essential similarity between lucid dreaming and the
maintenance of transcendental consciousness during dreaming
is that in both cases at least some form of wakefulness is
experienced during dreaming. Given this similarity, however,
there are several important differences between the two states.
    First, while lucidity is typically associated with
dreaming, transcendental consciousness is described as a self-

sufficient state of pure awareness that can be experienced
either in isolation or with any mental state. It is not
linked specifically to dreaming or sleep. Rather, in these
experiences there is a separation or gap between the peaceful,
non-changing awareness of transcendental consciousness and
the changing mental activity of these other states. The following is a description of witnessing dreaming described by a
subject (63):

> Often during dreaming I am awake inside, in a very
> peaceful, blissful state. Dreams come and go,
> thoughts about the dreams come and go, but I re-
> main in a deeply peaceful state, completely
> separate from the dreams and the thoughts. My
> body is asleep and inert, breathing goes on regu-
> larly and mechanically, and inside I am just aware
> that I am.

From this experience the nature of transcendental consciousness can be seen as completely simple and self-sufficient
awareness, which is separate from the process of dreaming or
thinking about dreaming, beyond mental activity of any kind,
displaying the quality of bliss or contentment. In contrast to
the explanation of lucidity as involving the active intellect
and discriminative processes similar to the waking state, the
essential feature of transcendental consciousness and witnessing is maintenance of an underlying, silent continuum of pure
awareness, regardless of whether or not more active levels of
mind are engaged in reflective thinking and/or dreaming.

Transcendental consciousness is not a process of waking
up the executive cognitive functions, and does not involve
gaining a perspective on the dream experience by reflecting
upon the dream content or the dream state, as some researchers
have said of lucidity (46;64). No self-reflective thinking
or logical discrimination is involved in deep sleep, but witnessing of deep sleep and dreaming both spontaneously occur
as the fifth state of consciousness, cosmic consciousness,
develops. In transcendental consciousness and all higher
states of consciousness described by Vedic psychology, the
Self, the witness, is totally de-embedded from the mental
faculties of the intellect, memory, and perception.

If transcendental consciousness were very similar to
lucidity, one would expect phenomenal descriptions of transcendental consciousness (like those given above) to be frequently
reported by lucid dreamers. However, Gackenbach et al. (63)
estimate that a very small percentage of the people they surveyed reported having spontaneously experienced at least once
in their lives a state which may have been transcendental con-

sciousness. By contrast, in other work (61) the majority of
those asked typically report having had a lucid dream at some
time in their lives. The experience of transcendental consciousness is infrequently described in the literature on lucid
dreaming and is conspicuous by the fact that such rare experiences, even in advanced lucid dreamers, are referred to
with enthusiasm (47).

In addition to these conceptual and phenomenological differences, the psychophysiological correlates of transcendental
consciousness differ from the findings on lucidity. As seen
in Table 13, transcendental consciousness is characterized by
silent awareness and deep physiological rest. In contrast,
lucidity during dreaming is associated with an increase in
some somatic arousal indices, suggesting an increase in cognitive processing rather than induction of a quiescent state (62).
Some researchers on lucid dreaming point out that events a
person experiences while asleep and dreaming produce effects
on the brain (and, to a lesser extent, the body) remarkably
similar to those that would be produced if the person were
actually to experience the corresponding events while awake.
As examples, they cite the correspondence between dreamed and
actual eye movements (65), voluntary control of respiration
during lucid dreaming (66), and singing and counting during
lucid dreams (67). These findings also differentiate the
psychophysiological correlates of lucid dreaming from transcendental consciousness, which is not associated with an active,
changing psychophysiological state, but with a stable, quiescent one.

Although the experiential and descriptive evidence clearly
suggests that lucidity and transcendental consciousness are
distinct types of experience, it is possible that future research will support the conception of a continuum of degrees
of lucidity, with the most advanced form being the state of
transcendental consciousness. Here we would like to speculate
on how lucidity might fit into a developmental framework based
on the conception of a continuum of levels of psychological
maturation.

Speculations on Lucidity
and the De-embedding Process

We suggest that lucidity as typically experienced may be
considered an indicator of the continuum of psychological
maturation related to the unfolding of higher order or self-
reflective thought (46). Human development unfolds in stages

from more concrete to increasingly abstract, subtle, and integrative cognitive states. Piaget has identified a sequence of four basic stages of cognitive development from birth to early adulthood: the sensorimotor stage, preoperational thought, concrete operational thought, and a level of abstract reflective thought termed "formal operations." Developmentally, dreaming generally appears to involve relatively primitive mental operations and, according to Piaget (68), has much in common with pre-operational thought, which is characterized by pre-logical mentation and impulsivity. Young children may be unable to distinguish clearly between waking and dreaming because the necessary waking discriminative functions are not yet developed. Even in the adult the dream state may, at times, be irrational and reflect a lack of discrimination. On the one hand, the adult dreamer may be performing a complex logical task, such as calculus, in the dream, but, on the other hand, may be satisfied with solutions which he would clearly identify as incorrect in the waking state. Adult dreaming may share features with preoperational thought, such as inability to distinguish fanciful and realistic experience, no clear definition of ego or self, and extended symbolic play (68).

The developmental process through preoperational thought, concrete operations, formal operations, and postformal operational thought (46) can be viewed in terms of the degree to which executive cognitive functions are de-embedded and begin to monitor immediate perceptions and increasingly abstract mental representations. After the onset of concrete operations, the waking state self is able to recall distinctly previous periods of the illusory reality of dreaming. Perhaps at a later stage when the nervous system is capable of supporting higher order reflective thought, the ability to have knowledge of dreaming during dreaming may become accessible to many individuals. These experiences may reflect a developed adult cognitive system, with relatively mature functions for differentiation and integration of experiences.

From the perspective of Vedic psychology, the human mind has a hierarchical structure, with levels of depth of functioning from gross to subtle to transcendental. The theory of levels of the mind in Vedic psychology identifies the following components of the individual psyche: the most expressed level, called *senses*; the deeper level of cognitive operations, such as representation and working memory, referred to as *mind*; the deep decision processes termed *intellect*; and, the most subtle, integrative aspect of individuality, the *ego*. Underlying these levels of the individual mind is the source of thought, the level of transcendental consciousness, the cosmic psyche. We have proposed (46) that the increasing functional

integration of the nervous system in ontogenesis may permit
the utilization of these increasingly subtle levels of mind.
The progressive enlivenment of each subtler level may provide
the *deep* structure for the expression of correspondingly
higher levels of cognitive operations. Enlivenment of a
deeper level of mind may allow that level to observe and
monitor the more expressed levels. As the level of intellect
becomes accessible to conscious awareness, it may be able to
monitor and add its discriminative functions to mental and
sensory operations; and as the ego becomes increasingly conscious and differentiated, the individual may be able to
hierarchically integrate more fully the operations of intellect, mind, and senses. If dreaming in its typical form
shares attributes with preoperational thought, the senses and
desires of the mind would tend to dominate during this experience, and the functioning of the intellect and ego would
not be in normal operation. In the case of lucid dreaming,
some of the monitoring functions of intellect and ego may be
operative. When conscious awareness comes to fully identify
with its transcendental foundation in pure consciousness,
then witnessing of the ego, intellect, and all levels of mind
would occur spontaneously.

Such a de-embedding process is also suggested by LaBerge
(47) as a potential aspect of lucid dreaming, which he calls
"de-identification." He points out that lucid dreamers

> know that the persons they appeared to be in the
> dream are not who they really are. No longer
> identifying with their [dream] egos, they are
> free to change them, correcting their delusions.
> ... [T]he fully lucid dreamer does not need to
> struggle to overcome his or her ego. He or she
> has become objective enough to no longer identify
> with it.... This knowledge puts the ego's impor-
> tance in modest proportion to the true, and, perhaps
> as yet undiscovered, *Self* (emphasis added). (pp.
> 242-243)

LaBerge's description seems also to point to the possibility
of extending the de-embedding process, such that the localized,
bounded ego of the dreamer, as well as the stable, walking
ego, is transcended and awareness identifies with the true
Self in its own self-referral state.

From the viewpoint of Vedic psychology and transcendental
consciousness, lucid dreaming can be seen as an indication of
a vast field of possibilities lying ahead. It is seen as an
experience of de-embedding of awareness from one representational state (dreaming) to a higher, more comprehensive state
(reflective thinking). This still does not reach the state of

complete transcendence, where knower, known, and process of
knowing are realized as one transcendental Self, pure consciousness, which is beyond representational thought. Maharishi
comments on this process of identifying one's awareness with
the Self in transcendental consciousness:

> Self has two connotations: lower self and
> higher Self. The lower self is that aspect of the
> personality which deals only with the relative
> aspect of existence. It comprises the mind that
> thinks, the intellect that decides, the ego that
> experiences. This lower self functions only in
> the relative states of existence--waking, dream-
> ing, and deep sleep. Remaining always within the
> field of relativity, it has no chance of experien-
> cing the real freedom of absolute Being (non-
> changing pure consciousness). That is why it is
> in the sphere of bondage. The higher Self is that
> aspect of the personality which never changes,
> absolute Being, which is the very basis of the
> entire field of relativity, including the lower
> self.
>   A man who wants to master himself has to
> master the lower self first and then the higher
> Self. Mastering the lower self means taking the
> mind (mind, intellect, ego) from the gross fields
> of existence to the subtler fields, until the
> subtlest field of relative existence is trans-
> cended.... This robs the lower self of its in-
> dividuality bound by time, space and causation and
> sets it free in the state of universal existence.
> (9, p. 339)

This is how the de-embedding process may be extended beyond the limits ordinarily imposed by the waking, dreaming,
and sleeping states of consciousness.

A Developmental Model of
Higher States of Consciousness

Fundamental cognitive, moral, and self-development typically come to a plateau during late adolescence or early adulthood with the stabilization of formal operations and adult
reflective thought. It is believed that psychological development freezes at this level because the central nervous system
generally stops developing during this period of life. The

high degree of functional interrelationship of mind and body
suggests, however, that not only can changes in the nervous
system act to change the level of awareness, but also changes
in the level of awareness can act back upon the nervous system
to influence the style of physiological functioning. We have
proposed that development may typically end at the level of
discursive adult thought because the experience of transcendental consciousness is not ordinarily available. As this
experience is regularly gained through the Maharishi Technology
of the Unified Field (MTUF), higher states of consciousness
naturally emerge.

Several cross-sectional and longitudinal studies employing
the State of Consciousness Inventory designed by Alexander (6)
indicate that regular practice of the TM technique enhances
frequency of transcendental consciousness and higher states
of consciousness in comparison to participation in other
treatment and control groups, even when controlling for score
on the SCI misleading items scale and relevant demographic
covariates. Further, statistical factor analyses revealed
that higher state experience items form a conceptually meaningful factor empirically distinct from adult waking state
and pathological classes of experience (6;60). Elevated
scores on the higher state of consciousness factor (6) or
separate higher state items (7;14) have been found to be significantly correlated with a wide range of physiological,
cognitive-perceptual, and personality effects that would be
expected to be associated with postconceptual growth beyond
the ordinary endpoint of human development. More frequent
experience of higher states of consciousness has been positively correlated with resting alpha and theta coherence,
suggestive of neurophysiological integration; greater resting
H-reflex recovery amplitude indicative of neurophysiological
efficiency; originality, fluency, and flexibility in creative
thinking; self-actualization; internal locus of control; participation in constructive social and work activities; reduction of symptoms of stress; capacity for absorption and non-
propositional information processing; and certain cognitive-
perceptual skills (6;7;12;20;46;69;70). Hence, higher states
of consciousness involve not only subjective experience but
profound behavioral changes.

As stated earlier in this chapter, habituation of the nervous system to sustain the state of transcendental consciousness throughout the states of waking, dreaming, and sleeping,
results in a fifth state of consciousness, called cosmic consciousness. The most unambiguous subjective indicator of
growth of cosmic consciousness is the experience of transcendental consciousness or witnessing even during the inertia of
deep sleep. Evidence of witnessing of sleep has also been

provided by two recent surveys of regular practitioners of the MTUF. In one study (60) 85% of the 235 respondents reported having had this experience; 40.4% reported occasional experiences of clear witnessing during a night's sleep, 7.4% frequent experiences, and 7.7% *regular* experiences. In the other study (63) involving 100 meditating freshmen students from Maharishi International University, 82.5% reported having had the experience of witnessing sleep. Similar reports have been obtained for witnessing during waking as well as during dreaming.

Once cosmic consciousness has been gained, further refinement of the nervous system, facilitated by the continued practice of the TM and TM-Sidhi program, is said to develop the state of refined cosmic consciousness. This state is characterized by refinement of perceptual and affective processes, resulting in the ability to appreciate what is described as the finest level of subjective and objective existence (6; 7;8;9).

Vedic psychology proposes that human development culminates in the seventh state of consciousness, unity consciousness. Unity consciousness is described as the highest state of enlightened development based upon optimal functioning of the nervous system. According to Vedic psychology, in unity consciousness the entire range of objective and subjective creation is spontaneously experienced in terms of the infinite self-referral nature of the Self, pure consciousness, and complete mastery is gained over all the laws of nature governing the individual and his interaction with the environment. All these higher states of consciousness are said to have their basis and their beginning in the self-referral state of transcendental consciousness.

Conclusion

Evidence of a fourth state of consciousness has been considered. The state of transcendental consciousness proposed by Vedic psychology has been distinguished from sleep, dreaming, lucid dreaming, and waking with respect to degree of awareness, response threshold, EEG activity, eye movements, metabolic rate, breathing pattern, GSR, paired H-reflex, evoked potentials, and concentrations of various hormones in the blood. These parameters identify transcendental consciousness as a state of coherent inner awareness and physiological quiescence, which is as different from the three ordinary states of consciousness as they are from one another.

In the context of the normal process of human development, the experience of transcendental consciousness, facilitated by practice of the Maharishi Technology of the Unified Field, appears to unfreeze human development, allowing natural growth of post-conceptual stages characterized by more comprehensive and adaptive cognitive and affective functioning, increased self-actualization, and improved social behavior.

The functions of deep sleep and dreaming appear to restore psychophysiological balance. The functions of the waking state appear to support activity for increased adaptation. According to Vedic psychology, the unique function of the fourth state of consciousness is the integration of the individual psyche with the cosmic psyche, the unified field of all the laws of nature, resulting in realization of the total potential of natural law in human life through the development of higher states of consciousness.

Notes

1. As certain physicists have recently recognized (71;72), current formulations in quantum field theory of an unmanifest field of all force and matter fields (laws of nature) at the source of the physical universe are remarkably similar to the studies of precise subjective descriptions in the Vedic literature of the unified field of consciousness said to be at the basis of the laws of nature (73).

According to Vedic psychology, the most parsimonious explanation for this striking isomorphism is that these are two descriptions of the same unified field viewed, respectively, from objective and subjective perspectives (8).

Because the unified field appears to display properties of consciousness on an infinite scale and is held to be the universal source of the individual psyche as well as objective existence, this field is also referred to in Vedic psychology as the *cosmic psyche* (8).

2. Transcendental Meditation is described as a simple, natural mental technique that allows one to effortlessly experience less excited, increasingly refined levels of mental activity until the mind transcends the subtlest state of thought and arrives at the source of thought, transcendental consciousness (9, p. 470). The TM-Sidhi program is said to foster the ability to think and perform activity from within transcendental consciousness and thereby enhance mind-body coordination to effortlessly achieve intentions and accelerate growth of higher states of consciousness (8).

The Maharishi Technology of Unified Field is held to be a sufficient condition for eliciting transcendental consciousness though it may not be a necessary one (46). Experiences of transcendental consciousness may occur spontaneously in some individuals (6;46). The function of TM is to systematically elicit this state in a highly efficient and effortless way (9).

3. The mathematical quantity called *coherence* is a measure of the consistency of the relationship between the phases of the EEG at a specified frequency when measured at two spatially separated points on the scalp. As such, it is a sensitive indicator of the degree of long-range spatial order in cortical activity—at least to the extent that such orderly activity is mirrored in the EEG (7). *Correlation* of brain waves refers to the correlation between the amplitude and power of the EEG measured at different areas on the scalp. *Synchrony* of two or more waves means that the two waves are in phase with one another. Both these measures have also been taken as indicators of orderliness in brain function (7).

4. Stress has also been directly implicated in the process of aging, and a recent literature review (74) suggests that changes in 34 physiological and psychological variables influenced by the TM program are in the opposite direction to that associated with aging. Several studies have shown that middle-aged (or younger) advanced TM practitioners are substantially younger biologically than chronologically on the Morgan scale (75). In fact, a recent prospective random-assignment experiment with the institutionalized elderly (which controlled for program structure and expectation-fostering conditions) indicated that subjects who learned TM literally lived longer than subjects who learned a comparable relaxation procedure over a three-year period. Also, greater reversals of decrements on cognitive and health factors were observed in the TM group (76).

References

1. Kleitman, N. (1963). *Sleep and Wakefulness*. Chicago: The University of Chicago Press.

2. Orme-Johnson, D.W., and Farrow, J.T. (Eds.). (1977). *Scientific Research on the Transcendental Meditation Program: Collected Papers: Vol. 1*. Livingston Manor, N.Y.: Maharishi European Research University Press.

   This volume includes 104 research studies on the Transcendental Meditation program from the first published study

in 1970 through 1977 (including three final papers on the
effects of the advanced TM-Sidhi program introduced in
1976).
    The volume is divided into five major parts: Physiology
(during and outside the practice of the TM technique),
Psychology, Sociology, Theoretical papers, and the TM-
Sidhi program. Each part is further divided into sections
as necessary, e.g., psychology is divided into two sections, one on Intelligence, Learning and Academic Performance and the other on Development of Personality.
An introduction to each section and brief annotations to
each study are provided by the editors. This is the most
complete compendium of papers on TM (plus the forthcoming
volumes 2-4) and is a must for any serious researcher in
this area.

3. Chalmers, R.A.; Clements, G.; Schenkluhn, H.; and Weinless,
    M. (Eds.) (in press). *Scientific Research on the Trans-
    cendental Meditation and TM-Sidhi Programme: Collected
    Papers: Vols. 2-4.* Vlodrop, The Netherlands: MIU Press.

    Volumes 2-4 include over 250 research studies on TM and
    TM-Sidhi programs from 1975 (with a few earlier ones)
    through 1984. Each volume is divided into four parts:
    Physiology, Psychology, Sociology, and Review Papers.
    An introduction to the sections and annotations for each
    paper are provided by the editors. A fifth volume is
    currently in press.

4. Wallace, R.K. (1970). "Physiological Effects of Transcen-
    dental Meditation: A Proposed Fourth Major State of Con-
    sciousness." Unpublished doctoral dissertation, School
    of Medicine, University of California at Los Angeles,
    California.

5. Wallace, R.K. (1970). "Physiological Effects of Transcen-
    dental Meditation." *Science, 167,* 1751-1754.

    This is the first research study ever published on the
    TM program and documents physiological correlates of the
    practice (e.g., decline in oxygen consumption and enhanced
    alpha EEG). Wallace's pioneering work stimulated wide-
    scale research on the correlates and effects of the TM
    program.

6. Alexander, C.N.; Alexander, V.K.; Boyer, R.; and Carlisle,
    T. (in press). "The Empirical Investigation of Higher
    States of Consciousness." *Journal of the Science of
    Creative Intelligence and Vedic Science.*

Exhaustive review of research on the physiological, cognitive-perceptual, and personality correlates of growth to higher states of consciousness as described by Vedic psychology. This paper appears in the first issue of a new interdisciplinary journal focusing on the systematic investigation of consciousness from the viewpoints of modern science and ancient Vedic science.

7. Orme-Johnson, D. (1977). "The Dawn of the Age of Enlightenment: Experimental Evidence that the Transcendental Meditation Technique Produces a Fourth and Fifth State of Consciousness in the Individual and a Profound Influence of Orderliness in Society." In D.W. Orme-Johnson and J.J. Farrow (Eds.), *Scientific Research on the Transcendental Meditation Program: Collected Papers: Vol. 1.* Livingston Manor, N.Y.: Maharishi European Research University Press.

8. Orme-Johnson, D.; Dillbeck, M.; Alexander, C.; and Van Denberg, V. (in press). "Unified Field Based Psychology: Vedic Psychology of Maharishi Mahesh Yogi." In R.A. Chalmers, G. Clements, H. Schenkluhn, and M. Weinless (Eds.), *Scientific Research on the Transcendental Meditation and TM-Sidhi Programme: Collected Papers: Vol. 5.* Vlodrop, The Netherlands: MIU Press.

This work is the first systematic exposition of Maharishi Mahesh Yogi's Vedic psychology. It includes sections on the relationship between the unified field as described by Vedic science and modern physics, the levels or functions of the human mind, the seven states of consciousness, the TM-Sidhi program, and the social-ecological effects associated with the practice of the Maharishi Technology of the Unified Field.

9. Maharishi Mahesh Yogi (1967). *On the Bhagavad-Gita: A New Translation and Commentary.* Baltimore, Md.: Penguin.

A highly original and thought provoking commentary on the *Bhagavad-Gita*, a classic text of the ancient Vedic literature. In his commentary, Maharishi describes transcendental consciousness in detail and how it provides the basis for higher states of consciousness. The emphasis in this book on the need for a scientific approach to the study of consciousness clearly lays the foundation for Maharishi's later work in Vedic psychology.

10. Dillbeck, M.C. (1983). "The Vedic Psychology of the *Bhagavad-Gita*." *Psychologia, 26,* 62-72.

In this theoretical paper Dillbeck locates the core
principles of Maharishi Mahesh Yogi's Vedic psychology
as brought to light in the *Bhagavad-Gita,* a classic text
of Vedic literature. He focuses on the distinction between transcendental consciousness and the three ordinary
states of consciousness, and the role of this fourth
state of consciousness in developing full human potential
or "enlightenment."

11. Dillbeck, M.C. (1983). "Testing the Vedic Psychology of
     the *Bhagavad-Gita.*" *Psychologia, 26,* 232-240.

     In this review paper Dillbeck cites considerable em-
     pirical evidence to support predictions derived from
     principles of the Vedic psychology of the *Bhagavad-Gita.*
     He shows how the research literature upholds the predic-
     tion that meditation--specifically transcendental medita-
     tion--can induce transcendental consciousness, neutralize
     stress, and foster growth of higher states of conscious-
     ness.

12. Orem, J., and Barnes, C. (Eds.) (1980). *Physiology in
     Sleep.* New York: Academic Press.

13. Lindsley, J.G. (1983). "Sleep Patterns and Functions."
     In A. Gale and J.A. Edwards (Eds.), *Physiological Cor-
     relates of Human Behavior: Vol. I: Basic Issues.* Lon-
     don: Academic Press.

14. Haynes, C.T.; Hebert, J.R.; Reber, W.; and Orme-Johnson,
     D.W. (1977). "The Psychophysiology of Advanced Par-
     ticipants in the Transcendental Meditation Program."
     In D.W. Orme-Johnson and J.T. Farrow (Eds.), *Scientific
     Research on the Transcendental Meditation Program:
     Collected Papers: Vol. 1* (pp. 208-212). Livingston
     Manor, N.Y.: Maharishi European Research University
     Press.

15. Farrow, J.T., and Hebert, J.R. (1982). "Breath Suspension
     during the Transcendental Meditation Technique."
     Psychosomatic Medicine; 44(2), 133-153.

     The most successful study in identifying distinctive
     psychophysiological changes during those subperiods of
     the practice corresponding to self-reported experience
     of transcendental consciousness. The results of four ex-
     periments indicated a significant increase in frequency
     and length of breath suspension episodes during TM in
     comparison to relaxation controls. Periods of transcen-

dental consciousness were especially correlated with episodes of breath suspension, increased alpha EEG coherence, and other acute changes.

16. Banquet, J.P. (1973). "Spectral Analysis of the EEG during Meditation." *Electroencephalography and Clinical Neurophysiology*, *35*, 143-151.

    The first study to explore in detail the EEG of regular practitioners of TM in comparison to relaxation controls. Banquet observed an increase in alpha and theta (and sometimes beta) spindles during TM, and was the original researcher to discover EEG synchronization during the practice of this technique.

17. Westcott, M. (1977). "Hemispheric Symmetry of the EEG during the Transcendental Meditation Technique." In D.W. Orme-Johnson and J.T. Farrow (Eds.), *Scientific Research on the Transcendental Meditation Program: Collected Papers: Vol. I.* Livingston Manor, N.Y.: Maharishi European Research University Press.

18. Kras, D.J. (1977). "The Transcendental Meditation Technique and EEG Alpha Activity." In D.W. Orme-Johnson and J.T. Farrow (Eds.), *Scientific Research on the Transcendental Meditation Program: Collected Papers: Vol. I.* Livingston Manor, N.Y.: Maharishi European Research University Press.

19. Levine, P.H., and Hebert, J.R. (1977). "EEG Coherence during the Transcendental Meditation Technique." In D.W. Orme-Johnson and J.T. Farrow (Eds.), *Scientific Research on the Transcendental Meditation Program: Collected Papers: Vol. I.* Livingston Manor, N.Y.: Maharishi European Research University Press.

20. Orme-Johnson, D.W., and Haynes, C.T. (1981). "EEG Phase Coherence, Pure Consciousness, Creativity and TM-Sidhi Experiences." *International Journal of Neuroscience*, *13*, 211-217.

    This seminal paper reveals that subjects with clear transcendental consciousness and TM-Sidhi experiences displayed higher alpha coherence and creativity scores than subjects who lacked these experiences.

21. Badawi, K.; Wallace, R.K.; Orme-Johnson, D.; and Rouzere, A.M. (1984). "Electrophysiological Characteristics of Respiratory Suspension Periods Occurring during the

Practice of the Transcendental Meditation Program."
Psychosomatic Medicine, 46(3), 267-276.

Badawi et al. replicated and extended Farrow and
Hebert's research on respiratory suspension and transcendental consciousness. They found that periods of natural
respiratory suspension during TM were accompanied by
greater total EEG coherence, in comparison to immediately
prior and subsequent periods of forced breath holding in
controls.

22. McEvoy, T.M.; Frumkin, L.R.; and Harkins, S.W. (1980).
     "Effects of Meditation on Brainstem Auditory Evoked
     Potentials." *International Journal of Neuroscience*,
     10, 165-170.

23. Wandhofer, A., and Plattig, K.H. (1973). "Stimulus-linked
     DC Shift in Auditory Evoked Potentials in Transcendental
     Meditation (TM)." *Pflugers Archiv* (Suppl. 343).

24. Wandhofer, A.; Kobal, G.; and Plattig, K.H. (1976).
     "Shortening of Latencies of Human Auditory Evoked Brain
     Potentials during the Transcendental Meditation Tech-
     nique." *Zeitschrift für Elektroenzephalographie und
     Elektromyographie EEG-EMG*, 7, 99-103.

25. Paty, J.; Brenot, P.H.; and Faure, J.M. (1977). "Modifi-
     cation of CNV Evoked Potentials through Transcendental
     Meditation." *Psychologie Medicale*, 9, 1235-1246.

26. Hebert, J.R., and Lehman, D. (1977). "Periodic Suspen-
     sion of Respiration during the Transcendental Meditation
     Technique." *Electroencephalography and Clinical Neuro-
     physiology*, 42, 397-405.

27. Kesterson, J. (October 1985). "Respiratory Changes
     during the Transcendental Meditation Technique." Paper
     presented at the annual Conference of the Society for
     Neuroscience, Dallas, Texas.

28. Orme-Johnson, D.W., and Dillbeck, M.C. (1986). "A New
     Perspective on Transcendental Meditation." Manuscript
     submitted for publication.

29. Jevning, R.; Wilson, A.F.; Pirkle, H.; O'Halloran, J.P.;
     and Walsh, R.N. (1983). "Metabolic Control in a State
     of Decreased Activation: Modulation of Red Cell
     Metabolism." *American Journal of Physiology*, 245 (Cell
     Physiol. 14), C457-C461.

State-of-the-art research by Jevning et al. reveals a substantial decline during the TM technique in whole blood metabolism accounted for mostly by decline of red cell glycolysis.

30. Jevning, R.; Wilson, A.F.; and Guich, S. (1985). "New and Unknown Metabolic Pathways Elicited by Acute Behavioral States of Decreased Activation." *American Journal of Physiology*, 245, C457–C461.

   A breakthrough study describing profound acute departure from "resting" metabolic functions during the TM technique. Jevning et al. discovered that during TM there was not only a substantial decline in O_2 consumption but literally a net forearm uptake in CO_2.

31. Jevning, R.; Wilson, A.F.; and Davidson, J.M. (1978). "Adrenocortical Activity during Meditation." *Hormones and Behavior*, 10, 54–60.

32. Jevning, R.; Wilson, A.F.; and Smith, W.R. (1978). "The Transcendental Meditation Technique, Adrenocortical Activity, and Implications for Stress." *Experientia*, 34, 618–619.

33. Jevning, R.; Wilson, A.; O'Halloran, T.; and Walsh, R. (in press). "Hormonal Control of Metabolism in States of Decreased Activation." *American Journal of Physiology*, 245, 110–116.

   Leading edge research showing substantial declines in thyroid stimulating hormones (TSH) during and immediately after TM. Basal TSH concentration was also significantly lower in the TM group than the rest group.

34. Werner, O.; Wallace, R.K.; Charles, B.; Janssen, G.; Stryker, T.; and Chalmers, R.A. (1986). "Long-Term Endocrinalogic Changes in Subjects Practicing the TM and TM-Sidhi Program." *Psychosomatic Medicine*, 48(1-2), 59–66.

35. Jevning, R.; Wilson, A.F.; and Vander Laan, E.F. (1978). "Plasma Prolactin and Growth Hormone during Meditation." *Psychosomatic Medicine*, 40, 4.

36. Janby, J. (1973). "Immediate Effects of the Transcendental Meditation Technique: Increased Skin Resistance during First Meditation after Instruction." In D.W. Orme-Johnson and J.T. Farrow (Eds.), *Scientific Research*

    on the Transcendental Meditation Program: Collected
    Papers: Vol. I. (pp. 213-215). Livingston Manor, N.Y.:
    Maharishi European Research University Press.

37. Laurie, G. (1973). "An Investigation into the Changes
     in Skin Resistance during the Transcendental Meditation
     Technique." In D.W. Orme-Johnson and J.T. Farrow (Eds.)
     Scientific Research on the Transcendental Meditation
     Program: Collected Papers: Vol. I (pp. 216-223).
     Livingston Manor, N.Y.: Maharishi European Research
     University Press.

38. Farrow, J.T. (1977). "Physiological Changes Associated
     with Transcendental Consciousness, the State of Least
     Excitation of Consciousness." In D.W. Orme-Johnson and
     J.T. Farrow (Eds.), *Scientific Research on the Trans-*
     cendental Meditation Program: Collected Papers: Vol. I.
     Livingston Manor, N.Y.: Maharishi European Research
     University Press.

39. Orme-Johnson, D.W. (1973). "Autonomic Stability and
     Transcendental Meditation." *Psychosomatic Medicine,*
     35, 341-349.

     This landmark study was the first to investigate the
     effects of TM on physiological stability and efficiency
     outside of the practice. It showed that regular prac-
     titioners of TM had fewer phasic GSR responses and more
     rapid habituation to stressful auditory stimuli with eyes
     open than control subjects.

40. Van Boxtel, A. (1976). "The Relationship between Mono-
     synaptic Spinal Reflex Amplitudes and Some EEG Alpha
     Parameters." *Electroencephalography and Clinical*
     Neurophysiology, 40, 297-305.

41. Wallace, R.K.; Mills, P.J.; Orme-Johnson, D.W.; Dillbeck,
     M.C.; and Jacobe, E. (1983). "Modification of the
     Paired H Reflex through the Transcendental Meditation
     and TM-Sidhi Program." *Experimental Neurology, 79,*
     77-86.

42. Pagano, R.R.; Rose, R.M.; Stivers, R.M.; and Warrenburg,
     R. (1976). "Sleep in Transcendental Meditation."
     Science, 191, 309-310.

43. Alexander, C.N., and Larimore, W.E. (in press). "Dis-
     tinguishing between Transcendental Meditation and Sleep

According to Electrophysiological Criteria." In R.A. Chalmers, G. Clements, H. Schenkluhn, and M. Weinless (Eds.), *Scientific Research on the Transcendental Meditation and TM-Sidhi Programme: Collected Papers: Vol. 3.* Vlodrop, The Netherlands: MIU Press.

44. Jevning, R.; Wilson, A.F.; and O'Halloran, J.P. (1982). "Muscle and Skin Blood Flow and Metabolism during States of Decreased Activation." *Physiology and Behavior, 29,* 343-348.

45. Jevning, R.; Wilson, A.F.; Pirkle, H.; Guich, S.; and Walsh, R.N. (1985). "Modulation of Red Cell Metabolism by States of Decreased Activation: Comparison between States." *Physiology and Behavior, 35,* 679-682.

46. Alexander, C.N.; Davies, J.; Dixon, C.; Oetzel, R.; and Muehlman, M. (in press). "The Vedic Psychology of Human Development: A Theory of Development of Higher Stages of Consciousness beyond Formal Operations." In C.N. Alexander, E. Langer, and R. Oetzel (Eds.), *Higher Stages of Human Development: Adult Growth beyond Formal Operations.* New York: Oxford University Press.

This is the first theoretical work to systematically integrate Vedic psychology with contemporary theories of human development. The authors propose that TM may act as an adult developmental technology to promote post-conceptual growth of higher stages of consciousness beyond Piaget's proposed endpoint of formal operational thought.

47. LaBerge, S.P. (1985). *Lucid Dreaming.* Los Angeles: Jeremy T. Tarcher.

48. James, W. (1890). *The Principles of Psychology.* New York: Holt, Rinehart and Winston.

49. Jevning, R.; Wilson, A.; Vander Laan, E.; and Levine, S. (1975). "Plasma Prolactin and Cortisol during Transcendental Meditation" (Summary). *Proceedings of the 57th Annual Meeting of the Endocrine Society,* 257.

50. Jevning, R.; Pirkle, H.; and Wilson, A.F. (1977). "Behavioral Alteration of Plasma Phenylalanine Concentration." *Physiology and Behavior, 19,* 611-614.

51. O'Halloran, J.P.; Jevning, R.A.; Wilson, A.F.; Skowsky, R.; and Alexander, C.N. (1985). "Hormone Regulation in

a State of Decreased Activation: Potentiation of Arginine Vasopressin." *Physiology and Behavior*, *35*, 591-595.

A recent study discovering a five-fold elevation in the level of the hormone arginine vasopressin (AVP) in the blood plasma of advanced subjects during TM in comparison to controls during relaxation. Potentiation of AVP may mediate reported effects of TM on learning, memory, and psychotherapeutic processes.

52. West, M.A. (1977). "Changes in Skin Resistance in Subjects Resting, Reading, Listening to Music, or Practicing the Transcendental Meditation Technique." In D.W. Orme-Johnson and J.T. Farrow (Eds.), *Scientific Research on the Transcendental Meditation Program: Collected Papers: Vol. I* (pp. 224-229). Livingston Manor, N.Y.: Maharishi European Research University Press.

53. Bujatti, M., and Riederer, P. (1976). "Serotonin, Noradrenaline, Dopamine Metabolites in Transcendental Meditation Technique." *Journal of Neural Transmission*, *39*, 257-267.

54. Walton, K.G.; Lerom, M.; Salerno, J.; and Wallace, R.K. (1981). "Practice on the Transcendental Meditation (TM) and TM-Sidhi Program May Affect the Circadian Rhythm of Urinary 5-hydroxyindole Excretion." *Society for Neuroscience Abstracts*, *7*, 48.

55. Wyatt, R.J. (1972). "The Serotonin-Catecholamine Dream Bicycle." *Biological Psychiatry*, *5*, 33-35.

56. Wirz-Justice, A. (1977). "Theoretical and Therapeutic Potential of Indoleamine Precursors in Affective Disorders." *Neuropsychobiology*, *3*, 199-233.

57. Walton, K.C.; McCorkle, T.; Hauser, T.; MacClean, C.; Jeni, J.; and Meyerson, L.R. (1986). "An Unidentified Modulator of Imipramine Binding and Serotonin Uptake Has Been Isolated from Human Urine." In Y.H. Ehrlich (Ed.), *Advances in Experimental Medicine and Biology: Vol. 7*. New York: Plenum.

Leading edge research has located high concentrations of an as yet unidentified biochemical in the urine of advance TM practitioners, which may be a candidate for a natural antidepressant agent.

58. Holmes, D.S. (1984). "Meditation and Somatic Arousal
     Reduction: A Review of Experimental Evidence." *American
     Psychologist*, *39*(1), 1-10.

59. Eppley, K.; Abrams, A.; and Shear, J. (August 1984).
     "The Effects of Meditation and Relaxation Techniques
     on Trait Anxiety: A Meta-analysis." Paper presented
     at the annual meeting of the American Psychological
     Association, Toronto, Canada.

60. Dillbeck, M.C., and Orme-Johnson, D.W. (in press). "The
     Vedic Psychology of Human Development." In C. Alexan-
     der, E. Langer, and R. Oetzel (Eds.), *Higher Stages of
     Development: Adult Growth beyond Formal Operations*.
     New York: Oxford University Press.

61. Gackenbach, J., and LaBerge, S. (1986). "An Overview of
     Lucid Dreaming." In A. Sheikh (Ed.), *International
     Review of Mental Imagery: Vol. 2*. New York: Human
     Sciences Press.

62. Moffitt, A.; Purcell, S.; Hoffman, R.; Wells, R.; and
     Pigeon, R. (1985). "Single-Mindedness and Self-Reflec-
     tiveness: Laboratory Studies." *Lucidity Letter*, *4*(1),
     5-6.

63. Gackenbach, J.; Cranson, R.; and Alexander, C.N. (June
     1986). "Lucid Dreaming, Witnessing Dreaming, and the
     Transcendental Meditation Technique: A Developmental
     Relationship." Paper presented at the annual conven-
     tion of the Association for the Study of Dreams, Ontario,
     Canada.

64. Hunt, H.T. (1985). "A Comparative Psychology of Lucid
     Dreams." *Lucidity Letter*, *4*(1), 1-2.

65. LaBerge, S.P.; Nagel, L.E.; Taylor, W.B.; Dement, W.C.;
     and Zarcone, V. (1981). "Psychophysiological Correlates
     of the Initiation of Lucid Dreaming." *Sleep Research*,
     10, 149.

66. LaBerge, S.P., and Dement, W.C. (1982). "Voluntary Con-
     trol of Respiration during REM Dreaming." *Sleep Re-
     search*, *11*, 107.

67. LaBerge, S.P., and Dement, W.C. (1982). "Lateralization
     of Alpha Activity for Dreamed Singing and Counting
     during REM Sleep." *Psychophysiology*, *19*, 331-332.

68. Piaget, J. (1962). *Play, Dreams and Imitation in Child-
     hood*. New York: Morton.

69. Alexander, C.N. (1982). "Ego Development, Personality
     and Behavioral Change in Inmates Practicing the Trans-
     cendental Meditation Technique or Participating in
     Other Programs: A Summary of Cross-sectional and Longi-
     tudinal Results." Unpublished doctoral dissertation,
     Harvard University, Cambridge, Massachusetts.

70. Alexander, C.N.; Grant, J.; and Stadte, C. Von (1982).
     "The Effects of the Transcendental Meditation Technique
     on Recidivism: A Retrospective Archival Analysis."
     Unpublished manuscript, Harvard University, Cambridge,
     Massachusetts.

71. Waldrop, M.M. (1985). "String as a Theory of Everything."
     Science, 229, 1251-1253.

72. Freedman, D.Z., and Nieuenhuizen, P. van (1985). "The
     Hidden Dimensions of Space-Time." *Scientific American*,
     252(39), 74-81.

73. Hagelin, J.; Clements, G.; and Sharma, P.K. (in press).
     "The Contribution of the Maharishi Technology of the
     Unified Field to Physics: A New Integrated Approach."
     In R.A. Chalmers, G. Clements, H. Schenkluhn, and M.
     Weinless (Eds.), *Scientific Research on the Transcen-
     dental Meditation and TM-Sidhi Programme: Collected
     Papers: Vol. 5*. Vlodrop, The Netherlands: MIU Press.

74. Jedrczak, A. (in press). "The TM-Sidhi Programme and
     Age-related Psychological Variables." In R.A. Chalmers,
     G. Clements, H. Schenkluhn, and M. Weinless (Eds.),
     *Scientific Research on the Transcendental Meditation
     and TM-Sidhi Programme: Collected Papers: Vol. 3*.
     Vlodrop, The Netherlands: MIU Press.

75. Wallace, R.K.; Dillbeck, M.; Jacobe, E.; and Harrington,
     B. (1982). "The Effects of the Transcendental Medita-
     tion and TM-Sidhi Program on the Aging Process." *Inter-
     national Journal of Neuroscience, 16*, 53-58.

Once again, Wallace pioneered a new area of research:
the long-term effects of the TM and TM-Sidhi program on
slowing--and possibly reversing--the process of biological
aging and its deleterious consequences.

76. Alexander, C.N.; Langer, E.; Davies, J.; Chandler, H.;
     and Newman, R. (1986). "Self-Regulation Procedures
     to Enhance Health and Longevity: Transcendental Medi-
     tation, Mindfulness, and the Elderly." Paper presented
     at the 36th annual conference of the National Council
     on Aging, Washington, D.C.

SECTION C
INTERDISCIPLINARY APPROACHES
TO THE STUDY OF DREAMING

Chapter 11
ETHNOGRAPHIC CONSIDERATIONS IN THE
CROSS-CULTURAL STUDY OF DREAMING

Robert Knox Dentan

The Nature of the Ethnographic Data

The huge ethnographic literature on dreaming may prove useful to psychologists. Would-be students need to be aware of the peculiarities of ethnographic data and of the criteria by which ethnographers judge them in order to avoid making the sorts of errors that blemish many earlier studies of non-Western dreaming.

The first part of this chapter sketches the pitfalls of ethnographic fieldwork and the resulting peculiarities of its products. The next summarizes the anthropological study of dreams so far. Documentation is extensive but not exhaustive. I have arranged the narrative chronologically in order to clarify the social and intellectual trends which influenced such studies. To avoid pitfalls myself, I have felt it necessary to include much contextual material not directly connected with lucidity and therefore perhaps of little interest to some readers.

What Is an Ethnographic Account of Dreams?

Dream accounts. Dream accounts are scientifically unsatisfactory because they are nonfalsifiable. An account is "falsifiable" to the degree that it is possible to imagine an event which would prove the account false. "You turn left here to get to City Hall" is a falsifiable statement; you can turn left and see what happens. "My head hurts" or "I had a dream" are nonfalsifiable statements, because no imaginable evidence would prove them false.

Falsifiability is a fundamental principle of positivist epistemology, which denies that nonfalsifiable statements are scientifically meaningful, however important they may be in

people's lives. Moreover, even giving up the attempt to
describe people's dreams and concentrating on what people say
about their dreams does not completely meet this criterion,
since the same person will give a somewhat different account
of the same dream the second time around. Only very general
assertions about what broad classes of people tend to say
under specifiable circumstances offer the possibility of replication and thus falsification. Some ethnographers, it will
become clear, fret about this "softness" of dream data.

Others find that the criterion of falsifiability eliminates
from scientific consideration many things in which people are
interested. They acknowledge sometimes that trying to present
ethnographic facts in falsifiable statements is a valuable
discipline and that confusing falsifiable with nonfalsifiable
data is obscurantist. They feel, nevertheless, that writing
off vast areas of common human experience as scientifically
meaningless (because falsifiable statements about those areas
are unfeasible) would result in a bleak corpus of scientific
statements which were reliable but not very interesting and
not representative of the richness of the data. Such experiences, moreover, tend to preoccupy people in organizing
their daily lives. "I have a toothache" is a nonfalsifiable
statement but, to the person making the statement (and thus
to an ethnographer), it may be the most important thing he
can think of saying.

Ethnographic dream accounts: Stage 1. Ethnographic dream
accounts are especially unsatisfactory data because they are
products of a process which involves at least two uneasy com-
promises. Ethnography is more like clinical psychology than
like astrophysics. A useful way to think about it is as a
two-step negotiation about the nature of reality. During
Stage 1, ethnographer and people try to arrive at statements
(about dreams, for example) which both can understand and with
which both are reasonably comfortable. Because neither party
has a clear idea about where the other "is coming from" this
tugging and hauling generates a welter of emotions--resentment,
elation, anxiety, despair, suspicion, and sometimes love.
The mystique of fieldwork among cultural anthropologists stems
from the difficulty of communicating this experience to people
who have not had it.

Since no one has direct access to dreams but the people
who dream them, people have to put their dreams into words to
tell an ethnographer about them. This verbalization brings
into play a congeries of factors extraneous to the dream itself
(see, e.g., 1, p. 163). The strengths and weaknesses of the
local lexicon, requirements of the local syntax, verbal skills
of the narrator, indigenous notions of what makes a good story
and what makes a good dream, propriety, ideas of what is

speakable and what is not, all come into play. Young Lakota
or Puritan men, for example, came under great pressure to
cast accounts of their dreams into a form acceptable to their
elders (2, pp. 134-135; 3, pp. 60-63; cf. 4, p. 22; 5, pp. 225-
227).

Moreover, telling dreams to an ethnographer, usually a
stranger with interests that seem obscure and bizarre, often
brings out special strategies of obfuscation, accommodation,
mistaken clarification, teasing, or elision (for funny examples
of which see, e.g., 6, pp. 12-13; 7). Psychiatrists encounter
similar phenomena. Jungian analysands report Jungian dreams,
Freudian patients report Freudian ones (8-11). The fact that
ethnographers' expectations are usually less systematized and
articulate than psychiatrists' can obscure the effect they
have on dream accounts. Since dream accounts themselves are
nonfalsifiable, the question of how extensive such observer
effects are is imponderable. Similarly, the race, gender,
class, and age of both ethnographer and informant affect dream
narratives; for instance, in many places, women would not be
comfortable discussing erotic dreams with a man.

Ethnographic dream accounts: Stage 2. Having come to an
uneasy compromise with the people about their experience and
how they categorize and interpret it, ethnographers must try
to translate this compromise into terms intelligible to their
own people or some other audience who have no direct contact
with the life being described. I know no ethnographers, certainly not I, who feel that they have carried off this enterprise successfully (e.g., 12, p. 7; 13, p. 254; Feld in 14, p.
107). "Translator = traitor" goes an Italian maxim. Any *gloss*
("rough translation") of a dream narrative differs from the
original. The alien new words chop up the experience in
inappropriate ways, the syntax and prose style reflect anomalous
interests and speech patterns, and so on, making meaningful
translations almost impossible (e.g., 15, p. 14; 16, p. 342n; 17).

Evaluating Ethnographic Accounts

Introduction. Anthropologists are beginning to articulate
the criteria by which they evaluate ethnographies (e.g., 18-
21). There are two critical areas: a) the duration and conditions of fieldwork (e.g., 22); and b) the way in which the
author handles problems of contextualization and translation.

Fieldwork. Ethnographic fieldwork should be intensive and
holistic. An ethnographer should live in a community long
enough, normally a year or more, to become familiar with both
the language and the daily routines. Living elsewhere and com-
muting to the people studied ("motel ethnography") or travelling

through an area without settling down ("tourist ethnography")
work against the personal rapport and sense of daily life that
inform good ethnographic writing. For instance, in the case
of Kilton Stewart, the fact that he did only motel and tourist
fieldwork vitiated the conclusions he drew about Senoi dreaming (14; 18; 22-24), although much of the material in his unpublished work (25) is valuable when it checks with other
reports.

Living with the people is important because any people's
accounts of their lives simplify, generalize, and often
idealize or mystify what they actually do. Deeds are as important as creeds. It is important not only to listen to
what people have to say about dreams but also to see how they
deal with their dreams in the humdrum of daily living. A
good ethnography conveys a holistic sense of quotidian life
extensive enough that the reader can imagine how the data on
which the author focuses fit into people's ordinary activities
(18).

Language. Translation and its attendant problems should
be in the foreground. This requirement entails being able to
put words into their contexts, for meaning *is* context. Simply
getting informants to give one gloss is inadequate. I could
usually get Semai Senoi to gloss Semai words into Malay,
which I could then gloss into English, only to find out much
later that the gloss was misleading. For instance, people
said that -*dat* meant *mati*, i.e., "die" (cf. Benjamin [26]:
s.v. "die"; Skeat and Blagden [27], II: s.v. D48). When, as
an ethnographer must, I could speak the language well enough
to carry on interviews in Semai, I found that going into trance
and collapsing during ceremonies was also -*dat*. The temptation was to think of the trance as somehow opening up a lane
into the land of the dead, but I am pretty sure that is wrong.
Nya'ni' dat-suui ("die-live affliction") is grandmal epilepsy
(28); swooning and detumescence are also -*dat*. Thus, the word
-*dat* means something like the English "die," but strongly emphasizes being limp and unsensitive. You can, in other words,
be "alive" in English and "dead" in Semai; and I suspect you
can be "dead" in English and "alive" in Semai. Anthropologists
look for signs of this sort of attention to difficulties of
contextualization and translation when they read ethnographies.
Readers interested in applying these principles to dream
studies might enjoy looking over the work of Roseman (29) and
Dentan (23;24;30) on Senoi dreams and trances.

History. As history is not an account of the past but an
interpretation of events selected by the historian, so ethnography is an interpretive account of selected aspects of other
people's present. Ethnographers must heed the interests of
their audience, which often differ from the interests of the

people whose ways of life are the topic (31;32). Thus, social
and intellectual trends in the ethnographers' own society
affect what they attend to, what they omit, how they interpret
data, and so on. For that reason, evaluating an ethnography
also entails having some understanding of the original social,
political, and intellectual currents on which it first floated.
The next section of this paper covers the anthropological
study of dreams as it developed in particular historical contexts.

Taking Dreams Seriously

A "Cultural Universal"

Individual variation. Most of the world's peoples take
dreams seriously, as real experiences of important, albeit
often obscure, significance. I write "peoples" rather than
"people," because intellectual diversity is the rule everywhere, as anthropologists in the 1970s came to realize (e.g.,
12, pp. 68-70, 93-95; 33, p. 26; 34; 35, pp. 462-464; 36, p.
450; 37, p. 200; 38, pp. 22-32, 109-120). In any population
some individuals are skeptical about, ignorant of, or indifferent to the significance of dreams (1, p. 3; 23, p. 52; 30, pp.
163-164; Quesalid in 39; 40, p. 125).
Internal inconsistencies in folk oneirology. Folk notions
of dreams and other altered states of consciousness (ASCs)
may be mutually inconsistent. Senoi hill people of West
Malaysia say that their lowland Malay neighbors set great
stock in dreams, and Malays do make great use of dream dic-
tionaries (*tabir*; 41, pp. 562-563, 666-669). But a Malay proverb
runs, "Put no trust in a dream; Day breaks, and where is it?"
(42, s.v. *mimpi*). Senoi, like positivists, agree that no one
can say what someone else thinks; the traditionalist Native
Americans I know agree. Besides being nonfalsifiable, statements about "the" Senoi or "the" ancient Hebrews suggest a
unitary body of people with an internally consistent dogma.
But there is no "the Senoi" in that sense, only many Senoi-
speaking individuals, holding a wide variety of often inartic-
ulate, incoherent, and mutually incompatible opinions about
dreams (24; 43-45). Similarly, ancient Hebrews were constantly
arguing about the truth value of dreams (e.g., 46, pp. 257-259;
47, pp. 53-65, 77-78, 85-86; 48, pp. 201, 211, 217), a quarrel
early Christians inherited (e.g., 49, pp. 6, 9, 152-153).
Universality. With these caveats, it is possible to say
that among any of the world's peoples, there is a body of lore
about dreams (*oneirology*), usually a way of interpreting them
(*oneirocriticism*), and often a way of using them (*oneiromancy*).

At least some individuals or classes within any ongoing society
will take dreams and dream lore seriously. Attending to dreams
is what anthropologists call a "cultural universal," a custom
found among all peoples, everywhere.

Anthropologists Rediscover Dreams

Historical Background

   Western "traditional intellectuals" and dreams. The 18th
century Enlightenment, in which positivism began to take shape,
tended to dismiss dreams as against Reason and thus tainted
with reactionary clericism. Although folk interest in dreams
remained unabated, Western "traditional intellectuals," who
from Roman times onward had been isolated by class and ethnici-
ty from other people in their countries, tended to hold folk
oneirology in contempt (31;33;50;51). Therefore, when after
a century of programmatic rationalism, Western imperialism
led this intelligentsia to study what they had come to call
the "primitive" world, they found other people's interest in
dreams exotic and striking. Such attitudes persist today.
For instance, Gross (10; pp. 38-40) intends to insult Western
psychotherapies by comparing them to shamanism, not recognizing that what Westerners "designate as being in the realm
of ASC appears primitive to us, merely because we have not
socialized or cultured it" (52, p. 85; cf. 53, pp. 102-122; 54).
   Nineteenth century anthropologists saw no need to explain
their own people's anomalous official dismissal of dreams but
wanted to understand why other peoples, "primitive" on the
self-serving scales Westerners constructed (e.g., 55), were
interested in dreams. After long study, the brilliant armchair
anthropologist Sir Edward Burnett Tylor (56) declared this
universal preoccupation the basis of religion: "ancient savage
philosophers" had inferred from dreams the existence of a
detachable "apparitional-soul." Belief in such souls, "ani-
mism" to Tylor, constituted a minimum definition of religion,
which by that definition was universal (cf. 57).
   The Freudian Revolution. As long as anthropologists
thought that only "primitive" peoples took dreams seriously,
the ethnographic study of dreams remained superficial. The
rise of Freudian thinking among young American intellectuals
coincided with a rush of sexual liberation and radical poli-
tics (58) in the

      first wave of White self-hatred and adulation of
      colored men which swept ... the United States in

>the twenties ... accompanied by ... a studied hos-
>tility to traditional notions of maturity. Wyndham
>Lewis in *Pale Face* ... associates it with Communist
>politics as well as with what he calls "the child
>culture" and the "homomotive." (59, p. 84)

Anthropology flourished in this cultural climate, which "had
as its object the recovery of primitive modes of thought, the
lost innocence of the race" (60, p. 144). Elsie Clews Parsons'
advocacy of total freedom, particularly in sexual relations (61),
is part of the same impulse that led to her still useful ethnographies of the Southwest (e.g., 62;63), where many of her
radical friends came to live with, or at least near, "the
Indians" (60, pp. 117-134, 147, 268n). Jung's visit to Taos
was as the guest of such enthusiasts (64, p. 739n; 65, pp. 246-
253).

The first ethnographic studies of dreams were in the
Freudian idiom of the time (e.g., 4;66-70). By mid-century,
dream ethnography became part of the subfield called "culture-
and-personality" (52, pp. 7-8; 71, pp. 65-80). The well-known
attentuation of Freudianism in America and the complexity of
non-Western lives changed such studies from sweeping cross-
cultural surveys to intensive work with particular peoples.
As the importance of local context in the meaning of dreams
became clear, ethnographic interpretations became more and
more limited and cautious, although still couched in American-
ized Freudian terms (e.g., 58; 72-80; cf. 81, pp. 170-171).
This increasing restraint in interpreting other people's dreams
(see, e.g., 15; 82) was congenial with the positivism which
increasingly pervaded American social and behavioral sciences
after World War II. That positivist emphasis diverted many
anthropologists from the interpretation of "latent symbolism"
to content analyses of manifest "dream elements" (36; 58; 83-
104).

Content analysis: Some drawbacks. The content analysis
which replaced Freudian hermeneutics permitted precise and
potentially replicable generalizations about the manifest content of dreams (cf. 94; 105, pp. 278-285; 106, pp. 488-490;
107). Moreover, this positivist technique served to discipline
the extravagances of psychoanalytic interpretations of "latent
symbolism." However, lumping dream elements together in order
to count them presupposes a valid way of identifying "dream
elements" and of classifying them. As Bertrand Russell remarks,
our ability to count things depends on the mathematical art of
calling different things by the same name. Each grouping of
dream elements into a category requires sloughing off information and obscures without resolving the question of whether they
belong together. Dream elements, "semblances" in Jung's word,
often seem polysemic, perhaps as a result of a process like
Freud's "condensation" (108, pp. 312-339) within the dream or

during its narration. Analysts of many persuasions, including
content analysts, recognize that in this sense a dream account is more like a work of art than a matter of public
positivist fact (e.g., 88, pp. 474-477; 106, pp. 504-505; 109;
110, pp. 48-52; 111, pp. 67-70). A sparrow may always be a
"bird" anywhere, but Shelley's skylark "never" was. Senoi
distinguish carefully between "real birds" and others which
more closely resemble Poe's raven. Kaluli fruitdoves,
the epitome of music, resemble Brancusi's "Bird in Flight"
more than they resemble chickens (112). Is a Ford Thunderbird
in an American dream a "bird"? Most peoples of the world do
not accept dream semblances as being what they seem. The
positivist insistence that what you see is what you get is
thus itself a sort of interpretation.

I would argue that Siberian "bird" dreams (e.g., 82, pp.
175-178; 113, pp. 48, 54) are radically distinct from Southeast
Asian ones (e.g., 23, pp. 41-44; 114, pp. 190-191). The
initial cross-cultural groupings, into a Siberian and a
Southeast Asian set, require taking dream elements out of their
personal and local context. Since, linguists aver, meaning is
context, this dissociation destroys a lot of meaning. For
historical reasons, however, the resulting groupings retain
some traditional ("emic") characteristics shared by all the
cultures of East Asia. Regrouping these with, say, eastern
Mediterranean bird dreams (115) under a rubric like "bird
dream" loses all meaningful context (cf. 116; 117). A broad
transculturally applicable category like "bird" may seem
"culture-free" ("etic" or "metalinguistic" in anthropologists'
jargon) but in fact is too close to demotic English to pass
unchallenged. Such problems are not fatal (106; 118), but the
progressive semantic impoverishment of the data merits comment.

Finally, some content analyses, particularly cross-cultural ones, treat all dreams as equally significant, lumped
under the purportedly culture-free but substantially English
rubric "dream." Non-Western dream analysis usually distinguishes between significant and meaningless dreams. Indeed,
writing this chapter was especially difficult because distinguishing "dreams" from "visions" often made no sense in
local terms; and conversely, conflating meaningful dreams
with insignificant ones warped the data (119, p. 226; 46-48;
120, pp. 8n, 18-19). Such conflation accounts for some errors
in Kilton Stewart's account of Senoi dreamwork (23), but he was
not alone in lumping together dreams Senoi think distinct (e.g.
27, vol. 2, p. 201). Indeed, he remarks in passing on a similar distinction among Sambali-speaking Ayta (121, p. 115).
Were Stewart's error egregious, it would be unnecessary to
stress that ignoring the disparities between Western and
indigenous classifications of dreams can stultify analyses,
while heeding it can prove enlightening.

Return of the Twenties. During the 1970s, dissatisfaction
with positivist analyses was part of a reaction against
dominant "depersonalizing" tendencies in American life. Young
radicals resurrected the memory of Jung and again turned to
native peoples for enlightenment. The publication of *Altered
States of Consciousness* (122) in 1969 influenced the continuing anthropological interest in dream phenomenology. This interest in dream states combined with the renewed interest in
interpretive ethnography (e.g., 29;21) to complement more narrowly positivistic studies (e.g., 123–132; cf. 133). The movement has been marred by fraud (134–139) but remains promising.

Transcultural Commonplaces in Oneirocriticism

What's in a Dream?

Uniformities. The morbidity of particular dream semblances
seems more uniform across cultural lines than cultural deter-
minism would predict (e.g., 1, p. 164; 91; 140; cf. 141). Some
symbols, notably feces for money and falling teeth for death,
occur in the oneirocriticism of historically unconnected
peoples (e.g., 4, pp. 107–131; 69; 70; 92; 142, pp. 299–302;
143–145), but exceptions are not rare (e.g., 1; 146). Males
of all ages in many societies report dreaming about males more
than women do (e.g., 85; 98, pp. 9–12; 99; 101; 104; 147–149).
Again, this tendency is not universal (e.g., 29; 150–152);
some evidence indicates it may reflect patriarchal social
arrangements (e.g., 153;154).

The frequency with which dream semblances occur seems
fairly stable over time (e.g., 148). They may resist accul-
turation and thus remain partially "archaic" in a culture-
historical sense, maintaining an adaptive connection between
past and present (e.g., 36; 58; 72, pp. 88, 100; 88; 96; 97, pp.
73–74; 155; 156, pp. 49–80; 157). However, many dreams are not
conservative in this sense (e.g., 79, pp. 89–93; 151; 158, p.
141; 159). Prophetic dreams or visions trigger many, if not
most, anti-colonialist popular movements, often with tragic
consequences (e.g., 79; 160; 161; 162, pp. 15–16; 163; 164;
165, pp. 30–38, 157–166, 209–215; 166).

Variability. Much transcultural diversity remains, however (e.g., 105, pp. 278–283; 142, pp. 308–316). Partly
because dream semblances often stem from local facts and folklore, different peoples report dreaming of different things
(e.g., 58; 89; 97; 167), just as clients undergoing a particular
psychotherapy tend to report dreams significant to that therapy.
For instance, some peoples report dreaming of death oftener
than Westerners do (e.g., 4, pp. 41–42, 218–245, 323–324; 90,
p. 277; 121, p. 91). Japanese dream accounts involve more fire

and color but less nudity than American ones (92). Ghanaian
peasants seem to dream often about being chased by cattle
(168). Almost half the accounts Siriono of Bolivia gave of
their dreams concerned food, regardless of the abundance of
food at the time of the dream, perhaps because their food
supply was generally unreliable (169). In short, dream content resembles most human behavior, showing wide diversity,
but with a few common themes.

What Do Dreams Mean?

   Culture pattern dreams. One way in which many of the
world's peoples manifest the seriousness with which they take
dreams is by distinguishing between mundane individual dreams
and what anthropologists call "culture pattern dreams" (e.g.,
4, pp. 22, 41, 189, 325-327; 84, p. 268; 128, pp. 126-129; 142,
pp. 313-316; 171, p. 342). Jung's study of non-Western dreams,
buttressed by his fieldwork with Kony and Pueblo peoples (65),
influenced him to mimic this dichotomy between "individual
dreams" and those which he felt tapped the "collective unconscious." Lincoln (4, pp. 23-24), an admirer, correctly
notes "that the images of the great cultural visions are
collective only for a given culture and not for all mankind."
   As noted, culture pattern dream narratives tend to conform
to local requirements. Such narratives often a) involve
guardian or familiar spirits, b) constitute part of a curer's
or diviner's tool kit, c) are prerequisite to achieving certain desirable statuses like "shaman" or "headman"; and, moreover, d) because people value such dreams, they resort to
culture-specific techniques like drugging or fasting to induce
them (128;142). This constellation of significantly intercorrelated traits seems itself to correlate with factors
which require a man's acting on his own, without reliable
support from other humans, viz., nonagricultural subsistence
economies or postmarital residence away from the husband's
father's family (89; 142; cf. 97, pp. 66-67).
   The prevalence of North American peoples in D'Andrade's
sample (142) may partially account for the high significance
he found for these correlations. The "vision quest" in native
North America is the most dramatic elaboration of culture
pattern dreaming (e.g., 4;36;72;82;89;95;103;105;109;142;171-
189).
   The salience of North American peoples in this sample
suggests that he might also have discovered a fifth factor
in the culture pattern dream complex, viz., the occurrence of
melodies in culture pattern dreams. Throughout the area
song is associated with spiritual power. For instance, the

word for "singing" in Iroquoian languages is glossable as
"holding out one's spiritual power" (190, pp. 39-40), in much
the same way that the Latin word for "song" (*carmen*) is cognate
with "charm." Similarly, a Navajo shaman is the "old man of
the songs" (184, p. 352). Culture pattern dream melodies are
widespread in native North America, Siberia, and Australia
(e.g., 4; 5, pp. 227-228; 36; 82, pp. 421-422, 431-432n; 103,
p. 49; 109; 113, p. 54; 191; 192, pp. 47-48; 193; 194, p. 28;
195, p. 28; 196; 197, pp. 219-220; 198; 199, pp. 320, 354-356;
for other areas, e.g., 16; 23; 24; 121; 125; 200). The most
remarkable example of a song passed down in dreams from generation to generation is the Tibetan "Gesar," probably the longest
ballad in the world: 106 episodes, a cast of thousands, over a
million lines. Balladeers, *zhongkan*, usually illiterate,
.typically claim not to have studied the song but to have
inherited it in a dream from which they woke with a compulsion
to sing (eyes half shut, with an air of intense concentration)
for days on end, without pause.

D'Andrade (142) found no correlation between this four-
or five-factor culture complex and the presence in a culture
of threatening oneiric supernaturals, specialized oneiromancers,
or rituals to avert oneiric predictions.

The match between people's accounts of their culture
pattern dreams and local stereotypes of such dreams raises
the perennial epistemological question in dream studies
(e.g., 5, p. 225; 201, p. 167). Do people remember and respond
to dreams or to dream interpretations? Are dreams clear and
vivid, or are these properties of how people recount interpreted and reconstructed dreams? Free associations to dream
semblances seem both idiosyncratic and culturally patterned
(e.g., 202, pp. 343-347). As discussed below, people normally
edit and interpret dream semblances as culture pattern elements
in disguise (e.g., as spirits in human form) in ways that
become clear to ethnographers only after careful and contexted
inquiry (e.g., 1, pp. 164-165, 170-172; 24; 84; 203). Where
dreams are prerequisite to full adult status, elders put heavy
pressure, deliberately or not, on youths to cast their dreams
or visions into acceptable form (e.g., 2; 3). Nevertheless,
circumstantial evidence indicates that non-Western peoples
rarely lie about their dreams (e.g., 5, pp. 8-14; 72, p. 87;
90, pp. 283-284; 142, pp. 314-315; 181; 187; 194, p. 28; 200,
pp. 111-112, 288-289; 204). "Political" dreams may be an
exception to this rule of thumb. Indigenous emphasis on culture pattern dreams probably elaborates the complexity of
both dreams and dream accounts (109, p. 1036). Bourguignon's
(84) typically insightful and sensible conclusions about her
Haitian materials probably apply to most culture pattern dream
narratives:

> While it is difficult to see to what extent
> dreams themselves may be culturally patterned, the
> cultural dogma of the dreams as the appearance of
> the gods interacts with the dream content in such

> a way that an interpreted version of the dream
> seems to be experienced by the dreamer. (p. 268)

Such hermeneutic flexibility makes it possible for most
people to have culture pattern dreams.

Ordinary dreams. Peoples with elaborated culture pattern
dreams tend to heed such dreams more seriously than ordinary
ones. Crow, for instance, found ordinary dreams too banal to
remember or recount to Lowie (171, pp. 317, 323, 342; cf. 158,
p. 141). But Menomini, equally wedded to the vision quest,
find ordinary dreams also significant, although in different
ways (103, pp. 46-54; 182, p. 47). Some peoples do not talk
freely about both kinds (1; 23; 24; 30).

Classical Chinese literature treats ordinary dreams (meng)
as illusory and deceptive (huan). The two words often go together in ordinary speech. Other "meng" words which refer to
unconsciousness and deception may be cognate. Yet the very
deceptiveness of dreams may instruct the dreamer, as the
idiom "a golden millet dream" (huang liang yi meng) suggests.
In the fable from which the set phrase comes (206), a youth
attains Enlightenment after a false dream reveals to him the
vanity of earthly pleasures and desires (cf. 207-211) and the
illusory nature of the empirical world (cf. 212;213). Even so,
not all dreams fall into the same category. There is, for
example, a word glossed as "nightmare" (yan). Moreover, re-
vitalization movements based on dreams and visions play an
important part in Chinese history (e.g., 162, pp. 15-16) and
imagination (e.g., 214). Despite traditional Chinese skepti-
cism about the supernatural (e.g., 215, p. 252), they would
agree that meaning is context or that the same dream narratives
may be of different import depending on who the dreamer is;
thus court historians thought the ominous dreams of the doomed
Qin emperors (221-206 B.C.) and the interpretations thereof by
imperial oneirocritics were worth recording (215, pp. 184, 193).

Among Tikopians

> the weight attached to a dream varies as the emo-
> tional intensity of the personal situation at the
> time.... [A] dream receives attention and credence
> largely in so far as it can be related to some
> question immediately at issue within the social
> horizon of the dreamer. It is this correlation of
> dream interpretation with the situation of the
> moment that explains the inconsistency frequently
> to be found in assigning a meaning to such experiences.
> (1; pp. 163-164)

Some peoples take all dreams fairly seriously. Tangu of
New Guinea, for instance, heed most dreams. Even

an "unsolicited" dream contains information to

> which thought must be given and action taken; and
> a man faced with a problem retires for the night
> with the hope that a dream will shed light on the
> matter and present him with a directive.... Even
> though a dream does not always solve the problem,
> it helps toward a solution, and Tangu feel that the
> information is always worth acting on. (216; pp.
> 40-41)

Nevertheless, like almost all peoples, Tangu distinguish significant from insignificant dreams. This differentiation, as
noted above, sometimes escapes Anglo-American investigators,
partly because in many languages it is no more terminologically
explicit than in their own (e.g., 4; 24, p. 195; 119, p. 226;
217, p. 368). Thus Trobrianders are sometimes said to be
indifferent to dreams because of their attitude toward ordinary
dreams (e.g., 105, p. 277), whereas Senoi are reputed to be
deeply involved in dreamwork because of their attitude toward
culture pattern dreams (but see 23; 24). In fact, the
Trobriand response to dreams parallels that of Senoi, whose
reputation for serious interest in dreams is widespread.

> Spontaneous dreams are not of any great importance....
> [T]he natives appear to dream but seldom, have little
> interest in their dreams, and do not often tell
> their experiences on waking or refer to dreams to
> explain a belief or justify a line of conduct.
> No prophetic meaning is ascribed to ordinary dreams,
> nor is there any system of code for their symbolic
> interpretation....
> Quite another class of dreams are those which
> are prescribed or defined by custom. These are
> expected of certain people by virtue of their posi-
> tion or of some task that they have performed, or
> which has been performed upon them, or of the in-
> fluence of spiritual beings. Such stereotyped or
> standardized dreams are expected, hoped for, and
> awaited; and this might easily account for the fre-
> quency of their occurrence and for the ease with
> which they are remembered....
> It should be noted that the distinction between
> free and standardized dreams is not made in native
> terminology nor even formulated in native doctrine.
> But as will presently be seen, it is embodied in
> behaviour and in the general attitude towards dreams.
> (218; pp. 326-327)

In summary, although different peoples treat dreams with
differing degrees of seriousness, almost all distinguish
meaningful from trivial dreams. Oneiric meaning is elusive.
Since people take their dreams interpreted, not raw, understanding local oneirocritical principles is vital.

Decoding dreams. The notion that certain dreams need interpreting seems to be another cultural universal (e.g., 4; 55,
pp. 121-122; 219, p. 124). Some interpretation is literal (e.g.,
98, pp. 22-23; 220, pp. 12-13). For instance, Malaysian Batek
De' take ordinary dreams as "merely a source of information
about the present" (125, p. 95): dreaming of a tiger, e.g., mean
a tiger is around. Similar beliefs among the related Semnam and
Sabum may have played a part in the genesis of Kilton Stewart's
"Senoi dream therapy" (e.g., 23, pp. 44-46; 221, pp. 51-59; cf.
121, pp. 69-70).

Oneirocritical complexity varies from place to place.
For instance, in Africa, Gusii and Kamba interpret dreams in-
formally and ad hoc, while their respective linguistic and
cultural kin, Maragoli and Zulu, have sophisticated hermeneutic
systems (58;97;222). Casual interrogation can usually elicit
from native informants lists of mechanical translations of
dream semblances, the sort of arbitrary decontextualized equations literate peoples put in dream books (e.g., 30; 55, p.
122; 100, pp. 122-123; 114, p. 191; 115; 119, pp. 225-227; 143,
p. 143; 223; 224, pp. 157-158; 225, p. 222; see the excellent
dream manual bibliographies in 98, pp. 32-38, 72-80; 108, pp.
37n-38n, 691-697).

A few additional questions might turn up some hermeneutic
principles, like the principle of contraries, by which dreams
portend the opposite of what they appear to. Early anthropologists were intrigued by the cross-cultural frequency of
this principle, which is found among such widely separated
peoples as Ashanti, Malays, Maori, Buffalo (New York) Polish-
American parochial schoolgirls, psychoanalysts, Semai, and
Zulu (4, pp. 38-39; 41, p. 305; 56, pp. 121-122; 58; 108, pp.
353-354). Such principles may stem from fundamental patterns
of human cognition or explication, in dreams (108, pp. 353-354)
or in dream narratives (e.g., 226, pp. 88-90, 99-103).

Simplistic principles or equivalence tables, however, are
probably artifacts of superficial investigations rather than
characteristics of non-Western oneirocriticism. Detached
questioning uproots dream interpretation from the two contexts
in which it makes sense: a) the system of symbols, metaphors,
folklore, and ideas which frame its intellectual power; and
b) the practicalities of quotidian life (cf. 1;17;23;30;58;
203;227). Take the instance of the Muslim dream manuals,
taawir or *tabir* (e.g., 41, pp. 562-563, 666-669), which Tylor
(56, p. 122) thought "far-fetched" and arbitrary (cf. 79, p.
89n). In quotidian praxis, people using *taawir* pay as much
attention to the circumstances surrounding the dream as Senoi
or Tikopians do, and *taawir* give alternative interpretations
for particular dream semblances (e.g., 46, p. 233; 120, pp. 7,
15; 228, pp. 48-49; 229; 230, p. 373).

In interpreted dreams, what you see is not what you get.
For example, natural entities like trees or animals with mystic
powers often appear as humans in interpreted dreams (e.g., 1,
pp. 164, 165, 170-172; 24; 128, pp. 68, 75-76; 146; 191, pp.

97-100; 202, pp. 139-144, 153, 207, 231-232; 231, p. 71; 232;
233, p. 83; 234, pp. 542-543). South American Jivaro say that
familiars appear as animals in visions but as people in
dreams (126, pp. 138-139). The reciprocal transformation of
people into animals provides "a kind of psychology; it is an
uncertain one, but its terms help to express the divisions and
conflicts a person can face in his own identity" (235, p. 348-
349). The potential polysemy of particular dream semblances
makes it possible to believe in dreams even when experience
proves them false; the interpretation, not the dream, erred
(e.g., 1, pp. 169-173).
      In short, indigenous oneirocriticism tends to be complex,
contextualizing, symbol-laden, and pragmatic. Studies of non-
Western dreams need take into account the fact that all dream
narratives have passed through an oneirocritical mixer.

Using Dreams: Oneiromancy

      Inducing dreams. Many peoples seek to induce dreams,
particularly culture pattern dreams. The technique may be
as simple as the Tangu or Zulu custom of "sleeping on" a problem. "Incubation," sleeping in sacred precincts to induce
meaningful dreams, is an elaboration of that practice (46, pp.
240-241, 250; cf. Jacob's ladder dream). People may sacrifice
or pray for prophetic dreams (e.g., 236, pp. 438-439) or seek to
make others dream, as when a young Cherokee swain sang midnight
serenades to make his beloved dream of, and fall in love with,
him (15, p. 97). In Chinese fiction Taoist priests often
induce dreams or visions (e.g., 206; 212; 213; 237) by magic
or by their mere presence. The literature or indigenous uses
of psychotropic drugs is far too extensive to cite here (see
bibliographies in 98; 127; 238-240). The literature on vision
questing covers inducing dreams by sexual abstinence, isolation,
fasting, and self-punishment. Many peoples combine several
tactics (e.g., 241, pp. 133-134). Altering body chemistry this
way is dangerous and may produce undesirable altered states of
consciousness like "kayak phobia" (82, pp. 54, 65-66; 242, p.
21n; 243, p. 242; 244). In short many peoples control the
onset of dreams.
      Learning in dreams. Several authors (e.g., 36; 109; 125,
pp. 95, 128-129, 134-135) show how ordinary conscious learning
affects dream learning. People learn the basics of mythology,
ritual, songs, spells, and so on by routine observation. This
learned material then reappears, often slightly altered, in
culture pattern dreams which validate the dreamers' expertise.
The flexibility of dream interpretation makes such validation
routinely possible and obviates the need to fake dream
narratives deliberately. Trying to separate dream from interpretation in such cases is probably pointless (84).
      Therapeutic aspects of dreams. Interpreted dreams may
have psychotherapeutic consequences. A dream may suggest that

a dreamer undertake a particular course of action, a sacrifice
(e.g., 245), or political revolution. To recognize the psychic
relief that results need not entail endorsing Horney's (246)
sense

> [t]hat in dreams we are closer to the reality of our-
> selves: that they represent attempts to solve our
> conflicts, either in a neurotic or in a healthy
> way: that in them constructive forces can be at
> work.... (p. 349)

Oneiromantic solutions are ideological, not medical.

> The general therapeutic function of any belief
> system is ... to alleviate the anxiety associated
> with ambiguity and uncertainty ... [in] a cognitive
> structure that creates meaning and purpose. The
> ideology will consist of beliefs that define the
> nature and causes of the problem, and values that
> specify goals to strive for and courses of action
> to obtain those goals. (247, p. 30)

Interpreting dreams resolves situations of uncertainty, trans-
lating anxiety-provoking events into familiar or understandable
forms and easing psychic conflict (235, pp. 348-349; 245, p.
368; 248, pp. 61-64; 249, p. 305). A Thai author (40) explains
one aspect of this clarifying process:

> When one has dreamed of anything, he must relate
> the dream to someone who knows how to interpret
> it. Interpreting dreams is a good thing, because
> if the dreamer has a dream that seems bad to him,
> it causes him worry and uneasiness; one who relates
> his dream and has it interpreted feels relieved.
> This applies only to people who still believe that
> dreams are signs of good or evil; if one does not
> believe in them, that is the end of the matter.
> (p. 124)

Ideological clarification and resolution involve the same
"placebo effect" that may account for one-third or two-thirds
of the cures Western medicine effects (250;251). Faith is
more important for placebo cures than veridical dream narratives or scientific diagnosis are (245;251). As the self-
doubting Kwakiutl shaman Quesalid told Franz Boas (39, vol. 2,
p. 13), he could cure a patient if the sick man "believed
strongly in his dream about me."

Besides clarity and placebo, oneiromantic solutions arouse
hope. Simplifying ambiguities and ambivalences lets people
organize their lives (189; 248, pp. 61-64). Performing the
prescribed act may vent anxieties or frustrations which have
no other outlet. Dream interpretations involve and affirm

assumptions dreamers share with other members of their group,
whose cooperation in working out the oneiromantic solution
bolsters faith in dreams, oneiromancy, and solution (245).
But the genocidal reaction of imperialist powers to revolutionary movements inspired by dreams shows that oneiromantic
solutions themselves may be illusory or worse: "the nocturnal
dream comes to reinforce a solution distant from common sense.
Reverie and dreams may thus undo the more realistic strivings
of the day" (9, p. 1455).

In other words, neither the veracity of dream accounts
nor the validity of oneirocriticism are crucial to the therapeutic effect of oneiromancy. An analogy may help clarify
this point. Cynical politicians have, from ancient times,
used dream narratives, especially retrospectively, to rationalize, justify, or mystify political undertakings on the basis
of someone's purported dream (e.g., 224, pp. 137-139; 236, pp.
35-36, 50, 56, 322; 252, p. 244). It would be strange if
private individuals did not also use dreams to rationalize,
justify, or mystify their own behavior.

Anthony Wallace's (187) classic account of Seneca and
Huron dream therapy describes how Iroquoian peoples used
dreams (cf. 4, p. 51; 38, pp. 59-75; 56, pp. 24-25; for other
such uses, see 80; 178; 253). Huron, Seneca, and other Long-
house People (Hodinosauni) say that ondinonk, "unconscious
wishes," appear in dreams and that failure to assuage ondinonk
imperils the dreamer and the community (4, pp. 37-38; 187; 254,
vol. 1, pp. 158, 206; 255, pp. 114-115). If the nature of the
ondinonk is unclear, a dreamer consults an interpreter. Mid-
winter, the New Year's ceremony, Ononharoia or "Turning the
Brain Upside Down," affords participants a chance to pantomime
their ondinonk for others to guess or to act out their feelings
in socially acceptable ways (187; 254, vol. 1, pp. 205-206; 255,
pp. 96-97; 256, pp. 227-233). Indeed, traditional Onondaga are
guessing each other's dreams as I write this passage in early
1984.

Summary. People around the world "control" their dreams
before having them, by inducing them, and afterward, by responding to them. The remaining question is whether they can
control dreams while having them, as in "lucid dreaming."
Here the ethnographic evidence is spotty, unsatisfactory, and
suggestive.

Lucid Dreams or Shamanic States?

Problems of evidence. The positivist or psychoanalytic
bias of much ethnographic research clouds the data which
might show whether lucid dreaming is cross-culturally a common
or rare phenomenon. States of consciousness elude the techniques these theoretical postures entail. Recently, however,
Bourguignon (123;124;257; cf. 258) and her colleagues have begun

to make some important distinctions on the basis of the subjective experiences involved in altered states of consciousness (ASCs). Besides dreams, there is "possession" in which a
person loses volition. In a willful visionary trance, however,
people move into a different state or states of consciousness,
which Harner (128) calls the SSC, "shamanic state of consciousness." Similarly, Endicott (125, p. 149) distinguishes between
"spirit mediumship" (e.g., 146, pp. 157-161, 179-180) and "soul-
leaving shamanism" (e.g., 259, pp. 116-120). Unfortunately, the
older literature is often vague on this topic; and in some
places, notably northeast Siberia, culture pattern dreams/
visions seem to involve a variety of states of consciousness
(e.g., 191; 198; 232). There is some ontological question
whether the "SSC" (128-130) has any empirical counterpart (e.g.,
133).

Nevertheless, shamanic trances involving "soul-leaving"
seem to resemble "lucid dreaming" more than any other ethnographic phenomena do (129;130;132). Batek oneirocriticism
parallels the way psychologists interested in lucid dreams
write:

> According to Batek theories, trancing is a sort
> of controlled dreaming, in that the shadow-soul
> can be deliberately sent to any part of the uni-
> verse ... guided by the songs that accompany the
> trance.... (125, p. 145)

Peters (131, pp. 35-38) explores the resemblances between such
culture-pattern dreams/visions on the one hand, and magical
flight, out-of-body experiences, Jungian therapy, and lucid
dreams on the other. Thus the tentative answer to the question
posed earlier seems to be: lucid dreams are a subset of trance
states, which in many places constitute a subset of culture
pattern dreams/visions. Perhaps, indeed, to call lucid
"dreaming" is misleading. The phenomenon seems more like
what anthropologists call "trance" (e.g., 257; 260, pp. 10-25;
261).

Summary and Conclusions

The ethnographic facts seem consonant with the following
assertations. a) Like speech, dreams originate in a perhaps
random firing of neurons which produces a sort of oneiric
babble. Babies' dreams may be as meaningless as cats'.
b) As individuals mature, however, daily experience encultur-
ates their dreams, giving them structure and meaning (e.g.,
261, p. 368). The distinction between such socialized dreams
and dream narratives, like the question whether "terms for

inner states are social more than they are experiential" (111, p. 88) is pointless from a positivist viewpoint, since there is no way to tell. The distinction also obscures the "surprising truth that our sense-data are primarily symbols" (110; p. 16). Finally, since people seem to experience their dreams as interpreted, contrasting private-individual-dream with public-social-narrative may more accurately reflect unresolved contradictions in the quotidian lives of industrialized peoples (263, pp. 199-201) than it clarifies processes by which people acquire social selves and the capacity to dream meaningfully from "significant others." c) The culmination of such enculturation is the culture pattern dream-vision, whose onset and sometimes content are under the dreamers' control and which they can match retrospectively to local stereotypes. d) These culture pattern dreams/visions and the subsequent trance states they legitimate are the ethnographic phenomenon most like lucid dreaming.

References*

1. Firth, Raymond (1967). "The Meaning of Dreams." In Raymond Firth (Ed.), *Tikopia Ritual and Belief* (pp. 162-173). Boston: Beacon.

2. Erikson, Erik H. (1950). *Childhood and Society*. New York: W.W. Norton.

3. Schneider, Herbert Wallace (1930). *The Puritan Mind*. New York: Henry Holt and Company.

---

*Deciding which sources to annotate involves an element of subjectivity which it would be dishonest to obfuscate or deny. Moreover, in China, where some of the annotations were written, most of the sources themselves are unavailable, so that comments must be from memory. Since O'Nell (98) gives a comprehensive and well-annotated bibliography, updated in the most recent edition (unavailable here), it seemed enough to annotate ten titles at most.

Within these limitations, two principles governed the selection of sources. a) The bibliography should represent the range of scientific approaches discussed in the article. The topical arrangement of the article should then make it easy to identify further readings. b) Each reading should embody a competent grasp of the relevant theory or method, deployed over a reasonably extensive body of data.

Recent work worth consulting includes, 264 on methodology, 265 and 266 on psi, and the 1981 issue of *Ethos* (vol. 9, no. 4) on the anthropology of dreams.

Ethnographic Considerations

4. Lincoln, Jackson Steward (1936). *The Dream in Primitive Culture*. Baltimore: Williams and Wilkins.

   The classic psychoanalytic comparative account, influenced by both Freud and Jung. The book contains many dream accounts usable for some purposes today, gathered under circumstances no longer extant. That fact alone makes it a valuable source.

5. Lowie, Robert H. (1948). *Primitive Religion*. New York: Liveright. Original work published in 1924.

6. Evans-Pritchard, Edward E. (1940). *The Nuer: A Description of the Livelihood and Political Institutions of a Nilotic People*. Oxford: Oxford University Press.

7. Griaule, Marcel (1965). *Conversations with Ogotemmeli: An Introduction to Dogon Religious Ideas*. (Ralph Butler, Audrey I. Richards, and Beatrice Hook, Trans.) London: Oxford University Press. Original work published in 1948.

8. Calestro, Kenneth M. (1972). "Psychotherapy, Faith Healing and Suggestion." *International Journal of Psychiatry, 10*, 83–113.

9. Munroe, Ruth L. (1959). "Other Psychoanalytic Approaches (Adler, Jung, Rank)." In Silvano Arieti (Ed.), *American Handbook of Psychiatry* (pp. 1453–1465). New York: Basic Books.

10. Gross, Martin L. (1978). *The Psychological Society: A Critical Analysis of Psychiatry, Psychotherapy, Psychoanalysis and the Psychological Revolution*. New York: Random House.

11. Whitman, Roy M. (1963). "Which Dream Does the Patient Tell?" *Archives of General Psychiatry, 8*, 277–282.

12. Dentan, R.K. (1979). *The Semai*. 2nd ed. New York: Holt, Rinehart and Winston.

13. Evans-Pritchard, Edward E. (1976). *Witchcraft, Oracles and Magic among the Azande* (Eva Gillies abridgement). Oxford: Oxford University Press.

14. Dentan, R.K. (1983). "Hit and Run Ethnograph [sic]." *Dream Network Bulletin, 2*(8), 12–13.

15. Ford, Clellan S., and Beach, Frank A. (1951). *Patterns of Sexual Behavior*. New York: Harper.

16. Herdt, Gilbert H. (1977). "The Shaman's 'Calling' among the Sambia of New Guinea." In B. Juillerat (Ed.), *Madness, Possession and Shamanism in New Guinea* (special issue). *Journal de la Société des Océanistes, 33*, 153-167.

17. Turzin, D.F. (1975). "The Breath of a Ghost: Dreams and the Fear of the Dead." *Ethos, 3*, 555-578.

18. Dentan, R.K. (1984). "Techniques and Antecedents: A Response to Gieseler." *Lucidity Letter, 3*(2;3), 5-7.

19. Marcus, George Emmanuel (1980). "Rhetoric and the Ethnographic Genre in Anthropological Research." *Current Anthropology, 21*, 507-510.

20. Marcus, George Emmanuel, and Cushman, Dick (1982). "Ethnographies as Texts." *Annual Review of Anthropology, 11*, 25-69.

21. Ruby, Jay (Ed.) (1982). *The Crack in the Mirror: Reflexive Perspectives in Anthropology*. Philadelphia: University of Pennsylvania Press.

22. Faraday, Ann, and Wren-Lewis, John (1984). "The Selling of the Senoi." *Dream Network Bulletin, 3*(4), 1-3.

23. Dentan, R.K. (1983). "A Dream of Senoi." *Council on International Studies, State University of New York at Buffalo, Special Study* (Vol. 150). Buffalo, N.Y.: State University of New York at Buffalo.

    This history-of-science approach to a classic study of Senoi dreamwork (see item 25) is of some interest, despite its narrow focus, because the self-reflexive history-of-science approach is fairly new in anthropology, so that few studies of how dream researchers make ethnographic errors are available.

24. Dentan, Robert Knox (in press). "Lucidity, Sex and Horror in Senoi Dreamwork." In J.I. Gackenbech and S. LaBerge (Eds.), *Lucid Dreaming: New Research on Consciousness during Sleep*. New York: Plenum.

25. Stewart, Kilton Riggs (1948). "Magico-Religious Beliefs and Practises in Primitive Society--A Sociological

Interpretation of Their Therapeutic Aspects." Unpublished doctoral dissertation, London School of Eco-
nomics.

This as yet unpublished but widely distributed account
reflects Stewart's most reliable work with Temiar Senoi.
His report belies the more extravagant claims of his
later work, but a careful reading reveals the seeds
which, in his retrospective imaginings, were to become
"American Senoi dreamwork" and "Jungian-Senoi dreamwork."
The large collection of dream narratives, amassed by
H.D. Noone and recorded by Claudia Parsons, remain of
some value today. There are also some comparative
materials from other areas Stewart visited.

26. Benjamin, Geoffrey (1976). "Austroasiatic Subgroupings
     and Prehistory in the Malay Peninsula." In Philip N.
     Jenner, Laurence C. Thompson, and Stanley Starosta
     (Eds.), *Austroasiatic Studies, Part I* (pp. 37-129).
     Honolulu: University Press of Hawaii.

27. Skeat, W.W., and Blagden, C.O. (1906). *Pagan Races of
     the Malay Peninsula*. London: Macmillan.

28. Dentan, R.K. (1968). "The Semai Response to Mental
     Aberration." *Bijdragen tot de Taal-, Land- en Volken-
     kunde, 124*, 135-158.

29. Roseman, Marina (1984). "The Social Structuring of
     Sound: An Example from the Temiar of Peninsular Malay-
     sia." *Ethnomusicology, 28*, 411-445.

30. Dentan, R.K. (1983). "Senoi Dream Praxis." *Dream Net-
     work Bulletin, 2*(5), 1-3, 12.

31. Gwaltney, John Langston (1976). "On Going Home Again--
     Some Reflections of a Native Anthropologist." *Phylon,
     30*, 236-242.

32. Gwaltney, John Langston (1976). "A Native Replies."
     Natural History, 85(12), 8-14.

33. Dunn, Fred L. (1975). "Rainforest Collectors and Traders."
     *Monographs of the Malaysian Branch of the Royal Asiatic
     Society* (#5).

34. Gardner, Peter M. (1966). "Symmetric Respect and Memor-
     ate Knowledge: The Structure and Ecology of Individualist

35. Gardner, Peter M. (1976). "Birds, Words, and a Requiem for the Omniscient Informant." *American Ethnologist*, *3*, 446-468.

36. Handleman, Don (1967). "The Development of a Washo Shaman." *Ethnology*, *6*, 444-464.

37. Vollweiler, Lothar Georg, and Sanchez, Alison B. (1983). "Divination--'Adaptive' from Whose Perspective?" *Ethnology*, *22*, 193-210.

38. Wallace, Anthony F.C. (1970). *Culture and Personality.* 2nd ed. New York: Random House.

39. Boas, Franz (1930). *The Religion of the Kwakiutl Indians: Columbia University Contributions to Anthropology* (Vol. 10). New York: Columbia University.

40. Rajadhon, Phya Anuman (1965). "Customs Connected with Birth and the Rearing of Children." In Donn V. Hart, Phya Anuman Rajadhon, and Richard J. Coughlin (Eds.), *Southeast Asian Birth Customs: Three Studies in Human Reproduction* (pp. 115-204). New Haven, Conn.: Human Relations Area Files.

41. Skeat, Walter William (1900). *Malay Magic: Being an Introduction to the Folklore and Popular Religion of the Malay Peninsular.* London: Macmillan.

42. Wilkinson, R.J. (1956). *A Malay-English Dictionary.* London: Macmillan.

43. Dentan, R.K. (1975). "If There Were No Malays, Who Would the Semai Be?" (J. Nagata, Ed.), *Pluralism in Malaysia: Myth and Reality: Contributions to Asian Studies* (Special issue) 7, 50-64.

44. Dentan, R.K. (1976). "Identity and Ethnic Contact: Perak, Malaysia, 1963." In T.S. Kang (Ed.), *Intergroup Relations: Asian Scenes* (Special issue). *Journal of Asian Affairs*, *1*(1), 79-86.

45. Dentan, R.K. (1978). "Notes on Childhood in a Nonviolent Context." In A. Montagu (Ed.), *Learning Non-aggression.* London: Oxford University Press.

46. James, E.O. (1960). *The Ancient Gods: The History and Diffusion of Religion in the Ancient Near East and Eastern Mediterranean.* London: Weidenfeld and Nicolson.

47. Knight, Harold (1947). *The Hebrew Prophetic Conscious-
    ness*. London: Lutterworth Press.

48. Lindblom, J. (1962). *Prophecy in Ancient Israel*. Oxford:
    Basil Blackwell.

49. Perkins, Pheme (1980). *The Gnostic Dialogue: The Early
    Church and the Crisis of Gnosticism*. New York: Paulist
    Press.

50. Gramsci, Antonio (1971). *Selections from the Prison Note-
    books of Antonio Gramsci*. (Quintin Hoare and Geoffrey
    Nowell Smith, Eds. and Trans.) New York: International
    Publishers.

51. Krippner, Stanley, and Hughes, William (1970). "ZZZGenius
    at WorkZZZ." *Psychology Today*, *4*(1), 40–43.

52. Price-Williams, Douglass R. (1975). *Explorations in
    Cross-cultural Psychology*. San Francisco, Calif.:
    Chandler and Sharp.

53. Leighton, Alexander H.; Adeyoe, T.; Lambo, Charles C.;
    Hughes, Dorothea C.; Leighton, Jane M. Murphy; and
    Macklin, David B. (1963). *Psychiatric Disorder among
    the Yoruba*. Ithaca, N.Y.: Cornell University Press.

54. Torrey, E. Fuller (1972). "What Western Psychotherapists
    Can Learn from Witchdoctors." *American Journal of
    Orthopsychiatry*, *42*, 69–76.

55. Tylor, Edward Burnett (1958). *The Origins of Culture*.
    New York: Harper Torchbooks. Original work published
    in 1871.

56. Tylor, Edward Burnett (1958). *Religion in Primitive
    Culture*. New York: Harper Torchbooks. Original work
    published in 1871.

57. Horton, Robin (1968). "Neo-Tylorianism: Sound Sense or
    Sinister Prejudice?" *Man*, *3*, 625–634.

58. Lee, S.G. (1958). "Social Influences in Zulu Dreaming."
    Journal of Social Psychology, *47*, 278–289.

59. Fiedler, Leslie A. (1969). *The Return of the Vanishing
    American*. Briarcliff Manor, N.Y.: Stein and Day.

60. Lasch, Christopher (1965). *The New Radicalism in America [1889-1963]: The Intellectual as a Social Type.* New York: Alfred A. Knopf.

61. Parsons, Elsie Clews (1915). *Social Freedom.* New York: G.P. Putnam & Sons.

62. Parsons, Elsie Clews (1919). "Increase by Magic: A Zuni Pattern." *American Anthropologist, 21,* 279-286.

63. Parsons, Elsie Clews (1925). *The Pueblo of Jemez.* New Haven: Yale University Press.

64. Ellenberger, Henri F. (1970). *The Discovery of the Unconscious: The History and Evolution of Dynamic Psychiatry.* New York: Basic Books.

65. Jung, Carl G. (1963). *Memories, Dreams, Reflections.* (Aniela Jaffe, Ed.) New York: Vintage.

66. Roheim, Geza (1945). *The Eternal Ones of the Dream, a Psychoanalytic Interpretation of Australian Myth and Ritual.* New York: International Universities Press.

67. Roheim, Geza (1949). "The Technique of Dream Analysis and Field Work in Anthropology." *Psychoanalytic Quarterly, 18,* 471-479.

68. Roheim, Geza (1952). *The Gates of the Dream.* New York: International Universities Press.

69. Seligman, Charles G. (1924). "Anthropology and Psychology: A Study of Some Points of Contact." *Journal of the Royal Anthropological Institute, 54,* 13-46.

70. Seligman, Charles G. (1932). "Anthropological Perspective and Psychological Theory." *Journal of the Royal Anthropological Institute, 54,* 13-46.

71. Leighton, Alexander H., and Murphy, Jane M. (1965). "Cross-cultural Psychiatry." In J.M. Murphy and A.H. Leighton (Eds.), *Approaches to Cross-cultural Psychiatry* (pp. 3-20). Ithaca: Cornell University Press.

72. Devereux, George (1951). *Reality and Dream: Psychotherapy of a Plains Indian.* New York: International Universities Press.

    An orthodox Freudian anthropologist presents one of the

few intensive ethnographic studies of an individual person's dreams. Like most good Freudians, Devereux is
simultaneously cranky and insightful, irritating and intriguing.

73. DuBois, Cora (1944). *The People of Alor*. Minneapolis:
     University of Minnesota Press.

74. Fortes, Meyer (1959). *Oedipus and Job in West African
     Religion*. Cambridge: Cambridge University Press.

75. Hallowell, A. Irving (1938). "Freudian Symbolism in the
     Dream of a Salteaux Indian." *Man*, *38*, 47-48.

76. Honigmann, John J. (1954). *Culture and Personality*.
     New York: Harper.

77. Horton, Robin (1961). "Destiny and the Unconscious in
     West Africa." *Africa*, *31*, 110-116.

78. Kluckhohn, Clyde, and Morgan, William (1951). "Some Notes
     on Navaho Dreams." In G.B. Wilbur and Werner Muenster-
     berger (Eds.), *Essays in Honor of Geza Roheim* (pp. 120-
     131). New York: International Universities Press.

79. Mannoni, Octave (1964). *Prospero and Caliban. The Psych-
     ology of Colonization*. (Pamela Powesland, Trans.)
     New York: Frederick A. Praeger.

80. Toffelmier, G., and Juomala, K. (1936). "Dreams and
     Dream Interpretation of the Diegueno Indians of Southern
     California." *Psychoanalytic Quarterly*, *2*, 195-225.

81. Hall, Calvin S., and Lindzey, Gardner (1954). "Psycho-
     analytic Theory and Its Applications in the Social Sci-
     ences." In Gardner Lindzey (Ed.), *Handbook of Social
     Psychology: Vol. I, Theory and Method* (pp. 143-180).
     Reading, Mass.: Addison-Wesley.

82. La Barre, Weston (1972). *The Ghost Dance: The Origins of
     Religion*. New York: Delta.

83. Bastide, Roger (1966). "The Sociology of the Dream."
     In G.E. von Grunebaum and Roger Caillois (Eds.), *The
     Dream and Human Societies* (pp. 166-211). Berkeley:
     University of California Press.

84. Bourguignon, Erika (1954). "Dreams and Dream Interpreta-
     tion in Haiti." *American Anthropologist*, *56*, 262-268.

85. Brenneis, C.B. (1970). "Male and Female Ego Modalities
     in Manifest Dream Content." *Journal of Abnormal
     Psychology, 76,* 434-442.

86. Dittman, Allen, and Moore, Harvey (1957). "Disturbance
     in Dreams as Related to Peyotism among the Navaho."
     American Anthropologist, 59, 642-649.

87. Eggan, Dorothy (1949). "The Significance of Dreams for
     Anthropological Research." *American Anthropologist,
     51,* 177-198.

88. Eggan, Dorothy (1952). "The Manifest Content of Dreams:
     A Challenge to Social Science." *American Anthropolo-
     gist, 54,* 469-485.

     This is an arbitrary selection from the opus of a
     pioneer who strove to treat ethnographic dream narratives
     as data independent of a possibly culture-bound Freudian
     interpretation. Her work remains seminal.

89. Eggan, Dorothy (1955). "The Personal Use of Myth in
     Dreams." *Journal of American Folklore, 68,* 445-450.

90. Eggan, Dorothy (1974). "Hopi Dreams in Cultural Perspec-
     tive." In Robert A. Levine (Ed.), *Culture and Personal-
     ity: Contemporary Readings* (pp. 265-286). Chicago:
     Aldine.

91. Grey, A., and Kalsched, D. (1971). "Oedipus East and
     West: An Exploration via Manifest Dream Content."
     Journal of Cross-Cultural Psychology, 2, 337-352.

92. Griffith, Richard M.; Miyagi, Otoya; and Tago, Akira
     (1958). "The Universality of Typical Dreams: Japanese
     vs. Americans." *American Anthropologist, 60,* 1173-1179.

93. Hall, Calvin S. (1959). *The Meaning of Dreams.* New
     York: Dell.

94. Hall, Calvin S., and Van de Castle, Robert L. (1966).
     The Content Analysis of Dreams. New York: Appleton-
     Century-Crofts.

     Two American post-Freudian psychologists wrote this
     classic work, which remains a useful methodological guide
     to the positivist study of manifest dream content.

95. Hallowell, A. Irving (1966). "The Role of Dreams in
     Ojibwa Culture." In G.E. von Grunebaum and Roger

Callois (Eds.), *The Dream and Human Societies* (pp. 267–292). Berkeley: University of California Press.

96. LeVine, Robert A. (1966). *Dreams and Deeds: Achievement Motivation in Nigeria.* Chicago: University of Chicago Press.

97. LeVine, Sarah (1982). "The Dreams of Young Gusii Women: A Content Analysis." *Ethnology, 21,* 63–78.

98. O'Nell, Carl W. (1976). *Dreams, Culture, and the Individual.* Norato, Calif.: Chandler and Sharp.

    A leading anthropological student of dreams summarizes the field and gives an extensive annotated bibliography.

99. Paolino, A.F. (1964). "Dreams: Sex Differences in Aggressive Content." *Journal of Projective Techniques and Personality Assessment, 28,* 219–226.

100. Reichel-Dolmatoff, A. (1961). *People of the Aritama: The Cultural Personality of a Columbia Mestizo Village.* Chicago: University of Chicago Press.

101. Robbins, Michael C., and Kilbride, Philip L. (1971). "Sex Differences in Dreams in Uganda." *Journal of Cross-cultural Psychology, 2,* 406–408.

102. Simmons, Leo W. (1942). *Sun Chief: The Autobiography of a Hopi Indian.* New Haven: Yale University Press.

103. Spindler, George, and Spindler, Louise (1971). *Dreamers without Power: The Menomini Indians.* New York: Holt, Rinehart and Winston.

104. Van de Castle, Robert L. (1970). "His, Hers and the Children's." *Psychology Today, 4*(1), 37–39.

105. Barnouw, Victor (1973). *Culture and Personality.* Rev. ed. Homewood, Ill.: The Dorsey Press.

106. Berelson, Bernard (1954). "Content Analysis." In Gardner Lindzey (Ed.), *Handbook of Social Psychology: Vol. I, Theory and Method* (pp. 488–522). Reading, Mass.: Addison-Wesley.

107. Wolfenstein, Martha, and Leites, Nathan (1950). *Movies: A Psychological Study.* Glencoe, N.Y.: The Free Press.

108. Freud, Sigmund (1967). *The Interpretation of Dreams.*
     8th ed. (James Strachey, Trans.) New York: Avon
     Books. Original work published in 1930.

109. Devereux, George (1957). "Dream Learning and Individual
     Ritual Differences in Mohave Shamanism." *American
     Anthropologist, 59*, 1036-1045.

110. Langer, Susanne K. (1953). *Feeling and Form: A Theory
     of Art.* New York: Charles Scribner's Sons.

111. Needham, Rodney (1972). *Belief, Language, and Experience.*
     Chicago: University of Chicago Press.

112. Feld, Steven (1982). *Sound and Sentiment: Birds, Weep-
     ing, Poetics, and Song in Kaluli Expression.* Phila-
     delphia: University of Pennsylvania Press.

113. Graburn, Nelson H.H., and Strong, B. Stephen (1973).
     Circumpolar Peoples: An Anthropological Perspective.
     Pacific Palisades, Calif.: Goodyear Publishing Company.

114. Bernatzik, Hugo Adolf (1947). *Akha und Meau.* Innsbruck:
     Wagner'sche Universität-louchdruckerei.

115. Oppenheim, A. Leo (1956). *The Interpretation of Dreams
     in the Ancient Near East.* Philadelphia: University
     of Pennsylvania Press.

116. Reser, Joseph (1981). "Australian Aboriginal Man's In-
     humanity to Man: A Case of Cultural Distortion."
     American Anthropologist, 83, 387-393.

117. Triandis, Harry C.; Malpass, Roy S.; and Davidson,
     Andrew R. (1973). "Psychology and Culture." *Annual
     Review of Psychology, 24*, 355-378.

118. Dentan, Robert Knox, and Nowak, Barbara (1980). "Die
     soziale Stellung des Minderbegabten." In Wolfgang M.
     Pfeiffer and Wolfgang Schoene (Eds.), *Psychopathologie
     im Kulturvergleich* (pp. 203-219). Stuttgart: Enke
     Verlag.

119. Glover, T.R. (1975). *The Conflict of Religions in the
     Early Roman Empire.* New York: Cooper Square.

120. Haldar, Alfred (1945). *Associations of Cult Prophets
     among the Ancient Semites.* Uppsala: Almqvist & Wiksells.

121. Stewart, Kilton (1954). *Pygmies and Dream Giants*. New
      York: W.W. Norton.

122. Tart, C.T. (Ed.) (1972). *Altered States of Consciousness*
      Garden City, N.Y.: Anchor.

123. Bourguignon, Erika (Ed.) (1973). *Religion, Altered
      States of Consciousness, and Social Change*. Columbus:
      Ohio State University Press.

      One of the foremost anthropological students of dream-
      ing presents "holocultural" accounts of ASCs, including
      dreams. She and her students have done much significant
      work in this area, and her review of the literature
      (1972) is exemplary.

124. Bourguignon, Erika, and Evascu, T.E. (1977). "Altered
      States of Consciousness within a General Evolutionary
      Perspective: A Holocultural Analysis." *Behavior
      Science Research, 12*, 197-216.

125. Endicott, Karen Lampell (1979). "Batek Negrito Sex
      Roles." Unpublished Master's Thesis, Australian
      National University, Australia.

126. Harner, Michael J. (1973). *The Jivaro: People of the
      Sacred Waterfalls*. New York: Anchor.

127. Harner, Michael J. (Ed.) (1978). *Hallucinogens and
      Shamanism*. New York: Oxford University Press.

      A collection of articles in the tradition of psychedelic
      ethnography, edited by a leader in the study of "SSC,"
      the shamanic state of consciousness, who teaches shamanism
      in New York; it is based largely on his fieldwork with
      Jivaro in South America.

128. Harner, Michael J. (1982). *The Way of the Shaman: A
      Guide to Power and Healing*. New York: Bantam.

129. Noll, Richard (1983). "Shamanism and Schizophrenia: A
      State-specific Approach to the 'Schizophrenia Metaphor'
      of Shamanic States." *American Ethnologist, 10*, 443-
      459.

130. Noll, Richard (1984). "Reply to Lex." *American Ethnolo-
      gist, 11*, 192.

131. Peters, Larry G. (1982). "Trance, Initiation, and

Psychotherapy in Tamang Shamanism." *American Ethnologist, 9,* 21-46.

132. Peters, Larry G., and Williams, David Price (1980). "Toward an Experiential Analysis of Shamanism." *American Ethnologist, 7,* 398-418.

133. Lex, Barbara W. (1984). "The Context of Schizophrenia and Shamanism." *American Ethnologist, 11,* 191-192.

134. Carneiro, Robert L. (1980). "Chimera of the Upper Amazon." In Richard de Mille (Ed.), *The Don Juan Papers: Further Castaneda Controversies* (pp. 94-98). Santa Barbara, Calif.: Ross-Erikson.

135. DeHolmes, Rebecca B. (1983). "Shabono: Scandal or Superb Social Science?" *American Anthropologist, 85,* 664-667.

136. De Mille, Richard (Ed.) (1980). *The Don Juan Papers: Further Castaneda Controversies.* Santa Barbara, Calif.: Ross-Erikson.

Various anthropologists examine the work of Carlos Castaneda and others who treat ASCs as tapping into another dimension of reality. Most of the comments are hostile, perhaps, as Michael Harner might argue, unduly so. Historically, Castaneda enthusiasts have tended to be less critical of their data than was prudent.

137. Donner, Florinda (1982). *Shabono: A Visit to a Remote and Magical World in the Heart of the South-American Jungle.* New York: Delacorte Press.

138. Lamb, F. Bruce (1971). *Wizard of the Upper Amazon: The Story of Manuel Cordova-Rios.* Boston: Houghton Mifflin.

139. Picchi, Debra (1983). "Review of Shabono (Donner 1982)." *American Anthropologist, 85,* 674-675.

140. Hall, Calvin S. "Ethnic Similarities in Manifest Dream Contents: A Modest Confirmation of the Theory of Universal Man." Unpublished manuscript.

141. Leach, Edmund R. (1958). "Magical Hair." *Journal of the Royal Anthropological Institute, 88,* 147-164.

142. D'Andrade, Roy (1961). "Anthropological Studies of Dreams." In Francis L.K. Hsu (Ed.), *Psychological Anthropology* (pp. 296-334). Homewood, Ill.: Dorsey Press.

143. Gallenkamp, Charles (1981). *Maya: The Riddle and Redis-
      covery of a Lost Civilization.* 2nd rev. ed. Harmonds-
      worth: Penguin.

144. Griffith, Richard M. (1951). "Dreams of Finding Money."
      American Journal of Psychotherapy, 5, 521-530.

145. Karpman, Ben D. (1948). "Coprophilia: A Collective Re-
      view." *Psychoanalytic Review, 35,* 253-272.

146. Karim, Wazir Jahan begum (1981). "Ma' Betisek Concepts
      of Living Things." *London School of Economics Mono-
      graph on Social Anthropology* (#54). London: The Ath-
      lone Press.

147. Hall, Calvin S., and Domhoff, G. William (1963). "A
      Ubiquitous Sex Difference in Dreams." *Journal of Ab-
      normal and Social Psychology, 66,* 278-280.

148. Hall, Calvin S.; Domhoff, G. William; Blick, Kenneth A.;
      and Weesner, K.E. (1982). "The Dreams of College Men
      and Women in 1950 and 1980: A Comparison of Dream Con-
      tents and Sex Differences." *Sleep, 5,* 188-194.

149. O'Nell, Carl, and O'Nell, Nancy (1963). "Aggression in
      Dreams." *International Journal of Social Psychiatry,
      9,* 259-267.

150. Colby, Kenneth M. (1963). "Sex Differences in Dreams
      in Primitive Tribes." *American Anthropologist, 65,*
      1116-1122.

151. Johnson, Kenneth E. (1978). "Modernity and Dream Con-
      tent: A Ugandan Example." *Ethos: Journal of the So-
      ciety for Psychological Anthropology, 6,* 212-220.

152. Urbina, S.P., and Grey, A. (1975). "Cultural and Sex
      Differences in the Sex Distribution of Dream Characters
      Journal of Cross-Cultural Psychology, 6, 358-364.

153. Gonzalez, Nancie L. (1979). "Sex Preference in Human
      Figure Drawings by Garifuna (Black Carib) Children."
      Ethnology, 18, 355-364.

154. Heinrich, P., and Triebe, J.K. (1972). "Sex Preferences
      in Children's Human Figure Drawings." *Journal of Per-
      sonality Assessment, 36,* 263-267.

155. Anderson, Barbara Gallatin (1971). "Adaptive Aspects of Culture Shock." *American Anthropologist*, *73*, 1121-1125.

156. Devereux, George (1967). *From Anxiety to Method in the Behavioral Sciences*. The Hague: Mouton.

157. Kroeber, Alfred L. (1937). "Ethnographic Interpretation: 2 Ad Hoc Reassurance Dreams." *University of California Publications in American Archaeology and Ethnology*, *47*, 205-208.

158. Jung, C.G. (1958). *Modern Man in Search of a Soul*. (W.S. Dell and Cary F. Baynes, Trans.) New York: Harvest Books. Original work published in 1933.

159. Kilbride, Philip K. (1973). "Modernization and the Structure of Dream Narratives among the Baganda." In M. Robbins and Philip K. Kilbride (Eds.), *Psycho-cultural Change in Modern Buganda: Nkanga* (#7). Kampala: Makerere Institute of Social Research.

160. Burridge, Kenelm (1969). *New Heaven New Earth*. New York: Schocken.

161. Burridge, Kenelm (1970). *Mambu: A Study of Melanesian Cargo Movements and Their Social and Ideological Background*. New York: Harper Torchbooks.

162. Compilation Group (1976). *The Taiping Revolution*. ("History of Modern China" series.) Beijing: Foreign Language Press.

163. Mooney, James (1965). *The Ghost Dance Religion and the Sioux Outbreak of 1890* (A.F.C. Wallace abridgement). Chicago: University of Chicago Press. Original work published in 1891.

164. Wallace, Anthony F.C. (1959). "Cultural Determinants of Response to Hallucinatory Experience." *AMA Archives of General Psychiatry*, *1*, 58-69.

165. Wallace, Anthony F.C. (1966). *Religion: An Anthropological View*. New York: Random House.

166. Worsley, Peter (1968). *The Trumpet Shall Sound: A Study of 'Cargo' Cults in Melanesia*. 2nd ed. New York: Schocken.

167. Devereux, George (1966). "Pathogenic Dreams in Non-
      Western Societies." In G.E. von Grunebaum and Roger
      Callais (Eds.), *The Dream and Human Societies* (pp.
      213-228). Berkeley: University of California Press.

168. Field, M.J. (1960). *Search for Security: An Ethno-
      psychiatric Study of Rural Ghana*. Evanston, Ill.:
      Northwestern University Press.

169. Holmberg, Allan R. (1950). *Nomads of the Long Bow: The
      Siriono of Eastern Bolivia*. Smithsonian Institution
      Institute of Social Anthropology (Publication #10).

170. King, Arden R. (1943). "The Dream Biography of a Moun-
      tain Maidu." *Character and Personality, 11*, 227-234.

171. Lowie, Robert H. (1922). "The Religion of the Crow
      Indians." *Papers of the American Museum of Natural
      History, 25*, 309-344.

172. Boyer, L. Bryce; Boyer, Ruth M.; and Basehart, Harry W.
      (1978). "Shamanism and Peyote Use among the Apaches
      of the Mescalero Indian Reservation." In Michael J.
      Harner (Ed.), *Hallucinogens and Shamanism*. New York:
      Oxford University Press.

173. Fletcher, Alice, and LaFlesche, Frances (1972). *The
      Omaha Tribe*. Lincoln: University of Nebraska Press.

174. Jarvenpa, Robert (1982). "Intergroup Behavior and
      Imagery: The Case of Chipewyan and Cree." *Ethnology,
      21*, 283-300.

175. La Flesche, Francis (1925). "The Osage Tribe: The Rite
      of Vigil." *Annual Report of the Bureau of American
      Ethnology, 39*, 31-630.

176. Lame·Deer, John (Fire), and Erdoes, Richard (1972).
      Lame Deer: Seeker of Visions. New York: Simon and
      Schuster.

177. Landes, Ruth (1938). *The Ojibwa Woman*. New York:
      Norton.

178. Opler, Marvin K. (1959). "Dream Analysis in Ute Indian
      Therapy." In Marvin K. Opler (Ed.), *Culture and Men-
      tal Health: Cross-cultural Studies* (pp. 97-117). New
      York: Macmillan.

179. Park, Willard Z. (1934). "Paviotso Shamanism." *American Anthropologist*, *36*, 99.

180. Radin, Paul (1914). *Some Aspects of Puberty Fasting among the Ojibwa*. *Canada Department of Mines Museum Bulletin* (No. 2).

181. Radin, Paul (1936). "Ojibwa and Ottawa Puberty Dreams." In *Essays in Anthropology Presented to A.L. Kroeber*. Berkeley, Calif.: University of California Press.

182. Skinner, Alanson B. (1913). "Social Life and Ceremonial Bundles of the Menomini Indians." *Anthropological Papers of the American Museum of Natural History*, *13*(1).

183. Smith, D.M. (1973). "Inkonze: Magico-religious Beliefs of Contact-Traditional Chipewyan Trading at Fort Resolution, NWT, Canada." *National Museum of Man Mercury Series* (No. 6).

184. Stephen, Alexander M. (1893). "The Navajo." *American Anthropologist*, *6*, 345-363.

185. Stewart, Kenneth M. (1946). "Spirit Possession in Native America." *Southwestern Journal of Anthropology*, *2*, 323-339.

186. Swanson, Guy E. (1973). "The Search for Guardian Spirit: A Process of Empowerment in Simpler Societies." *Ethnology*, *12*, 359-378.

187. Wallace, Anthony F.C. (1958). "Dreams and the Wishes of the Soul: A Type of Psychoanalytic Theory among the Seventeenth Century Iroquois." *American Anthropologist*, *60*, 234-248.

188. Wallace, W.J. (1947). "The Dream in Mohave Life." *Journal of American Folklore*, *60*, 252-258.

189. Whitehead, Harriet (1981). "The Bow and the Burden Strap: A New Look at Institutionalized Homosexuality in Native North America." In Sherry B. Ortner and Harriet Whitehead (Eds.), *Sexual Meanings: The Cultural Construction of Gender and Sexuality* (pp. 80-115). Cambridge: Cambridge University Press.

190. Hewitt, John Napoleon Brinton (1902). "Orenda and a Definition of Religion." *American Anthropologist*, *4*, 33-46.

191. Bogoras, Waldemar (1901). "The Chukchi of Northeastern
      Asia." *American Anthropologist, 3,* 80–108.

192. Bowra, C.M. (1962). *Primitive Song.* New York: Mentor.

193. Cloutier, David (1973). *Spirit, Spirit: Shaman Songs,
      Incantations.* Providence, R.I.: Copper Beech Press.

194. Eliade, Mircea (1951). *Le Chamanisme et les techniques
      archaiques de l'extase.* Paris: Payot.

195. Lopatin, Ivan A. (1960). *The Cult of the Dead among
      the Natives of the Amur Basin.* The Hague: Mouton.

196. Nadel, S.F. (1950). "The Origins of Music." *Musical
      Quarterly, 16,* 538–542.

197. Oswalt, Robert L. (1964). "Kashaya Texts." *University
      of California Publications in Linguistics* (36).

198. Shirokogoroff, S.M. (1935). *The Psychomental Complex
      of the Reindeer Tungus.* London: Kegan Paul.

199. Teit, J.H. (1900). "The Thompson Indians of British
      Columbia." *Memoirs of the American Museum of Natural
      History, 2*(4).

200. Maybury-Lewis, David (1967). *Akse-Shavante Society.*
      Oxford: Clarendon Press.

201. Radcliffe-Brown, A.R. (1964). *The Andaman Islanders.*
      New York: Free Press. Original work published in
      1922.

202. Herdt, Gilbert H. (1981). *Guardians of the Flutes:
      Idioms of Masculinity: A Study of Ritualized Homosexual
      Behavior.* New York: McGraw-Hill.

203. Meggitt, Mervyn J. (1962). "Dream Interpretation among
      the Mae Enga of New Guinea." *Southwestern Journal of
      Anthropology, 18,* 216–229.

204. Opler, Marvin K. (1942). "Techniques in Social Analysis."
      Journal of Social Psychology, 15, 91–127.

205. Rycroft, Charles (1979). *The Innocence of Dreams.* New
      York: Pantheon.

206. Pu Zengyuan (1984). "A Golden Millet Dream." In *A Golden Millet Dream*. (Stories of Chinese set phrases 2: 1-16 [unpaginated].) Beijing: Zhaohua.

207. Du Fu (1984). "Dreaming of Li Bai." In Yang Xiangyi and Gladys Yang (Eds.), *Poetry and Prose of the Tang and Song* (pp. 50-51). Beijing: Panda Books. Original work published c. 750.

208. Li Bai (1984). "A Visit to Sky-Mother Mountain in a Dream, a Song of Farewell." In Yang Xiangyi and Gladys Yang (Eds.), *Poetry and Prose of the Tang and Song* (p. 29). Beijing: Panda Books. Original work published c. 750.

209. Li Gongzuo (1980). "Governor of the Southern Tributary State." In Yang Xiangyi and Gladys Yang (Eds.), *The Dragon King's Daughter: Ten Tang Dynasty Stories* (pp. 41-52). Beijing: Foreign Language Press. Original work published c. 800.

210. Su Shi (1984). "A Dream of My Wife." In Yang Xiangyi and Gladys Yang (Eds.), *Poetry and Prose of the Tang and Song* (pp. 249-250). Beijing: Panda Books. Original work published 1075.

211. Su Shi (1984). "Memories of the Past at Red Cliff." In Yang Xiangyi and Gladys Yang (Eds.), *Poetry and Prose of the Tang and Song* (p. 255). Beijing: Panda Books. Original work published in 1082.

212. Li Fuyan (1980). "The Spendthrift and the Alchemist." In Yang Xiangyi and Gladys Yang (Eds.), *The Dragon King's Daughter: Ten Tang Dynasty Stories* (pp. 75-81). Beijing: Foreign Languages Press. Original work published c. 820.

213. Pu Songling (1984). *The Taoist Priest of Laoshan Mountain* (Cao Zuori, Adaptor). Beijing: Foreign Languages Press. Original work published c. 1700.

214. Lu You (1984). "'A Poem' and 'The Great Storm on the Fourth of the Eleventh Month.'" In Yang Xiangyi and Gladys Yang (Eds.), *Poetry and Prose of the Tang and Song* (pp. 280-281, 284). Original work published c. 1190.

215. Sima Qian [Szuma Chien] (1979). *Selections from Records of the Historian*. (Yang Xiangyi and Gladys Yang, Trans.)

Beijing: Foreign Languages Press. Original work published 89 B.C.

216. Burridge, Kenelm O.L. (1967). "Social Implications of
Some Tangu Myths." In John Middleton (Ed.), *Myth and
Cosmos: Reading in Mythology and Symbolism* (pp. 27-46).
Garden City, N.Y.: The Natural History Press.

217. Littlejohn, James (1967). "The Temne House." In John
Middleton (Ed.), *Myth and Cosmos* (pp. 331-347). Garden
City, N.Y.: The Natural History Press.

218. Malinowski, Bronislaw (1932). *The Sexual Life of Savages
in North-western Melanesia*. 3rd ed. London: George
Routledge & Sons.

219. Murdock, George Peter (1945). "The Common Denominator
of Cultures." In Ralph Linton (Ed.), *The Science of
Man in the World Crisis*. New York: Columbia University
Press.

220. Kensinger, Kenneth M. (1978). "*Banisteriopsis* Usage
among the Peruvian Cashinahua." In Michael J. Harner
(Ed.), *Hallucinogens and Shamanism* (pp. 9-14). New
York: Oxford University Press.

221. Noone, R.O.D., with Holman, D. (1972). *In Search of the
Dream People*. New York: William Morrow.

222. Beresford, S.C. (1928). "Akamba Ceremonies Connected
with Dreams." *Man, 28,* 176-177.

223. Boushahla, Jo Jean, and Reidel-Geubtner, Virginia (1983).
The Dream Dictionary: The Key to Your Unconscious.
New York: Pilgrim.

224. Kramer, Samuel Noah (1963). *The Sumerians, Their History,
Culture, and Character*. Chicago: University of Chicago
Press.

225. Oppenheim, A. Leo (1964). *Ancient Mesopotamia: Portrait
of a Dead Civilization*. Chicago: University of Chicago
Press.

226. Lévi-Strauss, Claude (1963). *Totemism*. (Rodney Needham,
Trans.) Boston: Beacon.

227. Rattray, Robert S. (1927). *Religion and Art in Ashanti*.
Oxford: Clarendon.

228. Abdul Jalil bin Haji Noor (1961). *Pesaka orang tuatau (The Elders' Legacy).* Singapore: Al-Ahmadah Press.

229. Kilborne, Benjamin (1983). "The Handling of Dream Symbolism: Aspects of Dream Interpretation in Morocco." In Werner Muensterberger and L. Bruce Boyer (Eds.), *The Psychoanalytic Study of Society* (Vol. 9). New York: Psychohistory Press.

230. Resner, G., and Hartog, J. (1970). "Concepts and Terminology of Mental Disorder among Malays." *Journal of Cross-Cultural Psychology, 1,* 369-381.

231. Jilek, Wolfgang G. (1974). *Salish Indian Mental Health and Culture Change: Psychohygienic and Therapeutic Aspects of the Guardian Spirit Ceremonial.* Toronto: Holt, Rinehart and Winston of Canada.

232. Jochelson, Waldemar (1904). "The Mythology of the Koryak." *American Anthropologist, 6,* 413-425.

233. Park, Willard Z. (1938). "Shamanism in Western North America: A Study of Cultural Relationships." *North-Western University Studies in the Social Sciences* (No. 2).

234. Sapir, Edward (1907). "Preliminary Report on the Language and Mythology of the Upper Chinook." *American Anthropologist, 9,* 533-544.

235. Ruel, Malcolm (1970). "Were-animals and the Introverted Witch." In Mary Douglas (Ed.), *Witchcraft Confessions and Accusations* (pp. 333-350). London: Tavistock Publications.

236. Olmstead, A.T. (1948). *History of the Persian Empire (Achaemenid Period).* Chicago: University of Chicago Press.

237. Su Shi (1984). "A Second Visit to the Red Cliff." In Yang Xiangyi and Gladys Yang (Eds.), *Poetry and Prose of the Tang and Song* (pp. 260-262). Beijing: Panda Books. Original work published in 1082.

238. DeRopp, Robert (1960). *Drugs and the Mind.* New York: Evergreen.

239. Furst, Peter T. (1972). *Flesh of the Gods: The Ritual Use of Hallucinogens.* New York: Praeger.

240. Krippner, Stanley, and Hooper, Jeffrey (1984). "Shaman-
     ism and Dreams." *Dream Network Bulletin, 3/4,* 14-16.

241. Reichel-Dolmatoff, Gerardo (1971). *Amazonian Cosmos:
     The Sexual and Religious Symbolism of the Tukano
     Indians.* Chicago: University of Chicago Press.

242. Foulks, Edward F. (1972). "The Arctic Hysterias of the
     North Alaskan Eskimo." *American Anthropological
     Association Anthropological Studies, 10.*

243. Freuchen, Peter (1935). *Arctic Adventure.* New York:
     Farrar and Rinehart.

244. Gussow, Zachary (1963). "A Preliminary Report of Kayak-
     angst among the Eskimo of West Greenland: A Study in
     Sensory Deprivation." *International Journal of Social
     Psychiatry, 9,* 18-26.

245. Lambo, Thomas Adeoye (1978). "Psychotherapy in Africa."
     In James P. Spradley and David W. McCurdy (Eds.),
     *Conformity and Conflict: Readings in Cultural Anthro-
     pology* (pp. 364-373). 5th ed. Boston: Little, Brown.

246. Horney, Karen (1950). *Neurosis and Human Growth.* New
     York: Norton.

247. Suler, John (1984). "The Role of Ideology in Self-Help
     Groups." *Social Policy, 14*(3), 29-36.

248. Frank, Jerome D. (1961). *Persuasion and Healing.* Bal-
     timore: Johns Hopkins University Press.

249. Wechsler, H. (1960). "The Self-Help Organization in
     the Mental Health Field: Recovery, Inc.: A Case Study."
     Journal of Nervous and Mental Disease, 30, 297-314.

250. Frank, Jerome (1975). "Psychotherapy of Bodily Ill-
     ness: An Overview." *Psychotherapy and Psychosomatics,
     26,* 192-202.

251. Moerman, Daniel F. (1983). "Physiology and Symbols:
     The Anthropological Implications of the Placebo Ef-
     fect." In Lola Romanucci-Ross, Daniel E. Moerman, and
     Laurence R. Tancredi (Eds.), *The Anthropology of
     Medicine: From Culture to Method* (pp. 156-167). New
     York: Praeger.

252. Gadd, C.J. (1929). *History and Monuments of Ur*. London: Chatto and Windus.

253. Chen, Paul C.Y. (1975). "Medical Systems in Malaysia: Cultural Bases and Differential Use." *Social Science and Medicine, 9*, 171-180.

254. Morgan, Lewis Henry (1901). *League of the Ho-de-no-Sau-nee or Iroquois*. Herbert M. Lloyel, Ed. New York: Dodd Mead and Co. Originally published in 1851.

255. Trigger, Bruce G. (1969). *The Huron. Farmers of the North*. New York: Holt, Rinehart and Winston.

256. Wilson, Edmund (1960). *Apologies to the Iroquois: With a Study of the Mohawks in High Steel by Joseph Mitchell*. London: W.H. Allen.

257. Bourguignon, Erika (1972). "Dreams: Altered States of Consciousness in Anthropological Research." In Francis L.K. Hsu (Ed.), *Psychological Anthropology* (pp. 403-434). 2nd ed. Homewood: Dorsey Press.

258. Hultkrantz, A. (1973). "A Definition of Shamanism." *Temenos, 9*, 25-37.

259. Hood, H.M.S. (1979). "The Cultural Context of Semelai Trance." *Federation Museums Journal, 24*, 107-124.

    A meticulous ethnographic account of dreams and other ASCs by an author who grew up in a context where such experiences were taken seriously. Hood's work generally exemplifies the best of "native" ethnography.

260. Walker, S.S. (1972). *Ceremonial Spirit Possession in Africa and Afro-America*. Leiden: Brill.

261. Wilson, Robert R. (1979). "Prophecy and Ecstacy: A Re-examination." *Journal of Biblical Literature, 98*(3), 321-337.

262. Heelas, Paul (1983). "Indigenous Representation of Emotions: The Chewong." *Journal of the Anthropological Society of Oxford, 14*, 87-103.

263. Arendt, Hannah (1977). *Between Past and Future. Eight Exercises in Political Thought*. Enlarged ed. Harmondsworth: Penguin.

264. Hillman, Deborah Jay, and Patric Giesler (1986).
      "Anthropological Perspectives on Lucid Dreaming."
      Lucidity Letter, 5 (1), 6-25.

265. Murray, D.D. (1982). "A Survey on Psi and Related
      Phenomena in the Philippines." In W.G. Rall, R.L.
      Morris, and R.A. White (Eds.), *Research in Parapsychol-
      ogy 1981* (pp. 186-187). Metuchen, N.J.: Scarecrow
      Press.

266. Sheils, Dean (1978). "A Cross-cultural Study of Beliefs
      in Out-of-Body Experiences, Waking and Sleeping."
      Journal of the Society for Psychical Research 49, 697-
      741.

Chapter 12
DREAMS AND LITERATURE:
A READER'S GUIDE

Carol Schreier Rupprecht

It is no surprise that this chapter comes at the end of this
book; the wonder is that it appears here at all. From the
mid-twentieth century to the early 1980s, scientists and
social scientists dominated discourse on dreams in the United
States. Dream work in the humanities, if not irrelevant in
the booming enterprises of sleep laboratory research, clinical
practice, and general psychological experimentation, certainly
seemed less exciting and less promising. Whatever interdisciplinary cross-overs were occurring between psychology and
literature were almost exclusively psychoanalytic and involved
the application of psychoanalytic categories and concepts to
literary texts, their authors, and even their readers: the
oral fixation of Jaques in Shakespeare's *As You Like It*; the
"wounded narcissism" of Dickens. Even when the cross-overs
involved Jungian, Adlerian, Rankian, Reichian, or other psychologies, the methods and aims were similar: a search for
anima, persona, shadow, archetype.

The proportion of psychological commentary that emphasized
dreams was small and proceeded by the same methods: "Do literary dreams have a latent content?" (1). The effort seemed
always aimed at confirming psychological hypotheses through
evidence of their applicability not just to "real" human
beings, but also to "fictional" ones. Even ignoring the
often unacknowledged (unconscious?) ontological pitfalls in
treating literature as if it were life, characters as if they
were "real" persons, texts as if they were infallible documen-
taries on the inner lives of their creators, and readers'
responses as if they were revealing answers to an analyst's
subtly probing questions, the net effect may have been illumi-
nation in certain individual cases. The basic assumptions
of psychology were seldom challenged, however, and the fron-
tiers of literary criticism were not significantly advanced.

But literary scholars and others outside the psychoanalytic
tradition had not been asleep; a quiet revolution was in progress

against the single-minded, reductionist, deterministic approaches of any school of psychological criticism. The dream
was at the center of this revolution, along with the revivifi-
cation of ancient truths about the intimate kinship of dreams
and literature. And even within the psychoanalytic mainstream,
a very different mode of interdisciplinary interaction, set
in motion in different ways by both structuralism and feminism,
was taking shape. The twin-pronged assault on everything from
canon formation to the referentiality of words led to the
recognition that the presumed boundaries between dream and
literature, and thus the assumed parameters of psychological
analysis of texts, were artificial.

Shoshana Felman, special editor of a 1977 Yale French
Studies issue on Literature and Psychoanalysis, was among the
first and the clearest to articulate this insight:

> In view of this shift of emphasis, the tradi-
> tional method of application of psychoanalysis to
> literature would here be in principle ruled out.
> The notion of application would be replaced by the
> radically different notion of implication: ... not
> to apply to the text an acquired science, a pre-
> conceived knowledge, but to act as a go-between,
> to generate implications between literature and
> psychoanalysis--to explore, bring to light and
> articulate the various (indirect) ways in which
> the two domains do indeed implicate each other,
> each one finding itself enlightened, informed,
> but also affected, displaced, by the other.
> (2, pp. 55-56)

This allegedly new insight, however, was one that scholars
working in dreams and not blinded by Freudian (or Jungian)
orthodoxy had been continuously expressing, in the field of
archetypal theory, for example. Often presented under the
rubric of "Jungian psychology," from which it received its
initial impetus, archetypal theory was from its beginning
iconoclastic, imaginative, multi-disciplinary, and centered
on the dream. Dream and text were seen in a relation of
affinity and analogy, as two dynamic processes; neither was
subject or object to the other.

In *The Unsounded Center: Jungian Studies in American
Romanticism*, Martin Bickman demonstrated the heuristic potential of such a perspective:

> This book is an approach to American Romanti-
> cism through Jungian psychology. Its wider impli-
> cations, however, and the special character of its
> methodology will be missed if it is not read also

as an approach to Jungian psychology through American Romanticism.... The literature does not serve merely as illustrative material for the psychology, but also illuminates the origins and nature of that psychology. (3, p. 5)

Throughout the seventies James Hillman, an initiator of archetypal theory and editor of its annual journal, *Spring*, regularly re-visioned Jung's ideas and countered the tendency of Jungians to harden Jung's concepts, especially the archetype (4). Hillman's continual return to the dream, as in *The Dream and the Underworld*, was always a corrective against constraining the imaginal within the theoretical (5). In the *Myth of Analysis*, Hillman also exposed the fantastic, imaginal underside of allegedly objective, scientific theorizing:

Theory-forming is thus as free and fantastic as the imagination; it is limited perhaps even less by observational data than by the archetypal a priori dominants of the imagination, the preformations of ideas acting as preconceptions that determine how and what one observes.... Fantasy intervenes where exact knowledge is lacking.... (6, pp. 220-221)

Felman echoes this sentiment in her provocative suggestion that "in the same way that psychoanalysis points to the unconscious of literature, literature, in its turn, is the unconscious of psychoanalysis: ... the unthought-out shadow in psychoanalytical theory is precisely its own involvement with literature" (2, p. 10). Perhaps that shadow can begin to take on some substance if we consider briefly the role of literature in the genesis of Freudian and Jungian psychology.

Though Freud claimed insistently that his theories were derived from clinical experience and based on neurobiological models, even a cursory reading of Freud's texts forces one to conclude that Freudian psychology is derived at least as significantly from Freud's literary imagination. Among his most famous patients and most frequently cited cases we must place not only Dora and Little Hans, but also Oedipus and Hamlet.

For his revolutionary turn-of-the-century treatise, *The Interpretation of Dreams*, Freud chose an especially revealing literary epigraph from Virgil's first-century Roman epic, the *Aeneid*, "Flectere si nequeo Superos, Acheronta movebo" (If I cannot bend the Higher Powers, I will move all of Hell). Freud found his own movement into depth psychology, his own descent to the unconscious, analogous to the descent to the underworld in that ancient poem not of the epic hero Aeneas, but of the goddess Juno. As the wife of Zeus who was powerless to shape the destiny of her favored Latins and frustrated

in her attempts to thwart the mission of Aeneas, Juno erupts
into the resolve cited above, then descends to Hell to rouse
the spirits and incite war.

Jung was similarly engaged with literature, processing
his experiences of self and work through that medium. While
he insistently claimed to have withheld his ideas from publication until he could establish a scientific basis for them
through the amassing of 60,000 dreams as data, it is neither
of his analysands' dreams nor his own dreams that he spoke
in his earliest writings on the subject. As if enlisting
irrefutable proof for his hypotheses, Jung cites and analyzes
the dream of Gretchen, a character in Goethe's nineteenth-
century poetic drama *Faust* (7, pp. 4-7). In a later essay
published in 1913 as "The Psychology of Dreams," Jung had
begun to break away from Freud and proposed his new theory
of compensation: dreams effect a dynamic balance between the
conscious and unconscious leading to the self-regulation of
the psyche. What evidence did he triumphantly provide for
the validity of this theory?--a "compensatory" dream of
Nebuchadnezzar from the Old Testament Book of Daniel. The
dream offset the king's megalomania through the image of
destruction of a great tree. Further, Jung's prime examples
of his distinction between "visionary" and "psychological"
types of literature were Parts I and II of Goethe's *Faust*
(8, pp. 88-89).

The proposal that the process of conceptualization in the
major psychologies of the twentieth century is inseparable
from the experiences of their founders as readers of literature, especially "dream" literature, may still be met with
defensive incredulity by practitioners in both disciplines.
But contemporary corroboration of this view occurs with increasing frequency. In an interview in the January 19, 1986,
issue of the *New York Times Book Review*, child psychiatrist-
author-Harvard Professor Robert Coles quotes his undergraduate
literature professor's response to the announcement that Coles
planned to become a psychiatrist: "Get out your old copies of
Hawthorne, Emerson and Melville. Anything you learn in psychiatry is in those books." Coles goes further to say that
"Literature is a much-neglected reservoir for the teaching of
psychiatry and psychology. I think Freud himself learned as
much from the Greek tragedies as from anything in medical
school" (9, p. 28).

How does all this apply--or better, since we are learning
our lesson--what does all this imply for our topic of Dreams
and Literature? It implies that oneirology, the study of
dreams, and oneirocritics, the interpretation of dreams especially through its historically primary core of dream-and-
literature, is a burgeoning, compelling, energetic end-of-the-

century movement. To understand and forward this movement
wisely, however, we must foster creation of an interdisciplinary, cross-cultural cooperative venture which will include mutual respect among scientists, social scientists, and
humanists, as well as among the various, often competing
schools of psychology. And we must also look backward, as
Freud and Jung did in forming their psychologies, to the beginning of oneirocritics in poems like the Babylonian Gilgamesh
(2000 B.C.) and in dream treatises like Artemidorus' *Oneirocritica* (200 A.D.). (Freud and Jung cite Artemidorus, and
Freud, having read him in the Kraus translation, borrowed the
title for *Die Traumdeutung*, which, like the Greek *Oneirocritica*, translates into English as "the interpretation of
dreams.")

This chapter is offered as a contribution to oneirocritics which seeks (within the very limited space allotted)
to raise awareness of its past, assess its present state, and
propose a guide for further study. The next section will de-
lineate the dimensions of the topic and scan the wealth of
material, selecting for emphasis certain dream episodes,
authors, and literary texts which can be fruitfully consulted
by the oneirophile. Since we do not now have in English anything like a comprehensive bibliography on oneirocritics, the
last part of this chapter is a brief bibliographic guide.

All the literature selected for inclusion in this chapter
was originally written in English or, with two exceptions, is
available in acceptably accurate translations. For texts
presumed to be in the general public domain--i.e., the Bible,
Shakespeare, Chaucer, Dickens--no bibliographical information
beyond the basic reference is provided nor are such books included in the final reference list.

There are at least five categories within which one can
begin to explore the interrelation of dream and literature:
a) dreams in literary texts; b) literary texts as dreams;
c) the dreamed text; d) the literariness of dream treatises;
c) the dreamlikeness of literary texts. For our purposes,
the term "literature" refers to those constructs of language
traditionally labeled poetry, fiction, and drama; dream refers
to any psychophysical event occurring in sleep (or a borderline
state between sleeping and waking) and reported in words
during the waking state. There is time to touch on only the
first and most readily recognizable category: a) episodes explicitly named as dreams and incorporated into literary texts.
For this see the section, Dreams in Literature.

The other categories can be only briefly described.

b) Texts as dreams are presented within a framework,
usually supplied by a narrative voice at the beginning, which
presents the whole work as if it had been a dream. It opens

with the narrator falling asleep and ends with the narrator
waking up. In fourteenth-century England and France this
genre flourished as never before or since in European or North
American literature. Among the many great dream-and-vision
poems of the medieval period are the hauntingly lovely Middle
English *Pearl* whose author is unknown, the explicitly erotic
Romance of the Rose by Jean de Meun and Guillaume de Lorris,
and Chaucer's elegaic *Book of the Duchess*. James Joyce's
Finnegans Wake is a modern version of this genre.

c) The dreamed text is one whose genesis reputedly lies
in a dream or dreams of the author: i.e., Mary Shelley's claim
that her novel *Frankenstein* came to her in a presleep state
or Robert Louis Stevenson's contention that he owed entire
scenes and the central idea of his novel, *Dr. Jekyll and Mr.
Hyde*, to his dreams. This topic leads into questions about
artistic creativity, aesthetics, and the nature of the imagination.

d) The category of literariness of the dream treatises
would deal with the style, metaphors, structure, tone, and
imagery in theoretical texts. Freud, himself, who won the
Goethe prize for the "literary" qualities of his writing,
appeared bemused and not really displeased that "the case
histories I write should read like short stories" and that
"a detailed description of mental processes such as we are
accustomed to find in the works of imaginative writers" enabled him to obtain insights not available through electro-
prognosis and other neuropathological techniques (10, p. 520).
Here the alleged boundaries between theoretical (scientific?)
and imaginal (literary?) discourse quickly disappear.

e) The last category, the dreamlikeness of so many literary texts, suggests the innate affinities between dreams and
literature which have appeared since the beginning of human
record. Samuel Taylor Coleridge captured this quality best in
speaking of a sixteenth-century English epic, Edmund Spenser's
Faerie Queene, but he could have been describing with equal
felicity a short story by Borges, a novel by Joyce, or a play
by Becket: "You will take especiall note of the marvelous independence and true imaginative absence of all particular
space or time in the 'Faery Queene.' It is in the domains
neither of history nor geography; it is ignorant of all artificial boundary, all material obstacles; it is truly in the
land of Faery, that is, of mental space. The poet has placed
you in a dream, a charmed sleep" (11, p. 514).

This category also explicitly raises issues implicit in
all the other categories: What is a dream? What is a text?
What is language, image, symbol? What is the difference between "unconscious" dreaming and the process of "conscious"
imagining in literary creation and the act of reading?

Little attention will be directed here toward twentieth-
century texts because the influence on creative writers of
Freudian and Jungian psychology profoundly altered the interaction of dreams and literature. Writers of this century
are as knowledgeable as their critics and readers are about
psychological theories. Many keep dream journals and make
self-conscious use of dreams in their writings. Many knew
Freud and Jung personally and analyzed with them or other
clinicians. Where would we begin to sift through the riches
of John Berryman's *Dream Poems* or Galway Kinnel's *Book of
Nightmares*? Where would we begin "reading" such dream-fiction
as Franz Kafka's *The Trial* or James Joyce's *Finnegans Wake*?
It would take another chapter to describe this new climate
and the resulting interpenetration of dreams and texts. The
century does seem to be generating new critical perspectives--
some from the conjunction of psychology with philosophy and
anthropology--to unveil the mysteries of such texts, but these
writings are currently accessible only to the academic initiate
and cannot be briefly explored. Another approach, the one
underlying this chapter and taken, as we have seen, by Freud
and Jung, is to return to the earliest texts and re-read them.

Dreams in Literature

At the moment a society turns from an oral tradition to
a written one or from a language of the literate elite to the
vernacular, two of the first human impulses are to make poems
and record dreams. Whether inscribed on cuneiform clay tablets or woven papyrus, poetry and dreams overlap and interweave
and seem to emanate from the same human needs to imagine, to
express, to remember and, concomitantly, to understand, to
interpret. Dreams in early literature are almost always accompanied by interpretations and by an account of behavior
undertaken in response to the dream and its interpretation.
Three examples may clarify this assertion: the dream of Dumuzi
from Sumerian poem fragments assembled under the name of the
goddess Inanna around 2000 B.C.; the dream of Agamemnon from
the *Iliad*, a Greek epic written down in the 800s B.C. by an
author named as Homer; and an anonymously authored Old English
lyric poem, "The Dream of the Rood," composed between the 7th
and 10th centuries.

The Inanna poetry comes from inscriptions on clay tablets
unearthed less than 100 years ago in what is now southern
Iraq, the site of ancient Sumer. About 4000 years ago Sumerians
developed one of the world's earliest forms of writing--a

cuneiform or wedge-shaped system of pictographic signs. Among
the tablets discovered, transliterated, and translated are
many that record dreams and interpretations which turn dream
images--"a single growing reed trembles for me"--into symbols
of one's destiny--"your mother will mourn for you."

In one fragment Dumuzi tells his dream to his sister
Geshtinanna: "A dream! My sister, listen to my dream. Rushes
rise all about me; rushes grow thick." He then chronicles a
series of alarming incidents: the bottom of his churn drops
away; his drinking cup falls from its peg. Her horror matches
his own as she interprets each event; the rushes are demons
which will attack him; the broken churn means demons will
hold him; the falling cup means he will fall to earth (12, pp.
75-76).

Dumuzi's nightmare and his sister's interpretation are
prophetic. He is taken away by demons to the underworld.
But she first protects him by refusing to betray his hiding
place to the demons despite their torture and later helps to
soften his fate by substituting herself for him in the underworld half of the year.

There is total acceptance of the power, naturalness, and
importance of the dream, of the special process by which the
dream can be translated into "real life" terms by a selected
person through a special process: "My sister who knows the
meaning of words. My wise woman who knows the meaning of
dreams" (12, p. 76).

In subsequent periods and cultures in the West, for Sumerian descendants, the demons and the underworld of the poem
become, like the rushes, reed, cup, and churn of Dumuzi's
dream, symbols of "real life" events, persons, and objects.
In 2000 B.C. the dream reed signifies a real mother; the dream
demons turn out to signify real demons who present real dangers
to the awakened dreamer.

Approximately 1000 years later, in Greece, centuries of
oral transmission of tales about a great war in a city called
Troy were written down for the first time by a scribe to whom
we have given the name of Homer. At approximately the 650th
line of the 15,693-line poem, the greatest of the Gods, Zeus,
has the idea "to send an evil Dream to Atreus' son Agamemnon."
Thus one of the great Greek protagonists of the epic has a
dream reported by the narrator: "In Nestor's likeness the
divine dream spoke to him/'Zeus bids you arm the flowing-
haired Achaians for battle, in all haste.'" Impending victory
is implied.

Upon waking Agamemnon gives a verbatim report of this
message dream to his troops: "A dream divine came to me in
appearance and stature and figure of Nestor and said/'Zeus
bids you arm the flowing-haired Achaians for battle in all

haste.'" The "real" Nestor, prototype of the wise old man, responds that "had it been any other Achaian who told us this dream/we should have called it a lie." But since the dreamer was Agamemnon, the dream is accepted as true; the gods are on their side now and they should attack. They do. And they are routed. The dream was false.

More dimensions of dream lore appear here: divine genesis; possibility of misleading dreams; non-symbolic directly monitory dreams; disastrous consequences of acting on a dream; the dream figures assuming the guise of familiar people; the variability of interpretation depending on the dreamer's identity. Some dimensions of dreams-in-literature will be altered by changes in cultural context; others will remain the same.

Among the first documents written in the English language, in its earliest form as Old English, we find among hymns, genealogies, and word lists a luminous lyric titled "The Dream of the Rood" (i.e., the Cross). In this poem the tree hewn into the cross upon which Christ was crucified appears to the dreamer-narrator, saving his soul. In the words of translator Bernard F. Huppé: "Give heed! I will reveal the extraordinary vision/which came to me at midmost night/when speaking men remained asleep./It seemed to me I saw the seemliest of trees/ lifted in the sky enveloped in light" (13, p. 65). The tree, awesomely bedecked in golden jewels, but bleeding from the right side, then takes over the narration, telling its experience of the crucifixion, i.e., having nails hammered into it.

Here the virtuosity of Christianity in adapting to existing cultural beliefs appears: the unreal, illogical phenomenon, a talking tree, acquires the stature of the miraculous with a prophetic role not just in relation to one's future on earth, but also in the life after death. The traditional form of the dream in the text allows for the imaginative ingenuity of telling the crucifixion story from the point of view of the cross. And the traditional pagan beliefs in the divine/demonic origin of dreams and in the genre of the message dream provide a vehicle for the miraculous eschatological function of the poem.

In addition to appearing at critical junctures in the history of language and culture, the dream literature of the West has recorded every conceivable variety of dream along with many elements of the dreaming process, including some which researchers of the twentieth century think they have been the first to identify. We can recognize accounts of physiological stimuli and phases of sleep, forms and timing of arousal to wakefulness; pregnant women's anxiety dreams; dreams that are telepathic, recurring, parallel, lucid, pre-

cognitive; nightmares and night terrors, etc. There are a
great range, density, and variety not only in the dreams themselves within the texts, but also in the varied functions
they perform there. Dreams in texts have served to relativize
reality and to reinforce it; to advance or retard the plot;
to involve or distance the reader; to reveal character, or to
conceal it; to inform or mislead the reader. Some dreams are
significant in their content; others in their form. Some
delude the dreamers and interpreters; others bear life-saving
truths to them. Some texts mock their dreams; others divinize
them.

Through the centuries, certain dream episodes have taken
hold of the imagination of readers and spawned an industry of
admirers, interpreters, and imitators. These dreams appear
in different cultures, genres, languages, and periods with no
apparent pattern to ensure their status as classics. Below
are chronicled some of the most famous.

We have already looked at Inanna, the *Iliad*, and the
"Dream of the Rood." The Sumerian/Babylonian culture also
produced the epic *Gilgamesh* with the powerful, prophetic
dreams of its two protagonists, Gilgamesh and Enkidu.

Italian medieval literature offers the dreams of the
love-struck narrator in Dante's *Vita Nuova* (The New Life)
which are not only remembered and analyzed in the text but
are turned into lyric poems (14). Fourteenth-century England,
through Chaucer's *Canterbury Tales*, boasts the greatest
comic dream-narrator: Chauntecleer, the proud rooster in the
Nun's Priest's Tale who reports his monitory, prophetic, symbolic dream to his favorite hen, Pertelote. In their ensuing
dialogue, a full, critical review of ancient and medieval
dream theory occurs.

During the Renaissance the prominent genre of epic poetry,
based on ancient models like the *Iliad* but composed in a
Christian era, contains a spectrum of dream episodes. The
five prominent dreams in Edmund Spenser's late sixteenth-
century epic, the *Faerie Queene*, include erotic, anxiety,
prophetic, incubation, and divine dreams, as well as comments
on the day residue's role in dream etiology. Eve's demonic
dream in Milton's *Paradise Lost* prefigures the temptation and
fall of the first humans. Adam fatally underestimates the
significance of the dream when Eve communicates it to him.
Milton has used the dream as a way to make deeply ambiguous our
theological ideas about the entrance of evil into the lives
of our first parents, their individual and joint knowledge
and capacities for recognizing good and evil and choosing between them.

Spanish novelist Miguel de Cervantes also used the dream
as a device to expose the ambiguity and complexity of the
relationship between imaginal and objective realities in
The Ingenious Gentleman Don Quixote of La Mancha. His narrative
contains the "dream" of the Cave of Montesinos that is regarded
as Cervantes' commentary on the art of fiction. The relevant
chapter bears this subtitle: "Of the wonderful things the in-
comparable Don Quixote said he saw in the deep cave of Montesinos, the impossibility and magnitude of which cause this
adventure to be deemed apocryphal" (15).

Three nineteenth century novels contain dream episodes
that have become classics: Mr. Lockwood's nightmare in Emily
Brontë's *Wuthering Heights*; Raskolnikov's dream of the mare
in Fyodor Dostoevsky's *Crime and Punishment*; the dream of the
protagonist in Charles Dickens' *David Copperfield*.

There are two early texts with famous dreams in them which
are also primarily occupied with questioning the very nature
of dream and reality: they are from Renaissance English and
Golden Age Spanish drama: Shakespeare's *A Midsummer Night's
Dream* and Calderon de la Barca's *La vida es sueño* (Life is a
Dream).

Most of the rest of the pre-twentieth century dreams-in-
literature which have attained the stature of classics occur
in two sources to which readers, writers, theorists, and
critics turn again and again: the Bible and Shakespearean
drama. In the Bible, especially the Old Testament, all kinds
of people dream all kinds of dreams in all kinds of settings;
if not the candlemaker, certainly the steward and the baker
as well as kings, slaves, prophets, and pregnant women.

Thirty-seven plays have been authenticated as the Shakespearean canon; at least two-thirds of them contain explicit
dream episodes. Every kind of play—comedy, tragedy, history,
romance—contains significant dreams. Indeed the greatest
number of dream references occurs in an early history play,
Richard III. An extraordinary range of dream lore is represented in the canon. In the *Tempest* the monster Caliban's
dream world forms such a beautiful contrast to his troubled
existence that he "wak'd and cried to dream again." In
Richard III Clarence's precognitive dream of his own execu-
tion deepens the horror of the event because we then see the
nightmare "brought to life" by Richard. This is true of Cal-
purnia's premonitory dream of Caesar's assassination which he,
to his doom, chooses to ignore. Romeo's *liebestod* dream car-
ries out the ironic reversals of roles and failures of recognition central to *Romeo and Juliet*: "I dreamed my lover came
and found me dead and kissed my lips and I revived and was an
Emperor."

Serious oneirophiles will want to know all the authors
and texts cited above. Other authors who may be read with
great reward include the English and American Romantics and
others from the nineteenth century not previously mentioned:
John Keats (1795-1821), Percy B. Shelley (1792-1822), William
Blake (1757-1827), Walt Whitman (1819-1892), Herman Melville
(1819-1891), Nathaniel Hawthorne (1804-1864). Among those
who bridge the centuries, required reading would be Marcel
Proust (1871-1922), Franz Kafka (1883-1924), William Butler
Yeats (1865-1939).

A Bibliographic Guide

Caveat lector! The only thing more elusive and elliptical
than the topic "dreams and literature" may well be a good
book on the subject. Writing about dreams and literature too
often resembles the behavior of the child in the nursery rhyme:
when it is good, it is very, very good, and when it is bad, it
is horrid. And much of the very, very good material must be
extricated from the depths of texts written on other subjects.

The fact that no full, useful bibliography on dreams and
literature exists may be due to these two problems: great
variation in quality and inaccessibility. But additional
problems also exist. Texts with alluring dream titles often
have nothing to do with dreaming as a psychophysical process.
Conventional interdisciplinary journals like *American Imago*
and *Literature and Psychology* are usually exclusively Freudian
in orientation and often omit any consideration of dreams.
Individually authored books often attempt to cover too much
material and are missing any systematic methodology; the kind
of analysis varies with each text examined.

Bettina Knapp's promising collection of her own essays,
A Jungian Approach to Literature, suffers from some of these
limitations. She sweeps from Euripides and Montaigne to the
Finnish *Kalevala* and the Persian *Mantiq ut Tair* (The conference
of the birds), but she pays little attention to dreams.
Furthermore, she lapses occasionally into the literature-as-
therapy school of psychological criticism: "Reading now becomes not merely an intellectual adventure but an excitingly
helpful living experience" (16, p. x). Conversely, collections
of essays with inviting titles like *The Practice of Psychoanalytic Criticism* (17) and *Psychoanalysis and Literary Process*
(18) turn out to be too narrowly focused in Freudian theory
and also deemphasize dreams.

Another limitation is one reportedly discovered also in forms of "poetry therapy"; the literature that proves most effective in bringing relief from neurotic symptoms is often the least effective as art. Those literary texts which yield most readily to the dream investigator are often the least aesthetically satisfying and interesting. What readers have ever heard of or taken deep pleasure in reading George du Maurier's *Peter Ibbetson* or Wilhelm Jensen's *Gravida* or Rider Haggard's *She*? Yet these three obscure aesthetically uncompelling prose narratives serve Freud, Jung, and others as exemplary embodiments of their theories.

Another problem is that many interesting resources, primary as well as secondary texts, have not been translated. Two examples are Gerard de Nerval's *Aurelia ou le rêve et la vie* (Aurelia or the dream and life) (19), and an excellent study of the dream in German Romantic poetry: Albert Beguin's *L'âme romantique et le rêve* (The romantic soul and the dream) (20). Other fine texts treat literature outside of the Western tradition or appear in disciplines like religion, anthropology, and philosophy in forms unavailable to the general reader, i.e., encoded within the theoretical and linguistic conventions of each discipline. Some of the best insights currently offered come from movements within the academy like structuralism and French Freudianism, but these are even more encoded and less accessible to the uninitiated. We need multi-disciplinary anthologies, cross-cultural comparative studies, translations, a directory of international researchers, etc. Where is the literary dream interpreter to turn?

Despite the problems enumerated above, the prognosis for literary dream research is excellent. Needed resources are coming into existence almost daily. This sourcebook is an example. And so is the fact that a majority of books in the reference list at the end of this chapter have come out in the last decade. Several active and growing associations of dream workers are proving to be excellent dream educators, cultivators, and coordinators of resources offering classes, sponsoring public presentations and conferences, publishing periodicals, reports, and books. There are the Freudian Group for Applied Psychoanalysis and the Western New England Psychoanalytic Society. Jungian Societies in New York City (*Quadrant*), Los Angeles (*Harvest*), and San Francisco (*Perspectives*) all put out their own periodicals. The Toronto Jungians publish their own monograph series under the name *Inner City Books* and the London Jungians publish the *Journal of Analytical Psychology*.

The Analytical Psychology Society of Western New York has had interdisciplinary conferences such as one described this way in their brochure: "The Lunatic, the Lover, and the Poet: a conference on the relation between psychiatry, archetypal

psychology, and poetry." And the recently founded (1983)
national Association for the Study of Dreams holds an annual
multi-disciplinary international conference (California,
1984; Virginia, 1985; Ottawa, Canada, 1986) and publishes ac-
stracts from its conference in its newsletter.

A new journal, *Dreamworks*, published by Human Sciences
Press, defines itself ambitiously as "an interdisciplinary
quarterly devoted to the art of dreaming" which "brings together the latest thinking on the dream process from many
fields--aesthetics, anthropology, criticism, neurophysiology,
philosophy, psychology, religion--and gathers dream reports
and adaptations from artists working in various media." The
boldness and innovative format of *Dreamworks* have attracted
impressive contributors despite a sometimes awkward blend of
the experiential, critical, and artistic. A serious commitment to oneirocritics motivates the work of this periodical
which is building the foundation for a record of modern
oneirology with the beginnings of a dream and literature bibliography. "Dream and Poetry: A Preliminary Checklist" by
John D. Engle was printed in 1980 in Volume 1, No. 2, pp. 183-
191, and was followed in 1981 by "Dream and Fiction: A Checklist," Volume 2, No. 2, pp. 156-162, compiled by Lee Zimmerman
and Carolyn Hoche. These short and very sketchily annotated
book lists are worth consulting since they include early
literature and theory, as well as literature outside the
West. The expansion of this bibliographical project is eagerly
awaited.

There are two psychology and literature bibliographies
which can be useful in locating articles, essays, chapters,
and books on dreaming. Normal Kiell's *Bibliography of Psychology, Psychiatry, and Literature*, originally published in 1962
by the University of Wisconsin Press, has been updated, revised,
greatly expanded, and reissued in 1982 by Scarecrow Press of
Metuchen, New Jersey. But Kiell's orientation is primarily
Freudian; a more promising source is the eclectic *Bibliography
of Psychocriticism* compiled by Joseph Natoli and Frederick
Rusch, from Greenwood Press, Westport, Conn. (These books
illustrate another dilemma in dream research: much publishing
is done by small presses whose budgets do not permit much ad-
vertising, or university presses who print limited editions,
so even excellent books often go out of print quickly.) In
an interesting, intelligently composed preface reviewing
various schools of psychological criticism, the compilers
claim to have surveyed Freud, Jung, Reich, Fromm, Lacan,
Horney, and Norman Holland (*Dynamics of Literary Response*).

Exciting material appears in the host of unpublished dis-
sertations that have come out in recent years; many are eclectic, interdisciplinary, sensible, thorough, and imaginative,

with good bibliographies. One of the first was by Francis X.
Newman on medieval theories of dreaming and the form of dream
and vision poetry (21). A notable recent one was Teresa
Soufas' *Dreams, Nightmares, and Swoons: Calderon and Ancient
Psychology* (22).

Several articles published by literary scholars during
the 1960s have this same blend of sound scholarship, awareness
of tradition, common sense, and originality. Even when they
treat a single dream, like Eve's in *Paradise Lost*, they avoid
reductive analysis and place the dream in wider contexts,
similar to the Jungian process of amplifying, circumambulating
dreams. Such articles, however, are scattered throughout
journals like the *Modern Language Quarterly*, *English Literary
History*, *Harvard Theological Review*, and *Tennessee Studies in
Literature*. Manfred Weidhorn, author of some of these articles,
is also to be credited with his 1970 *Dreams in Seventeenth
Century English Literature*. This was a harbinger of the dream
dissertation and also apparently a model for them, given its
frequent citation. Weidhorn knows Freud but in his purpose
of seeing "how the individual dream functions within the overall
construction of a literary work" he chooses, perhaps naively,
but with great skill, to "see what seventeenth century writers
were consciously attempting to do with what they understood
dreams to be, in the light of traditional beliefs and literary
uses of the dream" (23, p. 8). Experience suggests that the
greatest understanding of early literature as well as late
comes from an integration of modern theories with traditional
modes of literary explication.

A recent spate of books has begun to increase coverage of
the dream in European/North American literature, e.g., Julian
Palley's analytical survey, *The Ambiguous Mirror: Dreams in
Spanish Literature* (24). Margot Norris does convincing structural analysis with emphasis on dreams in her recent study,
The Decentered Universe of Finnegans Wake (25). David Saliba's
A Psychology of Fear: The Nightmare Formula of Edgar Allan Poe
draws successfully on Jungian/archetypal theory to analyze the
dream structure of Poe's tales (26). In *Dreams in the Novels
of Galdos*, Joseph Schraibman eschews allegiance to any psychological orthodoxy and presents a general, insightful review
of this Spanish novelist which invites attention to his work
(27).

Models of books dealing with early literature and theory
written by literary scholars are Constance Hieatt's *The Realism
of Dream Visions: The Poetic Exploitation of the Dream-Experi-
ence in Chaucer and His Contemporaries* (28) and A.C. Spearing's
Medieval Dream-Poetry (29). Marjorie Garber's *The Dream in
Shakespeare* turns the explicit dream episodes into a metaphor
for the process of transformation pervasive in Shakespearean

drama (30). There are a handful of references to Freud, none
to Jung or any other dream theorist. There is little of interest to the oneirocritical reader here, as almost any other
content than dreams would have served as well for Garber's
speculations.

Hieatt and Spearing, of necessity for their subjects, go
back to earlier primary sources on dreams, including Aristotle
and Plato. The serious dream reader of any period will want
to follow their lead not only because of the abiding intrinsic
merit of some of these texts, but also because of their persistent influence through the centuries on poets and theorists.
The most specifically influential and imitated treatises are
those by the Greek Artemidorus, whose *Oneirocritica* we have
already mentioned as influencing Freud and Jung. It also influenced his most famous successor, Macrobius, whose *Commentary
on the Dream of Scipio*, composed during the Middle Ages, was
much translated and widely read.

Macrobius reiterates his predecessor's categories of dreams
and distinguishes two main types: the enigmatic, which includes
the prophetic and oracular, has implications for the future
and hence has value; the nightmare-apparition types result from
conditions in the dreamer's life and "are not worth interpreting since they have no prophetic significance," no importance,
no symbolic meaning. Virtually every major idea in Freud and
Jung can be found at least incipient if not fully developed
in these early texts. James Hillman, particularly in *Re-
Visioning Psychology* (4) and *The Dream and the Underworld* (5),
has taken full account of Graeco-Roman, medieval, and Renaissance dream lore and literature. His books provide a starting
point for the modern reader's venture into the roots of dream
and literature in the Western tradition.

Readers should also consult texts dealing with the psychology of image and symbol in art. A Freudian and a Jungian sample would include Ernst Kris, *Psychoanalytic Explorations in
Art* (31) and Erich Neumann's *Art and the Creative Unconscious*
(32). Many pieces in *Spring: An Annual of Archetypal Psychology
and Jungian Thought* treat image and symbol in a multi-disciplinary perspective which yields fresh insights into issues of
dream and literature while fostering new attitudes toward
psychology.

This guide cannot end without a review of two recent works
which are justly fated to become classics in the history of
oneirics: Meredith Skura's *The Literary Use of the Psychoanalytic Process* (33) and Wendy Doniger O'Flaherty's *Dreams,
Illusions, and Other Realities* (34). These books are not
featured in this guide because the former is fully Freudian
and not specifically focused on dreams and the latter is
written by a professor of religion about "non-Western" litera-

ture. Nevertheless, both the books are required reading for
the flourishing or aspiring oneirocritic if only for the grace
of their prose and the lucidity of their argumentation. These
two authors navigate skillfully between the Scylla of the
Freudians' drastic reductionism and the Charybdis of the
Jungians' infinite expansionism; there is a dynamic balance
between critical acuity and imaginal flexibility.

Like so many of her predecessors and contemporaries,
Skura reaches not to the modern novel for her focal text,
but to Shakespeare, and to a particularly problematic dark
comedy, *Measure for Measure*. Her provocative differentiation
among the ways of "using" literature and psychoanalysis as
mutually illuminating processes is manifest in her chapter
titles, e.g., Literature as Case History: Content; Literature
as Fantasy: Psychic Function; Literature as Dream: Mode of
Representation.

O'Flaherty, who is steeped in modern psychology as well
as in Eastern religion and literature and has worked in the
original Sanskrit, argues coherently about the significance
of the relativity of "reality" in Indian writing. She explains
the way this relativity, so foreign to the minds of Westerners, can expose the shortcomings of modern Western psychology
and open the way to new perspectives on dreams and similar
phenomena.

One may hope that such books will inspire the creation
of that elusive very, very good book on dreams and Western
literature which does not seem to be in existence as this
guide goes to press.

References

1. Porter, Laurence (1978). "Do Literary Dreams Have a
    Latent Content? A Jungian View." *Journal of Altered
    States of Consciousness*, 4(1), 37-42.

2. Felman, Shoshana (1977). "To Open the Question." *Yale
    French Studies: Literature and Psychoanalysis. The
    Question of Reading: Otherwise*, 55/56, 1-10.

3. Bickman, Martin (1980). *The Unsounded Centre: Jungian
    Studies in American Romanticism*. Chapel Hill: University
    of North Carolina Press.

4. Hillman, James (1975). *Re-visioning Psychology*. New
    York: Harper & Row.

5. Hillman, James (1979). *The Dream and the Underworld*.
    New York: Harper & Row.

6. Hillman, James (1971). *The Myth of Analysis*. Evanston,
    Ill.: Northwestern University Press.

7. Jung, C.G. (1974). *Dreams*. (R.F.C. Hull, Trans.)
    Princeton: Princeton University Press.

8. Jung, C.G. (1966). *The Spirit in Man, Art, and Litera-
    ture*. (R.F.C. Hull, Trans.) Princeton: Princeton
    University Press.

9. Postman, Neil (January 18, 1986). "A Singer of Their
    Tales." *The New York Times Book Review*, pp. 3, 28.

10. Schwaber, Paul (1975). "Scientific Art: The Interpreta-
    tion of Dreams." *The Psychoanalytic Study of the Child*,
    31, 515-533.

11. Coleridge, Samuel Taylor (1893). *Lectures and Notes on
    Shakespeare*. London: George Bell & Sons.

12. Wolkstein, Diane, and Kramer, Samuel Noah (1983). *Inanna:
    Queen of Heaven and Earth*. New York: Harper & Row.

13. Huppé, Bernard (1970). *The Web of Words: Structural
    Analysis of the Old English Poems*. Albany: State
    University of New York.

14. Dante (1973). *Vita Nuova* (New Life). (Mark Musa, Trans.)
    Bloomington: Indiana University Press.

15. Cervantes, Miguel de (1981). *Don Quixote*. (J.R. Jones
    and Kenneth Douglas, Trans. and Eds.) New York: W.W.
    Norton.

16. Knapp, Bettina L. (1984). *A Jungian Approach to Litera-
    ture*. Carbondale: Southern Illinois University Press.

17. Tennenhouse, Leonard (Ed.) (1976). *The Practice of
    Psychoanalytic Criticism*. Detroit: Wayne State Univer-
    sity Press.

18. Crews, Frederick (Ed.) (1970). *Psychoanalysis and Liter-
    ary Process*. Cambridge, Mass.: Winthrop Publishers.

19. de Nerval, Gerard (1965). *Aurelia ou le rêve et la vie*.
    Paris: Minard.

20. Beguin, A. (1960). *L'âme romantique et le rêve*. Paris:
    J. Corti.

21. Newman, Francis X. (1963). *Somnium: Medieval Theories
    of Dreaming and the Form of Vision Poetry*. Unpublished
    doctoral dissertation, Princeton University.

22. Soufas, Teresa Ann Scott (1980). *Dreams, Nightmares,
    and Swoons: Calderon and Ancient Psychology*. Unpub-
    lished doctoral dissertation, Duke University.

23. Weidhorn, Manfred (1970). *Dreams in Seventeenth Century
    Literature*. The Hague: Mouton.

24. Palley, Julian (1983). *The Ambiguous Mirror: Dreams in
    Spanish Literature: Albatros Hispanofila* (Vol. 27).
    Valencia: Artes Gráficas Saler.

25. Norris, Margot (1976). *The Decentered Universe of Fin-
    negans Wake: A Structuralist Analysis*. Baltimore: The
    Johns Hopkins University Press.

26. Saliba, David (1980). *The Nightmare Formula of Edgar
    Allan Poe*. Lanham, Md.: University Press of America.

27. Schraibman, Joseph (1960). *Dreams in the Novels of
    Galdos*. New York: Hispanic Institute.

28. Hieatt, Constance (1967). *The Realism of Dream Visions*.
    The Hague: Mouton.

29. Spearing, A.C. (1976). *Medieval Dream-Poetry*. Cambridge:
    Cambridge University Press.

30. Garber, M. (1974). *Dream in Shakespeare*. New Haven:
    Yale University Press.

31. Kris, Ernst (1952). *Psychoanalytic Explorations in Art*.
    New York: International University Press.

32. Neumann, Erich (1974). *Art and the Creative Unconscious*.
    (Ralph Manheim, Trans.) Princeton: Princeton University
    Press.

33. Skura, Meredith Anne (1981). *The Literary Use of the
    Psychoanalytic Process*. New Haven: Yale University
    Press.

34. O'Flaherty, Wendy Doniger (1984). *Dreams, Illusions, and
    Other Realities*. Chicago: University of Chicago Press.

AUTHOR INDEX
(Italicized Pages are for References and Bibliographies)

Aarons, L. 218, 220, *223*
Abdul Jalil bin Haji Noor
  333; *355*
Abrams, A. 293, *313*
Adam, K. 83, *103*
Adams, H. 153, *179*
Adeyoe, T. 322, *340*
Akerstedt, T. 35, 36, 49,
  56, *61*
Akpinar, S. 155, *182*
Albrecht, P. 66, *94*
Alexander, C.N. 289, 290,
  291, 292, 294, 295, 296,
  297, 300, *303, 310, 311,*
  313, 314, 315
Alexander, V.K. 290, 300,
  301, *303, 304*
Allen, M. 149, *173*
Al-Marashi. See under M.
Ambuehl, R. 155, *183*
Anch, A.M. 133, *140*
Ancoli-Israel, S. 121, *139*
Anders, T. 12, *28*
Anderson, B.G. 325, *349*
Andreae, L. 158, *185*
Angst, J. 148, *173*
Antrobus, J. 148, *172*
Arendt, H. 334, *357*
Arito, H. 72, 73, *98*
Arkin, A. 146, 148, 150,
  171, 172
Armitage, R. 147, *171*, 267,
  280
Arnheim, R. 253, 262, 263,
  276
Ascher, L.M. 119, 120, *138,*
  139
Aschoff, J. 33, 50, *55*

Aserinsky, B. 3, *27*, 63, *91*,
  145, *169*
Aserinsky, E. 209, *221*
Assens, F. 88, *104*
Association of Sleep Disorders
  Centers 39, *57*, 124, *139*

Badawi, K. 285, 292, *307*
Badia, P. 32, *55*, 152, *176*
Baekland, F. 189, 190, *202,*
  218, *223*
Baghdoyan, H.A. 88, *104*
Baker, E. 152, *176*
Balkin, T. 32, *55*, 152, *176*
Banquet, J.P. 284, 285, *307*
Baogoras, W. 327, 330, 334,
  352
Baridwell, T.J. 83, *102*
Barker, D. 154, *180*, 258,
  278
Barnes, C. 8, *28*, 284, 290,
  300, *306*
Barnouw, V. 323, 324, 325,
  329, *344*
Bartus, R.T. 131, *140*
Basar, E. 156, *183*
Basehart, H.W. 326, *350*
Bastide, R. 323, *342*
Batini, C. 65, *93*
Baumgarten, H.G. 68, *96*
Baurack, R. 83, *103*
Beach, F.A. 319, 323, 330,
  331, *337*
Bebillier, P. 75, *100*
Beersma, D.G.M. 48, *61*
Beguin, A. 371, *377*
Belicki, K. 187, 194, 197,

379

SUBJECT INDEX